THE RADIOCHEMICAL MANUAL

EDITED BY

GEOFF LONGWORTH

Associate Editors

Bob Carpenter, Richard Bull, Joe Toole and Alan Nichols

D1465175

Produced under the National Measurement System for Ionising Radiation Metrology
Programme 1995-1998, Department of Trade and Industry
AEA Technology plc
Analytical Services Group
Harwell

Published by AEA Technology plc
Harwell, Oxfordshire, OX11 0RA

First published 1998

ISBN 0-7058-1768-7

This book contains information obtained from authentic sources. Reprinted material is quoted with permission, and sources are indicated. A wide variety of references are listed. While every care has been taken in compiling the book to provide reliable data and information, neither the authors, AEA Technology plc nor the Department of Trade and Industry assumes any responsibility for the validity of all materials or accepts any liability for any loss or damage arising as a result of any errors or omissions in the information.

PREFACE

Many readers are aware of, or indeed are still using, the publication on which this book is modelled - The Radiochemical Manual, 2nd edition, published by The Radiochemical Centre, Amersham in 1966. Much of the Amersham manual was, not unreasonably, concerned with the production of radiotracers, the manufacture and design of radiation sources, and the synthesis and properties of radiolabelled compounds. Other topics such as the measurement of radionuclides, instrument calibration, and the safety and use of radioactive materials were also given useful coverage. The Table of Physical Data used nuclear data which were close to the best available at that time. Nuclear data were provided for approximately 360 different radionuclides.

The National Measurement System Policy Unit (NMSPU) within the UK Department of Trade and Industry (DTI) recognised that there was a requirement to produce a replacement publication, since the Amersham document was out of print and inevitably many aspects covered therein would be out of date. The NMSPU placed this contract with AEA Technology plc in 1996 following a competitive tender exercise. They also appointed the National Physical Laboratory (NPL), the UK's national standards laboratory, as programme co-ordinator charged with the task of seeing that the objectives of the programme were met. The deadline for production of the final proofs was set originally for January 1998, with full publication later that year. Funding for the project has been provided by DTI as part of the Ionising Radiation Programme of the National Measurement System.

The objective for AEA Technology was to build on the Amersham document by updating the information which was outdated, expanding into other areas and disciplines where radioactivity and radioisotopes were used routinely, and constructing a well-organised, well-referenced Manual. The target readership would be wide, including chemists, geochemists, physicists, radiopharmacists, metrologists, biochemists and environmental analysts.

A cross-section of people in the target readership were surveyed by telephone or questionnaire to solicit views on their key needs, the physical form and cost of the new Manual. Early drafts of chapters were produced by authors within AEA Technology, with contributions by external experts in two fields of discipline. Each chapter was subjected to external review by several experts in the particular field and by members of the DTI's Measurement Advisory Committee as part of their annual review and programme progress meetings. Following these series of quality checks, the entire manual contents were sent for further external reviews, mainly to obtain feedback on overall balance and style, but additional comments were accepted.

A key feature of the Manual is the Nuclear Data Table. The requirement for accurate nuclear data is shared by virtually all scientific disciplines where radioactivity is used; a recommended set of reasonably comprehensive decay data was found to be the most frequent requirement in the initial survey of potential users of the Manual. An extensive amount of checking was carried out on the nuclear data presented here, covering nearly 300 radionuclides.

The use of SI units has been adopted throughout the Manual, although other units have also been given where they are in common usage. Terms in bold print are defined in the glossary. Since the DTI required that the Manual should be principally for the UK user community, certain sections, in particular those covering legislation, are very much biased towards the UK.

Due to the wide target readership, each chapter had to be limited in length and therefore depth of coverage. Hence it proved imperative to provide an extensive bibliography to direct readers to further key texts and publications.

The authors recognise that some of the information presented here can and will become out of date, owing to changes such as the forthcoming revision of the Ionising Radiation Regulations, the new POPUMET regulations expected in 2000, and to the ever-changing degree of accuracy of nuclear data. It is believed that much of the present manual contents will still be up-to-date for many years to come, while timely revisions would be in order for the type of information which ages more quickly.

This book has been produced as a collaborative effort by Geoff Longworth (Editor), Bob Carpenter, Alan Nichols and Joe Toole (AEA Technology plc) and Richard Bull (Consultant on Radiological Protection). Valuable contributions have also been made by Susan Scrivens (Environmental Consultant, Susan Scrivens & Associates), John Cobb and Emma Hunt (AEA Technology plc), Martin Finlan (Physical Sciences Consultant to Nycomed Amersham) and Susan Parry (Centre for Environmental Technology, Imperial College at Silwood Park).

The authors would like to acknowledge the invaluable advice given by many reviewers together with advice and assistance from many colleagues. The book has benefited from thorough reviews by an *ad hoc* working party from the Ionising Radiation Working Group under the auspices of the DTI and in particular thanks are due to Tom Conlon, Penny Allisy-Roberts, Barry Senior, Gerry Sutton and Steve Waters for their painstaking work. In addition the authors have benefited from many useful comments from Phil Warwick (University of Southampton) and Susan Scrivens (Environmental Consultant) who read the whole manuscript, and from many readers of particular chapters who are acknowledged at the end of those chapters.

The authors wish to thank Natasha Longworth (Central St. Martins College of Art and Design) who designed the front cover, Neil Buchan (Imaging Centre, AEA Technology plc) for assistance with the figures, Peter Wells and Hazel King, (Marketing Services, AEA Technology plc) for the design and preparation of this manuscript and Eve Thornton and colleagues at the Information Centre, AEA Technology plc, for tracking down some of the many references.

Last but not least the authors are indebted to DTI for funding the project and to Roy Crouch, Joan Cocksedge and Lee Vousden of the National Measurement System Policy Unit (NMSPU) of DTI for their encouragement and patience, as well as to Mike Woods, (National Physical Laboratory) who monitored the project, gave advice and provided much valuable discussion.

June 1998

TABLE OF CONTENTS

CONTRIBUTORS

Richard Bull, Dosimetry Consultant, AEA Technology plc, 551 Harwell, Didcot, Oxfordshire OX11 0RA

Bob Carpenter, AEA Technology plc, Analytical Services Group, 551 Harwell, Didcot, Oxfordshire OX11 0RA

John Cobb, AEA Technology plc, Analytical Services Group, 551 Harwell, Didcot, Oxfordshire OX11 0RA

Martin Finlan, Physical Sciences Consultant to Nycomed Amersham plc, Amersham Place, Little Chalfont, Buckinghamshire, HP7 9NA

Emma Hunt, AEA Technology plc, Analytical Services Group, 551 Harwell, Didcot, Oxfordshire OX11 0RA

Geoff Longworth, AEA Technology plc, Analytical Services Group, 551 Harwell, Didcot, Oxfordshire OX11 0RA

Alan Nichols, AEA Technology plc, Products and Services, 477 Harwell, Didcot, Oxfordshire OX11 0RA

Susan Scrivens, Susan Scrivens & Associates, Environmental Consultancy, The Wetlands, Sodbury Lane, Westerleigh, Bristol BS17 4RR

Joe Toole, AEA Technology plc, Analytical Services Group, 551 Harwell, Didcot, Oxfordshire OX11 0RA

GLOSSARY

TECHNICAL TERMS

A

Absorbed dose
The energy deposited per unit mass of material when exposed to radiation. The SI unit of absorbed dose is the Gray (Gy). $1Gy = 1$ J kg^{-1}. An older unit, the rad (0.01 J kg^{-1}) is still encountered in some literature.

Absorption
1. The retention, in a material, of energy removed from radiation passing through it.
2. The removal of radiation or the reduction of its energy on passing through matter.
3. The process whereby a **neutron** (or other particle) is captured by a **nucleus.**
4. The uptake of a radionuclide by body organs or tissues.

Abundance sensitivity
The ability of a mass spectrometer to resolve neighbouring peaks for different masses. In the presence of a large peak, the abundance sensitivity is the ratio of the measured signal of the tail of the major peak at the mass of interest to the measured signal of the major peak.

Activation product
Radionuclide formed in a neutron capture reaction, for example, with either the nuclear fuel or the components of a nuclear reactor.

Activation cross-section
See **Cross-section.**

Activity
Of a quantity of radioactive material, the number of nuclear transformations which occur in this quantity in unit time. (See also **becquerel**, below).

ADC (Analogue to Digital Converter)
Electronic device used to produce a digital signal which is proportional to the amplitude of an input pulse originating, for example, from a radiation detector.

ALI (Annual Limit on Intake)
A secondary quantity used in Internal Radiation Protection. It is defined as the intake of a radionuclide which would result in a committed effective dose equal to the dose limit.

Alpha decay
Form of radioactive decay involving the emission of alpha particles.

Alpha particle
A helium (^{4}He) nucleus.

AMU (Atomic mass unit)
One-twelfth of the mass of an atom of carbon 12. Approximately 1.66×10^{-27} kg.

Annihilation radiation
The electromagnetic radiation resulting from the mutual annihilation of two particles of opposite charge. In the case of a collision between an **electron** and a **positron**, the annihilation radiation consists of two **photons,** each of energy about 0.511 MeV, emitted in directions opposite to each other.

Anthropogenic radionuclides
Radionuclides introduced into nature by man.

Anticoincidence counting
  See **coincidence counting**

Antineutrino
Particle with no mass, charge or spin which is emitted in β⁻ decay. The antineutrino and the **neutrino** emitted in β⁺ decay are referred to collectively as electron neutrinos.

Atom
A unit of matter consisting of a single **nucleus** surrounded by one or more orbital electrons. The number of electrons is normally sufficient to make the atom electrically neutral.

Atomic number (Charge number)
Of an **element,** the integer Z, equal to the number of protons in the nucleus, giving Ze as the nuclear charge where e is the charge of a **proton.**

Atomic weight
The average mass of the atoms of an element at its natural isotopic abundance, relative to that of other atoms, taking carbon 12 as the basis. Roughly equal to the number of protons and neutrons in its nucleus. See **Mass Number.**

Attenuation
Reduction in the intensity of a beam of radiation or particles due to interactions with matter.

Auger electrons
Those **electrons** emitted from an atom due to the filling of a vacancy in an inner electron shell.

B

Background
1. In discussing radiation levels and effects, it refers to the general level of natural and man-made radiations against which a particular added radiation component has to be considered.
2. In discussing radiation measurement techniques, it may also include spurious readings due to the 'noise' characteristics of the instrument and its power supplies, and to the presence of local radioactive contamination etc.

Barn
A unit of nuclear reaction **cross-section**. 1 barn=10^{-28} m^2; 1 millibarn=10^{-31}m^2.

Becquerel, Bq
The unit of activity in the SI System. It is equivalent to 1 disintegration per second or roughly 2.70 ×10^{-11} curie.

Beta decay
Type of radioactive decay involving the emission of electrons or positrons along with neutrinos or antineutrinos

Beta particle
An electron, of positive or negative charge, emitted in the beta transformation. (See also **Electron**).

Binding energy
The energy needed to separate a nucleus into its constituent protons and neutrons. It gives a measure of the stability of the nucleus. See **Mass Defect.**

Biocide
Any substance that kills or inhibits the growth of micro-organisms such as bacteria, moulds, fungi etc.

Biological Monitoring or Sampling
The analysis of urine or faecal samples to estimate intakes of radionuclides or in-vivo monitoring of retained nuclides.

Body burden
The amount of radioactive or toxic material in a human or animal body at any time.

Bone seeker
An element which, if ingested, tends to be deposited in bone in preference to other tissues of the body.

Brachytherapy
The practice of inserting small sealed radioactive sources in or near a cancerous tumour for treatment.

Branching fraction or Branching ratio
When a radionuclide can decay by more than one mode, the branching fraction (ratio) gives the proportion of radionuclides that decay by a given mode.

Bremsstrahlung
Literally 'braking radiation'. The electromagnetic radiation resulting from the change in velocity of charged particles.

Build-up
Increase in the flux through a shield arising from scattering of the radiation in broad-beam geometry, making the shielding less effective than predicted from a simple exponential decay law.

C

Capture
Process in which a particle, for example, a neutron, collides with a nucleus and is absorbed in it.

Carrier-free
Production of a radionuclide to which no carrier has been added, and for which precautions have been taken to minimise contamination with other radionuclides.

Cerenkov radiation
Coherent radiation produced when a charged particle traverses a medium at a velocity greater than the phase velocity of light in that medium.

Charge number
  See **Atomic number**

Chelation
The formation of a closed ring of atoms by the attachment of compounds or radicals to a central metal ion. This process is exploited in many radiochemical separations.

Chromatography
A method of chemical analysis in which a mobile phase carrying the sample to be analysed is caused to move in contact with a selectively absorbent stationary phase.

Coherent
A scattering process is described as coherent, if in a wave picture, the phase of the scattered wave has a definite phase relationship to that of the incident wave.

Coincidence counting
Counting circuitry in which an output signal is produced only when two input signals arrive within a specified time interval. This is often used in low-level counting. Conversely, an anti-coincidence circuit gives no output when two input signals arrive together.

Committed equivalent dose/Committed effective dose
The time-integral of the dose-equivalent rate to an organ (committed equivalent dose) or of effective dose-equivalent (committed effective dose) resulting from the intake of a radionuclide. The integration time is usually 50y for adults and 70y for children. In ICRP 26 terminology these quantities were known respectively as committed dose equivalent and committed effective dose equivalent.

Compound nucleus
A highly excited nucleus, of short lifetime, formed as an intermediate stage in a nuclear reaction.

Compton scattering
The process by which a photon is scattered by an effectively free electron resulting in a loss of energy by the photon.

Controlled area
An area where workers follow established procedures in order to control radiation exposures.

Cosmic radiation or cosmic rays

Radiation originating both from the sun and from our own and other galaxies consisting mainly of high energy protons which produce a large number of new particles in the earth's atmosphere.

Cosmogenic nuclide

A nuclide formed by the action of cosmic rays on a target material.

Counter

An instrument for counting pulses of radiation or the electric pulses that it causes, and displaying or recording them in digital form. See also **Scaler, Ratemeter**. Also used loosely for any form of radiation detection or measuring instrument.

COSHH

Control of Substances Hazardous to Health

Critical

A nuclear reactor or other assembly of fissile material is said to be 'critical' when its chain reaction is just self-sustaining.

Cross-section, nuclear

The target area presented by a nucleus to an approaching particle relating to a specified nuclear interaction, for example, capture, elastic scattering or fission. The cross-section varies with the type of nucleus, the type and energy of the incident particle and the specified interaction. Cross-sections are measured in barns, and give a measure of the probability of the particular reaction.

Curie, Ci

An obsolete unit of radioactivity, being the quantity of radioactive material in which 3.7×10^{10} nuclei disintegrate every second. Originally it was the activity of 1 gram of radium-226. The curie has now been superseded under the SI system by the **becquerel** (Bq), equal to 1 disintegration per second.

Cyclotron

An accelerator in which charged particles follow a spiral path in a magnetic field and are accelerated by an oscillating electric field.

D

DAC (Derived Air Concentration)

Concentration of airborne activity such that a worker with standard breathing rate will inhale one **ALI** over the 2000 hr of a working year.

Dating, radionuclide

Determination of the age of an archaeological or geological specimen by measuring its content of a radionuclide in relation to that of its precursor or decay product or of its stable isotope. Applied particularly to **radiocarbon dating** of archaeological specimens.

Daughter product

The nuclide immediately resulting from the radioactive decay of a parent or precursor nuclide.

Dead time
The time after registering a count for which a radiation detector is inoperative and unable to detect further particles. Dead time must be allowed for in calculating true count rates.

de Broglie wavelength
Wavelength associated with a particle, given by **Planck's constant** divided by the momentum of the particle.

Decay chain
A series of radionuclides each of which disintegrates into the next until a stable nuclide is reached.

Decay constant
The probability for the decay of a radionuclide per unit time.

Decay, radioactive
The disintegration of a nucleus through emission of radioactivity. The decrease of activity due to such disintegration.

Delayed neutron
This arises as a result of fission when the series of decay steps of a **fission product** produces a nuclide which emits a neutron after beta decay.

Delta rays
Secondary electrons with sufficient energy to create an ionisation track of their own.

Deterministic effects
An effect on the body caused by exposure to radiation, such that the severity of the effect increases with dose above some clinical threshold. Called **non-stochastic** effects in ICRP 26.

Deuterium
Heavy isotope of hydrogen with one proton and one neutron in the nucleus.

Deuteron
Nucleus of deuterium containing one neutron and one proton.

Diagnostic imaging
The use of radionuclides to study the functioning of body tissues via measurement of the radiation distribution from accumulation of the radionuclide in the tissue after administration to the patient.

Disintegration
Any transformation of a nucleus, either spontaneous or by interaction with radiation, in which particles or photons are emitted. Used in particular to mean radioactive decay.

Dose, radiation
Generally, the quantity of radiation energy absorbed by a body. See **Absorbed dose**.

Dose commitment
Future radiation doses inevitably to be received by a person or group, for example, from radioactive material already incorporated in the body. See **Committed dose equivalent**.

Dose equivalent

Absorbed dose multiplied by a **quality factor** (ICRP 26) or **radiation weighting factor** (ICRP 60) to take account of the differing effectiveness of radiations in causing biological damage. In ICRP 60 it is renamed **equivalent dose.** The SI unit of **dose equivalent** and **equivalent dose** is the **sievert**.

Dose limits

Limits placed on the **equivalent dose** (dose equivalent in ICRP 26 terminology) received by workers or by members of the public. They should not be regarded as 'safe' doses and the overriding requirement is to keep doses as low as reasonably practicable (ALARP). The limit on effective dose to workers is 20 mSv per year averaged over defined periods of 5 years. The limit on effective dose to members of the public is 1 mSv per year.

Dose rate

The absorbed dose deposited in unit time, which is typically expressed in units such as mGy y^{-1}.

Dosemeter, Dosimeter, Dose rate meter

An instrument which measures radiation doses or dose rates.

E

Effective dose

The sum of the equivalent doses in all tissues and organs in the body weighted by the **tissue weighting factors** which allow for the differing relative sensitivities of the various tissues and organs.

Electrodeposition

The process of depositing by electrolysis, used in the preparation of sources for counting.

Electron

A negatively charged particle (charge $\cong 1.602 \times 10^{-19}$ C, mass $\cong 9.11 \times 10^{-31}$ kg) present in all **atoms**. However, the word electron is sometimes used to include both negative electrons (negatrons) and positive electrons (positrons).

Electron capture (EC)

A nuclear transformation whereby a **nucleus** captures one of its orbital **electrons**.

Electron volt (eV)

A unit of energy equal to the kinetic energy acquired by an electron when accelerated through a potential difference of 1 volt (1 eV $\cong 1.60 \times 10^{-19}$ C). See also **keV, MeV**.

Element

Substance that cannot be decomposed by normal chemical changes.

Emission probability

All emission probabilities of the various forms of decay are expressed in this manual as absolute probabilities of the specific emission per decay, that is, as fractional decay.

Energy resolution

of, for example a gamma ray peak is usually expressed as the full width at half maximum height of the peak (FWHM) in energy units, divided by the energy of the gamma ray or the mean energy of a particle and expressed as a percentage.

Enriched material
Material containing an element in which the abundance of one of the **isotopes** has been increased above that which it normally possesses.

EPD (Electronic Personal Dosemeter)
A personal dosemeter, usually based on a solid-state diode, which gives an instant read-out of dose rate or accumulated dose.

Epithermal neutrons
Neutrons with an energy in the approximate range 0.5-1eV.

Equivalent activity
Of a radiation source, the activity of a point source of the same **radionuclide** which will give the same exposure rate at the same distance from the centre of the source.

Equivalent dose
The absorbed dose averaged over a tissue or organ multiplied by the **radiation weighting factor**. This replaces the **dose equivalent** of ICRP 26. The SI unit of equivalent dose is the **sievert**.

Excitation
The addition of energy to a system, transforming it from its **ground state** to **an excited state**.

Exciton
A bound electron-hole pair formed as a result of photon absorption in a semiconductor which can migrate through the crystal with a definite half-life.

Exposure
The amount of radiation producing 1 coulomb of ionisation per kilogram of air.

F

Fall-out
Deposition of radioactive material from the atmosphere, resulting from the explosion of nuclear weapons or from accidental release.

Fast neutrons
Neutrons travelling with a speed close to that with which they were ejected from a fissioning nucleus, typically about 2×10^7 m s^{-1}. See **Thermal Neutrons**.

Film Badge
A small plaque worn by people working in radiation areas containing a masked piece of photographic film. The degree of darkening of the film on development is a measure of the radiation dose received. See **Thermoluminescent Dosimeter**.

Fission
  See **Nuclear Fission**

Fission yield
The percentage of fissions that give rise to a particular nuclide.

Fission fragments
The initial group of nuclides formed as a result of nuclear fission.

Fission products
Nuclides formed as a result of nuclear fission.

Fluence
The total number of particles or photons crossing a sphere of unit cross-section surrounding a point source.

Fluorescence yield
The number of X rays emitted per vacancy in an electron shell of an atom.

Flux or Fluence rate
The product of the number of particles or photons per unit volume and their average speed. Now referred to as fluence rate.

G

Gamma-rays
Highly energetic form of electromagnetic radiation in the approximate range keV-MeV, of nuclear origin emitted during radioactive decay, electron-positron annihilation and nuclear fission.

Geiger-Müller counter or Geiger counter
A simple and well-established form of radiation detector which produces electrical pulses at a rate related to the intensity of the radiation. Commonly called a 'Geiger Counter'.

Genetic effects (of radiation or mutagenic chemicals)
Effects produced in the descendants of the person or organism exposed. See **Somatic effects**.

Glove box
A form of protection often used when working with alpha-emitting radioactive materials. Gloves fixed to ports in the wall of a transparent box allow manipulation of work within the box without the risk of inhalation or contact.

Gray, Gy
The SI unit of absorbed radiation dose, one joule per kilogram. (1Gy = 100 rads).

Ground state
The state of lowest energy of a nucleus.

H

Half-life
The characteristic time taken for the activity of a particular radioactive substance to decay to half of its original value - that is, for half the atoms present to disintegrate. Half-lives vary from less than a millionth of a second to thousands of millions of years, reflecting the stability of the nuclide concerned.

Half-life, biological
The time required for the amount of a particular substance in the body to be halved by biological processes when the rate of removal is approximately exponential.

Hard radiation
Radiation having a relatively high penetrating power, that is, energy.

Health physics
The study and administration of radiological protection.

Heavy water
Water in which some or all of the hydrogen is replaced by 'heavy hydrogen' or deuterium.

Hereditary effects
Stochastic radiation effects expressed in the progeny of the exposed person. See **genetic effects.**

High-level waste
Radioactive waste of high activity in which the temperature may rise significantly as a result of their radioactivity. (Review of Radioactive Waste Management Policy - Final Conclusions, Cm.2919 (1995), para.53).

Hot
Jargon for highly radioactive.

Hydrology
The study of the Earth's waters, including underground water, surface water and rainfall.

I

ICP-OES (Inductively Coupled Plasma-Optical Emission Spectroscopy)
Technique used in multi-element analysis in which an argon plasma is used to excite analyte atoms. Decay of the excited states involves emission of light at specific wavelengths which are detected in a multichannel polychromator.

ICP-MS (Inductively Coupled Plasma-Mass Spectrometry)
Technique used in multi-element and multi-isotopic analysis which incorporates an argon plasma source as in ICP-OES as input to a quadrupole or sector **mass spectrometer**.

Inhalation types
A default solubility classification for inhaled material used in **ICRP** 60, to be used in the absence of detailed information on lung clearance. Types F (fast), M (medium) or S (slow) correspond to the classes D,W and Y, respectively of ICRP 30.

Intermediate-level waste
Waste in which radioactivity levels exceed the upper bounds for **low-level waste** but do not generate heat in sufficient quantity that it requires to be taken into account in the design of storage or disposal facilities. (Review of Radioactive Waste Management Policy - Final Conclusions, Cm.2919 (1995), para.53).

Internal conversion
A process in which an excited nucleus de-excites with the ejection of an orbital electron from an inner shell.

Internal conversion coefficient
The ratio of conversion electrons to the number of gamma rays emitted in a transition between two nuclear energy states.

Ion
An atom which has lost or gained one or more orbital electrons, thus becoming electrically charged.

Ion exchange
A technique, widely used in radiochemistry, in which ions are removed from a solution or exchanged for other ions, when the solution is passed through a resin bed.

Ionisation
The process of creating ions by dislodging or adding orbital electrons.

Ionisation chamber
A device for measuring the intensity of ionising radiation. The radiation ionises the gas in the chamber and the rate at which ions are collected (on oppositely-charged electrodes) is measured as an electric current.

Ionising radiation
Radiation which removes orbital electrons from atoms, thus creating ion pairs. Alpha and beta particles are more densely ionising than gamma-rays or X-rays of equivalent energy. Neutrons do not cause ionisation directly.

Ion pair
A positively charged ion together with the electron removed from the original atom by ionising radiation.

IRRs (Ionising Radiations Regulations)
UK legislation on Radiation Protection based on the recommendations in **ICRP** 26. New regulations based on ICRP 60 are due by 2000.

Irradiate
To expose to radiation, particularly in penetrating forms such as gamma-rays and neutrons.

Isobars
Nuclides of different elements having the same **mass numbers** but different **atomic numbers**.

Isomers
Isomers or isomeric nuclides have the same mass number A and the same atomic number Z but different nuclear binding energies.

Isomeric states
States of a nucleus having different energies and observable half-lives.

Isomeric transition (IT)
A transition between two isomeric states of a nucleus.

Isotopes
Nuclides having the same **atomic number** but different **mass numbers**.

Isotopic abundance
The number of atoms of a particular isotope in a mixture of the isotopes of an element, expressed as a fraction of all the atoms of the element.

K

Kerma (Kinetic energy released per unit mass)
Sum of the initial kinetic energies of charged ionising particles (or photons) released by incident uncharged particles (or photons) per unit mass of stopping medium.

keV
Thousand electron volts = 10^3 eV.

L

Labelled compound
A compound in which one or more of the atoms in some of the molecules are replaced by radionuclides.

Label, radioactive
A relatively very small quantity of a radioactive substance added to a material or object, the subsequent movements of which can then be studied by detecting and measuring the radiation emitted from it. See **Tracer**.

Leaching
The slow dissolution of a substance from a solid containing it.

LET (Linear energy transfer)
The rate at which a charged particle loses energy as it passes through matter. It is high for alpha particles and low for electrons. See **Quality factor**.

LINAC (Linear accelerator)
An accelerator in which the accelerated particles move in a straight path.

Liquid scintillator
A liquid in which the absorption of radiation results in the emission of light. This is used as the basis for many low-level counting systems.

Low-level waste
Waste containing radioactive materials not exceeding 4 GBq/te of alpha activity or 12GBq/te of beta activity. (Review of Radioactive Waste Management Policy - Final Conclusions, Cm.2919 (1995), para.53).

M

Magic numbers
The charge and neutron numbers, 2, 8, 20, 28, 50 and 82, that are characteristic of many stable **nuclides**.

Mass defect
The difference between the mass of a nucleus and the sum of the masses of its constituent nucleons. It is related to the **Binding Energy** of the nucleus by Einstein's equation $E = mc^2$, where E is the energy of mass m and c is the velocity of light *in vacuo*.

Mass Number
The number of protons plus neutrons in the nucleus of an atom. See **Isotopes**.

Mass Spectrometer
An analytical instrument in which accelerated positive ions of a material are separated electromagnetically according to their charge to mass ratios. Different species can be identified and accurate measurements made of their relative concentrations.

MCA (Multichannel Pulse Height Analyser)
Electronic device used to sort signal pulses originating, for example, with source radiation stopped in a radiation detector, into parallel amplitude channels in order to produce an energy pulse height spectrum of the source radiation.

MDA (Minimum Detectable Activity)
Informally, the lowest activity in a sample that can be distinguished from background by a given counting system.

Mean free path
Average distance between collisions.

Metastable states
In a nucleus, **isomeric** states with energies above that of the ground state.

MeV
Million electron volts $= 10^6$ eV.

Mössbauer effect
Emission of gamma rays without loss of energy to recoil of the emitting radionuclide, leading to gamma lines of very small energy width.

N

Natural decay series
Three series of naturally occurring radionuclides originating with ^{238}U, ^{232}Th and ^{235}U. A fourth 'man-made' series originates with ^{237}Np.

Nebulisation
The production of a mist of small stable droplets.

Neutrino
Particle with no mass or charge which is emitted in β^+ decay. The neutrino and the **antineutrino** emitted in β^- decay, are referred to collectively as electron neutrinos.

Neutron
An elementary particle with mass of 1 atomic mass unit (approximately 1.66×10^{-27} kg), approximately the same as that of the proton. Together with protons, neutrons form the nuclei of all atoms. In isolation, neutrons are radioactive, decaying with a half-life of about 12 minutes by beta emission into a proton.

Neutron activation analysis
A technique for the quantitative determination of the atomic composition of a sample involving the measurement of radionuclide activities produced by neutron irradiation of the sample.

Neutron flux
The product of the neutron density and the average speed. The number of neutrons entering an imaginary sphere having a unit surface area in one second. (see **flux, fluence**).

Neutron yield
The average number of neutrons emitted per fission. Usually per thermal neutron absorbed in uranium-235.

Non-Stochastic effects
In ICRP 26 terminology, radiation effects such that the severity increases with dose above a clinical threshold. Replaced by the term **deterministic effects** in ICRP 60.

Nuclear borehole logging
Technique used in geological exploration for measuring physical or mineralogical properties of rock. In passive mode, natural radiation from the rock is measured in a detector on a probe lowered into a borehole while in active mode the probe also carries a radioactive source and the detector measures radiation scattered by the rock.

Nuclear control gauge
A device incorporating a radioactive source to measure and control, for example, the density, thickness or moisture content in an industrial process.

Nuclear fission
A nuclear reaction in which a heavy nucleus splits into two (or very rarely three or four) approximately equal fragments.

Nuclear reactor
A structure or part of a plant in which a neutron-induced chain reaction of nuclear fission can be maintained, controlled and used.

Nucleon
A proton or a neutron, the particles from which all atomic nuclei are composed.

Nucleus
The central part of an atom at which the positive electric charge, and nearly all the mass is concentrated, which is surrounded by the orbital electrons in the Bohr model of the atom. See **Nucleon**.

Nuclide
An individual species of atom characterised by its mass number and atomic number. See **Isotopes. Radionuclide**.

O

Oncology
The branch of medicine concerned with new growths (tumours) in body tissue.

P

Pair production
The process in which a photon is converted into an electron–positron pair in the field of an electron or nucleus.

Parent
Of a nuclide, that radioactive nuclide from which it is formed by decay.

Particle accelerator
Machine used to accelerate particles to high energies used, for example, in the production of radionuclides, see **cyclotron**.

PET (Positron Emission Tomography)
Tool for medical diagnosis in which a positron emitter is administered to the patient who is then positioned in a scanner consisting of rings of detectors. The emitted coincident gamma rays are detected in opposite detectors allowing an accurate quantification to be made of the position and uptake of the PET radionuclide.

Phantom
A model of part or all of the human body constructed of a material which simulates body tissue as an absorber of radiation. Used for radiological protection studies.

Phonon
The quantum of energy associated with an atomic lattice vibration, in analogy with the photon.

Photoelectric effect
The process in which a photon ejects a bound electron from an atom.

Photon
A quantum of electromagnetic radiation, possessing the energy $h\nu$ (h being **Planck's constant** and ν the frequency).

Planck's constant
A universal constant relating the energy of a quantum of radiation to the frequency of the oscillator emitting the radiation, equal to 6.626×10^{-27} erg sec.

Poisson statistics
Statistical distribution of random events applying to the case where the probability of occurrence in a given time interval is small. The basis of nuclear counting statistics.

Positron
The anti-particle of the electron, having a positive charge instead of the more usual negative charge.

Precursor
In a radioactive decay chain any nuclide which has preceded another.

Precipitation
The formation of an insoluble substance from a solution via a chemical reaction.

Primary ionisation
The direct removal of electrons from atoms and molecules as opposed to the secondary ionisation produced by **delta rays**.

Primordial radionuclide
A long-lived radionuclide present in the Earth since its formation.

Prompt
Of neutrons or gamma-rays, emitted immediately upon fission, or other interaction. See **Delayed Neutrons**.

Proportional counter
A radiation detector that produces electrical pulses proportional in size to the energy of the radiation.

Proton
A nuclear particle of mass number 1 having a charge of about 1.602×10^{-19} C equal and opposite to that of an electron and having a mass of 1.0076 amu or about 1.67×10^{-27} kg.

Pulse Height Analysis
The use of electronic circuitry to sort voltage pulses according to size. Since pulse-height is proportional to energy deposition in most systems, this technique allows the energy spectrum of the incident radiation to be constructed.

Q

QFE (Quartz Fibre Electroscope)
A pocket dosemeter based on the discharge of a quartz fibre.

Quality factor
A factor which takes account of the dependence of **stochastic effects** on radiation quality or **LET**. In ICRP 26 the absorbed dose at a point in a tissue was multiplied by quality factor to give **dose equivalent**. In ICRP 60 these are replaced by **radiation weighting factors**.

Quenching
A term used in connection with 1. gas-filled detectors and 2. liquid scintillation counting.
1. A means of preventing the positive ions in a **Geiger counter** from triggering further pulses when they reach the wall of the tube. Quenching can be achieved by lowering the anode voltage for a fixed time or by incorporating a gas such as a halogen into the tube filling.
2. A reduction in the light output of a liquid scintillant as a result of introduction of a sample.

Q-value
The energy released in a nuclear reaction.

R

Rabbit
A small container pneumatically propelled through a tube between a laboratory and an irradiation device, for example, a nuclear reactor. A sample can thus be irradiated and returned for investigation with a short transit delay and a minimum of handling.

Rad

A now obsolete unit of absorbed radiation dose, equivalent to 0.01 J kg^{-1}. The unit has now been replaced by the SI unit, the **gray (Gy)**, equal to 100 rads. See **Roentgen** and **Rem**.

Radiation

Electromagnetic waves especially (in the context of nuclear energy), X-rays and gamma-rays, or streams of fast-moving particles (electrons, alpha-particles, neutrons, protons).

Radiation area

An area to which access is controlled because of a local radiation hazard.

Radiation burns

Skin damage similar to heat burns caused by intense or prolonged exposure to radiation.

Radiation chemistry

The study of the influence of radiation on chemical properties and reactions, and its applications. See **Radiochemistry**.

Radiation source

A quantity of radioactive material used as a source of ionising radiation.

Radiation weighting factor

In ICRP 60, these factors are used to allow for the dependence of **stochastic effects** on radiation quality or **LET**. The absorbed dose averaged over a tissue or organ is multiplied by the radiation weighting factor to give the **equivalent dose.**

Radicals

A group of atoms with an unpaired electron. These are highly reactive and play an important role in, for example, radiation chemistry.

Radioactive concentration

The activity per unit quantity of any material in which a radionuclide occurs.

Radioactivity

The property of certain nuclides of emitting radiation by the spontaneous transformation of their nuclei.

Radioactive chain or series

A radioactive decay chain, showing the successive daughter radionuclides, for example, the natural decay series originating with ^{238}U.

Radioactive equilibrium

A steady state condition in which the rate of decay of a daughter radionuclide becomes equal to its rate of production from the parent radionuclide.

Radioactivity

The property possessed by some atomic nuclei of disintegrating spontaneously, with loss of energy through emission of a charged particle and/or gamma-radiation.

Radioactivity, induced

Radioactivity that has been induced in an otherwise inactive material, usually by irradiation with neutrons.

Radioactivity, natural
The radioactivity of naturally occurring elements, for example, uranium, thorium, radium, lead, potassium and carbon, due to one or more of the isotopes being radioactive.

Radiobiology
The branch of science dealing with the interactions of radiation or radioactive substances with biological systems.

Radiocarbon dating
Technique based on the measurement of residual ^{14}C content of a plant or animal after death.

Radiochemical purity
Of a radioactive material, the proportion of the total activity that is present in the stated chemical form.

Radiochemistry
That part of chemistry which deals with radioactive materials, including the production of radionuclides etc. by processing irradiated or naturally occurring radioactive materials. The use of radioactivity in the investigation of chemical problems. See also **Radiation Chemistry**.

Radiogenic
1. Resulting from radioactive decay.
2. Caused by radiation.

Radiography
A method of non-destructive testing in which a beam of penetrating radiation is passed through the object under examination, where the dense parts absorb more radiation. The resulting variations of radiation intensity can be recorded on photographic film or digitally in a computer. Medical diagnostic X-rays and industrial gamma-radiography are the best-known examples. In neutron radiography, a beam of thermal neutrons is used.

Radioimmunotherapy
The delivery of a therapeutic dose to a cancerous tumour by labelling a cell-killing radionuclide onto a monoclonal antibody whose uptake is very strong in the tumour.

Radioisotope
An isotope which is radioactive.

Radioisotope generator
Device for providing a means of obtaining short-lived radionuclides at places far away from nuclear reactors or cyclotrons. It consists of a longer-lived parent radionuclide which decays to a shorter-lived daughter, which can be removed ('milked') from the system for use as a tracer, for example, in a hospital.

Radiology
The branch of medicine specialising in the uses of ionising radiations for medical diagnosis, and in studying their effects. See **Radiobiology, Radiotherapy**.

Radiolysis
The decomposition of material by radiation, for example, water into hydrogen and oxygen.

Radionuclide
A nuclide which is radioactive.

Radiopharmaceutical
A radionuclide in one of several forms, such as ionic, organic or gaseous, administered to a patient in order to deliver dose to an organ for radiotherapy or radiodiagnostic purposes.

Radiotherapy
Treatment of disease by the use of ionising radiation.

Radiotoxicity
A measure of the harmfulness of a radioactive substance to the body or to a specified organ following its uptake by a given process.

Radiotracer
Tracer labelled with radioactive material.

Radon
A radioactive inert gaseous element of natural origin. It is estimated to cause about half of the average radiation exposure in the UK.

Ratemeter
An instrument for detecting electrical pulses and displaying them in terms of the average number of pulses arriving per unit time. Often used in conjunction with radiation detectors. See also **Counter**.

Reactor
  See **Nuclear Reactor**

Rayleigh scattering
Coherent elastic scattering of photons by bound electrons.

Recoil
The motion acquired by a particle through ejecting another particle or photon.

Recording level
The value of a dose or intake above which a result is of sufficient interest to be worth keeping and interpreting.

Reference man/women
A person with the anatomical and physiological characteristics defined in the report of the ICRP Task Group on Reference Man/Woman (see ICRP Publication No.23).

Rem (Roentgen equivalent man) An obsolete unit of dose equivalent. The absorbed dose in rads multiplied by the Quality Factor of the type of radiation. Now replaced by the **sievert**.

Rest mass
The mass of a body, for example, a particle, having zero velocity.

Roentgen
An obsolete unit of exposure of X- or gamma-radiation. One roentgen is an exposure of X- or gamma-radiation such that the associated corpuscular emission per 1.293×10^{-6} kg of

dry air at 0°C and 760mm Hg produces, in air, ions carrying 1 electrostatic unit of quantity of electricity of either sign.

Rutherford scattering
Elastic scattering of charged particles between which an inverse-square law force is operating.

S

Scaler
An instrument for counting electrical pulses and displaying their total in digital form, often used in the measurement of radiation levels. See also **Counter, Ratemeter**.

Scintillation counter
A radiation detector in which the radiations cause individual flashes of light in a solid (or liquid) 'scintillator' material. Their intensity is related to the energy of the radiation. The flashes are amplified and measured electrically and displayed or recorded digitally as individual 'counts'.

Sealed source
A radiation source totally enclosed in a protective capsule or other container so that no radioactive material can leak from it.

Secular equilibrium
The condition, that the activity of a daughter radionuclide is equal to that of its parent. A necessary prerequisite is that the daughter **half-life** is much less than the parent half-life.

Self-shielding
The shielding from external radiations of the inner parts of a body or mass of material by the absorption, in its outer parts, of some of the incoming radiation.

Semiconductor detector
A radiation detector which uses the effect of radiation on the electrical properties of semiconducting material.

Shell model
A concept that neutrons and protons in a nucleus may be arranged in shells or layers somewhat similar to the arrangement of the electron orbits in an atom.

Sievert, Sv
The SI Unit of radiation dose equivalent; the product of absorbed dose in **grays** and the **quality factor**. (1 Sv = 100 rem).

Single Channel Analyser
Electronic device which produces an output logic pulse only if the input pulse amplitude lies between two levels, used to select only a limited range of pulse amplitudes from a radiation detector.

Site licence
A licence issued by the Nuclear Installations Inspectorate covering safety of design, construction, operation and maintenance of facilities at a nuclear site.

Soft radiation
Radiation having little penetrating power.

Solubility class
Classification of compounds in ICRP 30 according to lung clearance time. See **inhalation class**.

Solvent extraction
A chemical separation method. Two immiscible liquids, one being a mixture of dissolved substances and the other a good solvent for the material to be extracted, are agitated together. The material required passes into the solvent from which it can be recovered when the two liquids are allowed to separate out.

Spallation
Used for reactions in which a number of particles are emitted as a result of a direct interaction.

Specific radioactivity
The activity per unit mass of an element or compound containing a radioactive nuclide.

Specific gamma ray constant (or emission)
Of a radioactive nuclide, the exposure dose rate produced by the gamma rays from a unit point source of that nuclide at unit distance.

Spike
A radiotracer, preferably of pure isotopic composition, used to determine the chemical yield of a given process.

Stable isotope
An isotope which is not radioactive.

Sterilisation plant, gamma-ray
A plant in which gamma-rays from cobalt-60 are used to sterilise packaged medical equipment etc. in bulk.

Stochastic effects (of radiation exposure)
Those where the probability of occurrence is assumed to be proportional to dose without a threshold; they include induction of cancer and genetic effects. See **non-stochastic effects** and **deterministic effects**.

Supervised areas
An area for radioactive work where conditions are kept under review but where special procedures are not usually needed.

Szilard–Chalmers reaction
A nuclear reaction in which the chemical bonds are broken. If after breaking the bonds the product atoms exist in a different chemical state from that of the original target atoms, they may be separated to produce a source of high specific activity.

T

Tandem accelerator, Tandem generator
A particle accelerator comprising a **Van de Graaff** generator in which the generated

voltage is in effect doubled by reversing the charge on the accelerated particles half-way along their path. The effect is that of two **Van de Graaff** generators in series.

Thermal fission
Fission induced by **thermal neutrons**.

Thermal neutrons
Neutrons in thermodynamic equilibrium, that is, moving with the same mean kinetic energy) with their surroundings. At room temperature their mean energy is about 0.025 eV and their speed about 2.2×10^3 m s^{-1}.

Tissue weighting factor
A factor which represents the relative contribution of an organ or tissue to the total detriment resulting from uniform irradiation of the whole body. They are used to weight the **equivalent doses** to organs when summing to yield the **effective dose**.

TLA (Thin Layer Activation)
Process in which a beam of high energy ions from an accelerator is used to produce radionuclides in the near surface layers of an object. Subsequent surface wear can be quantified by measurement of removed activity.

TLD (Thermoluminescent dosemeter)
A type of personal dosimeter in which the radiation energy is stored and from which it can be released by heating, in the form of light. The amount of light emitted gives a measure of the radiation absorbed. See also **Film Badge**.

Tracer
An easily detected material used in small quantities to label a larger quantity of material so that its subsequent movements can be studied.

Track–etch detectors
Polymers which record damage trails when irradiated by heavily ionising particles such as neutron recoils. These trails can be rendered visible by chemical etching. These detectors can be used as the basis for personal fast-neutron dosemeters.

Transformation
The change of one nuclide into another.

Transient equilibrium
The condition, that the ratio of daughter to parent activities in a given radioactive decay is constant. A necessary prerequisite is that the daughter **half-life** is less than the parent half-life.

Transition, nuclear
A change in the configuration of a nucleus, usually either a disintegration or a change in internal energy level, accompanied by emission of radiation.

Tritium
An isotope of hydrogen having a mass number of 3, with two neutrons and one proton in the nucleus.

U

Unsealed source
Radioactive material that is not encapsulated or otherwise sealed, and which forms a source of radiation, for example, radioactive material in use as a **tracer.**

Unsupported radionuclide
A daughter radionuclide, for example, in one of the natural decay series, which has become separated from its precursor radionuclides. An example is the quantity of ^{210}Pb falling with rain produced in the decay of ^{222}Rn which has diffused into the atmosphere.

Uranium Series Disequilibrium measurement
Technique in which the ratio of the radioactivities of a parent and daughter radionuclide in the **natural decay series** are measured, with applications in, for example, earth, marine and environmental sciences.

V

Van de Graaff generator
An electrostatic generator in which a high electrical potential is produced by the accumulation of electric charge conveyed to an insulated conductor by a continuously moving belt. The potential may be used for accelerating charged particles. See **Tandem Generator**.

W

Wastes, nuclear
Products of the nuclear industry which are deemed to be of no further value but which, because of their radioactivity, are subject to special regulations. Spent nuclear fuel is not 'waste' if it is intended to reprocess it to recover uranium and plutonium.

Whole body monitors
An assembly of large scintillation detectors, heavily shielded against background radiation, used to identify and measure the total gamma-radiation emitted by the human body. This will include radiation from normal constituents of the body, such as potassium and other minerals (including fall-out from weapons tests) taken in with foodstuffs. All this forms the background against which the desired measurements must be made of the gamma activity and/or X-rays due, for example, to radioactive materials inhaled or ingested accidentally or as a result of working conditions.

X

X-rays
Electromagnetic radiations having much shorter wavelengths and hence higher energies than those of visible light. X-rays with clearly defined energies are produced in atomic orbital electron transitions, and are very similar to gamma-rays but usually of lower energy. X-rays produced by the interaction of high energy electrons with matter have a continuous energy spectrum used in medical X-ray machines.

X-ray fluorescence
A technique whereby an element may be identified and measured by the characteristic discrete X-rays emitted when it is irradiated by radiation of a slightly higher energy.

SELECTED ORGANISATIONS ON THE INTERNET

http://nuke.westlab.com	Nuclear information
http://paprika.saclay.cea.fr/uk/index.html	CEA (France)
http://www.aeat.co.uk/	AEA Technology plc
http://www.aecl.ca/hom_e.htm	AECL (Canada)
http://www.anl.gov/	Argonne National Lab
http://www.ansi.org	American National Standards Institute
http://www.bbsrc.ac.uk	Biomolecular Science Research Council
http://www.bnfl.co.uk/	BNFL, all sites
http://www.bnms.org.uk/bnms/	British Nuclear Medicine Society
http://www.british-energy.co.uk/	British Energy
http://www.chemsoc.org	Royal Society of Chemistry
http://www.eml.doe.gov/procman/intro1.htm	Access to the HASL manual
http://www.epsrc.ac.uk	Engineering and Physical Sciences Research Council
http://www.iaea.or.at/	International Atomic Energy Agency
http://www.ijs.si/	Jozef Stefan Institute in English
http://www.iop.org/	Institute of Physics
http://www.lanl.gov/external/index.html	Los Alamos National Laboratory
http://www.lbl.gov/	Livermore National Laboratory
http://www.lgc.co.uk	Laboratory of the Government Chemist
http://www.mrc.ac.uk/MRC/	Medical Research Council
http://www.ncrp.com	National Council on Radiation Protection
http://www.nerc.ac.uk	Natural Environmental Research Council
http://www.nirex.co.uk/	NIREX
http://www.nist.gov/	National Institute of Standards and Technology
http://www.npl.co.uk/	National Physical Laboratory
http://www.nrpa.no	Norwegian Radiation Protection Authority
http://www.nrpb.org.uk	NRPB, all sites
http://www.nuclear electric.co.uk/	Nuclear Electric, all sites
http://www.nycomed-amersham.co.uk	Nycomed Amersham
http://www.ornl.gov/	Oak Ridge National Laboratory
http://www.pharmacopoeia.co.uk	The British Pharmacopoeia
http://www.ukaea.org.uk	United Kingdom Atomic Energy Authority
http://www.who.ch/	World Health Organisation
http://www/jaeri.go.jp/	Japanese AEA

SELECTED ACRONYMS

ACSNI
Advisory Committee on the Safety of Nuclear Installations

ARSAC
Administration of Radioactive Substances Advisory Committee

AURPO
Association of University Radiation Protection Officers

BCR
Community Bureau of Reference, Commission of the European Communities

COMARE
Committee on Medical Aspects of Radiation in the Environment

DTI
Department of Trade and Industry

EML
Environmental Measurements Laboratory, U.S. Department of Energy, formerly **HASL** – Health and Safety Laboratory

EPA
Environmental Protection Agency

GLP
Good laboratory practice

HSC
Health and Safety Commission

HSE
Health and Safety Executive

IAEA
International Atomic Energy Agency

ICRP
International Commission on Radiation Protection.

ICRU
International Commission on Radiation Units and Measurement

IRAC
Ionising Radiations Advisory Committee

IRR
Ionising Radiations Regulations

MIRD
Medical Internal Radiation Dose Committee of United States Society of Medicine

MRC
Medical Research Council

NAMAS
National Accreditation of Measurement and Sampling

NEA
Nuclear Energy Agency

NERC
Natural Environment Research council

NCRP
National Council on Radiation Protection and Measurements

NII
Nuclear Installations Inspectorate

NIST
National Institute for Standards and Technology

NPL
National Physical Laboratory

NRC
National Research Council, Canada

NRPB
National Radiological Protection Board

OECD
Organisation for Economic Development

RADREM
Radioactivity Research and Environmental Monitoring Committee

RADWASS
Radioactive Waste Safety Standards

RIDDOR
Reporting of Injuries, Diseases and Dangerous Occurrences Regulations

RMMG
Radioactivity Monitoring Management Group

RWMAC
Radioactive Waste Management Advisory Committee

SEPA
Scottish Environment Protection Agency

UKAEA

United Kingdom Atomic Energy Authority. Note, AEA Technology plc is a private sector company which was formerly part of UKAEA

UKAS

The United Kingdom Accreditation Service

UNSCEAR

United Nations Scientific Committee on Effects of Atomic Radiation

DECIMAL MULTIPLES AND SUBMULTIPLES TO BE USED WITH SI UNITS

Prefix	Symbol	Power
exa	E	10^{18}
peta	P	10^{15}
tera	T	10^{12}
giga	G	10^{9}
mega	M	10^{6}
kilo	k	10^{3}
hecto	h	10^{2}
deca	da	10^{1}
deci	d	10^{-1}
centi	c	10^{-2}
milli	m	10^{-3}
micro	μ	10^{-6}
nano	n	10^{-9}
pico	p	10^{12}
femto	f	10^{-15}
atto	a	10^{-18}

CHAPTER 1 INTRODUCTION

GEOFF LONGWORTH

1.1 HISTORY

The history of radioactivity dates from its discovery by Becquerel a century ago in the three months between February and May 1896 [1-5]. The discovery arose following his studies of luminescence, from the observation that uranium salts placed in contact with a photographic plate produced a blackening of the plate in the absence of any excitation by sunlight. This property of uranium of 'radiant activity' was called **radioactivity** by Marie Curie. There followed the realisation that the radiation was emitted by other elements, such as thorium and the discovery of polonium and radium by the Curies [6,7].

Three types of radiation, **alpha particles**, **beta particles** and **gamma rays** were identified. Rutherford and Soddy suggested in 1903 that the atoms of radioactive elements disintegrate spontaneously to form atoms of different elements accompanied by the emission of alpha or beta particles [8]. This led to the theory of radioactive growth and decay. It was realised that the known radioactive elements could be divided into three series, originating with either uranium or thorium and ending with lead. There was a discrepancy between the existence of about 40 radioelements in the three series but only 11 chemically different elements between uranium and lead. This was resolved by Soddy and Fajans in 1913 who formulated the rules governing the production of new elements following alpha and beta decay [9]. Radioactive elements having different **mass numbers** that fell in the same place in the Periodic Table were identified as **isotopes** which had been postulated by Soddy in 1910 and established experimentally by Thomson in 1912 [10].

In the pioneering studies of the scattering of alpha particles by thin metal films between 1906 and 1909, Rutherford, Geiger and Marsden observed that a small number of the alpha particles suffered large deflections [11,12]. This led Rutherford in 1911 to postulate the current model of the atom with the positive charge contained in a very small central nucleus [12]. In 1919 Rutherford bombarded nitrogen atoms with alpha particles and observed the emission of high energy **protons**. This experiment established the possibility of nuclear reactions [13].

The discovery of artificial **radionuclides** by the Joliot-Curies in 1934 [14] was followed by the development of the cyclotron which was used to produce radionuclides from the bombardment of a range of elements by high energy light particles. The discovery of **nuclear fission** in 1939 [15] led to the first **nuclear reactor** in 1942 [16] and to the Manhattan Project during the Second World War. Since that time many hundreds of nuclear reactors have been built mainly for nuclear power but they have also been used to produce an enormous range of artificial radionuclides. In the following chapters some of the uses of such radionuclides in industry, biochemistry and medicine are presented. It is as well to remember alongside the destructive power of radioactivity, the tremendous advantages gained from its applications particularly in diagnostic and therapeutic medicine.

1

1.2 ATOMS, NUCLEI, ELECTRONS, PROTONS AND NEUTRONS

All elements consist of atoms which in the semi-classical theory of Bohr may be regarded as being composed of a central, heavy and positively charged nucleus surrounded by a series of shells containing light, negatively charged electrons. For a neutral atom the negative charge due to the electrons is equal in magnitude to the positive charge on the nucleus. The electrons in the outer shells determine the chemical properties of the atoms.

The existence of a positively charged particle, the **positron** with the same mass and charge magnitude as the electron (negatron) was discovered by Anderson in cosmic ray tracks in a Wilson cloud chamber [17].

The nucleus is made up of protons and neutrons which are collectively known as **nucleons**. The proton has an associated positive charge equal in magnitude but opposite in sign to that of the electron while the neutron has no associated charge. The total number of protons in a given nucleus (Z) is known as the **atomic number** or **charge number** while the total number of neutrons (N) is known as the neutron number. The total number of nucleons in a given nucleus is known as the **mass number** or the **nucleon number** (A) and hence A = N + Z. The identity and the chemical properties of an element are determined by the atomic number.

A given element, may be composed of atoms that have the same numbers of protons in the nucleus but differing numbers of neutrons. Such atoms with the same Z value but different N values are known as isotopes of the element and a **radioisotope** is a radioactive isotope. The general term **nuclide** is used to describe any specific nuclear species while **radionuclide** refers to any radioactive nuclear species. The term **isobar** is used to describe nuclides with the same mass number (A). The various nuclides are identified using a symbol such as $^{238}_{92}U$ where the superscript refers to the mass number, the subscript to the atomic number and the letter is the chemical symbol for the element. Other examples are the isotopes of hydrogen, $^{1}_{1}H$ (hydrogen or light hydrogen), $^{2}_{1}H$ (**deuterium** or heavy hydrogen) and $^{3}_{1}H$ (**tritium**). Usually the subscript is omitted since the mass number and chemical symbol are sufficient to define a given nuclide.

The atomic mass of a nuclide is the nuclide mass measured in atomic mass units. The **atomic mass unit** (amu) is defined as one twelfth of the mass of the ^{12}C atom which then has an atomic mass of 12 amu. The absolute mass of the ^{12}C atom, 1.993×10^{-23} g or 1.993×10^{-26} kg, is given by the mass number (12) divided by Avogadro's number (6.022×10^{23} atoms per g.atom). The mass of the electron is 0.000549 amu while the proton and neutron masses are 1.007825 amu and 1.008665 amu respectively.

The atomic mass of an element would be expected to be close to the total number of nucleons, that is, the mass number. This is frequently not the case due to the fact that many elements have several stable isotopes with different relative abundances which each contribute to the net mass of the element. For example, chlorine has two stable isotopes ^{35}Cl (75.77%) and ^{37}Cl (24.23%), where the relative percentage abundances are shown in parentheses. The average mass of the chlorine atoms, or **atomic weight**, is 35.453.

It is found that the measured mass of any nucleus is slightly less than the mass sum of its constituent nucleons. The difference is known as the **mass defect** and is usually expressed in units of energy using the Einstein equation relating mass (m) with energy (E), $E = mc^2$, where c is the velocity of light *in vacuo* (2.997925×10^8 m.s^{-1}) and 1 amu is equivalent to

931.5 MeV). This energy is known as the nucleon or nuclear **binding energy** which holds the nucleons together. For example, the atomic mass of the deuterium ($_1^2H$) nucleus, a **deuteron**, would be expected to be the sum of the atomic masses of one neutron and one proton, that is, 1.007825 amu + 1.008665 amu = 2.01649 amu. The measured deuterium mass is 2.01410 amu so that the mass defect is -0.00239 amu, equivalent to a binding energy of 2.226 MeV or binding energy per nucleon of 1.113 MeV. This binding energy will be released when deuterium is formed by the capture of a neutron by a proton. The average binding energy per nucleon as a function of atomic mass increases from about 1 MeV for deuterium to about 7 MeV for ⁴He. For heavier nuclides it has a value in a narrow range between about 7.4 MeV and 8.8 MeV with a broad maximum at around mass number 60 [18].

The positive binding energy implies that there are attractive nuclear binding forces within the nucleus. These are in addition to the repulsive Coulomb force between protons which becomes increasingly important for higher atomic numbers (Z).

Isomers or isomeric nuclides are nuclides which have the same atomic number and mass number but different nuclear binding energies and hence different energy states. Each energy state has its own measurable lifetime. The lowest energy state is known as the ground state and states with higher energy are usually called excited states. The term metastable **isomeric states** is used to describe longer lived isomeric states that typically exist for times longer than a microsecond. Isomers formed in an excited state will decay to the ground state frequently with the emission of gamma radiation (see Section 1.4.3). Examples are:

$$_{27}^{60m}Co \rightarrow _{27}^{60g}Co \qquad\qquad t_{\frac{1}{2}} = 10.5 \text{ m}$$

$$_{43}^{99m}Tc \rightarrow _{43}^{99g}Tc \qquad\qquad t_{\frac{1}{2}} = 6.01 \text{ h}$$

where m and g signify metastable and ground states and $t_{\frac{1}{2}}$ is the half-life of the excited state (see Section 1.3). ⁹⁹ᵐTc is widely used in medical diagnostic imaging (see Sections 4.2.1.3 and 5.5.7.1).

Finally, the energy states of nuclei are unique or quantised with an important parameter or quantum number being nuclear spin [18].

1.3 NUCLEAR STABILITY AND RADIOACTIVE DECAY

Out of about 1700 known nuclides only about 275 are stable and do not change with time. In Section 1.2 it was noted that nuclides with nucleon numbers around 60, that is iron, cobalt etc., have greater nuclear binding energies/nucleon implying they are more stable than nuclides with higher or lower nucleon numbers About 60% of the total number of stable nuclides contain even numbers of both protons and neutrons (even-even nuclei) and the remaining 40% are approximately equally divided between those having an even number of protons and odd number of neutrons (even-odd nuclei) and those having an odd number of protons and even number of neutrons (odd-even nuclei). This is explained in terms of the greater stability gained by having pairs of like nucleons. A plot of the number of protons (Z) against the number of neutrons (N) for stable nuclides indicates that for lighter nuclides, below about Z=10, N/Z = 1 while for heavier nuclides N/Z increases to a value of about 1.5 for bismuth (Z=83). Thus stability depends both on a given N/Z ratio as well as on the pairing of nucleons. Further discussion of the factors that govern the stability of nuclides is outside the scope of the present volume, but may be found in most nuclear physics text-books such as Burcham [18-20].

Each of the approximately 1400 remaining nuclides is unstable, that is, it is radioactive and will undergo one or successive spontaneous nuclear transformations or decays until a stable nuclide is reached.

The radioactive decay process is largely insensitive to conditions outside the nucleus and therefore for a given nuclide, it may be characterised by a fixed decay probability as well as by the mode and energy of decay. It is a statistical process such that although the decay probability is constant, the moment of decay of a particular atom of an unstable nuclide cannot be predicted.

The radioactive decay law, established experimentally by Rutherford and Soddy [8] states that:

$$N_t = N_0 e^{-\lambda t} \qquad (1.1)$$

where N_t and N_0 are the number of radioactive atoms at time t and time t=0 respectively and λ is the **decay constant**. The decay constant λ is the probability that an atom will decay in unit time. It has a characteristic value for each radionuclide and is related to the **half-life** $t_{1/2}$ which is the time in which the number of original or parent radionuclides is reduced by a factor of two and is given by:

$$t_{1/2} = \frac{\ln(2)}{\lambda} \cong \frac{0.693}{\lambda} \qquad (1.2)$$

Values of half-life cover an enormous range from, for example, 1.65×10^{-4} for ^{214}Po to 1.405×10^{10} y for ^{232}Th.

The number of atoms decaying in unit time, that is, the activity A, is given by:

$$A = N\lambda = -\frac{dN}{dt} \qquad (1.3)$$

The decay equation may be rewritten in terms of activities as:

$$A_t = A_0 e^{-\lambda t} \qquad (1.4)$$

The unit of activity is the **becquerel** (Bq) corresponding to one decay or disintegration per second. An older unit used is the **curie** based on the nominal activity of 1g of ^{226}Ra. 1 curie (Ci) is equal to 3.7×10^{10} disintegrations per second (Bq).

In many instances the radioactive decay of one parent nuclide is then followed by the decay of the daughter nuclide. This may be followed by successive decays until a stable nuclide is reached. Examples of these decay chains are the three **natural decay series** originating with ^{238}U, ^{232}Th and ^{235}U (Section 1.7.1). The decay law may be extended to the case of successive decays where the parent nuclide 1 decays to a daughter 2 which then decays to a grand-daughter 3 which is stable. The rate of decay of the daughter nuclide $\left(\dfrac{dN_2}{dt}\right)$ is given by the difference between its rate of loss and its production rate from parent 1. Thus, if the decay constants for nuclides 1 and 2 are λ_1 and λ_2, then:

4

$$\frac{dN_2}{dt} = N_1\lambda_1 - N_2\lambda_2 \qquad (1.5)$$

On the assumption that at time t = 0 there are N_0 parent nuclides of type 1, then at time t, N_2 is given by:

$$N_2 = N_0 \frac{\lambda_1}{\lambda_2 - \lambda_1}\left(e^{-\lambda_1 t} - e^{-\lambda_2 t}\right) \qquad (1.6)$$

The activity of the daughter nuclide (2) is given by $A_2 = N_2\lambda_2$ while the activity A_1 for the parent (1) is given by:

$$A_1 = N_1\lambda_1 = N_0 e^{-\lambda_1 t} \qquad (1.7)$$

Thus the ratio of daughter (2) to parent (1) nuclides, $\frac{A_2}{A_1}$ is given by:

$$\frac{A_2}{A_1} = \frac{\lambda_2}{(\lambda_2 - \lambda_1)}\left(1 - e^{-(\lambda_2 - \lambda_1)t}\right) \qquad (1.8)$$

If the half-life of the daughter (2) is less than that of its parent (1) then the activity ratio (A_2/A_1) first increases with time and then becomes constant. For all times:

$$t \gg \frac{1}{\lambda_2 - \lambda_1}$$

the ratio of daughter to parent activites is given by:

$$\frac{A_2}{A_1} = \frac{\lambda_2}{\lambda_2 - \lambda_1} = \frac{t_{1/2}(1)}{t_{1/2}(1) - t_{1/2}(2)} \qquad (1.9)$$

where $t_{1/2}(2)$ and $t_{1/2}(1)$ are the daughter and parent half-lives. This condition is known as **transient equilibrium** and clearly the ratio A_2/A_1 is constant and greater than unity.

An example of transient equilibrium occurs in the decay of ^{99}Mo ($t_{1/2}$ = 2.748d) to ^{99m}Tc ($t_{1/2}$ = 6.01h), used as an **radioisotope generator** (see Section 4.2.1.3). In this particular case the activity ratio A_2/A_1 becomes less than unity since ^{99m}Tc is produced in only 87.2% of the decays.

If the half-life of the daughter (2) is much less than that of the parent (1), such that $\lambda_1 \ll \lambda_2$ then expression (1.8) simplifies to :

$$\frac{A_2}{A_1} = 1 - e^{-\lambda_2 t} \qquad (1.10)$$

Thus, the daughter (2) activity increases exponentially at a rate governed by its own decay constant λ_2 and for long times when $t \gg t_{1/2}$, the ratio of daughter to parent activities approaches unity, and the two nuclides are said to be in **secular equilibrium**.

An example of this is in the decay of ^{234}U ($t_{1/2} = 2.457 \times 10^5$y) to ^{230}Th ($t_{1/2} = 7.54 \times 10^4$y). However, in nature, for example, in the near surface layers of a rock, the activity ratio ^{230}Th/^{234}U may be disturbed due to the differing chemical properties of the parent and daughter. Use of this feature is made in uranium series disequilibrium studies (Section 5.4.1).

These equations for a chain of three nuclides have been generalised to the case of many nuclides in a decay series - the Bateman equations [21] which are discussed in, for example, Evans [22].

1.4 MODES OF DECAY

It was noted in Section 1.3 that the stable nuclides had a neutron to proton ratio (N/Z) within a narrow range of $\cong$ 1-1.5. Nuclides with higher N/Z are neutron rich and will undergo radioactive decay in order to reduce the N/Z ratio. This can be achieved by the conversion of a neutron to a proton within the nucleus with the emission of an electron (negatron). Conversely nuclides with too low a N/Z ratio for stability will decay by the conversion of a proton to a neutron and the emission of a positron. Both these processes are known as beta decay which is the dominant decay process for nuclides with charge numbers (Z) less than about 80. **Electron capture** is an alternative process to positron emission, leading to the same daughter nuclide. In this process the parent nuclide is converted to the daughter nuclide by the capture of an extranuclear electron and the conversion of a proton to a neutron.

Above Z $\cong$ 80 another decay process becomes dominant, namely alpha decay involving the emission of an alpha particle (helium nucleus = 2 protons and 2 neutrons). The spontaneous emission of an alpha particle arises because the Coulomb repulsion forces within the nucleus increase with nuclear charge at a higher rate than the nuclear binding forces. The alpha particle is favoured because of its large binding energy and relatively small mass.

Radioactive decay involves a transition from a well-defined energy state of the original nuclide to a well-defined and lower energy state in a product nuclide. The difference in these energies corresponds to the decay energy which appears in the form of either electromagnetic radiation or as the kinetic energy of the decay products. The principal modes of radioactive decay are alpha decay, beta decay, electron capture and gamma emission. Alpha decay involves the emission of alpha particles which consist of helium nuclei. Beta decay involves the emission of either electrons or positrons. In electron capture the nucleus captures one of its own electrons. In gamma emission, short wavelength electromagnetic radiation in the form of gamma rays is emitted in a transition between two energy states of the same nucleus. Internal conversion represents a competing process to gamma ray emission in which the surplus energy is transferred to an atomic electron causing it to be ejected from the atom.

An alternative mode of decay for heavy nuclides of atomic mass A>230 is by spontaneous fission in which the nucleus dissociates into two roughly equal parts - fission fragments with the release of large amounts of energy of about 200 MeV per fission. Most of this energy goes into the kinetic energy of the fission fragments. These are accompanied by the emission of neutrons and electromagnetic radiation. The fission fragments then undergo a series of radioactive decays such that several hundred radionuclides - **fission products** - are produced which have a wide range of half lives. Fission may also be induced in heavy nuclides via bombardment, for example, with neutrons or charged particles.

The changes in mass number and atomic number for the main types of radioactive decay are illustrated schematically for a general location on the chart of the nuclides [23], in Figure 1.1. Here each square represents a different radionuclide arranged in order of increasing atomic number Z and neutron number N. In β⁻ decay Z is increased by 1 and N reduced by 1, whereas in β⁺ decay or electron capture Z is reduced by 1 and N is increased by 1. Emission of a neutron will reduce N by 1 but leave Z the same while emission of an alpha particle will reduce both N and Z by 2. In the next four sub-sections, the types of decay are discussed in more detail.

RADIOACTIVE DECAY

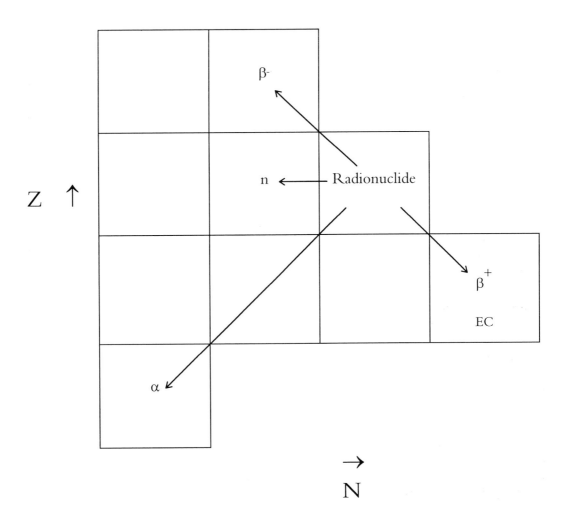

Figure 1.1   **Changes in atomic mass and atomic number for the main types of radioactive decays depicted on a section of chart of the nuclides (from G. Choppin, J. Rydberg and J.O. Liljenzin, Radiochemistry and nuclear chemistry, by permission of Butterworth-Heinemann, Oxford).**

1.4.1 Alpha decay

Alpha decay involves the emission of an alpha particle or helium nucleus $_2^4He^{2+}$ (2 protons and 2 neutrons). After the alpha decay the mass number A has decreased by 4 and the atomic number Z by 2. Alpha decay becomes predominant for nuclides with Z greater than about 80. In general for the lighter nuclides, alpha decay occurs directly to the ground state of the daughter nuclide and the emitted α particles are monoenergetic.

$$_{84}^{210}Po \rightarrow _{82}^{206}Pb \qquad t_{1/2} = 138.376d \qquad E_\alpha = 5.305 \text{ MeV}$$

Alpha decay in heavier nuclides is more complex leading to several excited states in the daughter nuclide and hence several discrete alpha particle energies. Examples of this are the decay of ^{238}U (section 5.4.1) which results in the emission of two alpha particles at discrete energies:

$$_{92}^{238}U \rightarrow _{90}^{234}Th + \alpha, \quad t_{1/2} = 4.468 \times 10^9 \, y \qquad E_\alpha = 4.150 \text{ MeV and } 4.199 \text{ MeV}$$

and the decay of ^{228}Th with the emission of four alpha particles at discrete energies:

$$_{90}^{228}Th \rightarrow _{88}^{224}Ra + \alpha, \quad t_{1/2} = 1.913y \qquad E_\alpha = 5.177, 5.211, 5.340 \text{ and } 5.423\text{MeV}$$

Figure 1.2 shows the energy level diagram for the ^{228}Th decay. As a result of these transitions the product nuclide ^{224}Ra is left either in its ground state or in one of three excited states which then decay to the ground state by γ emission.

The energy released in alpha decay is given by the release of the binding energy. In the decay ^{238}U → ^{234}Th + α, the energy released, the reaction **Q-value** is given by (m_{238} – m_{234} – m_α) × 931.5 MeV ≅ 4.3 MeV (see Section 1.2), where m_{238}, m_{234} and m_α are the masses of the ^{238}U, ^{234}Th and alpha particle in amu). Since the emitted alpha particle has kinetic energy, conservation of momentum and energy in the decay process ensures that the product nuclide will recoil with a given energy. As a result of the conservation of momentum, $m_{234} v_{234} = m_\alpha v_\alpha$, where v_{234} and v_α are the velocities of the ^{234}Th nuclide and the alpha particle. The kinetic energy of the ^{234}Th nuclide is then given by:

$$\frac{1}{2}m_{234}v_{234}^2 = \frac{1}{2}\frac{m_\alpha^2 v_\alpha^2}{m_{234}} = E_\alpha\left(\frac{m_\alpha}{m_{234}}\right) \qquad (1.10)$$

where $E_\alpha = \frac{1}{2}m_\alpha v_\alpha^2$ is the kinetic energy of the alpha particle. Since $E_\alpha \cong 4.2\text{MeV}$ and

$\frac{m_\alpha}{m_{234}} \cong \frac{4}{234} = 0.017$, then $E_{234} \cong 0.07\text{MeV}$. Although this energy is much less than the kinetic energy of the alpha particle, it is much larger than the chemical binding energies (several eV) and thus the recoiling daughter nuclide will break the chemical bonds and indeed may be ejected from the near surface of a compound (see Chapter 4 on isotopic fractionation produced by alpha decay).

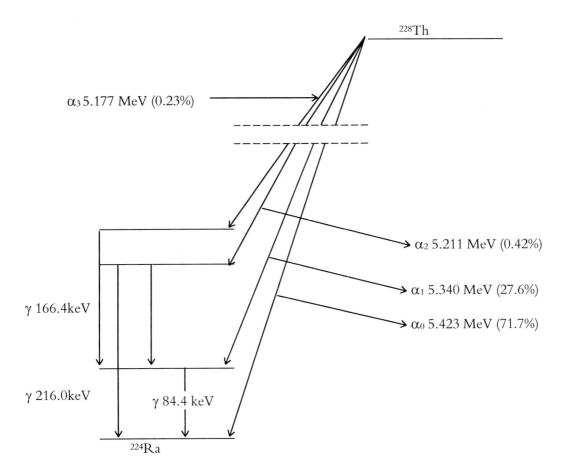

α_3 5.177 MeV (0.23%)

α_2 5.211 MeV (0.42%)

α_1 5.340 MeV (27.6%)

α_0 5.423 MeV (71.7%)

γ 166.4keV

γ 216.0keV

γ 84.4 keV

^{224}Ra

Figure 1.2   Alpha decay of ^{228}Th.

1.4.2 Beta decay

Beta decay involves the emission of either an electron (negatron) β^- or a positron β^+. The process may be represented as a transformation of one nucleon in the nucleus into another, either a neutron is transformed into a proton in negatron decay (β-decay):

$$n \rightarrow p + \beta^- + \bar{\nu}$$

or a proton is transformed into a neutron in positron decay (β^+ decay):

$$p \rightarrow n + \beta^+ + \nu$$

Where p and n denote a proton and a neutron and ν and $\bar{\nu}$ denote a **neutrino** or an **antineutrino**. β^- decay occurs for radionuclides with an excess of neutrons including those produced in a nuclear reactor by neutron capture and **fission products** (see Section 1.5). β^+ decay is preferred for nuclides with a neutron deficit. The number of nucleons (mass number) does not change but the atomic number is either increased or decreased by one.

In both β^- and β^+ decays the beta particles are emitted with a range of energies up to a maximum energy β_{max} [24], see Figure 1.3. In this figure the two peaks (conversion lines) at discrete energies are not related to beta decay and are explained in the section on gamma emission (Section 1.4.3). The presence of a range in particle energies is due to a sharing of available energy between the beta particle and the neutrino (antineutrino) in variable proportions. The neutrino, with no electric charge and no **rest mass** was originally postulated both to account for the distribution of emitted beta particle energies and also to conserve nuclear spin in the decay, see, for example, [18].

9

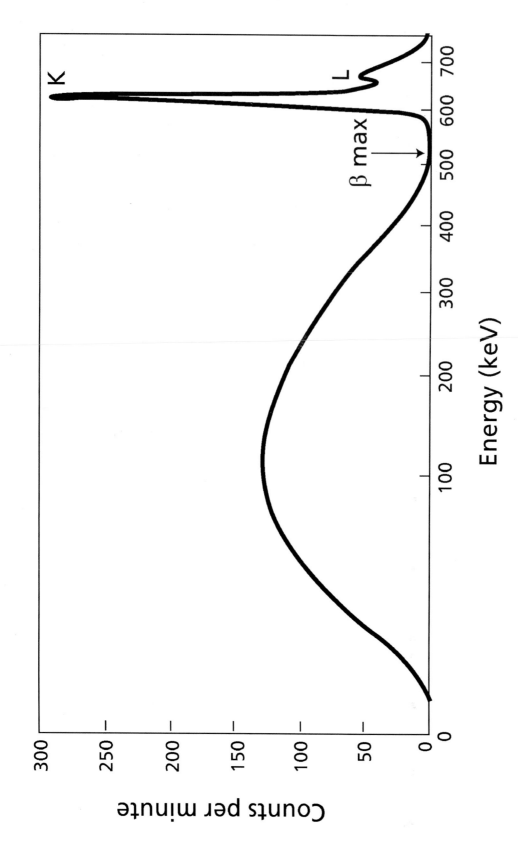

Figure 1.3   Spectrum of electron energies from β- decay of ^{137}Cs to ^{137}Ba plotted as a function of the square root of the energy.   The narrow lines K and L are due to conversion electrons. (From D. Halliday, Introductory Nuclear Physics, by permission of John Wiley & Sons Inc.).

1.4.2.1 β- decay

As with alpha decay, β- decay may proceed to the ground state of the daughter radionuclide either directly or via excited states which then decay to the ground state. An example of a simple β- decay is that of ^{90}Sr to ^{90}Y which is followed by the decay of ^{90}Y to ^{90}Zr. Here the beta particles have maximum energies of 546keV and 2279keV as shown in the energy level diagram (Figure 1.4).

An example of a complex decay is the beta decay of ^{38}Cl to ^{38}Ar which proceeds via two excited states to the ground state of the daughter nuclide with emission of three beta particles with maximum energies of 1107keV, 2749MeV and 4917keV (see Figure 1.5). Here the two excited states of ^{38}Ar decay to the ground state with the emission of gamma radiation (see Section 1.4.3).

Two well-known examples of β- decay are those for tritium with a half-life of 12.33y and a maximum beta energy of 18.57keV and ^{14}C with a half-life of 5730y and a maximum energy of 156.5keV (see Section 1.7.2 for the production and Sections 5.3.4 and 5.4.2 for applications of tritium and ^{14}C).

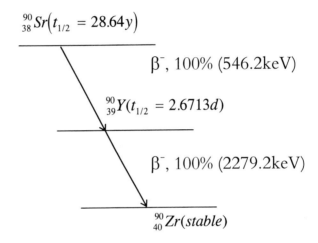

Figure 1.4   Beta decay of ^{90}Sr.

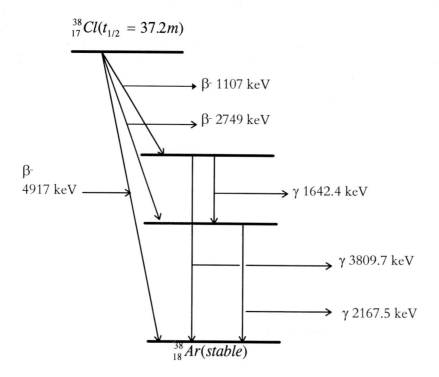

Figure 1.5   Beta decay of [38]Cl.

1.4.2.2   β⁺ decay

Positrons are emitted with a range of energies up to a maximum energy due to the available energy being shared between the β⁺ particle and the neutrino. However they lose energy in collisions and then combine with electrons to produce two gamma rays each with an energy of 0.511MeV emitted in opposite directions - the **annihilation radiation.** Thus, the annihilation radiation may be used to indicate β⁺ decay. Such a decay can only occur if the difference in the initial and final energy states is greater than 1.022MeV. Examples of positron emitters are ^{68}Ga used in positron annihilation studies and ^{11}C, ^{13}N and [15]O used in **Positron Emission Tomography** (PET) (see Section 5.5.7).

1.4.2.3   Electron capture

When the difference in the initial and final energy states is less than 1.022MeV no positron emission can occur and the decay of the parent nuclide occurs via **electron capture** (EC). When the energy difference is greater than 1.022MeV positron emission and electron capture are competing processes with the probability of electron capture increasing with increasing atomic number. Electron capture involves the capture of an inner electron by the nucleus in the transformation of a proton to a neutron, with the emission of a neutrino. It may be represented as:

$$p + e^- \rightarrow n + \nu$$

The daughter nucleus will be identical following decay of the parent nucleus by either electron capture or positron emission. An example of electron capture is the decay of [22]Na to [22]Ne represented as:

$$^{22}_{11}Na + ^{0}_{-1}e \rightarrow ^{22}_{10}Ne + \nu$$

The most likely electron to be captured is one from the K shell. This then leaves a hole in the K shell which is filled by the capture of a more distant L electron and the process is repeated in the more distant shells. The resulting energy release may then be used to emit the characteristic X-rays of the daughter nuclide. Alternatively the energy may result in the emission of electrons from more distant shells (**Auger electrons**). The competition between the emission of either a K X ray or an Auger electron is described by the K **fluorescence yield**, which is defined as the number of K X rays emitted per vacancy in the K shell. Auger electrons are also emitted following the photoelectric absorption of gamma rays (see Section 2.1.4) and their contribution to the dose delivered to the body by appropriate radiopharmaceuticals is discussed in Section 5.5.4.

In general, positron emission and electron capture are competing processes, for example, the decay of ^{22}Na to ^{22}Ne has a 90.5% probability of occurring by positron emission and a 9.5% probability of occurring by electron capture.

1.4.3 Gamma ray emission and internal conversion

As a result of either alpha or beta decay the daughter nucleus may be left in an excited state which will decay to the ground state usually but not always with the emission of gamma radiation. Emitted gamma rays have energies typically in the range 5keV to 7MeV.

In the above transition the ground state energy is well-defined but that of the excited state has an uncertainty (ΔE) which is related to its lifetime (τ) by the Heisenberg Uncertainty Principle:

$$\tau \Delta E \geq h/2\pi$$

where h is **Planck's constant** equal to 6.62618×10^{-34} J.Hz^{-1}. Thus the emitted gamma ray will have a small spread in energy, which is about 5×10^{-9}eV for the 14.41kev gamma ray emitted in the decay of the first excited state of ^{57}Fe, a **Mössbauer** nuclide, an energy resolution of several parts in 10^{13}.

In a gamma transition the decay energy Q is shared between the gamma ray (E_γ) and the kinetic energy of the recoiling nucleus (E_r), thus:

$$Q = E_\gamma + E_r$$

If the final nucleus is in a higher excited state, it will decay to the ground state via intermediate energy states resulting in the emission of successive gamma rays each with a discrete but different energy - a cascade. An example of this is the decay of ^{38}Cl (Figure 1.5) where one of the original β^- decays is followed by the emission of two gamma rays with energies of 1642keV and 2167keV. Clearly in the case of gamma ray emission, there is no change in mass number or atomic number. Usually emission of a gamma ray (prompt gamma) follows essentially immediately following alpha or beta decay but in some cases the nucleus remains in its excited state for a measurable time (delayed gamma). Such longer-lived metastable states are known as isomeric states and the decay is known as an isomeric transition (see Section 1.2).

For a given transition the energy difference between the initial and final nuclear states does not always give rise to a gamma ray but rather it may be used to overcome the binding energy of an inner shell electron which is then emitted. This process is known as **internal conversion** in which a conversion electron is emitted. Part of the decay energy (Q) is used to overcome the binding energy (E_b) and the remainder is shared between the emitted electron (E_e) and the recoiling nucleus (E_r), thus:

$$Q = E_b + E_e + E_r.$$

In Figure 1.3 the two peaks at the upper end of the beta spectrum from ^{137}Cs are due to the K and L conversion electrons for the product barium atom.

As in the case of electron capture (Section 1.4.2.3) the resulting vacancy in an inner electron shell then results in the emission of characteristic X-rays and Auger electrons. For a given transition, the internal conversion process competes with gamma ray emission and the ratio of conversion electrons emitted to the number of gamma rays emitted is known as the internal **conversion coefficient**. These effects are illustrated in Figure 1.6 [25] in the decay of the first excited state (14.41keV) in the Mössbauer radionuclide ^{57}Fe [26] (see Section 5.2.8).

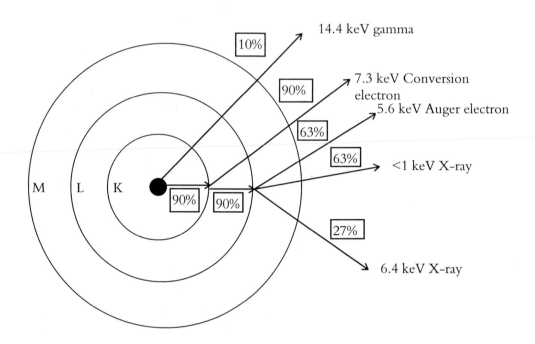

Figure 1.6   Illustration of emission of Auger electrons and conversion electrons and X rays from the decay of the 14.4 keV excited state in ^{57}Fe, after [25].

1.5 NUCLEAR FISSION

Heavy nuclei may decay by **fission** into two roughly equal fragments, fission fragments, with the release of large amounts of energy, of the order of 200MeV per fission. Nuclides with A > 230 such as ^{240}Pu, ^{244}Cm, and ^{252}Cf are observed to decay by spontaneous nuclear fission. In only a few radionuclides is spontaneous fission the main decay process, for example, ^{238}U decays by alpha decay with a half-life of 4.468 × 10^{9}y but has a half-life of 8 × 10^{15}y for spontaneous fission. Fission may also be induced by bombardment either with neutrons or charged particle such as protons or electrons or by gamma ray excitation (photofission). Induced fission proceeds via the creation of an unstable intermediate **compound nucleus**.

In each type of fission the original nuclide is split into fission fragments together with the emission of neutrons and gamma rays. The fission fragments possess excess neutrons which are reduced both by the emission of prompt neutrons and by a series of β⁻ decays. In a small number of cases the resulting nuclides emit neutrons after β- decay, known as delayed neutrons. The fission fragments then undergo a series of decays to produce many other radionuclides, the **fission products**. About 400 radionuclides have been identified in the fission products produced by neutron bombardment of ^{235}U.

The isobaric fission yields resulting from the bombardment of ^{235}U with either 14MeV or thermal neutrons is shown in Figure 1.7 [25]. Here the fission yield for a nuclide of atomic weight A represents the number of such nuclides formed per 100 fissions. This curve shows two peaks indicating that the most common occurrence is a splitting into two nuclides with mass numbers of about 96 and 140. These nuclides possess respectively 50 and 82 neutrons, the so-called magic numbers corresponding to particularly stable nuclides (for either the neutron or proton number).

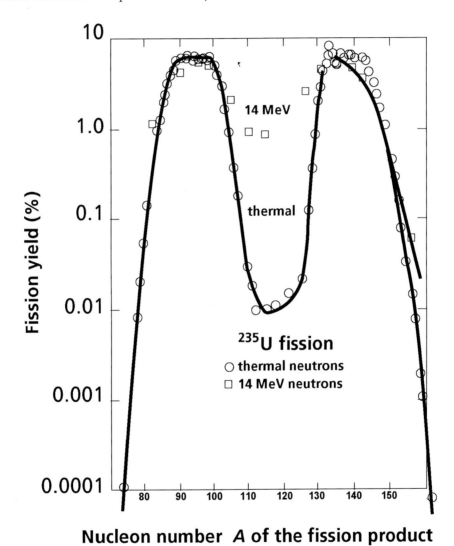

Figure 1.7:   Isobaric fission yields for ^{235}U for 14 MeV and thermal neutrons after [25].

1.6 NUCLEAR REACTIONS

As stated in Section 1.1, the upsurge in the production and use of artificial radionuclides came as a result of the availability of nuclear reactors and accelerators that could be used as a source of neutrons or charged particles, respectively in order to produce specific nuclear reactions. One such reaction is the interaction of alpha particles with nitrogen atoms, first observed by Rutherford [13]. This resulted in the emission of protons and the transformation of the nitrogen atoms into oxygen atoms in the reaction:

$$^{14}N + \alpha \rightarrow {}^{17}O + p \qquad \text{or} \qquad {}^{14}N(\alpha,p)^{17}O.$$

The energy change in the reaction ΔE is given by:

$$\Delta E = (m_N + m_\alpha - m_O - m_p)c^2$$

Where ΔE is negative, the difference in energy for the reaction is supplied by the kinetic energy of the incident particle.

Nuclear reactions are usually written in the form:

$$A(n,\gamma)B \quad \text{or} \quad C(n,p)D \quad \text{or} \quad E(n,\alpha)F$$

Where A, C and E are the target nuclides and B, D and F are the product nuclides.
The incident particle can be either a neutron or a charged particle and for the production of artificial radionuclides (see Chapter 5) the former class is the largest, including the reactions (n,γ), (n,p) and (n,α). The probability that a given nuclear reaction will occur is known as the cross-section and is usually measured in barns (1 barn = 10^{-28} m^2).

Incident charged particles having the same sign of charge as the target nucleus must have sufficient kinetic energy to overcome the potential barrier set up by the Coulomb repulsion. An example of such a reaction is the (d,n) reaction on ^{56}Fe to produce ^{57}Co used in Mössbauer spectroscopy [26] (see Section 5.2.8). Here d represents a deuteron which is the nucleus of deuterium ($^{2}_{1}H$) consisting of a neutron and proton. In this case the ^{56}Fe target is bombarded by 9.5 MeV deuterons in a cyclotron.

$$^{56}Fe + d \rightarrow {}^{57}Co + n$$

The changes in mass number and atomic number for common nuclear reactions are indicated schematically in Figure 1.8 for a general section of the chart of the nuclides. Here each square represents a different radionuclide arranged in order of increasing atomic number Z and neutron number N. For example, for the (d, α) reaction where alpha particles are emitted following bombardment with deuterons, both the atomic number (Z) and the neutron number (N) of the target nuclide decrease by one (+n+p-2n-2p). The same product radionuclide is also produced in a (γ,pn) reaction.

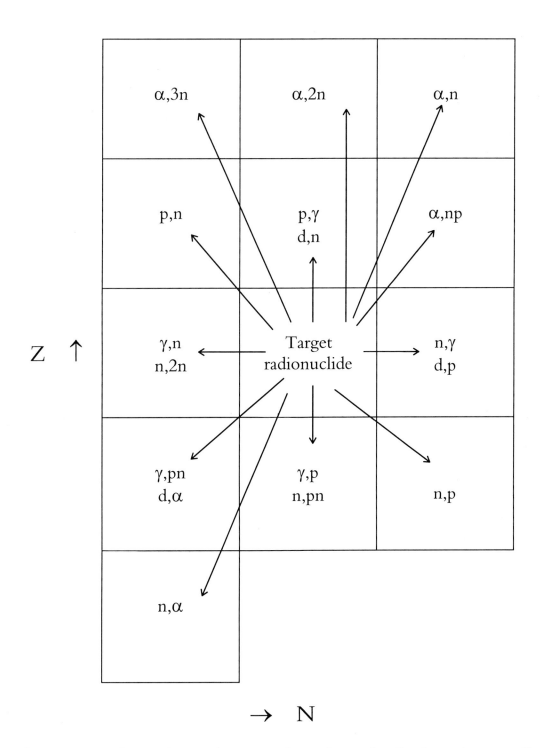

Figure 1.8   **Changes in atomic mass and atomic number for the main types of nuclear reactions depicted on a section of chart of the nuclide (from G. Choppin, J. Rydberg and J.O. Liljenzin, Radiochemistry and nuclear chemistry, by permission of Butterworth-Heinemann, Oxford).**

The amount of radioactivity produced in a given nuclear reaction is proportional to the amount of starting nuclide to the flux of bombarding particles and to the cross-section for the given nuclear reaction. The amount of radioactivity, in becquerels, is given by:

$$\text{Activity} = \sigma \phi w N_0 q \left(1 - e^{-\lambda t}\right) / A \qquad (1.11)$$

where σ is the reaction cross-section (m^2), ϕ is the incident flux ($m^{-2}.s^{-1}$), N_0 is Avogadro's number (6.022×10^{23} atoms per g.atom), w is the mass of the target element (g), q is the isotopic abundance of the nuclide of interest in the target element, A is the atomic mass of the target element, t is the bombardment time and λ is the decay constant (s^{-1}) of the product radionuclide. This equation is also used in Section 3.9 in the discussion of neutron activation analysis and in Section 4.2.1.1 with reference to the production of radionuclides.

1.7 RADIOACTIVITY IN THE ENVIRONMENT

Most natural materials contain some radioactive nuclei although frequently at such low concentrations that their quantification requires sensitive measuring techniques. Such radionuclides may be divided into two types, the **primordial radionuclides** having half-lives comparable to the age of the earth and the **cosmogenic radionuclides** produced by interaction of cosmic radiation with matter. A third type, **anthropogenic radionuclides**, produced in the environment by man, is discussed in the following section on artificial radioactivity.

As a consequence of the ubiquity of natural radioactivity, the population receives a small radiation dose from gamma rays from primordial radionuclides in the earth, from the gas radon produced in the natural decay series, by ingestion of foodstuffs containing small amounts of radioactivity and from cosmic rays. Additional doses comes from medical procedures, occupational exposure, weapons fallout, nuclear discharges and consumer products. Approximately half of the average dose to the population of the United Kingdom comes from radon and its daughter nuclides while the dose from occupational exposure, weapons fallout, nuclear discharges and consumer products together forms < 1% of the total dose [27].

1.7.1 Primordial radionuclides

These may be divided into the radionuclides present in the natural radioactive decay series originating with uranium or thorium (Figure 1.9) and those lighter radionuclides some of which occur in short decay series [23] (Table 1.1). Comparison of their half-lives with the age of the earth suggests that they were formed at around the formation time of the solar system and of the Earth about 5×10^9y ago. The most common primordial radionuclide is ^{40}K with a half-life of 1.28×10^9 y with an isotopic abundance of 0.0118% leading to an activity of about 30Bq g^{-1} of potassium.

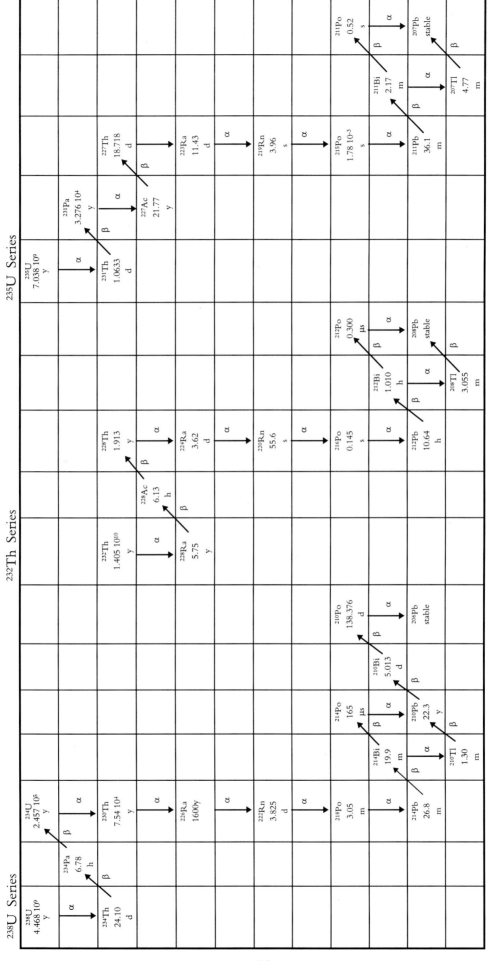

Figure 1.9 The three natural decay series.

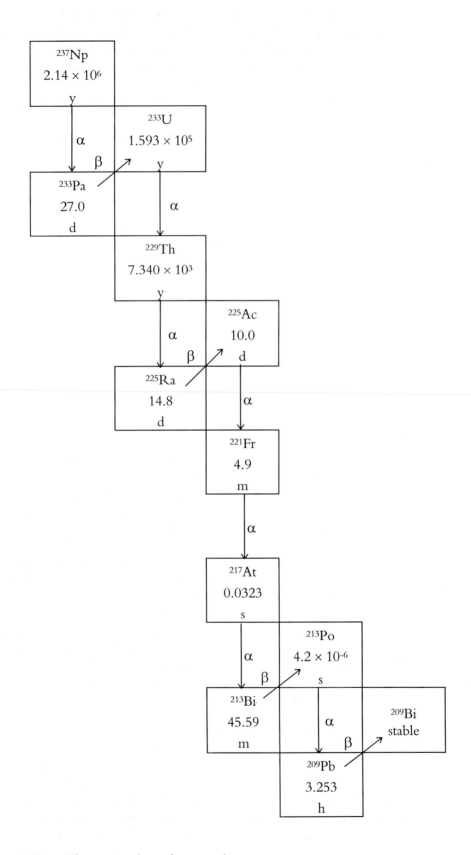

Figure 1.10   The neptunium decay series.

Table 1.1   **Selected list of primordial radionuclide with atomic number Z < 82, after [23]. (α, β^-, β^+ – alpha decay, β^- decay, β^+ decay and EC – electron capture). (Adapted from G. Choppin, J. Rydberg and J.O. Liljenzin, Radiochemistry and nuclear chemistry, by permission of Butterworth-Heinemann, Oxford).**

Nuclide	Isotopic abundance %	Decay mode	Half-life (years)
^{40}K	0.0117	β^- EC	1.28×10^9
^{50}V	0.250	β^- EC	1.5×10^{17}
^{87}Rb	27.83	β^-	4.8×10^{10}
^{115}In	95.72	β^-	4.4×10^{14}
^{123}Te	0.905	EC	9.99×10^{12}
^{138}La	0.092	β^- EC	1.05×10^{11}
^{144}Nd	23.80	α	2.1×10^{15}
^{147}Sm	15.0	α	1.06×10^{11}
^{148}Sm	11.3	α	7×10^{15}
^{174}Hf	0.162	α	2.0×10^{15}
^{187}Re	62.60	β^-	5.0×10^{10}
^{190}Pt	0.012	α	6.6×10^{11}

There are three main radioactive decay series originating with ^{232}Th, ^{238}U and ^{235}U. The thorium series starts with ^{232}Th (Figure 1.9), also known as the 4n series since all radionuclide mass numbers are evenly divisible by 4. The stable end product ^{208}Pb is reached via 6 alpha and 4 beta decay steps. The uranium series, or (4n+2) series, originates with ^{238}U (Figure 1.9), and the stable end product is ^{206}Pb reached by a series of 8 alpha and 6 beta decay steps. The actinium series, or (4n+3) series originates with ^{235}U (Figure 1.9) and the stable end product is ^{207}Pb, reached by a series of 7 alpha and 4 beta decay steps. There is a further 'man–made' radioactivity decay series, the neptunium or (4n+1) series (Figure 1.10). Since the half-life of ^{237}Np is 2.14×10^6y which is much less than the age of the earth, primordial ^{237}Np no longer exists on Earth.

Thorium is present in crustal rocks at a concentration of about 7ppm [28] corresponding to about 30mBq g^{-1} rock. Uranium exists in three isotopes ^{238}U (99.2745% abundance), ^{235}U (0.7200% abundance) and ^{234}U (0.0055% abundance). Crustal rocks contain on average about 2ppm of uranium corresponding to approximately 25mBq g^{-1} rock [28]. The average Th/U ratio for crustal rocks is therefore 3.5.

The situation was discussed in Section 1.3 in which daughter/parent radionuclide activity ratios within each of the three decay series will approach a value of unity after several daughter half-lives, provided the daughter half-life is much less than that of its parent. Such secular equilibrium is observed in nature but it is modified due to the differing chemical properties of the elements in the decay series, for example uranium, thorium and radium. The past geochemical behaviour of natural series radionuclides may be investigated in measurements of daughter/parent disequilibrium – uranium series disequilibrium (see Section 5.4.1) [28].

Two of the more important radionuclides in each of the three decay series are radium and radon due to their high radiotoxicities [27]. Although there are three radon isotopes, the most important one is ^{222}Rn, from the ^{238}U series with a half-life of approximately 3.825 days. Radon will diffuse out of permeable uranium/thorium-bearing minerals into the groundwater and may escape into the atmosphere, increasing the radioactivity level both due to itself and to its daughters. Since many rocks and indeed building materials contain small amounts of uranium the concentration of radon in the air inside a house may be significant, depending on the site, material and house construction.

As shown in Table 1.1 there are a number of lighter radionuclides having long half-lives which do not fall within the three natural decay series. Several of these and in particular ^{40}K ($t_{1/2} = 1.28 \times 10^9$y) and ^{87}Rb ($t_{1/2} = 4.8 \times 10^{10}$y) have been used in nuclear dating techniques. Thus the K-Ar and Rb-Sr dating techniques depend upon measuring the concentrations of daughter and parent activities. The techniques can be used to date the oldest K- and Rb-bearing minerals [29].

1.7.2 Cosmogenic radionuclides

The interactions between neutrons and protons associated with cosmic radiation and nitrogen, oxygen and argon atoms produce a series of radionuclides (Table 1.2), the most abundant of which are ^{14}C and tritium (^{3}H). Equilibrium is established between the production rate of these radionuclides and their residence times, for example in the atmosphere, oceans and the soil, leading to approximately constant specific activities in each reservoir.

Table 1.2   **Selected list of long-lived cosmogenic radionuclides found in meteorites and rain-water (a) and short lived cosmogenic radionuclides found in rain-water (b). (Adapted from G. Choppin, J. Rydberg and J.O. Liljenzin, Radiochemistry and nuclear chemistry, by permission of Butterworth-Heinemann, Oxford).**

1.2a Long-lived cosmogenic radionuclides in meteorites and rain-water

Nuclide	Half-life (years)	Decay Mode	Atmospheric production rate (atoms m^{-2} s^{-1})
^{3}H	12.33	β-	2500
^{10}Be	1.6×10^6	β-	300
^{14}C	5730	β-	17 000 – 25 000
^{22}Na	2.603	β-	0.5
^{26}Al	7.2×10^5	β+	1.2
^{35}S	87.5 d	β-	14
^{36}Cl	3.02×10^5	β-	60
^{39}Ar	269	β-	56
^{53}Mn	3.7×10^6	EC	
^{81}Kr	2.1×10^5	EC	

1.2b Short-lived cosmogenic radionuclides in rain–water

Nuclide	Half-life	Decay mode	Atmospheric production rate (atoms m^{-2} s^{-1})
^{7}Be	53.24 d	EC	81
^{24}Na	14.965 h	β-	
^{28}Mg	20.9 h	β-	
^{32}P	14.27 d	β-	
^{33}P	25.4 d	β-	
^{39}Cl	55.6 min	β-	16

EC – electron capture
β- – β- (negatron) decay
β+ – β+ (positron) decay

Carbon–14 (^{14}C) is produced by the reaction of slow neutrons with nitrogen

$$^{14}N + n(slow) \rightarrow {}^{14}C + p$$

This results in a global inventory of about 8.5×10^{18} Bq [23]. In addition there have recently been smaller contributions of ^{14}C from nuclear weapons tests, and nuclear reactors. All living material contains a ^{14}C concentration of about 227 Bq kg^{-1} carbon.

It is assumed that on the death of the organism containing this living material, all exchange of carbon atoms with its surroundings stops and the remaining unsupported ^{14}C activity decays by β- decay with a half-life of 5730 years:

$$^{14}C \rightarrow {}^{14}N + \beta^- + \bar{\nu} \qquad \beta_{max} = 156.5 keV$$

A measurement of the present ^{14}C concentration may then be used to determine the age of the biological material - the technique of ^{14}C dating (see Section 5.4.2).

Tritium is produced by the interaction of fast neutrons with nitrogen:

$$^{14}N + n(fast) \rightarrow {}^{12}C + {}^3H$$

It is rapidly incorporated into water with a residence time in the atmosphere of about 2 years. Large amounts of tritium were released to the atmosphere during the hydrogen bomb tests in the decade 1950-1960. Since this latter input was greater than the natural production, methods of dating waters from their tritium concentration are very limited. The peak in tritium activity in about 1963 was about 2000 TU, where 1 Tritium Unit (TU) is defined as one tritium atom per 10^{18} hydrogen atoms and is equivalent to 0.118 Bq per litre of water. Present day levels of tritium in waters are about 20-40 TU.

Tritium decays by β- decay with a half-life of 12.33 years:

$$^3H \rightarrow {}^3He + \beta^- + \bar{\nu} \qquad \beta_{max} = 18.57 \ keV$$

1.7.3 Artificial radioactivity

Anthropogenic sources of radioactivity include nuclear weapon tests, nuclear power plant accidents and the controlled release of small amounts of radioactivity to the environment mainly by the nuclear power industry. In addition there will be an input from the use of radionuclides in medicine and in industry (Chapter 5).

Several hundred radionuclides have been produced in nuclear weapons tests and in irradiated reactor fuel although only a limited number, including fission products (see Section 1.1) and **activation products**, may give a significant contribution to the population dose. Activation products are formed, for example, in reactions between neutrons and either the nuclear fuel or the components of a nuclear reactor. Thus successive neutron captures in ^{239}Pu produce ^{240}Pu and ^{241}Pu. Subsequent β^- decays and neutron captures leads to the production of ^{241}Am, ^{242}Am and ^{242}Cm.

A selected list of radionuclides produced in fission and activation processes which may contribute significantly to human exposure is given in Table 1.3 [30,31]. The variation of fission yields with mass number shows the characteristic double-peaked behaviour, see Section 1.5 and Figure 1.7.

Before the ending of the atmospheric testing of nuclear weapons in 1964 it has been estimated that there had been a total release of about 2×10^{20} Bq of fission products [23]. Since that time the fission products have decayed leaving only ^{90}Sr, ^{137}Cs, as well as the longer-lived plutonium radionuclides, with sufficiently long half-lives to retain any radioactivity. Their activities are negligible when compared to the global natural radioactivity. This leaves nuclear accidents as a more significant source of fission product radionuclides [31].

In the last 40 years there have been three major accidents resulting in the injection of large amounts of radionuclides into the atmosphere [23]. In the fire at the Advanced Gas Cooled Reactor (AGR) at Windscale in 1957 about 7×10^{14} Bq of ^{131}I were released while in the partial core melt-down in a reactor at Three Mile Island, Pennsylvania in 1979, about 10^{12} Bq of the noble gases Xe and Kr were released. In the more serious accident at Chernobyl in the Soviet Union in 1986, an explosion and fire in one of the power reactors resulted in the release of fission products and actinides, involving of the order of 10^{18} Bq over a period of several days. This resulted in a plume of radionuclides including ^{137}Cs spreading over the Soviet Union, Scandinavia and Central Europe with deposition determined by local wind and rain patterns.

The organised release of radionuclides from the nuclear power industry is carefully controlled by national regulatory bodies. Those isotopes for which authorised limits have been set include the release of noble gases, tritium, ^{14}C and ^{131}I to the atmosphere and the release of ^{3}H, ^{14}C, ^{35}S, ^{60}Co, ^{65}Zn, ^{90}Sr, ^{134}Cs, ^{137}Cs, ^{237}Np ^{241}Am ^{234,235,238}U and ^{238,239,240}Pu as liquid effluents.

Table 1.3   Selected list of fission products and activation products, which may contribute significantly to human exposure, after [30,31]. Where two radionuclides are quoted on one line, the second one is produced as a result of the subsequent decay of the first. Adapted from Measurement of radionuclides in food and the environment, a guidebook, IAEA Technical Reports Series, No. 295 by permission from the International Atomic Energy Agency, Vienna.

	Radionuclide	Half-life	Fission yield* (%)	Major Decay
Fission products	Sr–89	50.52d	4.77	β-
	Sr–90, Y–90	28.64y, 2.671d	5.76	β-,β-
	Zr–95, Nb–95	64.03d, 35.02d	6.51	β-γ, β-γ
	Mo–99, Tc–99m	2.748d, 6.01h	6.09	β-γ, β-γ
	Tc–99	2.113×10^5y		β-γ
	Ru–103, Rh–103m	39.26d, 56.12m	3.03	β-γ, β-γ
	Ru–106, Rh–106	1.008y, 30.1s	0.4	β-, βγ
	Te–129m	33.8d	0.661	β-γ
	I–131	8.04d	2.875	β-γ
	Te–132	3.23d	4.282	β-γ, β-γ
	Cs–137, Ba–137m	30.2y, 2.553m	6.136	β-γ
	Ba–140, La–140	12.74d, 1.6785d	6.134	β-γ, β-γ
	Ce–144, Pr–144	284.9d, 17.28m	5.443	β-γ, β-γ
Activation products	H–3	12.33y		β-
	C–14	5730y		β-
	Fe–55	2.74y		EC
	Fe–59	44.502d		β-γ
	Mn–54	312.3d		EC, γ
	Co–60	5.272y		β-γ
	Ni–63	99y		β-
	Zn–65	244.3d		EC, γ
	Cs–134	2.0652y		β-γ
	Np–239	2.355d		β-, γ
	Pu–241, Am–241	14.4y, 432.7y		β-αγ
	Cm–242	162.94d		α
	Pu–238	87.7y		α
	Pu–239	2.41×10^4y		α
	Pu–240	6.563×10^3y		α
	Pu–242	3.74×10^5y		α

* – fission of ^{235}U by slow neutrons

ACKNOWLEDGEMENTS

The author is grateful to Bill Newton, Chairman, Royal Society of Chemistry, Radiochemical Methods Group, 1997-98 and to Mike Woods, NPL for their careful reading of the chapter and for useful comments.

REFERENCES

1. H. Becquerel, *Sur les Radiations émises par Phosphorescence*, C.R. Acad. Sci. **122**, 420-421, 1896.

2. H. Becquerel, *Sur les Radiations Invisibles émises par les Corps Phosphorescents*, C.R. Acad. Sci. **122**, 501-503, 1896.

3. H. Becquerel, *Sur quelques Propriétés Nouvelles des Radiations Invisibles émises par divers Corps Phosphorescents*, C.R. Acad. Sci. **122**, 559-564, 1896.

4. H. Becquerel, *Sur les Radiations Invisibles émises par les Sels d'Uranium*, C.R. Acad. Sci. **122**, 689-694, 1896.

5. H. Becquerel, *Emission de Radiations Nouvelles par Invisibles émises par l'Uranium Métallique*, C.R. Acad. Sci. **122**, 1086-1088, 1896.

6. P. Curie and M. Curie, *Sur une Substance Nouvelle Radio-active, contenue dans la Pechblende*, C.R. Acad. Sci. **127**, 175-178, 1898.

7. P. Curie, M. Curie and G. Bémont, *Sur une nouvelle substance fortement radio-active, contenue dans la pechblende*, A.R. Acad. Sci. **127**, 1215-1217, 1898.

8. E. Rutherford and F. Soddy, *Radioactive change*, Phil. Mag. **5**, 576-591, 1903.

9. F. Soddy, Chemistry of the radio-elements, Part II, Longmans, Green & Co., London, 1914.

10. J.J. Thomson, *Rays of positive electricity*, Proc. Roy. Soc. London **89**, 1-20, 1914.

11. H. Geiger and E. Marsden, *On a Diffuse Reflection of the α-particles*, Proc. Roy. Soc. **A82**, 495-500 1909.

12. E. Rutherford, *The Scattering of α and β Particles by Matter and the Structure of the Atom*, Phil. Mag. **21**(6), 669, 1911.

13. E. Rutherford, *Collision of α particles with light atoms, IV An anomalous effect in nitrogen*, Phil. Mag. **37**, 581, 1919.

14. F. Joliot and I. Curie, *Artificial production of a new kind of radio-element*, Nature, **133**, 201, 1934.

15. O. Hahn and F. Strassman, Naturwiss., *Über den Nachweis und das Verhalten der bei der Bestrahlung des Urans mittels Neutronen entstehenden Erdalkalimetalle*, **27**, 89, 1939.

16. E. Fermi, *Elementary theory of the chain-reacting pile*, Science **105**, 27-32, 1947.

17. C.D. Anderson, *Cosmic-ray positive and negative electrons*, Phys. Rev., **44**, 406, 1933.

18. W.E. Burcham and M. Jobes, An Introduction to Nuclear and Particle Physics, Longman, 1997.

19. W.N. Cottingham and D.A. Greenwood, An introduction to nuclear physics, Cambridge, 1992.

20. A. Das and T. Ferbel, Introduction to nuclear and particle physics, J.Wiley & Sons, 1994.

21. H. Bateman, *Solution of a system of differential equations occurring in the theory of radioactive transformations*, Proc. Cambridge Phil. Soc. **15**, 423-427, 1910.

22. R. D. Evans, The Atomic Nucleus, Krieger, New York, 1982.

23. G. Choppin, J. Rydberg and J.O. Liljenzin, *Radiochemistry and Nuclear Chemistry*, Butterworth-Heinemann Ltd. 1995.

24. D. Halliday, Introductory Nuclear Physics, John Wiley & Sons, 1955.

25. C. Keller, Radiochemistry, Ellis Horwood Limited, 1988.

26. N. N. Greenwood and T. C. Gibb, Mössbauer spectroscopy, Chapman and Hall, London, 1971.

27. R.H. Clarke, *Natural Sources*, in Becquerel's legacy: A century of radioactivity, Radiat. Prot. Dosim., **68(1/2)**, 37-42, 1996.

28. M. Ivanovich and R.S. Harmon, Uranium Series Disequilibrium: Application to earth, marine and environmental sciences, 2nd Edition, Clarendon Press, Oxford, 1992.

29. G. Faure, Principles of isotope geology, John Wiley & Sons, 1977.

30. Food and Agriculture Organization, *Organization of surveys for radionuclides in food and agriculture*, FAO Atomic Energy series No. 4, Rome, 1962.

31. International Atomic Energy Agency, *Measurement of radionuclides in food and the environment, a guidebook*, International Atomic Energy Agency Technical Reports Series, No. 295, Vienna, 1989.

CHAPTER 2   MEASUREMENT OF RADIONUCLIDES

RICHARD BULL, GEOFF LONGWORTH AND JOHN COBB

2.1   INTERACTIONS OF RADIATION WITH MATTER

The ways in which radiations interact with matter are of importance both to the shielding of these radiations and to the methods by which they are detected. An outline of these interactions is given in this section. For further details a standard nuclear physics text such as Burcham and Jobes [1] or Evans [2] should be consulted.

2.1.1   General principles

When photons and particles (alpha particles, electrons, neutrons etc.) pass through a stopping medium they may interact with the electrons or nuclei via a number of scattering or absorption processes. The probability of collision with a scattering or absorption centre is described by an area σ ascribed to each centre. This is known as the **cross-section**[1] for the interaction. Consider a parallel beam of n_0 particles incident on a thin layer of material of thickness t, containing N interaction centres per unit volume. The probability that a single particle undergoes an interaction in passing through a distance dx is:

$$N\sigma dx = \frac{dx}{\lambda}$$

where $\lambda = 1/N\sigma$ is the **mean free path** for the collision. The product $N\sigma$ is often referred to as the macroscopic cross-section for the process. If the interaction leads to removal of particles from the beam and the number of particles passing through the layer dx is n, then the change in number $dn = n-n_0$ which will depend on the number of incident particles $n_0 \cong n$ and on the interaction probability $N\sigma dx$, thus:

$$dn = -nN\sigma dx = \frac{-ndx}{\lambda} \qquad (2.1)$$

Here the negative sign indicates that the number of particles decreases on passing through the material. The number of particles n remaining after passage through the total layer t is obtained by integrating (2.1) to give:

$$n = n_0 e^{-N\sigma t} = n_0 e^{-\mu t} \qquad (2.2)$$

where $\mu = N\sigma = 1/\lambda$ is the linear attenuation coefficient. A related quantity which is frequently used is the mass attenuation coefficient μ/ρ, where ρ is the density of the stopping medium.

---

[1]   The usual unit of cross-section is the **barn**. 1 barn = 10^{-28}m^2.

2.1.2 Interactions between charged particles

Charged particles will exert electromagnetic forces upon the orbital electrons and nuclei of the media they pass through. At velocities small compared with that of light, the interaction can be described by the familiar Coulomb force so that for a particle of charge ze interacting with a stationary centre of charge Ze at distance r, the force exerted on each is:

$$F = \frac{zZe^2}{4\pi\varepsilon_0 r^2}$$

where ε_0 is the permittivity of free space. This interaction leads to the well-known Rutherford scattering law which yields a cross-section $\sigma(\theta)$ for scattering of the incident particle through an angle between θ and $\theta + d\theta$ given by:

$$\sigma(\theta) = \left(\frac{zZe^2}{2M_0 v^2}\right)^2 \mathrm{cosec}^4 \frac{\theta}{2} \qquad (2.3)$$

where v is the velocity of the incident particle and M_0 is the reduced mass of the system, $mM/(m+M)$, where m and M are the masses of the incident particle and scattering centre, respectively.

The derivation of the Rutherford law depends on the classical notion of well-defined particle trajectories. It can be shown that this procedure is valid only when the least distance of approach between the incident particle and the scatterer is much larger than the **de Broglie wavelength** for the incident particle. When this condition does not hold, the quantum mechanical description of the process must be used. However, the quantum mechanical formula agrees with the Rutherford scattering law when the scattering interaction is a pure inverse-square force.

2.1.3 Energy losses for charged particles

In most cases a charged particle passing through matter loses most of its energy via interactions with the orbital electrons of the atoms of the stopping material. Electrons can be removed from their orbits to produce **primary ionisation** or they can be raised to high-energy orbits, a process known as **excitation**. If the energy transferred to an electron in ionisation is large, the released electron will itself be able to produce further ionisations. Such energetic primary electrons are called **delta-rays** and the ionisation they produce is secondary ionisation.

When a fast-moving charged particle suffers a change in velocity it will emit electromagnetic radiation. This process is known as **bremsstrahlung**.

Other processes are possible. A **positron** (the antiparticle of the electron) when slowing down in matter, can annihilate with one of the electrons in the stopping medium (see Section 1.4.2.2). This process results in the release of two 511 keV gamma rays. When a charged particle passes through a transparent material at a speed greater than the speed of light in the material, **Cerenkov radiation** is emitted (see Section 2.2.3). This is coherent light emission caused by polarisation of the atoms in the stopping material. Charged particle nuclear reactions can occur but these are rarely of importance for the radiations emitted by radionuclides.

If in passing through a thickness dx, a charged particle with kinetic energy E loses an amount of energy dE, the ratio -dE/dx is called the specific energy loss or stopping power. The stopping power includes components due to radiative processes as well as collisions with electrons.

For a particle of mass m and charge ze incident on target nuclei of charge Ze the intensity of bremsstrahlung radiation is proportional to z^2Z^2/m^2. Because of the $1/m^2$ term, the energy loss due to bremsstrahlung is most significant for electrons. The energy loss rate is given by:

$$-\left(\frac{dE}{dx}\right)_{brem} = NE_{TOT}Z^2f(Z,E) \qquad (2.4)$$

where N is the number of atoms per unit volume of the stopping material and $E_{TOT} = E + mc^2$ is the total energy of the particle, c is the velocity of light *in vacuo*. $f(Z, E)$ is a slowly varying function of Z and E. A 10 MeV electron loses 50% of its energy via bremsstrahlung whilst a 100 MeV electron loses 90% of its energy in this way.

The collision component of the stopping power is given by the Bethe-Bloch formula for non-relativistic particles of energy E, which may be approximated as:

$$-\left(\frac{dE}{dx}\right)_{coll} = \frac{z^2e^4NZ}{8\pi\varepsilon_0E}\ln\frac{4E}{I} \qquad (2.5)$$

where I is a mean atomic excitation potential. Figure 2.1 shows the collision stopping power as a function of energy for electrons and protons in water [3]. Tables of stopping power are given, for example, by Northcliffe and Schilling [4].

The modulus of the stopping power – the energy deposited per unit of path length in the stopping medium – is known as the **linear energy transfer** or **LET**. Typical units of LET are keV/μm.

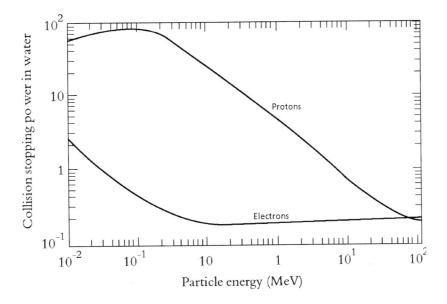

Figure 2.1　　Collision stopping-power (in keV μm⁻¹) for electrons and protons in water, after ICRP 21 [3]. Adapted from ICRP by permission of the International Commission on Radiological Protection.

2.1.4 Photon interactions

Photon emissions from radionuclides extend from the low-energy X-ray region of a few keV to gamma ray energies of a few MeV. Over this energy range the important photon interactions are as follows:

(i)   Photoelectric effect

A photon of energy E may be absorbed by a bound electron, ejecting it from its orbit with energy T given by:

$$T = E - E_b$$

where E_b is the ionisation energy of the electron. This process is called the photoelectric effect and has a cross-section σ_{pe} given approximately by:

$$\sigma_{pe} = Z^5 E^{-3.5}$$

The photoelectric effect is, therefore, most important for low-energy photons incident on high-Z materials. As a result of this interaction there is a vacancy in one of the electron shells. This can be filled by electrons from higher shells, a process which results in the emission of X-rays. This de-excitation of the ionised atom can also result in the emission of low-energy electrons, a process known as the **Auger** effect (see also section 1.4.2.3).

(ii)   Compton Scattering

For photon energies above a few hundred keV, the photon can be scattered by electrons with a resultant decrease in photon energy. The electron can be regarded as effectively free in such a process, which is known as **Compton scattering**. The energy E' of the scattered photon is given by

$$E' = \frac{E}{1 + \frac{E}{m_e c^2}(1 - \cos\theta)} \qquad (2.6)$$

where E is the initial photon energy and θ is the angle through which the photon is scattered and m_e is the electron **rest mass**. The kinetic energy of the recoil electron, T is given by:

$$T = \frac{E}{1 + \left(\frac{E}{m_e c^2}(1 - \cos\theta)\right)^{-1}}$$

The cross-section (per electron) σ_C for Compton scattering is independent of Z and is a rather slowly decreasing function of photon energy.

(iii)   Pair production

At photon energies in excess of $2m_e c^2$ (where m_e is the electron mass) the photon energy can be completely converted into the production of an electron-positron pair. In order that momentum be conserved this **pair production** process must take place in the field of an electron or a nucleus. The kinetic energy of the electron-positron

32

pair will be E - 2m$_e$c^2. The pair production cross-section σ increases roughly linearly with E - 2m$_e$c^2 and as Z^2. Pair production becomes the dominant photon attenuation process for energies of 10's of MeV and above.

(iv)   Rayleigh Scattering

Rayleigh scattering is **coherent** scattering from the electrons of an atom, resulting in no change in photon energy. The cross-section σ$_R$ varies as Z^2 and approximately as E^{-3}. This process is important only at photon energies of less than a few hundred keV.

The total linear attenuation coefficient, μ is given by:

$$\mu = N\left(\sigma_{pe} + \sigma_{pp} + \sigma_R\right) + ZN\sigma_c \qquad (2.7)$$

where N is the number of atoms per unit volume. The factor Z multiplies σ$_C$ because the Compton effect takes place with individual electrons rather than atoms as a whole. Figure 2.2 shows the contributions to the total attenuation coefficients as a function of photon energy for lead and aluminium [5].

a)

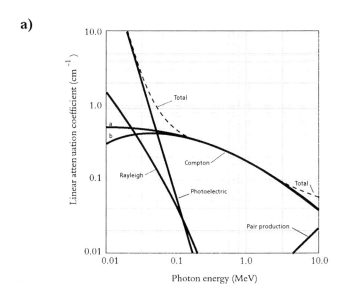

Figure 2.2

Linear absorption coefficients as a function of photon energy in

(a) aluminium and

(b) lead, after NCRP 58 [5].

Adapted from NCRP 58 by permission of the National Council on Radiation Protection and Measurements.

b)

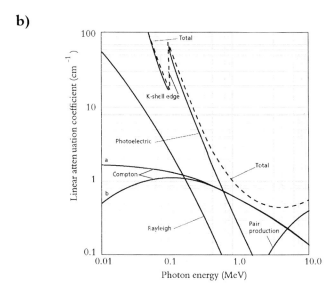

2.1.5 Neutron interactions

Neutrons interact with the nuclei of a stopping material by a variety of processes.

(i)   Elastic scattering

An incident neutron can strike a nucleus and be scattered leaving the nucleus in its ground state. Kinetic energy is conserved in this process, which is known as elastic scattering. The energy of the scattered neutron after a head-on collision is given by:

$$E' = E\left(\frac{M - m}{M + m}\right)^2 \qquad (2.8)$$

where m, M are the neutron and target nucleus masses. If the stopping material is hydrogen then $m \cong M$ and the neutron can lose all of its energy in a single elastic collision.

(ii)   Compound nucleus formation

In this process the neutron is absorbed by the target nucleus, which results in the formation of a **compound nucleus** in an excited state (see also Section 1.5). The excitation energy of the compound nucleus is determined by the bombarding energy. Its lifetime is relatively long and its properties are independent of its formation mode. The compound nucleus can dissociate in one of several ways, for example, via a nuclear transformation or a scattering process.

Alternatively a proton or an alpha particle is emitted in (n,p) or (n,α) reactions. An important reaction of the latter type is neutron capture by boron:

$$^{10}B + {}^{1}n \rightarrow {}^{11}B^* \rightarrow {}^{7}Li + \alpha$$

where the asterisk indicates that the compound nucleus is in an excited state.

Dissociation via emission of a gamma ray, denoted (n,γ) is called radiative capture.

When the emitted particle is a neutron the process is referred to as scattering. If in this process kinetic energy is not conserved and the target nucleus is left in an excited state, (from which it will return to the ground state by the emission of a photon) the interaction is called inelastic scattering. If a neutron is re-emitted without leaving the nucleus in an excited state, we have another form of elastic scattering called resonance scattering to distinguish it from the potential scattering in which elastic scattering occurs without formation of a compound nucleus.

In certain heavy elements, absorption of a neutron can induce fission (see Section 1.5). Nuclides such as ^{235}U and ^{239}Pu can undergo fission by **thermal neutrons** (E $\cong 0.03$eV), whereas ^{238}U, for example, undergoes fission only when bombarded by neutrons with energies >5.9MeV [1,2].

2.1.6 Variation in cross-sections with neutron energy

Elastic scattering cross-sections are in the region of 2-10 barns for most materials. For chemically unbound hydrogen, σ_s is about 20 barns at low neutron energies. Cross-sections tend to decrease with increasing neutron energy.

Capture cross-sections, particularly for heavier nuclei, tend to show a decrease with increasing neutron energy with $\sigma \propto 1/v$, where v is the neutron velocity. This behaviour occurs in the low-energy region, up to ~1eV. Beyond these energies, cross-sections usually show a series of sharp peaks or resonances. At neutron energies beyond a few keV, cross-sections tend to exhibit a continuous decrease with increasing energy.

2.1.7 Particle ranges

Photons are removed from a narrow beam via a one-hit process. It is not possible to define a unique range in such a case. The typical range of a gamma ray may be given by the attenuation length which is defined as the inverse of the linear attenuation coefficient. Gamma ray attenuation coefficients are listed in Table 6.6.

Charged particles generally lose energy via a large number of interactions. The range of a charged particle can be formally defined by the equation:

$$R = \int_{E_0}^{0} \left(-\frac{dE}{dx}\right)^{-1} dE$$

In practice, formulae such as the Bethe-Bloch equation (2.5) break down at very low energies. A semi-empirical approach can be used to produce range-energy tables for ions in various media (see, for example [6,7]). There are statistical variations in the number of energy-loss collisions suffered by a charged particle. As a result of this, the ranges of charged particles of a given type and energy are statistically distributed about a mean value – a phenomenon known as straggling. Whilst the track of a heavy ion through a stopping medium approximates to a straight line, an electron can undergo deflections through large angles and the concept of an electron range is less well-defined. If a beam of beta particles is attenuated by various thicknesses of absorber, an absorption curve such as that given in Figure 2.3 is obtained [8]. The absorber thickness at which the beta count rate drops to background levels defines a range for beta particles of a given maximum energy. It is found that, for a given beta energy, the range in terms of mass thickness is only weakly dependent on the absorber material. It is therefore possible to give a single range-energy curve for beta particles, as shown in Figure 2.4.

The mean range of an alpha particle is defined as the absorber thickness that reduces the alpha particle count rate from a collimated beam to one half of its value in the absence of an absorber. Range straggling is a small effect for alpha particles so that alpha ranges show a narrow distribution about the mean. Figure 2.5 shows range-energy curves for alpha particles in various stopping materials.

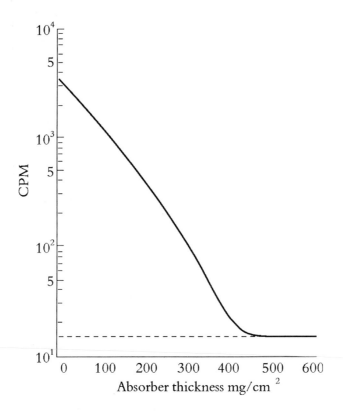

Figure 2.3 Absorption of 1.17 MeV [210]Bi particles in aluminium. The dashed line indicates the mean background count rate, after Cember [8]. Adapted from H. Cember, Introduction to Health Physics, by permission of McGraw Hill, New York.

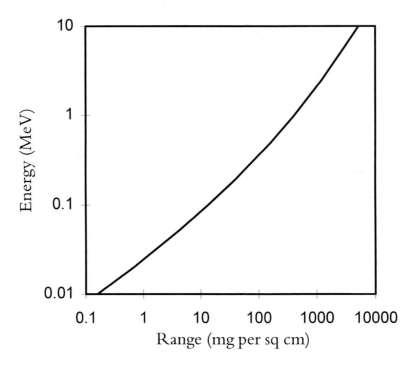

Figure 2.4 Range energy relation for beta particles.

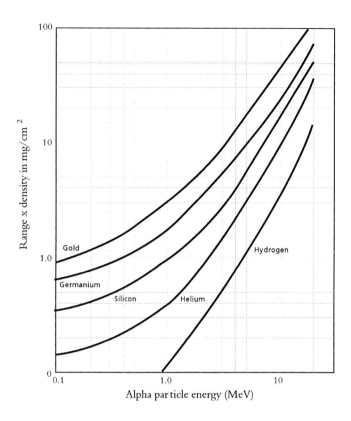

Figure 2.5   Range–energy curve for alpha particles, after Knoll [16]. Adapted from G.F. Knoll, Radiation Detection and Measurement, by permission of John Wiley & Sons. Inc.

2.2   RADIATION DETECTORS

In the radiochemical laboratory, radiation detectors are used not only to characterise the emissions from radioactive sources but also to monitor for contamination and to measure radiation dose rates. In this section, the principles of operation and characteristics of some of the more frequently encountered detectors are described.

2.2.1 Gas-filled detectors

When an ionising particle or gamma ray passes through a gas-filled enclosure some of the gas molecules are ionised to produce positive ions and free electrons (ion pairs). The energy needed to create an ion pair is typically 35eV. Therefore, a 1MeV particle, if stopped within the gas, will create about 30,000 ion pairs. In the presence of an electric field, the electrons and positive ions will drift in opposite directions constituting an electric current. In a gas-filled detector the electric field is generated by applying an external voltage across two electrodes. Movement of the ion pairs produces a voltage pulse at the electrodes.

Figure 2.6 shows a schematic representation of a cylindrical-geometry gas-filled counter, with the associated circuitry. The voltage pulse appears across resistor R which is usually the input resistance of the circuit connected to the detector. The detector and the measuring circuit will have an equivalent capacitance C. When the collection-circuit time-constant (CR), which represents the time over which a charge in the system will decay, is much larger than the collection time, the voltage pulse increases as the charges drift towards the electrodes. The maximum value V_{max} is given by Q/C, where Q is the total charge generated within the detector and is independent of the position at which the ion pairs were produced in the detector. Since C is usually fixed for a gas-filled detector, the amplitude of the voltage pulse is then proportional to the number of ion pairs generated within the detector and hence to the energy deposited by the incident particle.

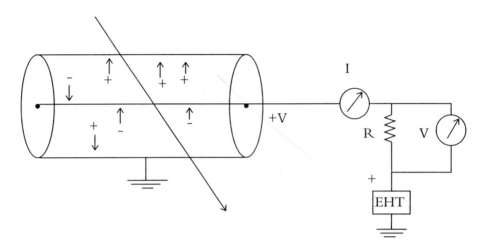

Figure 2.6   A cylindrical gas-filled counter.

There are three main types of gas-filled detector, the ionisation chamber, the proportional counter and the Geiger Müller counter. The main difference is in the magnitude of the electric field applied to the electrodes. When a charged particle passes through the chamber ion-pairs are produced. The electrons are drawn towards the central anode wire whilst the positive ions move more slowly towards the wall which is at a negative potential relative to the wire. The total charge collected by the external circuit depends on the voltage V between the anode and the wall and is shown schematically in Figure 2.7.

In region I, the voltage is so low that many of the ion pairs recombine. In region II, recombination is negligible and essentially all of the ion pairs are collected. This is the ion chamber region. As is clear from the diagram, a highly ionising alpha particle produces far more ion pairs for collection than does a lightly ionising particle such as a beta particle. In region III the electrons moving towards the central wire are greatly accelerated by the high field gradient near the wire and reach energies such that they can produce further ion pairs in collisions with gas molecules. The electron released in this secondary ionisation will in turn be accelerated and can produce a further ionisation. The gas multiplication process therefore produces a cascade or avalanche of ionisation. The total charge collected now exceeds the initial charge released by the ionising particle by several orders of magnitude but it is still proportional to that initial charge. This region is therefore known as the proportional region. In region IV non-linear effects occur due to the effect of the large positive ion concentrations on the electric field gradient near the wire and proportionality is lost. Eventually at very high voltages the ionisation cascade or avalanche will spread along the whole length of the central wire and will only stop when the positive ion concentration is high enough to reduce the electric field below the value needed for further ionisation. A very large amount of charge is collected which is independent of the original amount of ionisation. This is the Geiger Müller region.

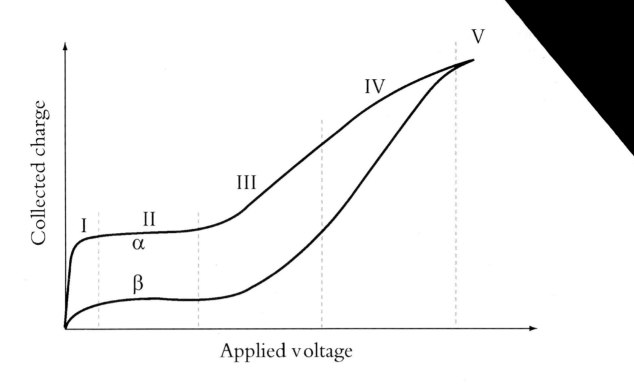

Figure 2.7 **Variation of collected charge with applied voltage for a gas-filled counter.**

(i) Ionisation chambers

These can be operated in two different modes. In pulse mode the detector output is recorded for each individual ionising particle. As discussed earlier in this section, the energy deposited by the particle can be determined from the amount of charge collected or the output voltage pulse. The amplitudes of such pulses will depend upon the energies of the incident particles and on any fluctuations in the detector response to monoenergetic particles. Thus, measurement of a pulse height distribution can be used to determine the energy spectrum of the particles. A 1 MeV particle stopping in a chamber with a capacitance of 50 pF (1 pF $=10^{-12}$F, where F - farad, the SI unit of capacitance) produces a voltage pulse in the external circuit of $\sim 10^{-4}$ V. Such small pulses require amplification by a high-gain external amplifier. If the typical collection time for ions is $\cong \tau$ sec, then pulse counting can only be performed when the rate of incidence of particles on the detector is $\leq$ $1/\tau$ per second. Problems associated with the slow collection of positive ions can be overcome by the use of gridded ion chambers in which only the fast voltage drop occurring between an intermediate voltage grid and the anode, due to passage of electrons, is detected.

At higher fluxes the ion chamber can be used in the ion-current mode in which the average current from the detector is measured. This corresponds to a time average of each pulse caused by separate ionisations. Under saturation conditions where all charges are collected, the ionisation current produced in the chamber is proportional to the rate of ionisation due to the incident particles. A dose rate of 1 mGy/h (Gy - gray, the S.I. unit of absorbed dose which is equal to one joule per kilogram) will produce a current of $\sim 10^{-11}$A in a chamber containing 1 litre of air at S.T.P. (Standard Temperature and Pressure, 760mm of mercury and 0°C). The voltage drop across a large load resistor is measured using a sensitive voltmeter.

ambers form the basis for many survey instruments used in area dosimetry 5.3.1). Ion chambers have excellent long-term stability and the ionisation perated in the saturated region depends only on the radioactive source and try. Thus, calibration of gamma ray sources is often carried out by ionisation current from an unknown source with that from a standard ame geometry.

Proportional counters

If n is the number of electrons produced by the initial ionising particle, the final number N of electrons collected at the anode is given by:

$$N = Mn$$

where M, the multiplication factor, is a constant, usually in the range 100–1000 for a given detector and applied voltage. The gas filling for proportional counters is usually argon or xenon with 5–10% methane.

The multiplication of electrons leads to the production of larger voltage pulses so that the requirements on external amplifiers are less stringent than with ionisation chambers. However, since the size of a voltage pulse is very sensitive to applied voltage, a very stable high-voltage power supply must be used if good energy resolution is to be achieved (see Section 2.2.6).

Proportional counters can be used as energy spectrometers for ionising particles which are stopped by the gas filling. The ranges of alpha particles ($\cong$ MeV) in the counter gas are frequently less than the detector dimensions so that each particle can be measured with close to 100% efficiency. Energy losses in the entrance window are reduced by the use of window-less flow counters. Beta particles of typical energies have ranges that are greater than the detector dimensions and hence the number of ion pairs is proportional to only that small fraction of the particle energy lost in the gas. The amplitudes of pulses from beta particles are therefore lower than those from alpha particles with equivalent kinetic energy.

Low energy X-rays or gamma rays ($\cong$ 5–100 keV) are often measured in proportional counters where the stopping power of argon, krypton and xenon can be up to 70–80%. Above these energies the interaction probability with the gas becomes very small and either scintillation (Section 2.2.2) or solid state detectors (Section 2.2.4) are used.

Neutrons can be detected by using BF_3 as the filling gas. Slow neutrons produce charged particles via the reaction $^{10}B(n,\alpha)^7Li$. For fast neutrons, the BF_3 proportional counter can be shielded by light materials such as polythene which slow down the neutrons via elastic collisions (a process known as moderation) to energies where the (n,α) reaction on boron has an appreciable cross-section (see Section 6.5.2).

(iii) Geiger–Müller counters

In the Geiger–Müller region, photons produced by energetic electron collisions with gas molecules spread the discharge along the length of the anode. The resulting output pulse is independent of the initial energy deposition so that **Geiger–Müller (G–M) counters** or Geiger tubes cannot be used for energy spectrometry. Rapid collection of the electrons leaves a positive ion sheath which moves slowly outwards towards the cathode. This sheath lowers the effective potential of the anode and makes the detector inoperative for a period of several hundred microseconds until the positive ions reach the cathode. Neutralisation of positive ions at the cathode can lead to the emission of photoelectrons which can initiate new, unwanted, pulses. To prevent this happening Geiger tubes are quenched either by lowering the anode voltage after a pulse, until all positive ions have been collected or by the use of a quenching agent such as a halogen gas to quench the discharge by absorbing excitation energy from neutralised atoms of the filler gas (usually argon or neon) without emission of photons.

The heights of voltage pulses produced by a Geiger tube are strongly dependent on applied voltage. The pulse-counting circuitry will normally include a discriminator (see Section 2.2.5) which rejects small, spurious pulses. As the applied voltage is increased, the output pulses from a Geiger tube become larger than the discriminator threshold and the observed count rate rises to a plateau. The count rate varies only slowly with applied voltage in this plateau region until finally a voltage is reached at which large numbers of spurious pulses are produced by electrical breakdown of the gas filling.

The motion of the positive ion sheath (and also the use of anode voltage reduction during quenching) leads to a dead time τ after a pulse, during which no further pulses are counted. When counting a radiation source allowance must be made for this. The true count rate N_0 is related to the observed count rate n by:

$$N_0 = \frac{n\tau}{1 - n\tau}$$

Voltage pulses from a Geiger counter are relatively large, typically a few tenths of a volt and a low-gain amplifier (or even no amplifier) is sufficient.

Because of their ruggedness and reliability, Geiger counters are frequently used in the counting of radiation sources and in radiation-dose monitoring. For the latter application they must be fitted with a metal screen to reduce the response to low energy radiations so that a roughly dosimetric overall response is produced (see Section 6.5.3.1). Gas-filled detectors are discussed in more detail by Price [9], England [10] and Kase, Bjärngard & Attix [11].

2.2.2 Scintillation counters

When radiations are incident on certain solids, some of the energy of the ionisation is converted to the production of photons. This scintillation process can be used in a class of detectors called **scintillation counters**. The scintillators include organic compounds and inorganic crystals. The scintillation process in inorganic crystals such as sodium iodide (activated with thallium) is briefly described as follows. An insulating crystal has an electronic band structure as shown in Figure 2.8. The filled valence band is separated from an empty conduction band by a forbidden gap. Ionisation raises electrons from the valence to the conduction band, leaving 'holes' in the valence band. Certain impurities (such as thallium in NaI) produce localised levels within the forbidden band called luminescence centres. An electron–hole pair can interact via lattice phonons to form weakly bound **excitons**. These excitons can be trapped at luminescence centres where the electron–hole pair recombine with the emission of light photons.

The photons released in this way are then allowed to strike a semi-transparent photocathode from which they release electrons. The number of electrons is greatly increased by a device called a photomultiplier which consists of a series of electrodes or dynodes which are maintained at successively higher positive potentials. Each electron which is accelerated onto a dynode releases ~2-5 further electrons. These are accelerated towards the next dynode where each releases further electrons. A cascade of electrons eventually reaches the anode and produces a voltage pulse across a resistor. The final voltage pulse is proportional to the initial energy deposition. The response time of scintillation counters is related to the time constant which characterises the emission of photons from the scintillator. This is typically ~1 μs for inorganic crystals such as sodium iodide NaI (Tl) or caesium iodide CsI (Tl) whereas organic scintillators such as anthracene have response times of a few tens of nanoseconds.

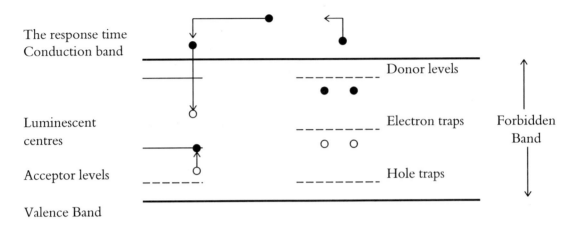

Figure 2.8 **Electronic band structure of a crystal, showing defect levels. Closed circles represent electrons and open circles represent vacancies (holes).**

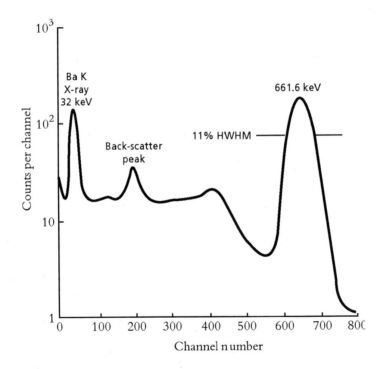

Figure 2.9 **Energy spectrum for ¹³⁷Cs gamma source with 76.2 mm × 76.2 mm Na(Tl) crystal, after NCRP 58 [5]. Reproduced by permission of NCRP.**

Figure 2.9 shows the pulse height (energy) spectrum (see Section 2.2.6) obtained from a ¹³⁷Cs source and a 76.2mm x 76.2mm NaI(Tl) crystal. The main peak or photopeak is produced when all of the gamma energy is deposited in the crystal. When photons undergo Compton scattering with electrons the scattered photon may escape from the crystal. A varying amount of energy is deposited in the crystal depending on the angle of scatter. This results in the broad Compton continuum of pulse heights below the photopeak which terminates at the Compton edge (see Figure 2.9), corresponding to the maximum kinematically allowed energy transfer in a single collision in which the photon is back-scattering through 180° relative to the incident photon direction. For further details see Birks [12] and references [9-11].

A backscatter peak may be produced when a gamma ray interacts via Compton scattering with the materials surrounding the detector (see Figure 2.9).

When the incident gamma ray energy is high enough to result in pair-production (see Section 2.1.4 (iii)), for a 'small' detector the annihilation gamma rays will escape from the detector and only the kinetic energies of the electron and positron are deposited. This adds a so-called double escape peak to the spectrum at an energy $2mc^2$ below the photopeak.

An escape peak may also be observed following photoelectric absorption (see Section 2.1.4 (i)), for example, in an argon filled proportional counter. In this situation a characteristic argon X-ray with an energy of about 2keV is produced which may escape from the counter if the photoelectric absorption occurs near to the surface of the counter. This results in an additional peak about 2keV below the gamma ray peak corresponding to full energy deposition in the counter.

Additional peaks in the pulse height spectrum due to summation effects are produced by the coincident detection of two (or more) gamma rays. This situation could arise when an excited state of a nucleus decays via an intermediate state with the emission of two successive gamma rays. If the lifetime of the intermediate state is less than the response time of the detector, then the gamma rays are in effect emitted in coincidence and a summation peak will be recorded at a pulse height given by the sum of the gamma ray energies.

In **liquid scintillation** counting of alpha or beta particles, the radioactive source is combined with a liquid scintillator (liquid scintillation cocktail) [13] and the emitted light photons are converted into electronic pulses in a photomultiplier as described above. In its simplest form, a liquid scintillator comprises an organic solute that is capable of fluorescing, dissolved in an organic solvent.

When an ionising particle passes through a liquid scintillator, the kinetic energy of the particle is transferred to the solvent/solute molecules present. Although most of the particle's kinetic energy is converted into kinetic energy of the molecules, the remainder may produce ionisation and excitation of the solvent molecules. The ionised molecules rapidly recombine with electrons resulting in the formation of excited solvent molecules. The solvent excitation energy effectively migrates through the solution by transfer from one solvent molecule to another until it is transferred to solute molecules. The resulting excited solute molecules de-excite by the emission of light photons (scintillations). These light photons are converted into electronic pulses in a photomultiplier as described above. The intensity of the scintillation, hence the electronic pulse height, is proportional to the energy of the radiation deposited in the scintillator solution and the number of electronic pulses produced in a given time is proportional to the activity present.

Many liquid scintillators contain more than one solvent, a primary solvent, whose role is to dissolve the solutes and to take part in the energy transfer process as described above and a secondary (or blending) solvent whose role is to aid miscibility between the radioactive sample and the liquid scintillator. Primary solvents used in liquid scintillators are aromatic with a p system of electrons that can be easily excited by ionising radiation, for example, xylene, linear alkylbenzenes, phenyl-ortho-xylylethane and di-isopropylnapthalene. Examples of secondary solvents include 2-ethoxy ethanol, ethane-1,2-diol and several surfactants. Many liquid scintillators also frequently contain a primary and a secondary solute. The requirements of the primary solute are that its emission range should match the response range of the photomultiplier and that the spectral range of the emission and absorption spectra do not overlap. Typical primary solutes used in liquid scintillators are 2,5-diphenyloxazole (PPO), 2-phenyl-5-(biphenyl)-1,3,4 oxadiazole (PBD) and (2-4'-t-butylphenyl)-5-4' biphenyl) 1,3,4 oxadiazole(butyl-PBD). The original role of the secondary solute was to adjust the wavelength of the primary solute emission to provide a better spectral match to the photomultiplier. Modern photomultipliers have eliminated the need for a secondary solute in this role, however, they are still used to reduce the effect of certain colour quenchers (see below). Commonly used secondary solutes are 1,4-bis-2- (5-phenyloxazolyl) benzene (POPOP), 1,4-di-2- (4-methyl-5-phenyloxazolyl) benzene (DMPOPOP) and p-bis (o-methylstyryl) benzene (bis-MSB).

The presence of materials other than solutes or solvents in a liquid scintillator, for example, from the sample being measured, may result in a reduction in the number of light photons produced by an ionising particle. This effect is called quenching and occurs in two principal forms, impurity(chemical) quenching and colour quenching. Impurity (chemical) quenching occurs when a non-fluorescent material present in the liquid scintillator dissipates the excitation energy of the solvent molecules prior to energy transfer to the solute molecules. Colour quenching occurs when a material present in the liquid scintillator absorbs the light emitted by the solute prior to detection by the photomultiplier. Some materials present in samples may promote luminescence reactions in a liquid scintillator, which has the effect of enhancing light production. The procedures used to correct for the effects of quenching and luminescence are referenced in Chapter 3 (Section 3.7.4).

Any background noise pulses from the photomultiplier, originating in the spontaneous emission of thermionic electrons from the photocathode, may be eliminated by the use of two photomultipliers in line at each side of the scintillation vial. Only pulses from the photomultipliers observed in **coincidence** are counted since the noise pulses in each photomultiplier will be uncorrelated and therefore coincidence pulses should only correspond to events within the liquid scintillator. Such an arrangement also gives an approximate 4π geometry and a high counting efficiency. An additional guard detector such as a chamber filled with liquid scintillant surrounding the sample and connected in **anticoincidence** with the main detector is used to remove the effects of signals produced by **cosmic rays** and background in general. Pulse shape analysis may be used to distinguish between alpha and beta particles. Recent developments in liquid scintillation counting are summarised in [14].

2.2.3 Cerenkov detectors

When a fast charged particle passes through an optically transparent medium it may lose energy by emitting a coherent pulse of light, **Cerenkov** light [15]. Energy is lost in this way provided the particle velocity $v_p > v_l$, the velocity of light in the medium where $v_l = c/n$ in which c is the velocity of light *in vacuo* and n is the refractive index of the medium. Cerenkov light is emitted in a cone whose axis lies along the particle track and whose half-angle θ is given by $\cos \theta = v_l/v_p = c/nv_p$. It is responsible for the bluish light observed in certain radioactive solutions and around reactor fuel rods submerged in water. The pulse of light is emitted for a very short time of the order of picosecond until the particle velocity falls below the threshold value and may be detected in a photomultiplier.

For particle energies below several MeV only electrons have sufficient velocities to produce Cerenkov light. This leads to applications involving radionuclides emitting beta particles (see Section 3.7.5). It is possible to detect Cerenkov light in a liquid scintillation counter in the absence of a scintillant in the sample vial (see Section 3.7.5).

2.2.4 Solid state devices

In principle, insulating or semiconducting solids can be used in place of gases in ion-chambers. Incident radiations produce electron-hole pairs which can be collected by electrodes attached to the surface of the solid. In practice there are a number of difficulties with this simple scheme. Charge carriers can be trapped at defects in the crystal and also scattered by **phonons** so that very large fields are required for efficient charge collection. Furthermore, impurities present in the crystal can result in electron donor levels just below the conduction band (Figure 2.8) or acceptor levels just above the valence band. These levels result in the presence of large electron densities in the conduction band or hole densities in the valence band, causing a large current to flow when an electric field is applied. This current will swamp any additional signal generated by radiation. Practical solid-state devices employ a number of different strategies to overcome these problems.

Semiconductors with electron-donor impurities or electron-acceptor impurities are known as n-or p-type materials, respectively. When n- and p-type materials are placed in contact the electron distributions in each are brought into equilibrium and a contact potential is established between the two sides. This potential difference is produced over a region free of charge carriers called the depletion zone. If an external voltage is applied to the junction so that the n-type region is made more positive with respect to the p-type region (the junction is reverse-biased) the width of the depletion zone is increased.

Radiation passing through the depletion zone creates electron-hole pairs which are rapidly swept down the potential gradient and can be collected at the electrodes. Such p-n junctions form the basis of the surface-barrier detectors. A thin layer of n-type silicon is connected to a voltage supply via an evaporated film of gold. Particles pass through the gold and the n-type layer into the depletion zone from which electron-hole pairs, formed by ionisation, are collected. The resultant voltage pulse is proportional to the amount of energy deposited in the depletion layer. In order to determine the total energy of a particle, it must come to rest in the depletion layer. Since depletion layers of ~100 μm are typical, surface barrier detectors have found most frequent application in alpha spectrometry. Detectors with thicker depletion layers are now available.

If a semiconductor such as germanium contains a p-type impurity, the effects of this impurity on the conductivity of the crystal can be neutralised by incorporating an n-type impurity, for example, lithium into the lattice. In the region where the number of donors is equal to the number of acceptors the number of free charge carriers is reduced to intrinsic levels. In practice, Li^+ is drifted into germanium at high temperatures in the presence of an electric field. This compensation process can produce active volumes of the order of $10^5 mm^3$ and Ge (Li) detectors can be used for gamma spectrometry. They have the disadvantage that they must be maintained at liquid nitrogen temperatures in order to prevent unwanted diffusion of lithium and to reduce the leakage current caused by thermal excitation of electrons across the narrow (~0.7 eV) band gap in germanium.

Nowadays, reasonably large single crystals of germanium can be produced with sufficient purity to obviate the need for lithium drifting. Such high-purity germanium (HPGe) detectors have the advantage that they need not be constantly maintained at very low temperatures, since lithium mobility is no longer a problem. However, HPGes must still be held at liquid-nitrogen temperatures whenever the high voltage supply is connected, in order to reduce the thermal leakage current.

Figure 2.10 shows a comparison between the pulse-height spectra for gamma rays from ^{40}K and ^{214}Bi as measured with a germanium detector and a scintillation counter. The much narrower peaks in the germanium detector spectrum are due to its superior energy resolution (see Section 2.2.6).

Semiconductor detectors are described in more detail by England [10].

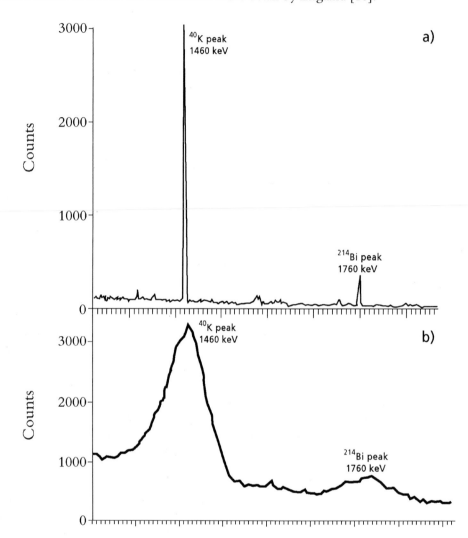

Figure 2.10   **Comparison of the pulse height spectra obtained with a high resolution germanium detector (a) and low resolution sodium iodide scintillation counter (b) showing the gamma ray peaks due to ^{40}K and ^{214}Bi.**

2.2.5 Counting systems

A typical counting system is shown in Figure 2.11. In the majority of detectors described above, for example, gas-filled detectors and solid state detectors, an electric field is applied via a high voltage (bias voltage) in order to collect the ion pairs produced by the incident particles. When the detector is operated in the pulse mode its output consists of a number of pulses of differing amplitudes produced at a rate determined by the rate of interactions between the incident particles and the detector medium.

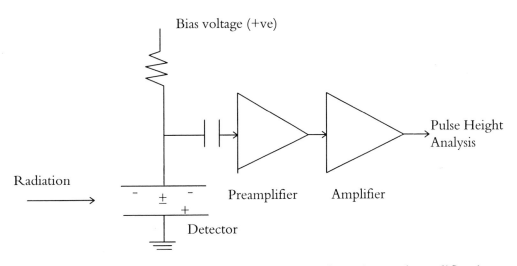

Figure 2.11   Schematic diagram of a basic detection and amplification system.

The functions of the preamplifier are to convert the charge pulses to voltage pulses, to amplify them, to match the high impedance of the detector with the low impedance of the coaxial cables to the amplifier, and to provide some pulse shaping. The rise time of the preamplifier output pulse is determined by the detector collection time while the decay time is set by the   time constant of the preamplifier which is longer than the rise time (long-tailed pulse).   A charge sensitive preamplifier is normally used with solid state detectors to provide an output voltage pulse which is proportional to the charge input while being independent of the capacitance of the detector which may change with variation in operating conditions.

An amplifier is used to provide further amplification and to shape the pulse to a suitable form for measurement. Consecutive pulses from the preamplifier may overlap due to the long decay time of pulses.   The pulses are therefore differentiated to provide a baseline reference level when the slow decay time is removed while keeping the information in the rise time. The pulse is then integrated to reduce its noise content and shaped to produce a near Gaussian shape.   If the time in-between pulses is low (high count rate) then this unipolar pulse is differentiated to produce a bipolar pulse. The magnitude or height of each pulse delivered by the amplifier is proportional to the energy deposited in the detector.   A ratemeter may be used to measure the average number of pulses per unit time (the count rate).

Each pulse from the amplifier carries information about the charge generated in the detector by a particular radiation/particle interaction with the detector medium. In general there will be a range of pulse amplitudes arising both from a range of radiation/particle energies and from fluctuations in the detector output for monoenergetic radiation or particles.   Thus, analysis of the distribution of pulse amplitudes or pulse heights may be used to measure the energy distribution of the radiation and to examine the operation of the detector (see Section 2.2.6).   This pulse height distribution or energy spectrum is usually displayed as the number of pulses per unit height increment against the pulse height.

Pulse height analysis is based on the use of an energy (voltage) discriminator which will produce an output logic pulse if the input pulse is greater than a certain adjustable level. The use of two discriminators in a **single channel analyser** (SCA) produces an output logic pulse whenever the input pulse falls within the voltage window set by the two discriminators. In order to produce the whole energy spectrum, the pulse height analyser can be stepped sequentially through a range of voltages (energies).

In modern systems a **multichannel pulse height analyser** (MCA) is used. The MCA collects voltage pulses in all ranges, converts them into digital information using an **Analogue to Digital Converter** (ADC) and stores them in the appropriate locations in a memory according to their voltage amplitudes. They are then displayed in real time on an oscilloscope. In this way an energy spectrum of the radiation is obtained, for example, of alpha particles or gamma radiation from a radioactive source. The energy spectrum is usually displayed as the variation of counts per multichannel analyser channel against the channel number (see Figures 2.9 and 2.12). The multichannel analyser may be a stand-alone analyser or be based on a personal computer both of which may be portable for field analysis. Commercial software packages are available which combine an acquisition function with the ability to make a simple measurement of peak areas, the so-called emulators.

2.2.6 Radiation spectroscopy

In many applications of radiation detectors the object is to measure the energy distribution or spectrum of the incident particles or radiation. This is achieved by analysing the pulse height distribution produced by the detector and associated amplifiers (Figure 2.12). In this figure the peak centred at channel number N_0 could represent pulses originating from monoenergetic particles or gamma rays from a radioactive source and the area under the peak from channel numbers N_1 and N_2 is a measure of the rate of particle (gamma ray) emission from the source, its radioactivity. If in addition the source emits particles (gamma rays) with different energies these will appear as peaks at other locations in the energy spectrum. The horizontal scale in channel numbers can be converted into an energy scale by calibration using, for example, several gamma sources of known energies.

The peak arising from monoenergetic particles is spread over a range of channels, around N_0 due to the fact there are fluctuations in the heights of pulses produced by the detector even though in each case the same energy was deposited in the detector (see next paragraph). If the fluctuations in pulse height are smaller the peak will be narrower and the energy resolution is said to be better.

The **energy resolution** is usually expressed as the full width at half maximum height of the peak (FWHM) in energy units, divided by the energy of the gamma ray or the mean energy of a particle and expressed as a percentage. In some applications, such as in alpha spectrometry or high resolution gamma spectrometry, the energy resolution is defined simply as the FWHM in energy units.

Fluctuations may occur due to drifts in the detector operating conditions, or in the electronic system or statistical noise due to the fact that the charge deposited in the detector is not a continuous variable but represents a discrete number of charge carriers. The number of charge carriers, for example, ion pairs, is subject to random fluctuations from event to event even though the same amount of energy is deposited in the detector in each case.

If a total energy E is deposited and the energy needed to create a pair of charge carriers is ε, the average number of pairs produced is $N = E/\varepsilon$. The statistical fluctuation in this number is given, from Poisson counting statistics, by $\sqrt{N}$. There is therefore, an intrinsic component to the energy resolution of a detector of about $\sqrt{N}/N$. About 35eV is required to produce an electron ion pair in a gas, whereas only ~3eV is required to produce an electron-hole pair in a semiconductor. The intrinsic component of the energy width in a solid state detector is therefore about $\sqrt{10}$ better than in a gas-filled detector.

A variety of other factors affect the energy resolution and in practice typical values for the detection of 661.66 keV gamma rays are about 0.2% for solid-state detectors, about 7% for scintillation detectors and about 2% for proportional counters. For further details see Knoll [16].

In order to identify and quantify the radionuclides present in the source, the peaks in the analyser spectrum must be identified. A background spectrum, obtained in the absence of the source is subtracted and the multichannel analyser spectrum is calibrated in terms of energy. The calibration process consists of recording the channel positions on the multichannel analyser spectrum of the peaks arising from a series of radionuclides whose radiation energies are known.

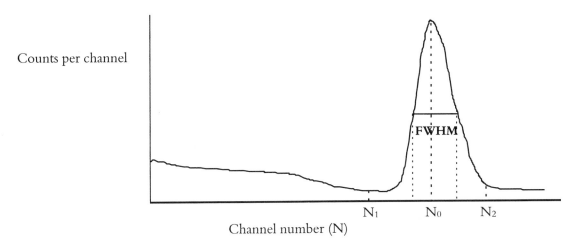

Figure 2.12 **Energy spectrum expressed as number of counts per channel as a function of channel number N. N_1 and N_2 represent approximate extent of peak with centroid N_0, FWHM is Full Width at Half Maximum.**

This allows a function, connecting channel number to energy, to be determined. The radionuclides present in the source may then be identified by comparing their radiation energies with those in a library of known radionuclides. The nuclear data table in Chapter 8 represents information available on a subset of selected radionuclides. The activity of a source radionuclide can be calculated from the peak areas knowing the detector efficiency/ies. For more complex spectra where, for example, there are overlapping energy peaks, some degree of spectral fitting is required (see Sections 3.7.1 and 3.7.7).

A discussion of counting statistics and their effect on a determination of a minimum detectable activity is given in Section 3.10.

2.3 RADIATION DOSEMETERS

A number of radiation detection devices have been described in Section 2.2. In the radiochemical laboratory such detectors are mainly used for measuring the activity of sources and for determining the energy spectra of radiations emitted by sources. Whilst some of these detectors may be adapted for use in radiation dosimetry, a further class of detectors are designed specifically for this purpose. The essentials of such dosemeters are described here. Their application to dosimetry is discussed in Chapter 6.

2.3.1 Photographic emulsions

Photographic emulsions have long been used in the study of nuclear radiations [17,18]. In the form of the film badge, they have been widely used in personal dosimetry. A photographic emulsion consists of a suspension of silver bromide grains in a matrix of gelatine, supported by a glass or plastic backing. When an ionising particle passes through the emulsion some of the Ag^+ ions are converted to Ag atoms. Complexes of such silver atoms can, under the action of the developer, catalyse the conversion of the entire grain to silver metal. The image formed by these silver grains is then fixed by using a suitable chemical to dissolve away all the undeveloped silver bromide grains.

Emulsions for nuclear research employ very fine (~0.25 μm) grains which are well separated in the matrix, so that well defined particle tracks can be developed. Nuclear emulsions of this sort are sometimes used for fast neutron dosimetry [19]. In photon and beta dosimetry there is no requirement to detect individual tracks, the overall degree of blackening being used to determine the degree of exposure of the film. A film which yields a high optical density for a low exposure is called a 'fast' emulsion whilst one showing much less optical density at low exposures is 'slow'. Because of the presence of the high-Z element silver, the emulsion over-responds to low-energy photons (via the photoelectric effect) so that a single emulsion does not have a good dosimetric response - equal doses of low and high energy photons will give different optical densities. For this reason, the film dosimetry badge (see Chapter 6 and references therein) consists of films of different speeds in addition to various filters, so that the dose may be calculated [19].

2.3.2 Thermoluminescence

Thermoluminescent dosemeters (**TLD**s) are increasingly being used for personal dosimetry. Thermoluminescence (TL) is best explained with reference to the electronic band diagram for an insulator, as shown in Figure 2.8. Radiation releases electron–hole pairs. Electrons or holes (or both) can be trapped at defect sites (electron or hole traps) within the crystal. For any given crystal, the amount of trapped charge is proportional to the radiation dose. When the crystal is heated electrons can gain thermal energy and escape from traps to the conduction band. From there they may recombine with holes at luminescence centres. This recombination is accompanied by the emission of light. The light output, which can be measured using a photomultiplier tube, is proportional to the amount of trapped charge and hence to the original radiation dose. When light intensity is plotted against temperature during a controlled heating cycle (usually with temperature increasing linearly with time) a series of peaks are obtained. This plot is known as the glow curve. For a thermoluminescent phosphor to be of practical use it is important that it should yield glow curvepeaks which are stable against fading (due to electron detrapping) at ambient temperatures.

Ideally, the dose absorbed by a phosphor should correspond closely to the dose absorbed by human tissue in the same radiation field. This requirement implies that the effective atomic number of the phosphor (Z) should be close to that of tissue ($Z \cong 7.4$).

An example of a TL phosphor is lithium fluoride doped with magnesium and titanium, which is widely used in TL dosimetry systems. In this material it is believed that defect complexes containing Mg^{2+} ions and Li^+ vacancies act as trapping centres whereas the Ti ions are associated with recombination (luminescent) centres. TL dosimetry is described in detail in books by McKinlay [20] & Oberhofer and Scharmann [21] and McKeever [22].

2.3.3 Pocket electrometer

The pocket electrometer can be used to monitor personal doses in real time. This device consists of a small ($\cong 10^3 \text{mm}^3$) ionisation chamber similar in shape and size to a pen. The central anode wire is connected to a quartz fibre. When the anode is charged to a positive potential, the fibre is repelled by electrostatic forces so that it is deflected away from the anode. When the chamber is exposed to radiation, the ionisation created in the chamber discharges the electrostatic field so that the elasticity of the fibre tends to return it to its original position. Thus, the degree of deflection is related to the degree of exposure to ionising radiation. The displacement of the fibre is viewed with a built-in lens. Some electrometers are charged externally, others have built-in chargers. Pocket electrometers have the advantage that they are direct-reading devices which can give an indication of exposure during a period of work in a radiation field. Electrometers are discussed in more detail in the IAEA report 109 [19].

2.3.4 Electronic personal dosemeters

Electronic Personal Dosemeters (EPDs) are potentially valuable devices for personal dose control. These operate on essentially the same principles as the solid-state detectors described in Section 2.2.3. A depletion layer typically 200 μm thick is contained between thinner p- and n-type regions of silicon. The bias on this p-i-n diode is provided by a long-life battery. The over-response at low photon energies due to the non-tissue equivalence of silicon can be corrected by shielding or by pulse height analysis [23]. Commercial systems claim a dosimetric response to photons from 20 keV to 10 MeV and a sensitivity to doses as low as 1 μSv. A discussion of dosimetric units is given in Chapter 6.

The dosimeter is equipped with a microprocessor and memory so that the wearer can read off dose rate or accumulated dose at any time. Alarm levels can be set to warn of high dose rates.

2.3.5 Track-etch detectors

Track-etch Detectors are sometimes useful for personal fast neutron dosimetry. When highly ionising particles pass through certain polymers a linear trail of polymer chain breaks and reactive species is formed. This damaged region has a diameter of ~100 nm. If the polymer is then treated with a suitable chemical etchant the damaged region is preferentially dissolved. The etchant can then proceed outwards from this narrow channel, forming a micron-sized hole which is visible under an optical microscope [24,25]. If the etching process is accompanied by a high-voltage, alternating electric field, the etched tracks develop into dielectric breakdown 'trees' of ~100 μm across. These electrochemically etched tracks are readily viewed using low-power microscopy or even a microfiche reader. Such track-etch detectors have been used to detect recoil nuclei from fast-neutron collisions [26]. The polymer CR-39 will detect proton recoils and has been used as the basis for a personal fast neutron dosimeter with a response down to neutron energies of a few hundred keV [26].

ACKNOWLEDGEMENT

The authors are grateful to Ian Adsley, AEA Technology, plc for several valuable discussions and to Bill Newton, Chairman, Royal Society of Chemistry, Radiochemical Methods Group, 1997-98 for his careful reading of the chapter and useful comments. They thank Pat Collis for her careful typing of the manuscript.

REFERENCES

1. W.E. Burcham, and M. Jobes, An Introduction to Nuclear and Particle Physics, Longman, 1997.

2. R.D. Evans, The Atomic Nucleus. Krieger, New York, 1982.

3. ICRP, Data for protection against ionizing radiation from external sources: Supplement to ICRP Publication 15, ICRP Publication 21, Pergamon Press, Oxford, 1973.

4. L.C. Northcliffe and R.F. Schilling, Nuclear Data Tables, **A7**,233-263, 1970.

5. NCRP, A Handbook of Radioactivity Measurements Procedures, NCRP Report No. 58, NCRP, Bethesda Maryland, 1985.

6. R.P Henke and E.V.Benton, Report TR-67-122, U.S. Nav. Rad. Def. Lab., San Francisco, 1967.

7. C.F. Williamson, J.P. Boujot and J. Picard, CEA-R3049, 1966.

8. H. Cember, Introduction to Health Physics, Pergamon Press, New York, 1983.

9. W.S.Price, Nuclear Radiation Detection, 2nd Edition, McGraw-Hill, New York, 1965.

10. J.B.A. England, Techniques in Nuclear Structure Physics, Part 1, Macmillan, London, 1973.

11. K.R. Kase, B.E Bjärngard, and F.H Attix, (Eds.), The Dosimetry of Ionising Radiation, Vol. II., Academic Press, Orlando, Florida, 1987.

12. J.B. Birks, The Theory and Practice of Scintillation Counting, Pergamon Press, Oxford, 1970.

13. D.L. Horrocks, *The mechanisms of the liquid scintillation process*, in Liquid scintillation, science and technology, A.A. Noujam, C. Ediss and L.I. Weibe, Eds., Academic Press, 1976.

14. G. T Cook, *Recent developments and applications in liquid scintillation counting*, Anal. Proc., **29**, 4-6, 1992.

15. J.V. Jelley, Cerenkov Radiation and its Applications, Pergamon Press, London, 1971.

16. G.F. Knoll, Radiation Detection and Measurement, 2nd edition, John Wiley & Sons, New York, 1989.

17. C.F Powell, P.H. Fowler, and D.H. Perkins, The Study of Elementary Particles by the Photographic Method, Pergamon Press, 1959.

18. J. Rotblat, *Photographic Emulsion Technique*, Prog. Nucl. Phys. **1**, 37, 1950.

19. IAEA, Personnel Dosimetry Systems for External Radiation Exposures, IAEA Technical Report 109, Vienna, 1970.

20. A.F. McKinlay, Thermoluminescence Dosimetry, Adam Hilger, Bristol, 1981.

21. M. Oberhofer, and A. Scharmann, (Eds), Applied Thermoluminescence Dosimetry, Adam Hilger, Bristol, 1981.

22. S.W.S. McKeever, Thermoluminescence of Solids, Cambridge University Press, Cambridge, 1985.

23. D.T. Bartlett, *Electronic Dosimeters: Use in Personal Dosimetry*, Rad. Prot. Dosim., 1/4, 335-339, 1993.

24. R.L.Fleischer, P.B. Price and R.M.Walker, Nuclear Tracks in Solids: Principles and Applications,University of California, Berkeley, 1975.

25. S.A.Durrani and R.K. Bull, Solid State Nuclear Track Detection - Principles, Methods & Applications, Pergamon Press, Oxford, 1987.

26. L. Tommasino, G. Zapparoli, R.V. Griffith and J.C. Fisher, Electrochemical etching of CR-39 foils for personnel fast neutron dosimetry, Proc. 5th Int. Congress of IRPA., **II**, 205-209, 1980.

CHAPTER 3
THE RADIOCHEMICAL ANALYSIS LABORATORY

BOB CARPENTER, JOHN COBB, JOE TOOLE AND GEOFF LONGWORTH

3.1 GENERAL LABORATORY SAFETY AND GOOD HOUSEKEEPING

Employers are responsible for maintaining a clean and healthy workplace and employees have a responsibility to work safely and maintain good standards of housekeeping. Good housekeeping should be regarded as a routine part of the job and means more than just neatness, it includes keeping all reagents, equipment etc. close to hand and in good working order. Good housekeeping can improve safety by minimising carelessness and clutter which are two common causes of accidental injuries and fires and can improve efficiency by keeping an orderly workplace and reducing lost time and frustration from constantly looking for papers, reagents, equipment etc.

Designated staff members should be made responsible for the safe operation of laboratories and these staff should be aware of all operations (and associated hazards) which are being carried out. It is recommended that a check list should be constructed which should include safety and housekeeping items and should be completed at regular intervals. This check list should review such items as general tidiness, clear exits, fire extinguishers, spillage kits, eye protection, clear passages, fume cupboard air flows and air input.

The Reporting of Injuries, Diseases and Dangerous Occurrences Regulations (RIDDOR, 1995 [1]) came into effect on the 1st April 1996 and place a legal obligation on employers to comply with the procedures. These cover specific dangerous occurrences, reportable diseases, fatal accidents, major injuries and other lost time accidents of greater than three days duration - all of which must be reported to the Health and Safety Executive (HSE). Most employers extend this requirement to local recording of actual and potential incident and accident situations, including near-misses.

The requirements and procedures are normally laid down in Company Safety Management Regulations and a defined level of management is given the responsibility to ensure both that all accidents, incidents and near misses are reported to the Head of Safety (or equivalent) and that all are investigated and appropriate actions taken to respond to any recommendations. All employees or their supervisors have a responsibility to generate the initial report to their management and this can conveniently be carried out by means of a pro-forma. Companies will have adopted their own local systems, for example, the reporting form currently in use within AEA Technology plc is reproduced in Figure 3.1.

UNUSUAL OCCURRENCE
IMMEDIATE REPORT FORM

Location of occurrence	
Site/Town/Country	Building/Room

Time of occurrence (Date and Time)

Person involved in occurrence:	Circle as appropriate:
Name:	
Contact Tel No.:	Employee
	Contractor
	Visitor
Company	

Home Address

Responsible Manager
Responsible Contract Superintending Officer (for contractors)

Name:	Tel No.:
	Fax No.:

Description and consequences of occurrence	Circle as appropriate:
	Near miss
	Property damage
	Radiation/contamination
	Release to environment
	Injury
	Visit to medical
	Possible lost time accident

Report made by	Date:
Name:	Address:
Telephone no.:	

Figure 3.1   Example of pro-forma for reporting unusual occurrences.

3.2 SAFETY AND ANALYTICAL OPERATIONS

3.2.1 Handling of chemicals

All staff who work in Radiochemical Analysis Laboratories (and, of course, other analytical laboratories) may handle materials which are potentially hazardous. Handling of certain types of samples can present hazards from skin contact, eye splash, infection, inhalation or ingestion. Basic laboratory safety procedures (which should be mandatory) will eliminate the potential severity of these hazards. References [2-10] provide more details of these hazards, relevant procedural requirements and legislation.

These include the following for all laboratory areas:

- no smoking, eating or drinking or application of make-up;

- wearing of laboratory coats and eye protection;

- protection of open wounds with waterproof dressing (obtain medical advice if necessary);

- wearing of suitable protective gloves for potentially hazardous operations;

- use of fume cupboards or fume hoods for handling operations involving hazardous materials;

- keeping acidic solutions covered where possible;

- always adding acid to water when diluting;

- handling mineral acids or organic solvents in fume cupboards;

- when using hydrofluoric or perchloric acids ALWAYS do so in a fume cupboard. Note particularly that perchloric acid fume cupboards must be of an approved construction material and cupboard and ductwork washdown facilities must be available;

- an age limit of 18 years of age applies for Classified Radiation Workers and

- a dose limit of 1 mSv applies to a foetus. Pregnant females should alert their supervisor as soon as pregnancy is confirmed or suspected. (see Chapter 6 for more detailed dose information).

Sample preparation procedures may employ hazardous chemicals, for example, acids, alkalis and organic solvents etc. In addition to the previous safety procedures it is recommended that full face masks (not safety glasses) should be used for all operations where splashing or spillage could be a problem.

In the event of spills or splashes on skin the affected area must be irrigated with copious quantities of water. If the severity of the incident is high, for example, hot or boiling reagents (including water) this treatment should be continued while medical advice or assistance is obtained. Much tissue damage from boiling water scalds can be prevented by the rapid and prolonged irrigation of the affected area with cold water – a minimum of 10 minutes irrigation will be necessary.

In the event of eye splashes of any chemical, the affected area should be irrigated immediately with copious quantities of water or, preferably, with 0.1% saline solution from a proprietary eye-wash bottle. This is a sterile solution from a sealed container but checks are needed on 'use by' date. Irrigation of the affected area should be performed for at least 15 minutes and medical advice or assistance must be obtained in all incidents involving potential eye damage.

Some reagents can present particularly severe hazards, for example, hydrofluoric acid (HF) which has the potential to cause deep tissue and bone damage. The use of this reagent in a laboratory area should be announced to all staff by displaying an 'HF IN USE' sign at the entrance to the area. Calcium gluconate gel must be readily available (checks are needed on 'use by' date) and in the event of a spill on skin the affected area should be immediately washed with water and the calcium gluconate gel constantly massaged into the affected area until medical advice is obtained.

An emergency shower or hand held sprays should be available to all staff working with acids and/or alkalis to enable prompt washing in the event of a major spillage incident.

3.2.2 High temperature preparations

The preparation of samples for radiochemical analysis may include ashing and/or high temperature fusion procedures which may involve handling glassware or metal crucibles at temperatures of ~300°C to ~1000°C. To facilitate the safe handling of these items they should be manipulated by an operator wearing a laboratory coat and full face mask and using suitable long reach tongs and heat resistant gloves.

The work area close to the oven or furnace should be designed so that hot vessels can be easily and quickly transferred to a heat resistant surface to cool.

3.2.3 The preparation and handling of biological samples

The preparation of biological samples can present particular infection hazards which are obviously at maximum severity in Clinical Laboratories. A Code of Practice exists to cover these situations [11] and classifies micro-organisms, viruses and materials into four groups depending on the level of hazard they present and the minimum safety conditions for handling. The use of biological materials is covered by The Control of Substances Hazardous to Health (COSHH) Regulations 1994, extended 1998.

Radiochemical analysis laboratories may analyse biological samples, for example, urine, faeces and blood to support routine dosimetry monitoring programmes for classified radiation workers. In addition, research programmes to investigate the behaviour of radionuclides in the human or animal body may require the analysis of body fluids, tissue and excretion products. Laboratories handling biological samples must have written procedures to cover the handling and disposal of samples, disinfection of work areas, dealing with spills, the disposal and cleaning of potentially contaminated sample containers and the transport of samples. Guidance can be obtained from the Code of Practice [11] but as samples are normally from a healthy population which should not contain the listed pathogens and hazardous materials, then a Category C Laboratory is a suitable classification.

3.2.4 Spillage of reagents

Procedures should be established to deal with spillages of acids, solvents and other hazardous materials. Minor spillages should be dealt with promptly and efficiently, proprietary absorbent and neutralising spill kits should be readily available and all staff should be trained in their use. In the event of a significant spillage, local procedures should be activated which should involve alerting a Safety Officer and/or local Fire Brigade (who should previously have been briefed of the potential hazards). If necessary, the Fire Brigade will employ a crew equipped with Breathing Apparatus (BA) to deal with the situation, but they should be informed of the actual hazards at the time of the incident.

If an immediate life-threatening situation exists, for example, a worker overcome with fumes then the Laboratory should have available suitable powered breathing helmets fitted with appropriate filters. Experienced supervisory staff should be trained in the use of this equipment for the sole purpose of dealing rapidly with a life-threatening situation. This equipment is ONLY for emergency use and should not be used for major spillage clean-up as the exhaustion of filters cannot readily be monitored.

3.2.5 Laboratory use of liquid nitrogen

Gamma Spectrometry Laboratories use liquid nitrogen (boiling point -196°C) to cool both Lithium Drifted and Intrinsic Germanium detectors. Suitable protective clothing including full face masks, laboratory coats and specialist gloves must be worn when handling this material and adequate ventilation must be provided [2].

3.2.6 Safety aspects of collection of environmental samples

The collection and handling of certain environmental samples can present hazards from infective organisms which may be present in the samples. As a minimum, all staff should be protected against Tetanus. Those collecting aquatic samples (especially in the vicinity of sewage discharges) should receive medical advice on the hazards and recognition of the symptoms of Leptospirosis which can be spread by rats.

Laboratory Operating Procedures should address the inherent hazards and control measures necessary for all operations. Risk assessments can most conveniently be carried out by the use of pro-formas which should cover a description of the job, solutions involved (including a hazard assessment), staff potentially at risk, control measures, personal protective equipment (PPE) needed, actions required and any training needs. Risk assessments should be reviewed annually or when a procedural change is introduced.

Further information can be obtained from:

HSE Information Centre
Broad Lane
Sheffield
S3 7HQ

3.2.7 The Control of Substances Hazardous to Health (COSHH) Regulations 1988 [3]

These regulations came into force on 1st October 1989 with a major revision in 1994 [3-6]. The Health, Safety and Environment Committee (HSEC) of the Royal Society of Chemistry (RSC) has published a guide booklet entitled 'COSHH in Laboratories'[5]. This booklet is aimed at chemists who are required to carry out assessments and provides sound, practical advice to assist with this process. This subject has also been covered by another very practical publication from Croner [6].

COSHH requires the following actions for compliance:

- **risk assessments** to be carried out on all work procedures which involve the use of hazardous substances;

- **testing and record keeping of equipment** used for the control and reduction of hazards (the measurement of fume cupboard flow rates is a common example);

- **monitoring of the work environment** or an individual's breathing zone will normally be determined by the assessment. Prevention or adequate control of exposure is a fundamental requirement and any exposure must be assessed against Occupational Exposure Standards and Maximum Exposure Limits [7];

- **training and instruction** of employees in hazards and procedures for their reduction and

- **reviews of procedures** to reduce exposure levels together with Occupational Health surveillance of employees who are potentially at risk.

The main responsibility for COSHH resides with the employer and action is normally delegated to local management. The local manager becomes responsible for carrying out assessments, decisions on control measures, training and record keeping (other than medical records).

Risk assessments are necessary to enable informal decisions to be made about the need for any necessary control measures to reduce occupational health hazards. Compliance can be achieved by identification of hazards, their severity and effects, risk assessments of work operations and documentation and demonstration of the adequacy of control measures.

3.2.8 Health and safety at work

A number of fundamental reference texts are available to provide information on legislation, dangerous substances and occupational hygiene. A selection of these are as follows:

Croner's Health and Safety at Work [8]

A loose-leaf binder which provides first points of reference to legislation, Codes of Practice and Guidance currently in force in the UK on Health and Safety at Work.

Croner's Dangerous Substances [9]

A loose leaf ring binder set which provides hazard information, classification and package labelling data on most hazardous substances in common use. It provides detailed guidance on the requirements of relevant safety legislation - mainly COSHH regulations.

Croner's Handbook of Occupational Hygiene [10]

A useful compendium of guidance on health matters associated with work activities. It takes the reader through identification of hazards, assessment of risks, measurement/ monitoring, control of risks and training guidance.

Essentials of Health and Safety at Work (The Health and Safety Executive (HSE)) [12]

This publication provides practical advice on coping with health and safety in the reality of business life. Interpretation of the Health and Safety at Work Act (1974) is provided together with distinctions between definite legal requirements and 'reasonably practical' guidance. The contents include sections on managing health and safety, premises, plant and machinery, substances, procedures and people and includes many useful references.

Principles of Health and Safety at Work (The Institution of Health and Safety at Work (IOSH)) [13].

This publication was written to coincide with the introduction of the 'six-pack' set of Regulations on health and safety at work resulting from EC directives. The contents include sections on safety technology, occupational health and hygiene, safety management techniques and law. It also includes a series of self-assessment questions and answers.

3.2.9 Ionising Radiation Regulations (1985)

The Approved Code of Practice [14] contains details of acceptable methods to meet the requirements of the Regulations. The Code provides guidance to put in place 'reasonably practicable' working practices and recognises that advancing knowledge may result in practices which are not described in the Code but which are perfectly acceptable.

A more detailed discussion of radiation protection is provided in Chapter 6 and the Regulations are outlined in Section 7.1.3.

3.2.10 Safety training

Safety training records must be maintained for all staff. The only mandatory training required is instruction in the use of Fire Extinguishers and this training must be renewed every three years, at a maximum. Recognition of local safety signs and alarms is a local requirement for all staff and contractors/visitors. Other training needs should be assessed on the basis of risk assessments.

An Occupational Health Department should be available for advice and medical assistance. Qualified First Aiders must be available in the absence of an Occupational Health Department and are desirable for all Laboratories. All staff should be encouraged to attend an Emergency First Aid course. A hydrofluoric acid training course must be attended by staff using this hazardous reagent.

A First Aid Manual should be available for qualified first aiders. The authorised manual of the St. John Ambulance, St. Andrew's Ambulance Association and the British Red Cross [15] is recommended.

3.3 STORAGE OF RADIONUCLIDE TRACERS AND STANDARDS

Radionuclide tracers and standards are invariably ordered in bulk quantities from approved suppliers and the regulations appropriate to the Transport (Section 7.4), Shielding (Section 7.4), Storage (Section 7.3) and Disposal (Section 7.3) of these materials must be obeyed. Because of the radioactivity levels of these materials they should be stored in a Designated Area which is under the control of a Radiological Protection Supervisor (RPS). The RPS should ensure that local written rules are available for all operations which will be carried out with radionuclide tracers and standards (see Chapter 6).

Standards and tracers usually need to be diluted before use and local precautions should be employed for these operations. Particular care should be exercised when opening sealed glass ampoules. These should be chilled before opening (to avoid pressure build-up) and carefully opened in the presence of a supporting staff member who can carry out immediate local monitoring with survey equipment. Special handling equipment may be required to reduce finger doses to staff opening glass ampoules.

Diluted radioactive standard and tracer solutions should ideally be stored in glass vessels and normally under acidic conditions to avoid adsorption losses on container walls. All dilutions of standard and tracer solutions should preferably be carried out by weight, they should be witnessed by a supporting staff member and records kept.

The shelf-life of the diluted standard should be recorded. This can be determined from the half-life of the radionuclide and the experience of the laboratory in previous, similar operations.

Standard solutions should be traceable to National or International Standards. Once the original sealed container has been opened, the standard becomes vulnerable to misuse. This can be controlled by the application of documented procedures for use but is obviously dependent upon the frequency of use and the experience of the staff involved. Ideally, tracers and standard solutions should be obtained which require the minimum number of dilution operations before they are suitable for use as working tracer and standard solutions. If a stable element carrier is present in the purchased standard, the concentration of this carrier should be maintained in the dilution.

3.4 COLLECTION OF SAMPLES

Sampling forms an essential part of any analytical procedure since, however carefully analyses are carried out, the final result will be dependent on the representative nature of the sample presented for analysis. Sampling procedures are normally developed locally to comply with local needs but guidance is available to establish these procedures [16]. General principles are covered in a Valid Analytical Measurement (VAM) article [17] which concentrates on the benefits of good sampling practice. Other VAM publications present a review of sampling systems [18], a bibliography of the literature of sampling [19] and an electronic reference source for Sampling for Valid Analytical Measurement [20].

3.5 STORAGE AND PRESERVATION OF SAMPLES

3.5.1 Site treatment

Samples may need some form of preservation or treatment at the sampling site for the following reasons;

- to reduce the loss of volatiles;

- to reduce bio-degradation;

- to reduce oxidation and reduction processes;

- to reduce wall losses;

- to reduce the transfer from one phase to another and

- to preserve anaerobic samples.

Stabilisation of bulk water samples with acid, for example, acidification to 2% nitric acid is commonly employed to retain plutonium and many other radionuclides in solution [16].

Rain-water samples, which may be collected over many days should be preserved by the addition of acidified stable carrier solutions. These can be formulated with reference to the particular radionuclides of interest but care should be taken to avoid any precipitation reactions [21]. Addition of **biocides** may be necessary for samples which may be contaminated with sewage but care must be taken to ensure that the chemical does not interfere with subsequent chemical separations. Addition of preservatives such as Formalin to milk [22] can prevent decomposition and subsequent analytical problems.

Filtrations of liquid samples may be necessary to avoid the exchange of radionuclides from aqueous to solid (particulate) phases. The elimination of air from sample containers is desirable and this is essential if the anaerobic nature of samples is to be preserved [23].

3.5.2 Laboratory preservation and storage

The above procedures are all relevant for laboratory preservation and storage. Refrigeration and freezing can be employed for the preservation of animal tissue, vegetation, soils and sediments but most laboratories would normally employ appropriate air drying or freeze drying prior to chilling. If extraction or acid digestion is required, these procedures should be carried out as soon as possible as the resulting solutions are then more stable for long term storage.

Ruckner and Johnson [24] established the criteria of holding times for aqueous samples and these are as follows:

- tritium: sealed to prevent isotopic fractionation;

- iodine: preserved in sodium hydroxide or sodium thiosulphate solution;

- caesium: 6 months, preserved to pH <2 in hydrochloric acid;

- plutonium: 6 months, preserved in 2M nitric acid and

- other radionuclides: 6 months preserved to pH <2 in nitric or hydrochloric acid.

These criteria (and others) should always be evaluated for the particular sample matrix to be analysed.

3.6 RADIOCHEMICAL ANALYSIS PROCEDURES

3.6.1 Introduction

Radiochemical separation becomes necessary when it is impossible to determine the activity of a radionuclide of interest by direct radiometric techniques. This occurs when the activity of the radionuclide is close to the detection limit of the direct technique or when the sample matrix interferes with the measurement. The interference may be due to the absorption of the radioactive emissions by the sample matrix or the presence of other radionuclides that emit particles or electromagnetic radiation of similar energy to the radionuclide of interest.

Radiochemical separation is usually required to determine low-levels of alpha and beta-emitting radionuclides in environmental samples. Gamma-emitting radionuclides are normally determined by direct counting, although when present at very low-levels, some degree of pre-concentration or separation may be required.

When it is clear that radiochemical separation is required, a suitable procedure must be chosen. The general requirements of such a procedure are as follows:

- the radionuclide of interest is isolated in high yield and with high purity;
- the radioactive emissions are detected with as high an efficiency as possible, taking into account background considerations and
- the analysis of a wide range of material types and radionuclide concentrations should be achievable.

In order to achieve the above requirements, labour intensive, multi-step procedures are usually required, although more efficient procedures are constantly being developed. Improvement of the selectivity and sensitivity of a procedure usually involves a more thorough removal of interfering components by the inclusion of more steps or of steps that are more selective to the radionuclide of interest.

Radiochemical analysis procedures can be divided into seven principal stages:

- sub-sampling;

- pre-treatment;

- solubilisation;

- concentration;

- separation and purification;

- source preparation and

- counting of sources.

Each of these stages is described in the following sections. Detailed descriptions of radiochemical procedures are outside the scope of this manual but can be found in published procedures manuals [25].

3.6.2 Sub-sampling and pre-treatment

The analytical result is only as good as the sample presented for analysis. Radiochemical analysis laboratories are frequently presented with samples for analysis which have been collected either by other organisations or by other parts of their own organisation. Sampling protocols and strategies have not been considered in this work but valuable assistance can be provided from the literature [26].

Samples provided for analysis are generally larger than the sample size required for analysis (an exception to this could be in the use of gamma spectrometry) and thus a representative sub-sample should be taken for analysis. The sub-sampling procedure used will depend on the sample type, size, nature and the radionuclides of interest to be determined (together with detection limit). The sub-sampling requirements (and problems) can be summarised as follows:

Aqueous samples	Take the total sample.
	Take an aliquot of the total sample.
	Filter to remove suspended particulate then take an aliquot of the filtered sample.
Soil, sediment, silt	Take the total sample.
	Sieve and take an aliquot of the sieved sample. NB this procedure should be used with care as sieving can remove an essential part of the sample which could affect the final result.
	Grind and homogenise and take an aliquot of the ground sample.
	Sub-sample the ground and homogenised sample by means of 'coning and quartering' or riffling [27].
Foodstuffs	Prepare as for culinary use.
	Separate bones from fish, poultry and meat by heating at ~150°C for 1 hour or dry at 100°C overnight.
	Air dry or freeze dry and homogenise.
Air filters	Take the total sample.
	Sub-sample the filter to take a known fraction.
Animals and fish	Take the total sample
	Dissect to remove the organ(s) of interest, for example, muscle, bone, liver, kidney etc.
	Air dry or freeze dry and homogenise.
Vegetation	Take the total sample.
	Sub-sample to take a known fraction.
	Air dry or freeze dry and homogenise.
Milk	Take the whole sample, evaporate to dryness and ash or freeze dry and ash.

The sub-sampling procedure should be carefully carried out to ensure that a representative sub-sample is acquired. Multiple analyses should be employed to demonstrate the adequacy of any sub-sampling procedure.

Wet and dry ashing techniques are commonly employed to remove organic constituents and convert samples into an inorganic form which is more readily solubilised. These ashing procedures also function as a pre-concentration step enabling bulk samples to be reduced in size and facilitating subsequent sub-sampling.

Dry ashing is normally carried out at temperatures between 300°C and 550°C and the selection of conditions must take into account the sample matrix and radionuclides of interest. Losses of volatile or semi-volatile radionuclides will occur to a greater or lesser extent. These will include ^{3}H, ^{14}C, Cs isotopes, I isotopes, ^{35}S, Ru isotopes, ^{210}Po and ^{99}Tc.

Tritium is normally determined as tritiated water (HTO) and can be extracted by freeze-drying [28-30], hetero-azeotropic distillation with xylene, benzene or cyclohexane [31-34] and distillation procedures at normal or reduced pressure. Of these techniques, the first two are preferred since they generally result in extraction of the total water content and do not suffer from any isotope fractionation effects which can occur in the distillation procedures.

Total loss of ^{14}C (from the organic component of the sample) will occur as a result of oxidation. Specialist combustion and trapping techniques are used for the analysis of this radionuclide [35].

Distillation losses of ^{210}Po (as the chloride) can occur during dry ashing and acid digestion techniques are normally employed for this determination.

Caesium-137 has been shown to be lost from biological samples when ashed at temperatures greater than 300°C [36] but careful control of conditions can eliminate or reduce these losses.

The volatility of ruthenium isotopes (as RuO_4) is often employed as a pre-separation technique using mineral acid digestion followed by distillation of the ruthenium into alkaline solution and precipitation as RuO_2 [37].

Losses of ^{99}Tc are more difficult to control during ashing and a variety of pre-treatments have been employed such as the addition of ammonia or mineral acids. Hydrochloric acid has been found to be the most useful in the ashing of vegetation [38].

A variety of chemical and combustion techniques have been developed over the years for the pre-treatment of environmental samples prior to the separation and determination of iodine isotopes [39-44].

The use of internal yield tracers, for example, ^{242}Pu, ^{243}Am, ^{232}U, ^{229}Th, is a commonly employed technique to ensure the accuracy of determinations for alpha emitting radionuclides (for more details see Section 3.6.10). These should be added as early as possible in the treatment of samples and appropriate oxidation/reduction steps carried out to ensure equilibration with the radionuclides present in the sample. A disadvantage of dry ashing is that it is not normally convenient to add yield tracers until the samples have been ashed. Thus, care should be taken in the choice of ashing containers and ashing conditions to reduce wall losses and combustion losses respectively.

Wet ashing techniques using mineral acids and/or oxidising reagents such as hydrogen peroxide can eliminate some of the disadvantages of dry ashing. For example, internal yield tracers can be added early and ashing processes can be more closely controlled [45-47]. Environmental radiochemical analysis can require the use of large samples which is problematic for wet ashing and these procedures are generally more time consuming than the simple dry ashing techniques.

3.6.3 Solubilisation

The dissolution of samples containing radionuclides can be achieved either by total dissolution or by leaching. The purpose of the analysis and final use of the analytical data should always be a consideration in the choice of the dissolution procedure. For example, the solubilisation procedure for the determination of the total uranium content of a soil sample could be different from the procedure employed for the determination of uranium deposited from the atmosphere. Whichever technique is employed, the objective should be to ensure that quantitative extraction is achieved and if the uranium is present in mineral phases then a total dissolution procedure is necessary. Leaching is more appropriate for the more readily soluble forms of uranium and, with careful choice of reagents, an initial form of separation can be achieved.

Leaching can be easier and quicker than total dissolution and reduces the quantity of sample which is taken into solution – this can simplify subsequent separations. Mineral acids are normally employed in leaching procedures and the advantages of this approach have been demonstrated for the determinations of artificial actinides in soils using hydrofluoric and nitric acids followed by hydrochloric acid extractions [48]. Similar approaches have used aqua regia [49], nitric and hydrofluoric acids [50], nitric acid and hydrogen peroxide [51,52].

Leaching procedures rely on the high solubility of the determinand and if any doubt exists or if the solubility is likely to be variable then total dissolution must be employed. Accreditation of analytical methods employing leaching procedures may require the demonstration of the effectiveness of the procedures by comparison with total dissolution techniques.

Total dissolution procedures normally either rely on extended treatments with mineral acids or fusion with a suitable flux to solubilise the material. Various combinations of mineral acids have been employed for dissolution and these usually consist of nitric, perchloric and hydrofluoric acids, [53-55]. The combination of mineral acid dissolution and the fusion of silicate residues is a very effective and widely used technique [56,57].

The use of heated pressure vessels [58] and microwave ovens [59] provide a very efficient approach for the dissolution of small samples of a gram or so in mass.

Fusion techniques have been used for the total solubilisation of resistant materials and require the samples to be thoroughly mixed with the flux and heated to high temperatures (800°C-1000°C) to disrupt mineral matrices [45,47,60]. Acid dissolution of the fused melt is the final process in this procedure.

Fusion procedures are commonly employed to eliminate preparation losses of semi-volatile radionuclides, for example, the determination of iodine isotopes in vegetation, soils and filters by subjecting the sample to an alkaline fusion to remove organic material [61]. The use of an alkaline fusion has been reported for the preparation of soil, milk and suspended particulates prior to leaching and extraction of ruthenium isotopes [62]. It has also been employed for the preparation of environmental samples prior to the determination of ^{99}Tc [63].

As indicated earlier, the choice of the dissolution procedure will depend upon the objectives of the programme and criteria such as the chemical form and solubility of the radionuclides must always be considered. A comparison of leaching and fusion techniques for the determination of plutonium isotopes and [241]Am in soil samples has been reported [64].

3.6.4 Concentration

The concentration step prepares the sample for the separation/purification stage by removing the bulk of the sample matrix. To some degree this is achieved during pre-treatment, for example, ashing removes the organic component of the sample. At this stage it is usually necessary to add isotopic or non-isotopic stable carriers to the sample to aid the separation process.

Evaporation of water or solubilised samples is the simplest method of concentration, although it is only suitable for samples of low salt content. For samples containing large quantities of dissolved solids, precipitation in the presence of stable isotopic carrier or co-precipitation in the presence of non-isotopic carrier is a convenient way of concentrating the analyte. Concentration may also be achieved by other approaches such as solvent extraction, **ion-exchange** and in the case of volatile radionuclides, trapping following combustion or wet oxidation.

Examples of concentration procedures used for some radionuclides of interest in environmental monitoring and geochemical applications are given below.

Actinides

Actinides are frequently concentrated from a wide range of sample matrices by co-precipitation from solution onto ferric hydroxide by the addition of aqueous ammonia solution [22,65-67]. In the case of uranium, it is essential that the sample and ammonia solution are carbonate-free otherwise uranium will not co-precipitate due to the formation of a carbonate complex [68]. Plutonium, americium, curium and thorium are co-precipitated onto lanthanum and neodymium fluorides precipitated from acidic solution [69,70], uranium and neptunium will also co-precipitate following their reduction to the tetravalent state. Calcium oxalate precipitated at pH 1.5 to 4.5 is used in procedures to co-precipitate plutonium, americium and curium from solubilised soil and sediment samples [22,51] the presence of excess oxalic acid prevents the precipitation of iron due to the formation of an oxalate complex. Other co-precipitants used to concentrate actinides include ferric phosphate, bismuth phosphate [71] and barium sulphate [72]. The precipitates are isolated by filtration or centrifuging and then dissolved in small volumes of acid to produce a low ionic strength solution for the subsequent separation procedure.

Radiostrontium

Radiostrontium is usually concentrated by precipitation in the presence of stable carrier as either a mixed alkaline-earth sulphate [73], carbonate [22], oxalate [74,75] or phosphate [22,76] from a wide range of sample matrices.

Radiocaesium

Radiocaesium may be concentrated from acidic solutions of a range of sample matrices onto ammonium molybdophosphate (AMP) [77,78,79]. The sample solution can be passed through the AMP dispersed on an inert support or the AMP can be mixed directly with the sample solution. The Cs-AMP complex is then isolated and gamma-counted.

Radiocaesium may also be concentrated from large volume water samples on a column of potassium cobaltiferricyanide [80].

Radioiodine

For vegetation and soil, radioiodine in the presence of stable carrier can be concentrated by trapping in alkaline solution following either combustion [81] or wet oxidative distillation [82]. For vegetation and foodstuffs, concentration can be achieved by solvent extraction or anion-exchange following ashing in the presence of sodium hydroxide and dissolution [83,84]. For water and milk samples, direct concentration onto anion-exchange resins can be used [84].

Radioruthenium

Precipitation of ruthenium dioxide from solution in the presence of stable ruthenium carrier is frequently used to concentrate radioruthenium from a range of sample matrices. The sample solution is heated at $90^{\circ}C$ under alkaline oxidizing conditions and ruthenium dioxide is precipitated at pH 4 by the addition of methanol [62].

Technetium-99

Concentration of ^{99}Tc from solution can by achieved by ion-exchange or solvent extraction [85,86].

Tritium

Tritium is usually concentrated from aqueous samples by electrolytic enrichment. The sample is made alkaline and then reduced in volume by electrolysis over a period of several days. The tritium is isotopically enriched in the remaining solution [7].

Carbon-14

For solid samples, concentration of ^{14}C involves its conversion to benzene which is then liquid scintillation counted. The benzene synthesis approach involves the conversion of the carbon to carbon dioxide by oxidative combustion followed by conversion to benzene via lithium carbide and ethyne [88,89]. Alternatively the ^{14}C can be concentrated as barium carbonate following conversion to carbon dioxide by combustion or wet oxidation [90]. Concentration of inorganic ^{14}C in water samples can simply be achieved by precipitation as barium carbonate.

Polonium-210 and lead-210

Polonium-210 can be concentrated from solution by co-precipitation onto manganese dioxide in the presence of potassium permanganate [91]. Lead-210 may be concentrated from solution by precipitation as lead chromate [92] or by co-precipitation on ferric hydroxide [93].

3.6.5 Separation and purification

The concentration step (or direct counting) may be all that is required to permit measurement by gamma-spectrometry. However, alpha and beta-emitting radionuclides generally require further purification prior to counting. Many radiochemical separation procedures are based on the use of ion-exchange or solvent extraction to purify the radionuclide of interest. The recent introduction of extraction chromatography resins has provided an alternative approach to these techniques.

3.6.6 Ion-exchange

Ion-exchange separations [94,95] are based on the adsorption-desorption characteristics of an analyte on ion-exchange resins. Ion-exchange resins are synthetic high molecular weight organic polymers containing a large number of ionic sites (functional groups) which can be either cationic, for example, sulphonic acid or anionic, for example, quaternary ammonium. A cation-exchange resin takes up cations from solution in contact with it, releasing an equivalent amount of cation associated with the resin into solution; an anion-exchange resin takes up anions in a similar manner. Ion-exchange resins can be used in the form of a vertical column. The sample solution is passed through the column to permit adsorption of ions of interest. By washing the column with carefully selected solutions (eluents) it is possible to separate the analyte from mixtures of interfering ions in a sample. An alternative to the column ion-exchange approach is a batch process where sufficient resin is mixed with the sample solution to permit adsorption of the analyte. The resin is then separated and treated to remove the analyte.

A few examples to illustrate the use of ion-exchange in radiochemical separations are presented here:

A sequential separation of the radionuclides of strontium, lead and radium can be achieved by cation-exchange. Initially, 1.5 M ammonium lactate at pH 7 is used to remove interfering magnesium and calcium, then strontium is eluted using the same eluent. Lead is then eluted with 1 M ammonium acetate at pH 6.2 and finally radium (with barium) is eluted with 0.25 M EDTA at pH 10 [96].

Sequential separation of radionuclides of the trivalent rare-earths (and americium) can be achieved by cation-exchange using 0.3M ammonium α-hydroxyisobutyric acid or ammonium hydroxyisobutyrate as eluents [97].

Although cation-exchange can be used in actinide separations, procedures involving anion-exchange are more frequently used. A procedure in common use involves the adsorption of nitrato-complexes of tetravalent actinides from 8 M HNO_3 onto an anion-exchange resin in the nitrate form. Plutonium, thorium and neptunium are retained by the resin whereas most other metals including iron, U(VI) and trivalent actinides are not retained. Thorium is eluted from the resin with concentrated hydrochloric acid. Plutonium is eluted by reduction to the trivalent state with 9 M HCl/0.1 M NH_4I and neptunium is finally eluted with 1 M HCl [22].

An important step in americium/curium determinations is their separation from rare-earth elements. This separation can be successfully achieved by anion-exchange from a mineral acid/alcohol medium. Americium and curium are adsorbed onto the anion-exchange resin from 1 M HNO_3-93 % MeOH. Lighter rare earths also retained by the resin are then eluted using 0.1 M HCl-0.5 M NH_4SCN-80 % MeOH. Americium and curium are then eluted with 1.5 M HCl-86 % MeOH [22,49].

In procedures for uranium/thorium separations in geological media, uranium and thorium can initially be separated from concentrated hydrochloric acid solution on an anion-exchange column in the chloride form. Uranium and iron are retained but thorium passes straight through the column. Uranium and iron are eluted with 0.1 M HCl. Thorium is further purified by adsorption onto an anion-exchange column from 7 M HNO_3 and subsequent elution with dilute hydrochloric acid. Uranium can be isolated from iron by adsorption onto an anion-exchange column from ammonium acetate solution at pH 4.5-5. Iron passes through the column, and then uranium is eluted in dilute hydrochloric acid [98]. Separation of uranium from iron can also be achieved by anion-exchange from nitric acid solution [67], but great care must be taken since uranium is only weakly adsorbed under these conditions.

3.6.7 Solvent extraction

In solvent extraction procedures [99] (also referred to as liquid-liquid extraction), the aqueous sample is shaken with an organic solvent containing an organic extractant. The extractant removes the analyte from the aqueous phase, whilst leaving interfering ions in the aqueous phase, by the formation of an analyte-extractant complex which is more soluble in the organic phase. The purified analyte can then be back-extracted from the organic phase into a separate aqueous phase by adjustment of the extraction conditions. Alternatively, solvent extraction can be used to remove interfering ions into the organic phase leaving the purified analyte in the aqueous phase. Extractants typically used include high molecular weight amines, for example, tri-iso-octylamine, β-diketones, for example, thenoyltrifluoroacetone (TTA) and organophosphate esters, for example, di-2-(ethylhexyl)phosphoric acid (HDEHP) and tri-butyl-phosphate (TBP).

A few examples are presented here to illustrate the use of solvent extraction in radiochemical separations.

Solvent extraction using HDEHP [100,101] or TBP [102,103] in hydrocarbon diluents can be applied to procedures for ^{90}Sr determinations via isolation and measurement of the ^{90}Y daughter. This can be illustrated using a sequential extraction procedure for the determination of ^{90}Sr, ^{147}Pm and ^{144}Ce. Initially, yttrium, promethium and cerium are extracted into HDEHP from 0.05 M HNO$_3$. Yttrium is then purified by back extraction of the cerium and promethium into 1 M HNO$_3$. Yttrium is then back extracted into 8 M HNO$_3$. Promethium and cerium are separated by extraction of cerium into HDEHP from 10 M HNO$_3$ - 1 M NaBrO$_3$. Cerium is then back extracted into 10 M HNO$_3$ - 6 % H$_2$O$_2$ [100].

Actinides are frequently separated by solvent extraction. For example, extraction using dibutyl-N,N-diethylcarbamylphosphonate (DDCP) is used in procedures to purify americium and curium. The americium and curium extracted into DDCP from 12 M HNO$_3$ and then back extracted into 2 M HNO$_3$ [22,49]. The procedure is quantitative but further purification is required to remove rare earths which follow americium in the extraction.

Extraction into TBP from 3-6 M HNO$_3$ in the presence of Al(NO$_3$)$_3$ is widely used to separate uranium from accompanying elements for a range of samples. Other elements that are extracted include iron and thorium. Iron can be removed by its back extraction into dilute HNO$_3$ and the extraction of thorium can be prevented by complexing it with EDTA prior to extraction. The purified uranium is back extracted into water or carbonate solution [104].

Plutonium can be purified by extraction into TTA in cyclohexane from 1 M HNO$_3$ followed by back extraction into 10 M HNO$_3$. Prior to extraction, the plutonium is converted to the tetravalent state using hydroxylamine hydrochloride.

3.6.8 Extraction chromatography

Extraction chromatography involves the use of resins which comprise highly selective organic extractants dispersed on an inert support. The recent commercial availability of the resins has resulted in an increase in their application in radiochemical separations. The resins are used in a similar manner to column ion-exchange, however, due to the highly selective nature of the extractant much smaller quantities of resin are required compared to column ion-exchange, resulting in the use of much lower volumes of reagents to effect efficient separation. Resins are available which comprise the following extractants: 4,4'(5')-bis(t-butyl-cyclohexano)-18-crown-6 (DtBuCH18C6); octyl (phenyl)-N,N-diisobutylcarbamoyl-methyl-phosphine oxide (CMPO); diamyl amylphosphonate and Aliquat-336. These resins have been used in procedures for separation of radiostrontium [105-107], actinides [108-110] and ^{99}Tc [111]. Two examples of radiochemical separations involving extraction chromatography are given here to illustrate its use.

Radiostrontium may be separated from soils using the DtBuCH18C6 resin. Strontium is concentrated from the solubilised sample as the oxalate and following destruction of the oxalate, the strontium is adsorbed onto the DtBuCH18C6 resin from 3 M nitric acid solution, other interfering ions are eluted in the load solution and in further 3 M nitric acid washes. The purified strontium is then eluted from the resin using water [106].

Americium may be sequentially separated from a variety of samples using the CMPO and Aliquat-336 resins. Americium is concentrated from the sample solution onto calcium oxalate, and, following destruction of the oxalate, americium, other actinides and lanthanides are adsorbed onto the CMPO resin from 2 M nitric acid. Americium and lanthanides are eluted from the resin in 4 M hydrochloric acid. The americium is then adsorbed onto the Aliquat-336 resin from a solution of 2 M ammonium thiocyanate in 0.1 M formic acid. Lanthanides are eluted in the load solution and thiocyanate/formic acid washes and then the purified americium is eluted in 2 M hydrochloric acid [109].

3.6.9 Other separation techniques

Not all radionuclide separations are best achieved by the techniques described above. A few examples of other purification procedures are summarised here.

Tritium

For aqueous samples, tritium is separated from non-volatile radionuclides and non-volatile quenching materials by distilling off tritiated water from the sample. The distillation is carried out in the presence of sodium carbonate and sodium thiosulphate to prevent the transfer of inorganic ^{14}C and radioiodine respectively [22].

Radon-222 and radium-226

Separation of ^{222}Rn from aqueous samples is achieved by purging helium through the sample in a closed system. The radon and helium are dried, carbon dioxide is removed and the radon is absorbed on activated charcoal. At the end of the separation, radon is desorbed and drawn into an evacuated alpha scintillation counting flask. The ^{226}Ra can then be determined by sealing the water sample and repeating the radon separation after the ^{222}Rn has ingrown towards secular equilibrium with the ^{226}Ra [67].

Radiostrontium

Radiostrontium may be separated by ion-exchange or solvent extraction in the case of ^{90}Sr (by extraction of the ^{90}Y daughter). However, the classical approach for radiostrontium involves the near specific precipitation of strontium nitrate from fuming nitric acid solution [22]. The precipitation permits the separation of strontium from large amounts of calcium due to the greater solubility of calcium nitrate under these conditions. Several precipitations may be required to achieve good separation. Barium and radium which are also precipitated are then removed by barium chromate precipitation and ingrown ^{90}Y is removed by co-precipitation onto ferric hydroxide.

3.6.10 The use of chemical yield tracers

Radiochemical separation procedures are rarely quantitative, it is therefore essential that the chemical yield is known for an accurate determination of the radionuclide of interest. This can be achieved by the addition of a suitable chemical yield monitor as early as possible in the separation procedure. Ideally the yield monitor should behave identically to the analyte during the separation procedure.

For radionuclides for which stable nuclides are available, this can be achieved by the addition of known quantities of the stable isotope which can be measured at the end of the separation by techniques such as gravimetry, titrimetry, atomic absorption spectrometry, emission spectrometry or mass spectrometry. If the stable isotope is already present in the sample, it is possible to measure it at the beginning and the end of separation to determine the isotopic and hence chemical yield.

For radionuclides that do not have stable counterparts, the yield monitor used will be a radionuclide which is not likely to be present in the sample. It is essential that the yield monitor establishes chemical equilibrium with the analyte at an early stage and that the yield monitor and analyte can be measured in the presence of each other. For alpha emitting radionuclides, a suitable yield monitor is an alpha emitter of the same element with alpha energies sufficiently different from those of the analyte to permit a simple measurement. In some cases radionuclides with a different mode of decay to the analyte have to be used as yield monitors, for example the beta emitter ^{239}Np is used as a yield monitor for the alpha emitter ^{237}Np. Radioactive yield monitors can also be used for radionuclides that have stable isotopes, for example ^{85}Sr is routinely used in ^{90}Sr determinations. Table 3.1 provides a list of radionuclide yield monitors suitable for the analysis of radionuclides of environmental interest.

In some cases it is not possible to use an isotopic yield monitor and recoveries have to be estimated using non-isotopic yield monitors that are chemically similar. Barium is frequently used as a yield monitor for ^{226}Ra and ^{243}Am is used for curium.

Table 3.1   Radionuclide yield monitors used in radiochemical separations after [16,112]

Analyte	Yield monitor
^{90}Sr	^{85}Sr measured by gamma counting.
^{99}Tc	^{99m}Tc measured by beta or gamma counting, ^{99}Tc measured after ^{99m}Tc decays or direct measurement by mass spectrometry-see Section 3.8.
^{210}Po	^{208}Po or ^{209}Po measured by alpha spectrometry
^{226}Ra	^{223}Ra measured by alpha spectrometry, ^{133}Ba measured by gamma ray spectrometry
^{228,230,232}Th	^{229}Th measured by alpha spectrometry
^{231}Pa	^{233}Pa determined by beta counting of ^{227}Ac daughter or alpha counting of ^{227}Th grand-daughter
^{234,235,238}U	^{232}U measured by alpha spectrometry, ^{236}U can be used for determination of ^{234,238}U in geological samples
^{237}Np	^{239}Np measured by beta or gamma counting
$^{238,239/240}$Pu	^{242}Pu or ^{236}Pu measured by alpha spectrometry
^{241}Am	^{243}Am measured by alpha spectrometry
^{242,243,244}Cm	^{243}Am measured by alpha spectrometry

3.7   PREPARATION OF AND COUNTING OF SOURCES

In order to determine the radionuclide content of a sample it is necessary to prepare a source in a suitable form for the alpha, beta or gamma measurement. The physical and chemical form of the source must be selected to be compatible with the chosen counting technique. The form of the source should be readily reproducible for consistency and calibration purposes and it should be sufficiently durable to enable storage (where possible) and re-counting if necessary.

For environmental measurements, gamma-emitters are usually determined by gamma spectrometry using high resolution intrinsic germanium or low resolution NaI(Tl) detectors, beta-emitters are determined by gas flow proportional counting, liquid scintillation counting or Cerenkov counting and alpha-emitters are determined by alpha spectrometry using silicon surface barrier or ion-implanted detectors. These counting techniques are discussed in Chapter 2 and practical aspects are briefly discussed here.

3.7.1   Gamma ray spectrometry

Sources for gamma-ray spectrometry generally require very little preparation unless homogenisation and sub-sampling are required for large samples or pre-concentration and separation steps are required to achieve low detection limits. It may be necessary to use appropriate pre-treatment and concentration procedures as described in Sections 3.6.2 and 3.6.4 to arrive at a sample which is suitable for counting. Ideally, sources should be uniform and symmetrical to ensure accurate calibration and the consistency of data. In principle, if a source or sample can be presented to the detector in a suitable form which can be calibrated, then an accurate and precise analysis can be carried out.

Solid sources may be in the form of a flat disc which is placed on top of the detector. To assist accuracy and reproducibility it may be necessary to grind soil samples or compress large area air filters with a hydraulic press. Alternatively the source may be contained in a cylindrical vial within an appropriate aperture in the detector crystal - a well type detector. The geometry in a well type detector is larger and is close to 4π geometry.

Liquid samples containing suspended particulate should be filtered before analysis to avoid uncontrolled geometry effects from settling of the particulate whilst the sample is being counted. Clearly if significant activity resides on the particulates this should also be measured. Re-entrant vessels are commonly employed for sample containment during counting (the Marinelli beaker) [113] and large samples, for example, up to 3kg of soil, can readily be accommodated.

In the simplest case, the activity of a gamma ray source is obtained by dividing a measured gamma ray count-rate by the gamma ray emission probability and by the counting efficiency. In practice, it is usually necessary to make a correction for the background count-rate. The counting efficiency is dependent on the energy of the gamma emitter, the source geometry and on self absorption in the source. Therefore, in order to determine counting efficiencies as a function of energy, mixed radionuclide standards are used (typically with an energy range of 5 to 2000 keV) which are in the same geometry and have the same physical characteristics as the source to be measured. The gamma ray activities of the radionuclides in these standards need to be known accurately. The standards are also used to energy calibrate the counting system.

Acquisition of data should be carried out over a suitable period to achieve the required precision taking into account the background count-rate and interferences from Compton scattering (see Section 2.2.2) and peak overlap. The counting system should be stable enough to prevent variation in the energy calibration over the counting period. The energy calibration and backgrounds should be regularly checked for fluctuations.

Analysis of gamma spectra requires knowledge of the nuclear properties of the radionuclides counted. As noted in Sections 1.4.2.2 and 2.1.3, positron annihilation results in the emission of two gamma rays at 511 keV. It is possible that there are peaks in the energy spectrum which do not correspond to radiation from a single gamma transition which clearly need to be understood before quantitative analysis is possible. Thus, there may be peaks in the background radiation, impurities in the source or photopeak summation effects. In the latter case, if two coincident gamma rays are detected simultaneously in the crystal, then the recorded peak is the sum of their two energies. Random summation due to accidental time coincidence between two events in the detector is also possible and will give rise to a sum peak. Such effects need to be considered when fitting a gamma-ray spectrum in order to identify and quantify the radionuclides present.

Gamma spectra are usually computer fitted to an analytical function taking into account the instrumental background. The major issues addressed by these computer codes are the calculation of the peak energies, the energy resolution and efficiency of the detector and the identification and quantification of the radionuclides or attribution of a peak to an escape peak (see Section 2.2.2), a backscattered peak or a summation peak due to coincident gamma rays. The codes generally require additional information relevant to each application, examples of these are given below:

Energy and resolution	details of the isotopes used and their emission energies
Efficiency	activities of standards used, date of measurement and relevant nuclear data
Radionuclide identification	user knowledge of expected radionuclides
Radionuclide quantification	user knowledge of actual radionuclides

Of key importance to the performance of spectral analysis software is the identification of photopeaks in the spectrum and the accurate determination of the areas of these peaks. Algorithms and computer codes to perform these tasks were initially developed in the late 1960s [114,115] and have been continually improved to the current high standards. Several excellent reference books on this subject are available [116-118].

Commercial software packages are available for the analysis of gamma spectra. There are two main types, the so-called emulators which combine an acquisition function with the ability to make a simple measurement of peak areas and those in which the spectra are computer fitted to an analytical function taking into account the instrumental background. In addition, various organisations have produced their own in-house computer-based analysis packages. The general problems that a user of the packages may encounter in their use have been highlighted in a comparison of spectral analysis software using a created set of test spectra [118]. Such test spectra should first be analysed as 'blind' spectra to provide a thorough test of a given package. This work, while suggesting that the packages in general performed well, emphasised the importance of a calibration step to establish the energy, peak shape and efficiency and pointed to some shortcomings in the estimation of uncertainties [119].

3.7.2 Gross alpha and gross beta measurements

These analyses can be carried out to screen both solid and liquid samples for total radioactivity content. Great care should be taken in the interpretation of the resulting data as they can be very method dependent. As samples are normally analysed 'as received' (albeit following drying and/or ashing) a considerable variety of source preparation techniques can be employed to present samples for counting. In addition, inconsistencies can occur from the use of different calibration radionuclides and counting procedures.

These measurements are popular because they are rapid and low cost procedures. For example, whole water samples can be evaporated down to provide counting sources and soils or sediments can be slurried onto counting trays for counting. To achieve consistency of data it is highly recommended that standard procedures are employed for the determinations such as those described for the analysis of waters and associated materials [120]. The quoted method for raw and potable waters recommends acidification, sulphation and ignition of the sample to produce a uniform thick source for counting. The quoted method for sludges and sediments recommends the determination of the solids content of samples, followed by pH adjustment, then drying, grinding prior to weighing of the prepared sample onto the counting tray and slurrying with methanol.

Simultaneous alpha and beta measurements can be made in gas filled proportional counters (argon/methane) (see Section 2.2.1). A typical counter set-up consists of 10 detectors with a high detection sensitivity for alpha particles and for beta particles. The background counts are greatly reduced by the use of suitable shielding and a guard counter operating in anti-coincidence so that events arising in both the guard counter and a sample counter, due to cosmic rays, are drastically reduced. Background count-rates of typically less than 1 cpm are obtained for modern instruments. Alpha particles have twice the charge and $\cong 8000$ times the rest mass of beta particles and therefore give rise to more intense ionisation and a consequently larger signal in the amplifier. The separation of pulses from either alpha or beta particles is then carried out using pulse height analysis (see Section 2.2.6) to discriminate between the two types of pulses. Recommended calibration radionuclides are ^{242}Pu (alpha) and ^{40}K (beta). Alternative radionuclides will give rise to different counting efficiencies and hence influence the results.

3.7.3 Beta counting

Beta particles are usually measured in gas-filled proportional counters as described in the previous section or by liquid scintillation counting (see Section 3.7.4 and Chapter 2).

The source for the proportional counter is usually a uniformly thick precipitate mounted on a planchet. The mass of precipitate produced by the radiochemical separation can vary slightly which results in variation in the counting efficiency due to increasing absorption of the emitted beta particles with increasing mass. Therefore, in order to calibrate the detector, a series of standard sources are prepared containing the analyte in the form in which it will be presented for counting, covering the mass range that will be encountered. A calibration curve of counting efficiency as a function of mass is plotted and the counting efficiency of a sample is interpolated from the curve. It is not possible to discriminate by this method between beta emitters of different energies that may be present in the source.

3.7.4 Liquid scintillation counting (LSC)

Liquid scintillation counting was developed primarily to overcome the low counting efficiency problems associated with measuring low-level beta emitters in gas-filled detectors but it is now widely used to measure both beta and alpha emitters. Beta-emitters may be measured with high counting efficiency, typically > 90% for intermediate to high energy beta emitters and low backgrounds, typically a few cpm (counts per minute) for modern low-level instruments. It has the advantage over proportional counting in that energy discrimination is possible which enables the accurate determination of the activity of the analyte in the presence of other beta emitters.

Liquid or solid samples are mixed with proprietary liquid scintillants in a vial and presented for counting. Samples can require very little preparation as water samples are miscible with the scintillants to produce homogeneous solutions. Water samples for ^3H determination normally require distillation prior to analysis but the determination of other beta emitters will be carried out on the total sample. However, as mentioned previously, overlap of beta emission energies may require a chemical separation to achieve accurate data.

Tritium or other beta emitters in non-aqueous samples will require some form of separation (see Section 3.6.9) and may be prepared as homogenous or heterogeneous sources, for example, a barium sulphate gel for ^{35}S determination or a phosphate gel for ^{32}P determination.

Counting is usually carried out in borosilicate glass, plastic or quartz vials and the choice of vial affects the counting characteristics. Glass vials contain ^{40}K and therefore provide higher backgrounds than quartz or plastic. but they have the advantage that they can be used as reaction vessels resulting in higher chemical recoveries. Plastic vials are commonly used but have the disadvantage that the solvents used in scintillants may permeate the vials resulting in variation in counting efficiencies during long counting times. The disadvantage of quartz vials is that they are expensive.

In liquid scintillation counting, the effects of quenching (impurity and colour) require that the counting efficiency be determined for each sample (see Chapter 2) and the effects of each type of quenching need to be corrected for separately. Colour quenching can be reduced by preparing colourless sources or using decolourisers prior to counting. A number of quench correction procedures are available to enable accurate determinations of counting efficiency. These are based on internal standardisation, sample channels ratio and automatic external standardization. The application of these techniques is discussed in detail in the literature [121-124].

Other problems which affect the count-rates in liquid scintillation counting are associated with chemiluminescence and static electricity. Chemiluminescence can be eliminated by careful choice of scintillant or by storing the sample in the dark prior to counting to permit the decay of the luminescence. Most modern instruments are capable of detecting and compensating for the effects of chemiluminescence. They also have anti-static devices and anti-static vials are commercially available.

3.7.5 Cerenkov counting

Cerenkov counting is a technique which permits the measurement of high energy beta emitters in solution without the addition of scintillant (see Section 2.2.3). The threshold energy for production of Cerenkov radiation in water is 263 keV but the practical threshold is in the region of 500-600 keV. Although Cerenkov detectors are available, Cerenkov radiation is routinely detected in liquid scintillation counters. Counting efficiencies of up to 65 % can be achieved and backgrounds are lower than in LSC. Advantages of the technique are that it discriminates against low-energy beta, alpha and gamma emitters, it permits the counting of samples solubilised in strong acids or alkalis, unlike LSC and the sample counted is in a form that permits further radiochemistry.

Cerenkov counting is not subject to impurity quenching but the counting efficiency is affected by colour quenching, sample volume and vial type. Therefore counting should be carried out at a predetermined optimum volume and quench correction techniques should be applied to compensate for any colour quenching. Plastic vials are most frequently used for counting since they provide higher counting efficiencies compared to glass vials.

3.7.6 Alpha counting

The use of liquid scintillation counting is generally limited to screening of alpha emitters, whereas alpha spectrometry is used for quantitative determination of individual radionuclides. Alpha emitters may be measured by liquid scintillation counting with a counting efficiency of almost 100 %. Unlike beta particles, the measurement of alpha particles is not subject to quenching although peak shifts to lower energies may occur. In general, the resolution of alpha particles of different energies is not sufficiently good to permit the determination of one alpha emitter in the presence of another.

3.7.7 Alpha spectrometry

Alpha particles are rapidly attenuated by solids and thus alpha spectrometry sources need to be prepared as thinly and uniformly as possible to avoid attenuation and hence degradation (peak tailing and poor resolution) of the alpha spectrum.

A variety of techniques have been reported for the preparation of alpha spectrometry sources [125]. These include the evaporation of an organic solvent, containing the alpha emitters of interest, onto a planchet [54,126]. Any residual organic material present is removed by flaming the source. Another approach for production of alpha spectrometry sources involves the co-precipitation of a purified radionuclide with a small quantity of inactive carrier. Co-precipitation of actinides with lanthanide hydroxides or fluorides has been used effectively to produce alpha spectrometry sources which provide good resolution in the resulting alpha spectra [127-129].

Electrodeposition is a well established and reliable technique for the routine preparation of high quality alpha spectrometry sources which can be carried out from either aqueous or organic solutions. The traces of alpha emitters are deposited from solution onto a cathode surface (usually a stainless-steel or platinum disc) using a stationary or rotating platinum rod as the anode. Although methods for the electrodeposition of alpha emitters from organic solution are reported (media used include acetone, butanol and isopropyl alcohol [130]), electrodeposition from mildly acidic or alkaline aqueous solution is more frequently used. Frequently, complexing agents are added such as ethylenediammineteraacetic acid (EDTA), diethylenetetraminepentaacetic acid (DTPA) and hydrofluoric acid to prevent deposition of any residual interferences present. Examples of aqueous electrolyte media are ammonium sulphate, ammonium sulphate-EDTA, ammonium chloride-oxalic acid and sodium sulphate-sodium hydrogen sulphate [67,131,132]. The optimum conditions for electrodeposition, such as time, current, electrolyte concentration, pH temperature and electrode spacing should be determined for each radionuclide. Some of these conditions change during the deposition and need to be controlled, for example, with the use of cooling jackets for temperature control and buffer electrolyte solutions to control the pH [132].

Polonium can be spontaneously deposited onto silver [133] or nickel [134] discs and this technique can be used to assist the separation of the required radionuclides from other alpha-emitting radionuclides. This method can suffer from the deposition of oxidants, organic materials and certain other elements that can also deposit onto silver but sample pre-treatment techniques can be used to eliminate these problems.

The quantitative measurement of alpha-emitters is usually achieved by alpha spectrometry using silicon surface barrier detectors or ion-implanted silicon detectors. Both types of detector provide high energy resolution, excellent stability and low backgrounds (typically 0.001 to 0.003 cpm). The detection efficiency over the energy range of 2.5 - 8 MeV is almost constant (typically 20 to 30 %). This range covers the region of most alpha emitters of interest which makes quantitative evaluation simpler for alpha spectra than for gamma spectra. Energy calibration of the alpha spectrometer is achieved using multi-nuclide sources and single nuclide sources are used to determine counting efficiency and resolution. Most determinations of alpha-emitters are carried out in the presence of internal yield monitors and the activity of the analyte is determined by comparing the peak integral of the analyte with that of the known activity yield monitor. Therefore knowledge of the absolute counting efficiency is not essential, but is useful to provide an estimate of the chemical yield.

Interferences that occur in alpha spectrometry are spectral interferences from radionuclides present on the counting source which emit alpha particles of similar energy to the analyte and degradation of the spectrum due to the presence of unwanted material on the counting source. Table 3.1 is a list of alpha emitting radionuclides of environmental interest and yield monitors that may be used. This also provides a guide as to which radionuclides may interfere with each other. For example, the presence of ^{228}Th interferes with the determination of ^{241}Am and ^{238}Pu. The spectral degradation that may occur is in the form of tailing of the alpha peak on the low energy side; this can result in overlapping of peaks which then need resolving. Both of these types of interference should be largely reduced by the radiochemical separation procedure.

In alpha spectrometry it is important to check background levels regularly. This is because a variable background component can be introduced due to recoil nuclei produced in alpha decay drifting across the gap between the source and detector resulting in increased backgrounds. Modern detectors can be cleaned to remove recoil nuclei thus preventing the gradual build-up of unacceptably high backgrounds. Alternatively it is possible to reduce the implantation of recoil nuclei either by applying a suitable back-bias voltage between the source and detector or by increasing the source/detector distance.

Alpha spectra from a thin source are in general simpler than gamma spectra and may consist of a number of well separated peaks with a very low background. The radionuclides present can be identified from the peak positions. Their activities are calculated by summing the counts under the appropriate peak, known as the region of interest (ROI) and multiplying the ratio of this peak count to that of the yield tracer radionuclide by the known activity of the tracer radionuclide [135]. However, the peak shape of a monoenergetic alpha particle is not simple because of the presence of a low energy tail arising from energy losses in the source and in the detector window. This behaviour then leads to the presence of overlapping peaks which become pronounced when more than one radionuclide is present, each of which may give rise to a series of alpha peaks at discrete energies (multiplet structure - see Chapter 1). The analysis of such spectra has been carried out in two ways, either by correcting the peak counts for those counts in the low energy tail or by assuming a given peak shape and carrying out either a least squares minimisation or a series of iterative approximations. In the first case the low energy tail is assumed to decrease, for example, either exponentially or by geometric progression [136-138]. In the second case the analytical function usually consists of a monoenergetic component, an exponential low energy tailing function folded with a Gaussian function for the detector and electronics response function [139,140].

3.8 MASS SPECTROMETRY

In recent years it has become apparent that alpha spectrometry has limitations in terms of its sensitivity. The activity levels of, for example, thorium in groundwaters are close to the detection limit achievable using alpha spectrometry. Instrumental methods of analysis which can act as alternatives to radiometric methods have been described and compared in a critical review of the literature by McMahon [141]. The most sensitive of the alternative methods tend to be the mass spectrometric ones because of the relatively high ionisation efficiencies attainable. The overall efficiency is the product of the ionisation efficiency (which lies in the range 0.1% to nearly 100%), the transmission efficiency and the detection efficiency. In the best cases, the overall efficiency, for example, for thorium, can be about 0.1%.

Various instruments share common components such as types of mass analyser and ion detector but differ in the type of ion source.

A wide range of mass spectrometric analytical techniques have been used for the determination of the concentrations of radionuclides in samples:

SSMS	spark source mass spectrometry
GDMS	glow discharge mass spectrometry
ICPMS	inductively coupled plasma–mass spectrometry
IC-ICPMS	ion chromatography ICPMS
ETV-ICPMS	electrothermal vaporisation ICPMS
LA-ICPMS	laser ablation ICPMS
HR-ICPMS	high-resolution ICPMS
TIMS	thermal ionisation mass spectrometry
AMS	accelerator mass spectrometry
SIMS	secondary ion mass spectrometry
LMS	laser mass spectrometry
RIMS	resonance ionisation mass spectrometry

To a first approximation, the techniques may be subdivided into those which can be applied to solid samples, either directly (SSMS, GDMS, LA-ICPMS, SIMS, LMS and RIMS) or following medium or extensive chemical separation steps (ICPMS, IC-ICPMS, HR-ICPMS, TIMS, AMS) and those applicable to solutions directly (ICPMS, IC-ICPMS, HR-ICPMS).

Ideally, for elemental analysis, the source will completely atomise the sample and efficiently generate singly-charged analyte ions. This is best accomplished by having separate atomisation and ionisation processes, as in GDMS and RIMS. SSMS, ICPMS, TIMS and SIMS techniques effect atomisation and ionisation in one step which requires a great deal of energy. Since it is difficult to control the amount of energy input into each process (vaporisation of the solid, molecular bond dissociation, ionisation), it is better to be able to adjust the energy of the vaporisation/atomisation step and the ionisation step independently. In a one-step process, either insufficient energy input will give rise to molecular interferences or too much energy will generate multiply-charged ions, for example, in SSMS.

When considering non-radiometric methods (mass spectrometry in this case), the relationship between radiometric units of measurement and the mass spectrometric units depends upon the half-life ($t_{1/2}$) of the radionuclide of interest. The relationship between activity (A, disintegrations per unit time) and half-life ($t_{1/2}$, unit time) is given by:

$$A = N\left(\frac{\ln 2}{t_{\frac{1}{2}}}\right)$$

where N represents the number of radionuclide atoms present. This comparison of radiometric and atomic methods of radionuclide detection is discussed further by Smith et al [142] and McMahon [141,143].

Figure 3.2 provides a useful guide for conversion of mass units into activity units for half-lives ranging from 10 years to 10^{12} years. As an example, 1 µg of a nuclide (log -6 on left hand axis), of a radionuclide with a theoretical atomic mass of 200 and a half-life of 10^5 years, would have an activity of about log 2.5 Bq, that is, 316 Bq (bottom axis), equivalent to about log 15.3 atoms, that is, 2×10^{15} atoms (right hand axis).

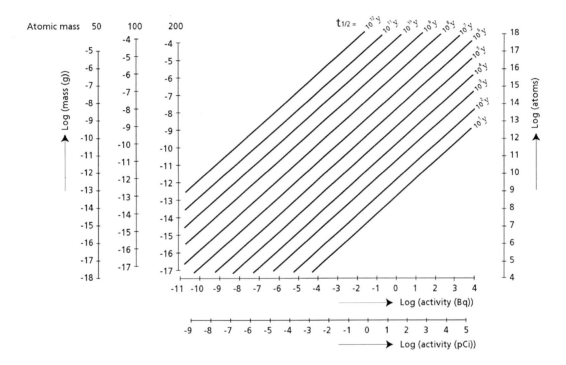

Figure 3.2   Conversion of non-radiometric to radiometric units.

The specific activities of those radionuclides which are often analysed by mass spectrometric techniques are given in Table 3.2. The data are given both as activity per gram (Bq g^{-1}) and as mass per Bq (g Bq^{-1}) for ease of conversion between units.

Table 3.2 Specific activities of radionuclides commonly measured by radiometric and mass spectrometric methods. Half-lives are taken from Chapter 8 and atomic masses from The 1995 Update to the Atomic Mass Evaluation (G. Audi and A.H. Wapstra, *The 1995 Update to the Atomic Mass Evaluation., Nucl. Phys.* A595, 409 (1995). (see also http://www.nndc.bnl.gov/nndcscr/masses/).

Radionuclide	Atomic mass	Half-life (years)	Specific activity (Bq/g)	Mass per Bq (grams)
Be-10	10.0135	1.60E+06	8.257E+08	1.211E-09
C-14	14.0032	5.73E+03	1.649E+11	6.065E-12
Al-26	25.9869	7.20E+05	7.070E+08	1.414E-09
Cl-36	35.9683	3.02E+05	1.218E+09	8.211E-10
K-40	39.964	1.28E+09	2.586E+05	3.867E-06
Ca-41	40.9623	1.03E+05	3.136E+09	3.189E-10
Mn-53	52.9413	3.68E+06	6.790E+07	1.473E-08
Ni-59	58.9344	7.60E+04	2.954E+09	3.386E-10
Rb-87	86.9092	4.80E+10	3.171E+03	3.153E-04
Sr-90	89.9077	2.86E+01	5.138E+12	1.946E-13
Tc-99	98.9063	2.11E+05	6.330E+08	1.580E-09
I-129	128.905	1.57E+07	6.541E+06	1.529E-07
Cs-135	134.906	2.40E+06	4.086E+07	2.447E-08
Cs-137	136.9071	3.017E+01	3.203E+12	3.122E-13
La-137	136.9065	6.00E+04	1.610E+09	6.209E-10
Ra-226	226.0254	1.600E+03	3.658E+10	2.734E-11
Ra-228	228.0311	5.75E+00	1.009E+13	9.911E-14
Th-228	228.0287	1.913E+00	3.033E+13	3.297E-14
Th-229	229.0318	7.34E+03	7.869E+09	1.271E-10
Th-230	230.0331	7.54E+04	7.627E+08	1.311E-09
Th-232	232.0381	1.405E+10	4.058E+03	2.464E-04
Pa-231	231.0359	3.276E+04	1.748E+09	5.721E-10
U-232	232.0371	6.98E+01	8.168E+11	1.224E-12
U-233	233.0396	1.593E+05	3.565E+08	2.805E-09
U-234	234.0409	2.457E+05	2.301E+08	4.347E-09
U-235	235.0439	7.038E+08	7.997E+04	1.250E-05
U-236	236.0456	2.342E+07	2.393E+06	4.178E-07
U-238	238.0508	4.468E+09	1.244E+04	8.040E-05
Np-237	237.0482	2.14E+06	2.608E+07	3.835E-08
Pu-236	236.046	2.90E+00	1.933E+13	5.174E-14
Pu-238	238.0496	8.77E+01	6.337E+11	1.578E-12
Pu-239	239.0522	2.411E+04	2.295E+09	4.357E-10
Pu-240	240.0538	6.563E+03	8.397E+09	1.191E-10
Pu-241	241.0568	1.44E+01	3.811E+12	2.624E-13
Pu-242	242.0587	3.735E+05	1.463E+08	6.834E-09
Pu-244	244.0642	8.00E+07	6.775E+05	1.476E-06
Am-241	241.0568	4.327E+02	1.268E+11	7.884E-12
Am-243	243.0614	7.37E+03	7.385E+09	1.354E-10

For a given activity level, it can be seen from Figure 3.2 and Table 3.2 that the longer the half-life of the radionuclide, the more atoms will be present for the atomic-based measurement method to detect. According to Smith et al [142], quadrupole inductively coupled plasma mass spectrometry is superior to radiometry in sensitivity for radionuclides whose half-lives exceed about 10^5-10^6 years, using pneumatic solution **nebulisation** for sample introduction. Using ETV-ICPMS, the crossover is around 10^3 years [128], while for HR-ICPMS with ultrasonic nebulisation it will be lower still.

Mass spectrometric methods can offer isotopic information, although like alpha spectrometry, for example, they can suffer from interferences. These interferences can arise from the presence of isobars, such as the co-interference of ^{238}U and ^{238}Pu or ^{99}Ru on ^{99}Tc, and from molecular interferences such as, for example, ^{204}Pb^{40}Ar on ^{244}Pu and ^{238}UH on ^{239}Pu.

Some of the features of the techniques listed are outlined below and references are provided for the techniques in general and for their application in the analysis of radionuclides.

GDMS

This method is best suited to analysis of homogeneous conducting materials. It has been used, for example, to analyse soil samples for uranium isotopes [144]. Detection limits are in the sub-ppb range in solids and precisions on isotopic ratios of better than 0.05% relative standard deviation (rsd) have been obtained [145]. GDMS is suited to the analysis of nuclear materials requiring minimal sample treatment and Betti et al [146] have adapted their instrument for glovebox operation.

ICPMS

There are many reported examples of quadrupole ICPMS being used to determine the concentration of the longer-lived radionuclides in environmental samples. The technique has been used for the actinides plutonium, uranium, neptunium and thorium [147-153], ^{99}Tc [154] and ^{129}I [155]. The technique is described in detail by Jarvis et al [156] with many publications on the interference problems, for example [156-158]. Detection limits are typically at pg ml^{-1} level in solution for the essentially interference-free heavy elements. The use of a variety of sample introduction techniques to improve sensitivity or performance or to analyse solids directly have also been reported. These include the use of ion chromatography [160,161], isotope-dilution ion chromatography [162], ultrasonic nebulisation (USN) [163], flow-injection concentration with USN [164], electrothermal vaporisation [142] and laser ablation [165]. More recently, high-resolution instruments (HR-ICPMS) have become available [166-169]. Compared to the quadrupole instrument, this double-focusing sector spectrometer shows improved transmission characteristics, particularly when operated in low-resolution mode, and has lower backgrounds. Detection limits for heavy elements are about 20 fg ml^{-1}. However, the costs of the instrument and associated clean-room facilities are very high and the capability is not widespread.

As in quadrupole ICPMS, if the conventional nebuliser and spray chamber sample introduction system to the HR-ICPMS instrument is replaced by an ultrasonic nebuliser (USN) with membrane desolvater, sample transport to the plasma can be improved by a factor of about 20. The desolvated sample is excited more efficiently by the plasma, with an overall effect that detection limits can be improved by a further factor of up to 50. For uranium, the detection limit is around 6 fgml^{-1} which is limited by the high-purity acid blank. For ^{244}Pu which is not as blank-limited, detection limits in solution of better than 0.1 fg ml^{-1} have been achieved [167].

TIMS

This is the most sensitive analytical technique for the measurement of isotopic composition of uranium and plutonium in environmental samples and in the verification of safeguarded nuclear materials [170-180]. TIMS has also been used to measure radium and its isotopic ratios in marine and geological samples [181,182]. Best results are obtained by the use of one or two spikes of the element of interest, for example, ^{233}U and ^{236}U to monitor and correct for instrumental fractionation. Because of isobaric interferences, for example, ^{238}U on ^{238}Pu, samples are radiochemically purified to provide microvolumes for loading on to a rhenium filament [170,171], or the resin bead technique is used to load one or more ion exchange beads on to the filament [175-177]. Femtogram levels of these actinides can be measured and the precisions for isotopic ratio measurements are usually better than 0.5%. With total sample volatilisation and a multicollector instrument, the precisions on uranium and plutonium isotopic ratio measurements can be better than 0.02% [180]. Isotope **abundance sensitivities** are about 10^{-12} for TIMS instruments. A good summary of TIMS instrumentation and spectral interpretation is given by Chen et al [183].

AMS

Accelerator mass spectrometry [184,185] employs **tandem accelerators** at MeV energies and works with multiply-charged ions. The technique probably represents the ultimate for achieving high abundance sensitivity and the elimination of isotopic, isobaric and molecular interferences, so that abundance sensitivities of 10^{-16} are achievable. AMS has mainly been applied to the precise determination of isotope ratios, particularly ^{14}C, where 1 part ^{14}C in 10^{15} parts of ^{12}C can be measured. The use of AMS systems has also been demonstrated extensively for the detection of long-lived radionuclides such as ^{10}Be, ^{26}Al, ^{36}Cl, ^{41}Ca and ^{129}I in a variety of applications including environmental and earth sciences, biomedicine, archaeology and materials science [186-190]. AMS systems for the measurement of actinides are also becoming available [191].

SIMS

Secondary ion mass spectrometry was developed as a surface analysis technique. The ion microprobe uses a primary beam of oxygen or argon charged atoms, focussed to micron dimensions. This can be rastered, that is, scanned over the sample, producing a cloud of sputtered ions above the surface. A selected portion of the secondary ions is extracted and analysed using a high-resolution mass spectrometer. In the natural series dating field, Compston et al [192] and Zindler et al [193] have used SIMS to perform in-situ uranium-lead age determination in zircon and measurement of ^{230}Th/^{232}Th ratios in volcanic rocks respectively. The latter authors reported an abundance sensitivity of 10^{-7} at mass 230 with respect to 232. Adriaens et al [194] used SIMS to analyse uranium and thorium in soils in a comparison of the technique with TIMS. The SIMS instrument can be used in a microscope or a microprobe mode. In the microprobe mode, it has been used recently to analyse individual uranium particles for their isotopic ratios [169].

RIMS

In a resonance photo-ionisation source, vapour produced on top of the sample surface (by heating, ion beam or laser sputtering) is ionised by laser beams tuned to specific excited states of the element of interest. Resonance ionisation schemes and isotope selectivity are usefully summarised by McMahon [141] and references therein. Towrie et al [195] describe their RIMS instrument being used for analysis of standard reference materials; problems with carbon cluster interferences are discussed. Fassett and Travis [196] review the analytical applications of RIMS. Using a three-step, three-colour excitation process,

Trautmann [197] achieved an overall detection efficiency of about 2×10^{-6} to give a detection limit of 1.6 fg of ^{99}Tc. RIMS applied to the analysis of uranium and plutonium is described by Donohue and co-workers [198,199].

3.9 NEUTRON ACTIVATION ANALYSIS (NAA)

Activation analysis, in general, is a method for elemental analysis based on the activation of a stable nuclide to an unstable radionuclide [26,200-206]. The mode of decay of the product radionuclide is used to identify the target element, and the activity of the product can be used to calculate the original concentration of the element. There are several activation analysis methods, characterised by the source of activation, such as charged particles, neutron or photon activation. Neutron activation is the most widely used activation method, principally because neutrons can penetrate a thick target and hence it is a bulk method, in contrast to photon or charged particle activation which may only be considered as surface techniques. Elements are activated by thermal, epithermal or fast neutrons. Most elements of interest produce at least one radionuclide on interaction with thermal neutrons, and the resulting radionuclides decay with half lives ranging from seconds to years.

NAA laboratories generally use a nuclear reactor to provide a high flux of thermal neutrons. Irradiation devices give access to a constant flux of thermal neutrons for the required irradiation time, from a few seconds to several weeks, to generate sufficient activity in the sample for detection and measurement. The analysis of the radionuclide will depend on its mode of decay. A single element target, with only one radioactive product, can be detected directly from its beta emissions but it is usually necessary to separate out the element of interest to measure the activity from a particular radionuclide in the presence of others. Gamma ray emissions from the radionuclide are easily identified in the presence of other emitters, using high resolution spectrometry with a semiconductor germanium detector. The gamma ray spectrum from a typical environmental or industrial sample may contain peaks at over one hundred energies, all readily resolved from one another using sophisticated software which can be used on a standard personal computer. Commercial software can assign a gamma ray to a particular radionuclide by its characteristic energy and, if there is more than one gamma ray emitted for a particular radionuclide, confirm the origin using the ratios of the emission probabilities. The resulting identification, using libraries of nuclear data, can provide very accurate qualititative analysis of complex materials. It should be noted that radiochemical separation of the radionuclide of interest may be performed before or after irradiation either to eliminate background effects or to achieve a concentration factor.

More importantly, neutron activation analysis can provide quantitative information about the element of interest. The way that activity induced in a target element is related to the mass of the element in the sample is expressed in the activation equation (identical to equation 1.12):

$$\text{Activity} = \sigma \phi w N_0 q \left(1 - e^{-\lambda t}\right) / A \qquad (3.1)$$

where, σ = neutron cross section, m^2
ϕ = neutron flux, neutrons $m^{-2}\ s^{-1}$
w = mass of the target element, g
N_0 = Avogadro's number
q = isotopic abundance
λ = decay constant, s^{-1}
t = length of irradiation, s
A = atomic weight

Quantitative information is obtained by measuring the integrated counts in the gamma ray photopeak, over a preset counting period. The activity or disintegration rate, is related to the gamma ray count-rate by the gamma ray **emission probability**, P. The activity is determined by dividing the measured count-rate, C, by the gamma ray detection efficiency, E measured for the same geometry, and by P:

Activity $= C / E P$ (3.2)

A correction is applied for decay during the time, t_d, between the end of irradiation and start of count: $(e^{-\lambda t_d})$. A further correction for decay during the counting period, t_c, may also be required: $\lambda t_c / (1 - e^{-\lambda t_c})$.

Equations (3.1) and (3.2) may then be combined to extract the mass of the target element. In situations where the cross-section is not known or the neutron flux cannot be measured, either internal or external standards are used.

3.10 DATA HANDLING

3.10.1 Introduction

A comprehensive treatment of errors and uncertainties in analytical measurement is outside the scope of this manual. A brief introduction to the main concepts is given while the reader is referred to the following references for a fuller treatment [207-212].

Analytical measurements of a given quantity are subject to error where an error is defined as the difference between the measured value and the true value. In general repeated measurements of a given quantity will yield different values. The term uncertainty is used to describe the dispersion in these measured values and may be characterised in terms of a probability function for the error, an error distribution. When a confidence interval is defined, the true value of the measured quantity is said to lie within a given range with a certain level of confidence, for example, 95%.

In a given set of measurements random effects can cause errors, which vary from one measurement to the next. Such random errors occur, for example, in the measurement of the count-rate from a given radionuclide due to the random nature of radioactive decay. This is discussed in the following Sub-section 3.10.2. The resulting uncertainty or precision may be defined in a statistical analysis by the determination of a mean value and a standard deviation [210, 212]. It can usually be reduced by increasing the number of observations.

A systematic error is one which remains either constant in a series of measurements or varies in a predictable way. It is thus independent of the number of measurements made. Examples of systematic errors are those due to contamination effects or to not taking account of a reagent blank. They will influence the accuracy of the measured value. A systematic error may be reduced if the systematic effect is recognised and the extent of the consequent error is known.

In a given set of measurements, an error distribution may be associated with each type of error and it is assumed that these distributions may be combined using statistical procedures to produce the overall uncertainty [209]. It is clearly important to identify and quantify all sources of error in a procedure. Ideally the possible sources of error should be identified and steps taken to minimise them before the procedure is carried out. Measurements on certified reference materials and interlaboratory comparisons provide good ways of assessing overall uncertainties since they give information on the combined effect of several sources of uncertainty (see Section 3.11).

3.10.2 Mean and standard deviation

If a given quantity x is measured n times then the mean value $\bar{x}$ is given by:

$$\bar{x} = \frac{1}{n}\sum_{j=1}^{n} x_j = \frac{x_1 + x_2 + x_3 + \ldots\ldots x_n}{n}$$

A useful measure of the spread in the measured values is given by the standard deviation s where:

$$s = \sqrt{\sum_{j=1}^{n} \frac{\left(x_j - \bar{x}\right)^2}{n-1}}$$

This set of n measurements is a sample from the very large number of measurements that could be made, called the population. The form of this population is described by a continuous curve giving the probability y_j that the measured value will be x_j. For random errors the curve is assumed to be a normal or Gaussian distribution, given by:

$$y = \frac{e^{-(x-\mu)^2/2\sigma^2}}{\sigma\sqrt{2\pi}}$$

The mean of the population μ is the true value of the measured quantity. $\bar{x}$ is an estimate of μ and similarly s is an estimate of the standard deviation of the population σ, given by:

$$\sigma = \sqrt{\sum_{j=1}^{n} \frac{\left(x_j - \sigma\right)^2}{n}}$$

This equation holds strictly only as $n \rightarrow \infty$.

The determination of $\bar{x}$ in the sample of measurements mentioned above is one determination in an infinite population of possible measurements of the mean. This distribution of sample means has the same mean as the population described above and its standard deviation, known as the standard error in the mean is given by $s/\sqrt{n}$ which is a measure of the uncertainty involved in estimating μ from $\bar{x}$.

Statistical theory allows us to estimate the range within which the true value of a quantity (μ) might fall within a given probability defined by the measured mean ($\bar{x}$) and the standard deviation (s) even when the number of data points is not large. This range is called the confidence interval and the range limits define the confidence limit, given by $\bar{x} \pm \frac{ts}{\sqrt{n}}$, where t is a statistical factor which depends on the number of degrees of freedom $\nu = n-1$ and the confidence level required. Values for t for different values of ν are available in the literature [213]. For 6 measurements and hence 5 degrees of freedom for a confidence level of 95% the confidence limit is $\bar{x} \pm \dfrac{2.571s}{\sqrt{n}}$ while for an infinite number of degrees of freedom the confidence limit is reduced to $\bar{x} \pm \dfrac{1.960s}{\sqrt{n}}$.

3.10.3 Statistics involved in counting radioactive sources

The quantitative estimation of the radioactivity present in a sample is made by measuring the number of counts n obtained in a suitable detector during time t. If we assume that the counting time is small compared to the half-life of the source then it can be shown [207] that the probability distribution of the counts n obtained in repeated (equal) counting times is given by a Poisson distribution, see, for example, [214]. When n is large the Poisson distribution tends to the normal (Gausssian) distribution.

If just one measurement is performed, our best guess of the true number of counts is n and the estimated standard deviation for a single measurement is $s = \sqrt{n}$.

Most results from counting experiments are obtained by combining two or more quantities which have their own associated standard deviation. For example, an activity determination will require a background count to be subtracted from the gross sample count. In order to determine the error on the final result, the standard deviation associated with each individual quantity which contributes to that result must be combined. The general expression used for combining random errors may be used, where a value y is to be calculated from a combination of independent measured quantities a, b, c.....etc., is:

$$\sigma_y^2 = \left(\frac{\partial y}{\partial a}\right)^2 \sigma_a^2 + \left(\frac{\partial y}{\partial b}\right)^2 \sigma_b^2 + \ldots$$

where σ_y, σ_a and σ_b, are the standard deviations in y, a and b.

Commonly used examples of this expression are:

i) Error propagated by addition or subtraction

If a value y is calculated from addition and/or subtraction of independent measured quantities a, b, c,.. etc. by:

$y = k + k_a a - k_b b + k_c c...$

where k, k_a, k_b, k_c etc. are constants, then the standard deviation of y, σ_y is given by

$$\sigma_y = \sqrt{\left(k_a \sigma_a\right)^2 + \left(k_b \sigma_b\right)^2 + \left(k_c \sigma_c\right)^2}$$

Thus, if a = 10000 counts are measured for a radioactive source in 100s, $\sigma_a = \sqrt{10000}$, of which b = 300 counts in the same time are due to instrumental background, then y = a − b and $\sigma_b = \sqrt{300}$, then $\sigma_y = \sqrt{\sigma_a^2 + \sigma_b^2} = \sqrt{10000 + 300} \cong 101$. Thus y = 9700±101 counts.

ii) Error propagated by multiplication or division

If y is calculated by an expression of the type:

y=kab/cd

where a, b, c and d are independent measured quantities and k is a constant then the standard deviation of y, σ_y is related to the sum of the squares of the relative standard deviations and is given by:

$$\sigma_y = y\sqrt{\left(\frac{\sigma_a}{a}\right)^2 + \left(\frac{\sigma_b}{b}\right)^2 + \left(\frac{\sigma_c}{c}\right)^2 + \left(\frac{\sigma_d}{d}\right)^2}$$

In the example given above, if the detector efficiency c = 0.30, with a standard deviation σ_c = 0.05, then the source activity =9700/(100×0.30) Bq = 323Bq and the standard deviation in the activity σ_y is given by:

$$\sigma_y = \frac{9700}{100 \times 0.30}\sqrt{\left(\frac{101}{9700}\right)^2 + \left(\frac{0.05}{0.30}\right)^2} = 54.0$$

Thus, the activity is 323±54Bq.

3.10.3 Low-level counting

3.10.3.1 Critical level, detection limit and minimum detectable concentration

The measurement of a sample containing low-levels of radioactivity may result in a gross count-rate that is similar to the background count-rate. In this case, the observed net count-rate may be due to either the presence of activity in the sample or simply to a statistical fluctuation in the background. A decision has to be made as to whether activity is present in the sample [215-219]. The decision may be subject to two kinds of error: deciding that activity is present when it is not (α; Type I error), and conversely failing to decide that activity is present when it is (β; Type II error).

In practice, low-level counting data are compared to a decision level to determine if the sample count-rate is statistically different to the background. This decision level, called the Critical Level (L_c) is defined as the net count-rate that must be exceeded before the sample is considered to contain any measurable activity above background.

Figure 3.3a shows the normal distribution expected for a mean net count-rate of zero in the presence of a background count-rate [215]. The value of L_c is expressed as a multiple of the standard deviation of the zero net count-rate, σ_0 by the equation

$L_c = k_\alpha\sigma_0$ (3.3)

where k_α is a one-sided confidence factor. Usually, k_α is chosen such that 95 % of the measurements of a true zero net count-rate are less than L_c and that there is only a 5 % chance that a true mean zero count-rate will be falsely reported as positive (Type I error). The value of k_α at this confidence level is 1.645.

A more useful way of expressing L_c is in terms of an experimentally determined background count-rate (R_b) [216,217], where:

$$L_c = k_\alpha \sqrt{\frac{2R_b}{T}} \qquad\qquad (3.4)$$

and T is the count time. This equation applies if the background and sample counting times are equal. In order to limit the chance of a Type I error to 5 %, equation (3.4) becomes:

$$L_c = 2.33 \sqrt{\frac{R_b}{T}} \qquad\qquad (3.5)$$

Another term used in low-level counting that is related to the Critical Level is the Detection Limit (L_d). The Detection Limit is defined such that the observed net count-rate of a probability distribution with a mean net count-rate L_d will exceed L_c with a specified degree of confidence. This means that for a specified measurement process, L_d is the smallest true net count-rate that is 'certain' to be detected with a specified degree of confidence where there is a built-in protection against deciding that activity is present when it is not. Figure 3.3b illustrates L_d in terms of a normal distribution with a mean and standard deviation of L_d and σ_d respectively and illustrates its relationship to L_c [215].

The value for L_d is given by:

$$L_d = L_c + k_\beta \sigma_d = k_\alpha \sigma_0 + k_\beta \sigma_d \qquad\qquad (3.6)$$

where k_β is a one-sided confidence factor. Usually, k_β is chosen such that 95 % of the measurements of a mean net count-rate of L_d are detected, that is, there is a 95 % chance of not having a Type II error. The values of k_α and k_β are usually set to be equal.

An equation for L_d can be derived in terms of an experimentally determined background count-rate (R_b). In the usual case where the values of k_α and k_β are usually set to be equal, L_d is given by:

$$L_d = \frac{k^2}{T} + 2k \sqrt{\frac{2R_b}{T}} \qquad\qquad (3.7)$$

where $k = k_\alpha = k_\beta$.

a)

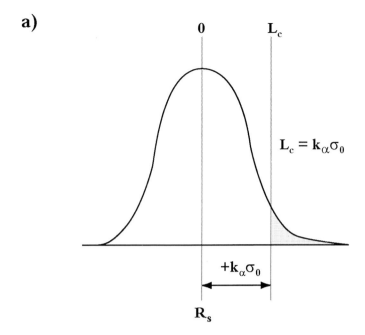

b)

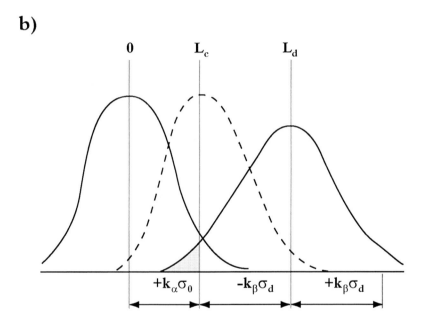

Figure 3.3   a. Normal distribution for a net count-rate of R_s, with a background count-rate of R_b and a critical level $L_c = k_\alpha \sigma_0$ where k_α is a one-sided confidence factor and σ_0 is the standard deviation of a zero net count-rate, after [215].

b. Graphical representation of the detection limit $L_d = L_c + k_\beta \sigma_d$ where σ_d is the standard deviation of a normal distribution and k_β is a one-sided confidence factor, after [215].

Reproduced with the permission of EG & G Ortec.

91

For a 5% chance of a Type I error and a 95 % chance of not having a Type II error, k is 1.645. Substituting this value into equation (3.7) gives:

$$L_d = \frac{2.71}{T} + 4.65\sqrt{\frac{R_b}{T}} \qquad (3.8)$$

The minimum detectable concentration (MDC) is the result of expressing L_d as an activity concentration. This requires correcting L_d using typical values of parameters that are used to correct a sample net count-rate to activity units. For example,

$$MDC = \frac{L_d}{VEF} \qquad (3.9)$$

where:

V= sample volume or weight,
E = counting efficiency,
F = chemical yield

and MDC is presented in units of Bq per unit volume or mass. MDC can be also be expressed in terms of a background count (B) as:

$$MDC = \frac{2.71 + 4.65\sqrt{B}}{TVEF} \qquad (3.10)$$

The MDC for a specified measurement procedure represents the smallest activity concentration that is 'certain' to be detected with a specified degree of confidence. It is the value that is quoted when it is required to specify the limit of detection of a procedure.

3.10.3.2 Reporting low-level counting data

In practice, the net sample count-rate is compared to L_c which is calculated from an experimentally determined background. If the net sample count-rate exceeds L_c, it is decided that activity is present in the sample and the result is reported as positive with its associated two sided confidence interval. Conversely, if the net sample count-rate is less than or equal to L_c, it is decided that the gross sample count-rate is not statistically different from the background at the specified confidence level. When reporting results that have net count-rates less than or equal to L_c, the problem arises how to present the data. Several approaches which are used are presented here.

One approach is to calculate the result as an activity value and report it (even if it is negative) or to report the value with a comment that the result was close to the background [16]. Alternatively, the result is not reported and is replaced by either a less than value or a comment that activity was not detected [216].

Less than values of the form '< MDC' or '< L_c*' are often reported, where L_c* is the Critical Level converted to units of activity concentration. However, some authors [217,219] recommend that the MDC and L_c should not be reported as less than values and that another value, the Less Than Level (L_t) should be used. L_t is defined as the maximum true count-rate that a sample could have, based on the measured count-rate R_s, where R_s is less than L_c. For a 95 % confidence that the activity present does not exceed L_t, the value of L_t in terms of count-rate is given by:

$$L_t = R_s + 1.645\sqrt{\frac{R_s + 2R_b}{T}} \qquad (3.11)$$

where R_s is the net sample count-rate, R_b is the background count-rate and T is the count time for both sample and background. Once calculated L_t is converted to activity concentration units ($L_t\star$) and is reported in the form '< $L_t\star$ '.

Since MDC, $L_c\star$ and $L_t\star$ are all used as less than values, it is important to state which value is being used when a less than value is reported.

3.11 STANDARDS AND REFERENCE MATERIALS

All determinations of radionuclide concentrations in analytical samples, whether by radiometric or mass spectrometric techniques, require to be validated by the use of appropriate standards and reference materials.

Detailed documentation of analytical procedures, staff training and indeed successful accreditation status, are no guarantee that all results for radionuclide activities generated by a laboratory are correct. Optimum performance will be demonstrated and achieved by the use of a variety of types of materials.

3.11.1 In-house method validation

In-house validation of radioanalytical procedures is normally carried out by the use of commercially available certified reference materials such as those obtainable from **NPL**, **IAEA**, **NIST**, **NRC** and **BCR**. Note that the certified values for some materials can be less well known (wider ranges) than others due to the number and pedigree of the laboratories contributing results for their characterisation. A variety of sample matrices are available, occasionally with high and low radionuclide activity levels of the radionuclide of interest. However, it is usually difficult to find a certified material which matches closely the characteristics of a sample presented for analysis.

Analytical reference materials can acquire their radionuclide concentration levels from *in situ* or *in vivo* contamination or they can be 'blank' environmental materials which are spiked in the laboratory. In the former category, sometimes referred to as NMRMs – natural matrix reference materials – are soils, sediments, vegetation, biota and samples of human or animal origin such as tissues, organs, bone, urine and faeces. Spiked reference materials can be any type of sample which can be obtained and reliably spiked and homogenised; examples would be waters, some foodstuffs, soils etc. If a sample type contains activity concentrations which are too high for testing of low-level analyses, then it may be blended with larger amounts of uncontaminated material of similar type. The advantages and disadvantages of using spiked or natural matrix materials have been discussed by Bowen and Volchok [220] and Sill and David [221]. Where differences in the relative behaviours of the contaminant and added yield tracer are suspected or known (this could be in an extraction from a solid sample or precipitation from a aqueous sample) then careful consideration should be given as to which type of reference material is used, assuming that they exist for the radionuclide in question.

Although the range of available certified reference materials is growing slowly, there are many instances where one has to use a material which is judged to be the closest in composition to the analytical sample of interest.

There is only a limited availability of these reference materials, and many laboratories produce their own *in-house* working standards. These can be used more frequently, for example, to test a variation in a procedure or to train a new member of staff. This is quite in order as long as there is evidence for the homogeneity of the material at the appropriate sample size and there is traceability between the *in-house* standard and a certified material of a similar type.

3.11.2 External validation

Participation in national and international intercomparison exercises or proficiency testing schemes is an essential component of a laboratory quality control programme. They are more informative than the use solely of certified reference materials because the correct answer is not known before analysis. The ultimate assessment of a laboratory's performance is in its successful analysis of samples from these schemes. Repeating schemes and new exercises are usually in progress for one or more analyte/matrix combinations. A selection of schemes where UK radioanalytical laboratories take part is shown in Table 3.3. Not all of the exercises are available to all-comers, either because the material is very limited in quantity or the organising laboratory requires the participation of experienced laboratories using specific techniques to provide data for the certification process.

Table 3.3   Selection of international and national intercomparison exercises for radioactivity measurements.

Organiser	Radionuclide(s)	Sample type	Comments
National Physical Laboratory, UK	α, β and γ emitters	acidified water	annual
	γ emitters	kaolin	
	tritium	water	annual
	^{134}Cs, ^{137}Cs	milk powder	
National Institute for Standards and Technology, USA	natural and artificial actinides, ^{210}Pb, ^{210}Po, ^{90}Sr	bone ash	limited participation
Commissariat à l'Energie Atomique, France (PROCORAD)	actinides	dried urine, faecal ash dried urine	limited to bioassay laboratories
	U, ^{137}Cs, ^{90}Sr, ^{3}H		
International Atomic Energy Agency, Vienna	variety of natural and artificial radionuclides	soil, sediment, biota, vegetation	intermittent
World Health Organisation (International Reference Centre for Radioactivity)	U, ^{226}Ra, ^{60}Co	mineral water	
	^{3}H, ^{14}C, ^{137}Cs	water	

There are in addition other proficiency testing schemes run in the UK from time to time.

3.11.3 Equipment calibration

Quite apart from the use of standard reference materials, there is a requirement for laboratories to calibrate and test their counting equipment on a routine basis using traceable standards. These can take the form of:

solid sources such as electrodeposited alpha nuclides for energy and efficiency calibration of alpha spectrometry systems;

point sources for energy calibration of high and low-resolution gamma detectors and

standard solutions for matrix spiking to prepare in-house standards, assess radiochemical recoveries (yield tracers) or for isotope dilution procedures.

A variety of suppliers exist for certified sealed and unsealed radionuclide standards. The radionuclides available to the radionuclide analysis laboratory have been outlined in Chapter 4 of this manual, which also covers some aspects of their purity and preparation.

3.11.4 Analytical protocols

Formal radiochemical analytical protocols rarely exist although they should be an essential part of the analytical process. In practice, the decision making process is normally carried out informally in order to define the problem and the analytical programme in order that the intended results can be achieved efficiently and reliably and be fit for purpose.

It cannot be stressed enough, that analysts should participate in the planning stages of environmental sampling programmes in order to establish exactly what is required, how the results will be used and what the expected results may be. The analytical planning process can then establish the most appropriate analytical methodology regarding sensitivity, accuracy, precision, selectivity, limitations, turnaround time and cost [222].

Good planning should produce valid and useful results and an important element in this is the incorporation of essential decision criteria into the overall analytical protocol. This protocol should describe the analytical process in detail and include information on the overall goals and data quality objectives together with a description of the quality assurance and quality control requirements, the sampling plan, analytical methods, calculations, documentation and report requirements.

The choice of the analytical method is an important factor influencing data reliability [223] and a number of data quality objectives have been proposed. These are as follows:

- The level of confidence for the analysis should be chosen with reference to the cost of the analysis and the consequences of an incorrect decision for the identification or quantification.

- Choice of the analytical method together with sample size, preparation and pre-concentration requirements will influence the accuracy, precision and cost of the analyses.

- Quality assurance procedures must include regular and rigorous checks on the quality of analytical data and procedures to deal with data which appear to be 'out of control'. The degree of analytical confidence will depend upon the selection of method, analysis of replicates and the design of the quality control programme. In general, the higher the level of quality required the higher will be the cost of the analysis.

- A suitable level of method validation must be chosen to confirm the required level of specificity, precision and accuracy.

3.12 LABORATORY FACILITIES

3.12.1 General introduction

Ideally, radiochemical analysis laboratories should be designed so that they are suitable for all operations which will be undertaken. In practice, laboratories tend to be inherited or refurbished where there is available space. Certain essential criteria must be specified as minimum requirements for effective laboratory operations, these can be summarised as follows:

- segregation of analytical operations to ensure the absence of cross contamination and permit valid analyses of samples ranging from ultra low-level measurements on, for example, urine samples for dosimetry purposes, to higher levels of activity in environmental samples and to enhanced activity in land remediation and decommissioning samples;

- effective co-ordination and control of sample types and appropriate audit trails;

- control of access to certain sensitive laboratories, for example, for dosimetric purposes (Health and Safety Executive requirement), and decommissioning analyses (Radiological Protection Supervisor requirement);

- adequate fume cupboard space for operations involving acidic digestions and evaporations. The fume cupboards should be 'fit for purpose', that is, equipped with acid and heat resistant linings and extract ductwork. Fume cupboard extracts should be 'scrubbed' to eliminate acid fume discharges to the environment. Operations involving the use of perchloric acid should only be carried out in suitable fume cupboards connected to ductwork where water spray washdown is available in both;

- laboratory fixtures and fittings should be 'fit for purpose' and control and monitoring should be in place for critical environmental conditions such as temperature, laboratory air changes and radiation exposure;

- the environment of counting rooms housing sensitive electronic equipment should be air conditioned to avoid temperature fluctuation which could adversely affect the operation of this equipment;

- sample preparation areas housing muffle furnaces, grinders etc. should have appropriate environmental controls, safety instructions and local operating procedures and

- samples should be stored in suitable accommodation to preserve their integrity. This may require facilities ranging from shelving, storage cupboards, cold rooms or freezers depending on the sample types and the needs of the customer.

3.12.2 High activity operations

This Chapter has concentrated on environmental levels of radioactivity although it is recognised that many organisations handle much higher levels of radioactivity, for example, radiopharmacies, industry, academia and the specialist Nuclear Industries. Section 6.6.2.3 provides useful basic information on the operation of controlled area facilities for handling unsealed radioactive sources. More detail can be found in the quoted references which provide information on the standards for radiochemical laboratories, the design of facilities and the requirements for safe handling of unsealed sources.

Information on surface and airborne monitoring is provided in Section 6.6.2.4 and the treatment of contaminated personnel in Section 6.6.2.5.

Operational standards for Nuclear Medicine and radiotherapy are specific for these organisations and briefly discussed in Section 5.5.6. Useful references are provided for guidance on standards for radiopharmacies which include information on the facilities, documentation required and the radiopharmaceuticals themselves.

3.13 QUALITY ASSURANCE AND ACCREDITATION

3.13.1 Introduction

A major objective of quality assurance is to ensure that analytical results have a high probability of being accurate and precise. The achievement of this objective is dependent on the analytical laboratory establishing quality management systems which can achieve the desired level of quality and demonstrate a consistency in the delivery of this level of quality.

The quality assurance sub-group of the Radioactivity Monitoring Management Group (RMMG) was established in 1983 to develop quality assurance standards for environmental radiochemical analysis following publication of the RMMG State of the Art Review of Radioactivity Monitoring Programmes in the United Kingdom [224].

In 1986 the Radioactivity Research and Environmental Monitoring Committee (**RADREM**) took over responsibility for the review and co-ordination of environmental radioactivity monitoring programmes.

The Quality Assurance Sub-Group to the RADREM published a report in 1989 entitled The Assurance of Quality in Environmental Radionuclide Analysis [225]. The terms of reference of this Sub-Group were as follows:

to advise on an appropriate quality assurance scheme that could be used within the United Kingdom to demonstrate the adequacy and compatibility of analyses of environmental material undertaken by operators of nuclear facilities, Government departments, other national organisations and contract laboratories.

The management, assessment, validation and accreditation of radiochemical analyses have improved immensely since the publication of this report which provided the guidelines for improvements. The report defined the elements of good practice affecting the quality of measurements of radionuclides in environmental media. These elements have been fundamental in the development of quality assurance programmes and their importance and relevance is such that they are summarised as follows:

1. There should be close co-operation between the customer and the analytical laboratory concerning the requirements for precision, accuracy and limit of detection. These should be agreed before sampling is carried out. Details of these requirements and any other relevant data should be specified in writing to the laboratory undertaking the analysis and a copy should accompany the sample.

2. Every effort should be made to ensure that the environmental sample is truly representative of the medium from which it was taken and that it is maintained in a stable form during storage and transport to the laboratory.

3. Each laboratory must operate an internal quality control programme which must be documented.

4. Each laboratory must use appropriate radioactive standards of established material of international traceability. However, the Sub-Group considers that there is an urgent need for the availability of pure radionuclide standards both for calibration purposes and for use as yield indicators, and for readily available natural matrix standard and reference materials containing a range of radionuclides at a range of known concentrations.

5. The mandatory use of only certain specific methods of analysis is not recommended. However, analytical procedures must be validated and documented. Any departure from the written procedure should be authorised and recorded. Where appropriate, a comment should be made in the final report.

6. Laboratories should participate in national and international intercomparisons. In particular, further regular intercomparisons between UK laboratories should be encouraged.

7. When analytical results are reported, the associated uncertainties and the method of deriving them must be quoted.

8. High quality results can only be obtained by laboratories that employ skilled and motivated analysts in well-equipped laboratories operated with strict adherence to the principles of good laboratory practice.

Analytical quality assurance was reviewed by the Laboratory of the Government Chemist in 1991 [226] and, although this paper did not include radiochemical analyses, the principles of quality assurance are still relevant. These principles have been presented in a number of published texts and the following have been clearly identified as vital components of analytical quality assurance:

1. the establishment of validated methods;

2. the establishment of maintenance and calibration regimes for equipment;

3. the availability and use of reference materials;

4. analytical quality control procedures;

5. national and International Intercomparison exercises;

6. well trained and motivated staff and

7. formal accreditation of laboratories and procedures.

3.13.2 Valid Analytical Measurement (VAM)

The Department of Trade and Industry (DTI) programme for Valid Analytical Measurement (VAM) is an integral part of the UK National Measurement System. The programme aims to assist analytical laboratories to demonstrate the validity of their data and to facilitate mutual recognition of the results of analytical measurements. A Quarterly VAM Bulletin published by the Laboratory of the Government Chemist presents regular information on, for example, the VAM principles, feedback from Laboratories, news, reference materials and contact points.

The programme does not specifically cover radiochemical analyses but the principles are relevant as they focus on good analytical practice, backed up by technical support and management guidance, to enable laboratories to deliver reliable results consistently and thereby improve performance. A recent article by the National Laboratory Service of the Environment Agency [227] provides a good example of effective implementation of the VAM principles to provide a high level of customer service. These fundamental principles are summarised as follows:

1. Analytical measurements should be made to satisfy an agreed requirement;

2. Analytical measurements should be made using methods and equipment which have been tested to ensure they are fit for their purpose;

3. Staff making analytical measurements should be both qualified and competent to undertake the task;

4. There should be a regular independent assessment of the technical performance of a laboratory;

5. Analytical measurements made in one location should be consistent with those made elsewhere and

6. Organisations making analytical measurements should have well defined quality control and quality assurance procedures.

It is clear that many common themes exist in these publications, all of which are vital for the operation of a high quality radiochemical analysis laboratory and are fundamental requirements for laboratories to achieve formal accreditation.

3.13.3 Accreditation of radiochemical analysis laboratories

All laboratories operate quality systems of some kind and whether these are formal or informal will be dependent upon the management, operation, standards and customer care of each laboratory. King [228] identified two major standards for quality systems. Firstly, the competence of laboratories may be assessed against defined professional standards, such as NAMAS (National Accreditation of Measurement and Sampling) in the United Kingdom, for analytical calibration and testing. The second standard is appropriate for work done by a facility for a customer. Registration or certification to such a standard establishes that the facility has the necessary procedures and systems in place, to ensure that contractual requirements are both agreed and delivered to the customer. Examples of this standard in the United Kingdom are the BS EN ISO 9000 series of standards and the GLP (Good Laboratory Practice) managed by the Department of Health.

The United Kingdom Accreditation Service (UKAS) can award accreditation both to testing and calibration laboratories (**NAMAS**) and to third-party independent certification bodies (NACB-National Accreditation of Certification Bodies)[2]. Such bodies may then assess and approve companies or organisations, for example, to the BS EN ISO 9000 standard.

All these Quality Systems are specific to particular needs and the Laboratory should have a clear understanding of the aims of the standards. The Laboratory is required to define and document the systems and procedures, detailing the organisational and administration of the Analytical Quality System, within which each of the quality standards places specific

---

[2] Prior to the establishment of a unified accreditation service (UKAS) in 1995, the National Accreditation Council for Certification Bodies (NACCB) and the National Measurement Accreditation Service (also abbreviated to NAMAS) were separate organisations.

emphasis on different aspects of the system. The operation and management of these and other systems have been reviewed and compared [229] and the following guidelines have been established.

NAMAS accreditation provides the necessary assurance that analytical testing conforms to defined professional standards, thus demonstrating and recognising the competence of the accredited laboratory for the analytical service they carry out.

BS EN ISO 9000 registration aims to ensure that an analytical facility has the necessary systems and procedures in place in order to deliver assured contractual requirements to the customer.

GLP (Good Laboratory Practice) compliance is an essential requirement for analytical facilities producing data supporting the registration of new therapeutic drugs and/or new chemicals. The aims are to impose consistent standards, improve the quality of safety data and to prevent malpractice and fraud within the analytical community.

GMP (Good Manufacturing Practice) is a Quality Assurance system applied to the production of medical devices and equipment used in the medical industry. This standard can be sensibly applied to the production of sources and radiotracers used in medical applications.

Three regulatory standards (UKAS, BS EN ISO 9000 and GLP) are compared in [229] and the benefits are stressed of holding compliance and accreditation to all three quality standards. Although this aim may be outside of the scope of the majority of radiochemical analysis laboratories, most will have achieved recognition or accreditation with one or more of these schemes and/or with others.

3.13.4 NAMAS - National Accreditation of Measurement and Sampling

This standard is most universally recognised by customers who have a requirement for radiochemical measurements and by the laboratories who provide these measurements. The **NAMAS** Accreditation Standard M10 [230] specifies the general criteria for the assessment and accreditation of calibration and testing laboratories in the UK. This Standard requires that all laboratories will meet the requirements of the Standard in terms of the provision of a service in compliance with the NAMAS regulations M11 [231]. Laboratories engaged in calibration, testing or both can find guidance in the compilation of a Quality Manual that meets NAMAS requirements in addition to those of the laboratory and the parent company [232].

Additional information can be obtained from NAMAS Information Sheets (NIS) such as NIS 45 [233] which gives detailed guidance for the interpretation of M10 and M11 for laboratories undertaking quantitative and qualitative examination of the composition, nature and properties of materials, products and substances. It is applicable to laboratories carrying out measurements ranging from routine analysis to ad hoc studies and research and development. NIS 0825 [234] provides information on the derivation and statement of uncertainty in radiological measurements.

3.13.5 BS EN ISO 9000 Series

The International Standards in this quality series specify the required elements of a quality system but not how an individual organisation should implement them. This series recognises that the needs of organisations vary and that the design and implementation of quality systems will be influenced by the individual Company objectives, processes, products and practices. This series of quality systems is very product orientated (a product can include a service) and recognises that the success of a Company will depend upon certain product criteria such as the definition of need, use or purpose, the satisfaction of customer expectations, the compliance with applicable standards, specifications and the requirements of society, reflection of environmental needs and the economic production and availability at competitive prices. Guidelines on the Quality Management and Quality System Elements can be found in BS EN ISO 9004-1:1994 [235]. Guidelines on the selection and use of Quality Management and Quality Assurance Standards can be found in BS EN ISO 9000-1 [236]. These documents provide a good introduction to the implementation of the BS EN ISO 9000 Quality Assurance System.

3.13.6 Good Laboratory Practice (GLP)

The Department of Health has the responsibility for monitoring laboratories for compliance with GLP principles. The GLP Monitoring Authority has the responsibility to inspect laboratories involved in the health and environmental safety testing of pharmaceuticals, agrochemicals, cosmetics, food additives and industrial chemicals. GLP is concerned with the organisational processes and the conditions under which studies are planned, performed, monitored, recorded and reported. The GLP compliance programme establishes that laboratories have implemented GLP principles for the proper conduct of laboratory health and environmental safety studies on chemical substances where the results will be submitted to regulatory authorities [237].

A supplementary leaflet [238] provides the guidelines to assist a Company's Management by defining the role of QA in terms of GLP compliance needs, resources and responsibilities and provides advice to QA personnel for their day to day organisational needs.

3.13.7 Local Authority Radiation and Radioactivity Monitoring and Collation Centre (LARRMACC)

This organisation was established to co-ordinate Local Authority (LA) monitoring throughout the country. Up to the end of November 1996 approximately 293 LA's subscribed to LARRMACC which establishes comparability of monitoring schemes and quality assurance procedures. LARRMACC Technical Contractors have accredited 141 LA's up to January 1997 and they report on the activities and findings of these LA's.

3.13.8 Approval of Dosimetry Services under the Ionising Radiation Regulations (IRRs), 1985

This scheme is operated by the Health and Safety Executive for the approval and assessment of Dosimetry Services for External Radiations, Internal Radiations and Co-ordination and Record Keeping [232], see also Section 6.6. Laboratories undertaking the analysis of excretion products, for example, urine and faeces for radiation dosimetric purposes, have a mandatory requirement to be accredited under these Regulations. These laboratories are normally associated with the Nuclear Industry and generally are part of a wider dosimetry approval.

ACKNOWLEDGEMENTS

The authors are indebted to Susan Parry, Centre for Environmental Technology, Imperial College at Silwood Park for the section on neutron activation analysis. They are grateful to Francis Livens, University of Manchester, Peter Warwick, Loughborough University and Pam Hart, AWE Aldermaston for reviewing this chapter and for suggesting valuable improvements, Tim Sanders, AEA Technology plc for reviewing the section on data handling, Mike Heslop, AEA Technology plc for his advice on safety matters and to Peter Penfold, AEA Technology plc, for his expert guidance on the sections involving Quality Assurance.

REFERENCES

1. The Reporting of Injuries, Diseases and Dangerous Occurrences Regulations, The Health and Safety Executive, 1985.

2. A Guide to Working with Hazardous Materials, P. N. Cheremisinoff, Pudvan Publishing Co., 1987. ISBN 0 934165 06 9.

3. COSHH Approved Codes of Practice - Control of Substances Hazardous to Health, Control of Carcinogenic Substances and Control of Biological Agents, HSE Books 1997 ISBN 0 7176 1308 9.

4. A Step by Step Guide to COSHH Assessment, HMSO Publication, 1993. ISBN 0 11 11886379 7.

5. COSHH in Laboratories, The Royal Society of Chemistry, 1989. ISBN 0 85186 3191.

6. R. M. Pybus, Guide to COSHH, Croner Publications Ltd., 1991. ISBN 1 85524 237 0.

7. Occupational Exposure Limits, EH 40/98, HSE Books, 1998. ISBN 0 7176 1474 3 7 (updated annually).

8. Health and Safety at Work, Croner Publications Ltd.

9. Dangerous Substances, Croner Publications Ltd.

10. Handbook of Occupational Hygiene, Croner Publications Ltd.

11. Code of Practice for the Prevention of Infection in Clinical Laboratories and Post-Mortem Rooms, HMSO Publication, 1979. ISBN 0 11 320464 7.

12. Essentials of Health and Safety at Work, The Health and Safety Executive, HSE Books, 1995.

13. A. St. John Holt and H. Andrews, Principles of Health and Safety at Work, The Institution of Health and Safety at Work, IOSH Publishing Ltd., 1993.

14. The protection of persons against ionising radiation arising from any work activity, Approved Code of Practice, L58, HSE Books, 1994.

15. First Aid Manual. The Authorised Manual of St John Ambulance, St Andrew's Ambulance Association and The British Red Cross, Dorling Kindersley, London. 1993. ISBN 0 86318 978 4.

16. Sampling and Measurement of Radionuclides in the Environment. HMSO Publication, 1989. ISBN 0 11 752261 9.

17. J.R.P. Clarke and C.L.P. Thomas, *The benefits of good sampling*, VAM Bulletin, Issue No. 15, 13-14, Autumn 1996.

18. K.G. Carr-Brion and J.R.P. Clarke, Sampling systems for process analysers, 2nd. edition, Butterworth Heinemann, 1996.

19. C.L.P. Thomas and H. Schofield, Sampling source book, Butterworth Heinemann, 1996.

20. Sampling for Valid Analytical Measurement, Software database and explanatory booklet, Butterworth Heinemann, 1996.

21. Determination of Radioactivity in Water by Multinuclide Gamma Ray Spectrometry. HMSO Publication, 1989. ISBN 0 11 752220 1.

22. Measurement of Radionuclides in Food and the Environment, IAEA, Vienna, 1989. ISBN 92 0 125189 0.

23. *Preservation Techniques for Samples of Solids, Sludges and Non-Aqueous Liquids*, in Principles of Environmental Sampling, Ed., L.H. Keith, American Chemical Society, 1988.

24. T.L. Rucker and C.M. Johnson Jr., Laboratory Data Validation Guidelines for Evaluating Radionuclide Analyses, Science Applications International Corporation (SAIC), 1991.

25. N.A. Chieco, D.C. Bogen and E.O. Knutson (Eds.), *EML Procedures Manual 27th Edition*, US Department of Energy, New York, 1990.

26. J. Tolgyessy and E.H. Klehr, Nuclear Environmental Chemical Analysis, Ellis Horwood Ltd., 1989. ISBN 7458 0176 5.

27. K.H.Head, Manual of Soil Laboratory Testing, Vol 1, Pentech Press, 1980.

28. J.J. Koranda, P.L.Phelps L.R.Anspaughand G. Holladay, Sampling and Analytical Systems for Measuring Environmental Radioactivity, in Rapid Methods for Measuring Environmental Radioactivity in the Environment, IAEA, Vienna, 1971.

29. M.L. Stewart, J.R. Kline JR and C.F. Jordan, *A Tritiated Water Recovery System*, Int. J. Appl. Radiat. and Isotopes, **23**, 387-388, 1972.

30. D.A. Wickenden, *Determination of Tritiated Water in Biological Matrices*, presented at the 6th Int Conf on Environmental Analysis, Manchester, UK, September 1990, Sci. Tot. Env., **130/131**, 121-128, 1991.

31. P. Daruschy, Eine Schnelle und Einfache Methode zum Nachwein von Tritium in Biologischem Material, Atompraxis, **11**, 273-274, 1965.

32. A.A. Moghissi, E.W. Bretthauer and E.H. Compton, *Separation of Water from Biological and Environmental Samples for Tritium Analysis*, Anal. Chem., **45(8)**, 1565-1566, 1973.

33. A.A Moghissi, *Application of Cyclohexane in the Separation of Water from Biological and Environmental Samples*, Health Physics, **41**, 413-414, 1981.

34. R. Moore and E.R. Bushkirk , *Differential Sublimation Rates of Light and Tritium-Labelled Water*, Nature, **189**, 149-151, 1961.

35. J.F. Lockyer and A.E. Lally, *The determination of tritium, ^{14}C and ^{35}S in milk and crop samples using a combustion technique*, Sci., Tot. Envir., **130/131**, 337-344, 1993.

36. A. Martin and R.L. Blanchard, *The Thermal Volatilisation of Caesium-137, Polonium-210 and Lead-210 from In-Vivo Labelled Samples*, Analyst, **94**, 441-446, 1969.

37. E. Steinbruggen and D.C. Auman, *Simultaneous Determination of Some Long-Lived Semivolatile Radionuclides in Environmental Samples*, J. Radioanal. and Nucl. Chem. Articles, **158(2)**, 367-382, 1992.

38. J. Rioseco, E. Holm and M. Garcia-Leon, *Radiochemical Analysis for Technetium-99: Progress and Problems*, Fourth Symposium on the Determination of Radionuclides in Environmental and Biological Materials, National Physical Laboratory, Middlesex, UK, 1983.

39. M.H. Studier, C. Postmus, J. Mech, R.R.Walters and E.N. Sloth, *The use of ^{129}I as an isotopic tracer and its determination along with normal ^{127}I by neutron activation-the isolation of iodine from a variety of materials*, J. Inor. Nucl. Chem., **24**, 755-761, 1962.

40. B. Keisch, R.C. Koch and A.S. Levine, *Determination of Biospheric Levels of I-129 by Neutron Activation Analysis*,Texas A&M University, USA, 284, 1965.

41. M.S. Boulos, V.J. Becker and O.K. Manuel, *Iodine-129 in Thyroid Glands*, Health Physics, **24**, 375-378, 1973.

42. J.J. Gabay, G.J. Paperiello, S. Goodyear, J.C. Daly and J.M. Matsusek, *A Method for Determining Iodine-129 in Milk and Water*, Health Physics, **26**, 89-96, 1974.

43. R.C. MacFarland, D.M. Walker and M.E. McLain, *Determination of Atmospheric Concentrations of Stable Iodine,* Nucl. Sci., **21**, 503-509, 1974.

44. F.P. Brauer and H. Tenny H, *I-129 Analysis Methodology*, Report No. BNWL-SA-5287, Battelle Pacific Northwest Laboratories, Richland, Washington, USA, 1975.

45. J.W.T. Meadows, J.S. Schweiger, B. Mendoza B and R. Stone R, *Procedure for Plutonium Analysis of Large (100g) soil and sediment samples*, in, Reference Methods for Marine Radioactivity Studies II, IAEA, Vienna, p 89, 1975.

46. N.P. Singh and M.E. Wren, *Tracers and Methods for Determining Thorium and Uranium in Biological Samples*, in, Actinides in Man and Animals, Proceedings of Snowbird Actinide Workshop, October 15th, 1979. Ed. ME Wrenn, RD Press, Salt Lake City, p 53, 1981.

47. H.L. Volchok and G. de Planque, Eds., *Environmental Measurements Laboratory Procedures Manual*, 26th Edition, HASL-300, US Dept of Energy, New York, 1983.

48. A.E. Lally and J.D. Eakins, *Some Recent Advances in Environmental Analyses at AERE, Harwell*, in Symposium on Determination of Radionuclides in Environmental and Biological Materials, CEGB, Sudbury House, London 9th October, 1978.

49. S. Ballestra S. and R. Fukai, *An improved Radiochemical Procedure for Low Level Measurements of Americium in Environmental Matrices*, Talanta, **30(1)**, 45-48, 1983.

50. M.H. Hiatt and P.B. Hahn, *Simultaneous Determination of Americium and Curium in Soil*, Anal. Chem., **51(2)**, 295-298, 1979.

51. K. Sekine, T. Imai and A. Kasai, *Liquid-Liquid Extraction Separation and Sequential Determination of Plutonium and Americium in Environmental Samples by Alpha Spectrometry*, Talanta, **34(6)**, 567-570, 1987.

52. A. Yamato, *An Anion Exchange Method for the Determination of Americium-241 and Plutonium in Environmental Samples*, J. Radioanal. Chem., **75(1-2)**, 265-273, 1982.

53. J.W.T. Meadows, J.S. Schwieger, B. Mendoza and R. Stone, *Procedure for Plutonium Analysis of Large (100g) Soil and Sediment Samples*, in, Reference Methods for Marine Radioactivity Studies II, IAEA, Vienna, pp89-90, 1975.

54. T.-L. Ku, *An evaluation of the $^{234}U/^{238}U$ Method as a Tool for Dating Pelagic Sediments*, J. Geophys. Res., **70**, 3457-3474, 1965.

55. L.B. Fischer, *Microwave Dissolution of Geologic Material, Application to Isotope Dilution Analysis*, Anal. Chem., **58**, 261-263, 1986.

56. C.W. Sill and F.D. Hindman, *Preparation and Testing of Standard Soils Containing Known Quantities of Radionuclides*, Anal. Chem., **46**, 113-118, 1974.

57. C.W. Sill, *A Critique of Current Practices in the Determination of Actinides*, in, Actinides in Man and Animals, Proceedings of Snowbird Actinide Workshop, October 15-17, 1979, Ed. M.E. Wrenn, RD Press, Salt Lake City, pp 1-28, 1981.

58. J. Korkisch, I. Steffan, G. Arrhenius, M. Fisk and J. Fraser, *Chemical analysis of manganese nodules. Part II. Determination of uranium and thorium after an ion-exchange separation*, Anal. Chim. Acta, **90**, 151-8, 1977.

59. W.R. Alexander and T.M. Shimmield, J. *Microwave oven dissolution of geological samples: novel application in the determination of natural series radionuclides*, Radioanal. Nucl. Chem. Lett., **145(4)**, 301-310, 1990.

60. A.A. Aarkrog, *Radiochemical Determination of Plutonium in Marine Samples by Ion Exchange and Solvent Extraction*, in, Reference Methods for Marine Radioactivity Studies II, IAEA, Vienna, pp 91-96, 1975.

61. S.N. Joshi and G.R. Doshi, *I-129 in the Environment Around a Nuclear Processing Plant*. Bull. Rad. Prot., **11(1-2)**, 119-124, 1988.

62. BNFL, *An Analytical Method for the Radiochemical Separation of Ruthenium-106 in Environmental and Biological Materials*, BNFL Report No. 464(W), 1984.

63. F. Patti, L. Capellini and L. Jeanmaire, Determination du Technetium-99 dans les Enchantillons Biologiques Marins, CEA Report No. CEA-N-2140, 1980.

64. L.L. Smith, F. Markin, and T. Ten Kate, *Comparison of Acid Leachate and Fusion Methods to Determine Plutonium and Americium in Environmental Samples,*Argonne National Laboratory, Argonne Report ANL/ACL 92/2, 1992.

65. J. Kronfield and J.A.S. Adams, *Hydrologic investigations of the groundwaters of central Texas using U-234/U-238 disequilibrium,* J. Hydrol., **22**, 77-88, 1974.

66. E. Holm and R. Fukai, *Determination of americium and curium by ion-exchange in nitric acid-methanol medium for environmental analyis,* Talanta, **23(11-12)**, 853-855, 1976.

67. A.E. Lally, Chapter 4 in M.Ivanovich and R. S. Harmon, Uranium series disequilibrium: Application to earth, marine and environmental sciences, 2nd Edition, Clarendon Press, Oxford 1992.

68. W.D. Urry and C.S. Piggot, *Apparatus for determination of small amounts of radium,* Am. J. Sci., **239**, 191-203, 1941.

69. D. Hindman, *Neodymium fluoride mounting for α spectrometric determination of uranium, plutonium and americium,* Anal. Chem., **55(14)**, 2460-2461, 1983.

70. B.R. Harvey and L.M. Thurston, *Aquatic Environment Protection: Analytical Methods,* Number 1, MAFF, Lowestoft, 1988.

71. M.B. Lovett, S.J. Boggis and P. Blowers, *Aquatic Environment Protection: Analytical Methods,* Number 7(1), MAFF, Lowestoft, 1990.

72. C.W. Sill, K.W. Purphal and F.D. Hindman, *Simultaneous determination of alpha emitting nuclides of radium through californium in soil,* Anal. Chem., **46(12)**, 1725-1737, 1974.

73. J.D. Eakins and P.J. Gomm, *The determination of radiostrontium in urine, AERE-R 4753,* 1964.

74. B R. Harvey, R.D. Ibbett, M.B. Lovett and K.J. Williams, *Aquatic Environment Protection: Analytical Methods,* Number 5, MAFF, Lowestoft, 1989.

75. K Bunzl and W. Kracke, *A simple radiochemical determination of ^{90}Sr in environmental samples,* J. Radioanal. Nucl Chem. Art., **148(1)**, 115-119, 1991.

76. J. Cobb, P. Warwick, R.C. Carpenter and R.T. Morrison, *Determination of strontium-90 in milk samples using a controlled precipitation clean-up step prior to ion-chromatography,* Sci. Tot. Environ., **173/174**, 179-186, 1995.

77. A. Morgan and G.M. Arkell, *A method for the determination of caesium-137 in sea water,* Health Phys. **9,** 857-862,1963.

78. J. Molero, A. Morán, J.A. Sanchez-Cabeza, M. Blanco, P.I. Mitchell and A., Vidal-Quadras, *Efficiency of radiocaesium concentration from large volume natural water samples by scavenging with ammonium molybdophosphate,* Radiochim. Acta, **62**, 159-162, 1993.

79. I.I.L. Cunha and L. Sakai, *Determination of cesium-137 in water by ion exchange,* J. Radioan. and Nucl. Chem., **131**, 105-109, 1989.

80. International Atomic Energy Agency, *Reference Methods for Marine Radioactivity Studies*, Technical Report Series 118, IAEA, Vienna, 1970.

81. Y. Muratsu, S. Uchida, M. Sumiya and K Ohomo, *Iodine separation procedure for the determination of ^{129}I and ^{127}I in soil by neutron activation analysis*, J. Radioanal. Nucl. Chem. Lett., **94**, 329-338, 1985.

82. G.R. Doshi, S.N. Doshi and K.C. Pillai, *^{129}I in soil and grass samples around a nuclear reprocessing plant*, J. Radioanal. Nucl. Chem. Lett., **155**, 115-127, 1991.

83. S. Foti, *Ashing of vegetation for the determination of ^{131}I*, Health Physics, **33**, 387-391, 1977.

84. S.J. Parry, B.A. Bennett, R. Benzing, A.E. lally, C.P. Birch and M. Fulker, *The determination of ^{129}I in milk and vegetables using neutron activation analysis*, Sci. Tot. Env., **173/174**, 351-360, 1995.

85. P. Robb, P. Warwick and D.J. Malcome-Lawes, *A method for the determination of technetium-99 in environmental waters*, J. Radioanal. Nucl. Chem. Art., **89(2)**, 320-329, 1985.

86. R.S. Grieve, *Low level determination of technetium-99 and antimony-125 in environmental samples*, Fourth Radiochemical Methods Group Symposium on the determination of radionuclides in environmental and biological materials, Teddington, UK, 1983.

87. G. Sauzay and W.R. Schell, *Analysis of low level tritium concentrations by electrolytic enrichment and liquid scintillation counting*, Int. J. Appl. Radiat. Isotopes, **23**, 25-33, 1972.

88. H. Polach, J. Gower and I. Fraser, *Synthesis of High Purity Benzene for Radiocarbon Dating by the Liquid Scintillation Method*, Proceedings of 8th International Conference on Radiocarbon Dating, **1**, 1972.

89. F.B. Johns, *The Analysis of Food and Milk for Carbon-14*, in *Handbook of Radiochemical Methods*, Report EPA-680/4-75-001, 1975.

90. B.W. Fox, *Techniques of Sample Preparation for Liquid Scintillation Counting*, Elsevier, London, pp213-233, 1976.

91. J.D. Eakins and R.T. Morrison, *A new procedure for the determination of lead-210 in lake and marine sediments*, Int. J. Appl. Radiat. Isotopes, **29**, 531-536, 1978.

92. M. Rama Koide and E.D. Goldberg, *Lead-210 in natural waters*, Science, **134**, 98-99, 1961.

93. H. Craig, S. Krishnaswami and B.L.K. Somayajula, *Lead-210-radium-226, Radioactive disequilibrium in the deep sea*, Earth Planet.Sci. Lett., **17(2)**, 295-305, 1973.

94. W. Rieman and H.F. Walton, Ion-exchange in Analytical Chemistry, Pergamon Press, Oxford, 1970.

95. J. Korkisch, *Handbook of Ion-Exchange Resins: Their Application to Inorganic Analytical Chemistry*, CRC Boca Raton, Florida, USA, 1989.

96. L.P.Gregory, *A simplified separation of strontium, radium and lead from environmental media by precipitation followed by fractional elution*, Anal. Chem., **44(12)**, 2113-2115, 1972.

97. G.R. Choppin and R.J. Silva, *Cation exchange separation of rare earth elements using alpha-hydroxyisobutyrate*, J. Inorg. Nucl. Chem., **3**, 153-154, 1956.

98. S.G. Bhat, S. Krishnaswami, D. Lal and W.S. Moore, *Thorium-234/uranium-238 ratios in the ocean*, Earth Planet Sci. Lett., **5**, 483-491, 1969.

99. G.H. Morrison and H. Freiser, *Solvent Extraction in Analytical Chemistry*, John Wiley New York, 1957.

100. G.H. Kramer and J.M. Davis, *Isolation of strontium-90, yttrium-90, promethium-147 and cerium-144 from wet ashed urine by calcium oxalate coprecipitation and sequential solvent extraction*, Anal. Chem., **54**, 1428-1431, 1982.

101. J. Borcherding and H. Nies, *An improved method for the determination of ^{90}Sr in large samples of seawater*, J. Radioanal. Nucl. Chem. Lett., **98**, 127-131, 1986.

102. E.J. Baratta and T.C. Reavey, *Rapid determination of strontium-90 in tissue, food, biota and other environmental media by tributyl phosphate*, J. Agric. Food Chem., **17(6)**, 1337-1339, 1969.

103. S.Zhu, A. Ghods, J.C. Veselsky, A. Mirna and R. Schelenz, *Interference of ^{91}Y with the rapid determination of ^{90}Sr originating from the Chernobyl fallout debris*, Radiochim. Acta, **41**, 157-162, 1990.

104. D.F. Wood and R.H. Mc Kenna, *Determination of small amounts of uranium in hafnium, zirconium and zircaloy-2*, Anal. Chim. Acta, **27**, 446-453, 1962.

105. E.P. Horwitz, M.I. Dietz and D.E. Fisher, *Separation and preconcentration of strontium from biological, environmental and nuclear waste samples by extraction chromatography using a crown ether*, Anal. Chem., **63**, 522-525, 1991.

106. N.Vajda, A. Ghods-Esphahani, E. Cooper and P.R. Danesi, *Determination of radiostrontium in soil samples using a crown ether*, J. Radioanal. Nucl. Chem. Art., **162**, 307-323, 1992.

107. H.W Jeter and B. Grob, *Determination of radiostrontium in milk using an extraction chromatography column*, Radioactivity and Radiochemistry, **5(3)**, 8-16, 1994.

108. E.P. Horwitz, R. Chiarizia, M.L. Dietz, H. Diamond and D.M. Nelson, *Separation and preconcentration of actinides from acidic media by extraction chromatography*, Anal. Chim. Acta., **281**, 361-372, 1993.

109. G.J. Ham, *Determination of actinides in environmental materials using extraction chromatography*, Sci. Tot. Env., **173/174**, 19-22, 1995.

110. J.H. Kaye, R.S. Strebin and R.D. Orr, *Quantitative analysis of americium, curium and plutonium isotopes in Hanford samples using exchange chromatography and precipitation plating*, in Proc. 3rd Intl. conference on Methods and applications of radioanalytical chemistry, J. Radioanal. and Nucl. Chem., **194(1)**, 191-196, 1995.

111. A.D. Banavali, J.M. Raimondi, E.M. Moreno and D.E. McCurdy, *The determination of technetium-99 in Low-Level Radioactive Waste*, Radioactivity and Radiochemistry, **6**, 26-35, 1995.

112. *Environmental Radiation Measurements*, NCRP Report No. 50, 1976.

113. J.D. Hemingway, *Investigations Towards an Improved Marinelli Beaker for Gamma Detectors*, J. Radioanal. Nucl. Chem. Articles, **99(2)**, 299-306, 1986.

114. M.A. Mariscotti, *A method for automatic identification of peaks in the presence of background and its applications to spectral analysis*, Nucl. Instr. Meth., **50**, 309-320, 1967.

115. J.T. Routti and S.G. Prussin, *Photopeak method for the computer analysis of gamma-ray spectra from semiconductor detectors*, Nucl. Instr. Meth., **72**, 125-142, 1969.

116. F. Adams and R. Dams, Applied Gamma-ray Spectrometry, 2nd Edition. Int. Ser. of Monographs in Analytical Chemistry, Vol. 41, Pergamon Press, Oxford, 1970.

117. K. Debertin and R.G. Helmer, Gamma- and X-ray Spectrometry with Semiconductor Detectors, Elsevier Science Publishers, 1988.

118. G. Gilmore and J.D. Hemingway, Practical Gamma-Ray Spectrometry, John Wiley & Sons, 1995.

119. S.A. Woods, J.D. Hemingway, N.E. Bowles and J.L. Makepiece, *Standard gamma-ray spectra for the comparison of spectral analysis software,* National Physical Laboratory, NPL Report CIRM 2, 1997.

120. Methods for the Examination of Waters and Associated Materials, HMSO, 1986. ISBN 0 11 751909X.

121. D.J. Malcolm-Lawes, Introduction to Radiochemistry, Macmillan Press Ltd, London, 1979.

122. D.L. Horrocks, *Absolute disintegration rate determination of beta-emitting radionuclides by the pulse height shift-extrapolation method*, in Liquid scintillation, science and technology, A.A. Noujam, C. Ediss and L.I. Weibe, Eds., Academic Press, 1976.

123. K. Rundt, *On the Determination and Compensation of Quench in Liquid Scintillation Counting,* Ph.D. Thesis, Abo Akademi, Finland, 1989.

124. H. Ross, J.E. Noakes and J.D. Spaulding, Eds*., Liquid Scintillation Counting and Organic Scintillators,* Lewis Publishers Inc., 1991.

125. A.E Lally and K.M. Glover, *Source Preparation in Alpha Spectrometry*, Nucl. Inst., Methods Phys. Res., **233**, 259-265, 1984.

126. A. Kaufman, *Thorium-230/uranium-234 Dating of carbonates from Lakes Laboratory and Bonneville*, Columbia University, PhD Thesis, 1964.

127. C.W. Sill and R.L. Williams, *Preparation of Actinides for Alpha Spectrometry Without Electrodeposition*, Anal. Chem., **53(3)**, 412-415, 1981.

128. S.R. Joshi, *Lanthanum Fluoride Coprecipitation Technique for the Preparation of Actinides for Alpha Particle Spectrometry*, J. Radioanal. Nucl. Chem. Art., **90**, 409-415, 1985.

129. F.D. Hindman, *Actinide Separations for Alpha Spectrometry using Neodymium Fluoride Coprecipation*, Anal. Chem., **58(6)**, 1238-1241, 1986.

130. W. Parker, H. Blidstein and N. Getoff, *Molecular plating. I. A rapid and quantitative method for the electrodeposition of thorium and uranium*, Nucl. Instr. Meth., **26**, 55-60, 1964.

131. N.A. Talvitie, *Electrodeposition of Actinides for Alpha Spectrometric Determination*, Anal. Chem., 44, 280-283, 1972.

132. I Kressin, *Electrodeposition of plutonium and americium for high resolution α spectrometry*, Anal. Chem., **49**, 842-845, 1977.

133. W.W. Flynn, *The Determination of Low Levels of Polonium-210 in Environmental Materials*, Anal. Chim. Acta, **43**, 221-227, 1968.

134. R.L. Blanchard, *Rapid Determination of Lead-210 and Polonium-210 in Environmental Samples by Deposition on Nickel*, Anal. Chem., **38(2)**, 189-192, 1964.

135. M. Ivanovich and R.S. Harmon, Uranium series disequilibrium: Application to earth, marine and environmental sciences, 2nd Edition, Clarendon Press, Oxford, 1992.

136. A.P. Fleer, and M.P. Bacon, *Determination of ^{210}Pb and ^{210}Po in seawater and marine particulate matter*, Nucl. Instr. Meth. in Phys. Res., **223**, 243-249, 1984.

137. H.W. Kirby and W.E. Sheehan, *Determination of ^{238}Pu and ^{241}Am in ^{239}Pu by alpha-spectrometry*, Nucl. Instr. Meth. in Phys. Res., **223**, 356-359, 1984.

138. J. Parus, W. Raab, H. Swietly, J. Cappis and S. Deron, *On the capabilities of isotope dilution alpha spectrmetry in the determination of plutonium concentrations*, Nucl. Instr. Meth. in Phys. Res., **A312**, 278-283, 1992.

139. E. Garcia-Toraño and M.L. Aceña, *NOLIN: nonlinear analysis of complex alpha spectra*, Nucl. Instr. Meth., **185**, 261-269, 1981.

140. W. Westmeier, *Computerized analysis of alpha-particle spectra*, Int. J. Appl. Radiat. Isot., **35(4)**, 261-270, 1984.

141. A. W. McMahon, *A critical intercomparison of techniques for the determination of low levels of radionuclides*, Harwell Report R-13617, 1989.

142. M. R. Smith, E. J. Wyse and D. W. Koppenaal, *Radionuclide detection by inductively-coupled plasma mass spectrometry: a comparison of atomic and radiation detection methods*, J. Radioanal. Nucl. Chem., Articles, **160**, 341-354, 1992.

143. A. W. McMahon, *An intercomparison of non-radiometric methods for the measurement of low levels of radionuclides*, Appl. Radiat. Isot., **43**, 289-303, 1992.

144. D. C. Duckworth, C. M. Barswick, D. A. Bostick and D. H. Smith, *Direct measurement of uranium isotopic ratios in soils by glow discharge mass spectrometry*, Applied Spectr., **47**, 243-245, 1993.

145. D. L. Donohue and M. Petek, *Isotopic measurements of palladium metal containing protium and deuterium by Glow Discharge Mass Spectrometry*, Anal. Chem., **63**, 740-744, 1991.

146. M. Betti, G. Rasmussen, T. Heirnaut, L. Koch, D. M. P. Milton and R. C. Hutton, *Adaptation of a glow discharge mass spectrometer in a glove box for the analysis of nuclear materials*, J. Anal. Atom. Spec., **9**, 385-391, 1994.

147. T. J. Shaw and R. Francois, *A fast and sensitive ICP-MS assay for the determination of ^{230}Th in marine sediments*, Geochim, Cosmochim. Acta, **55**, 2075-2078, 1991.

148. C. Pin, S. Lacombe, P. Telouk and J.-L. Imbert, *Isotope-dilution-inductively coupled plasma mass spectrometer: a straightforward method for rapid and accurate determination of uranium and thorium in silicate rocks*, Anal. Chim. Acta., **256**, 153-161, 1992.

149. J Toole, K. McKay and M.S. Baxter, *Determination of uranium in marine sediment porewaters by isotope dilution inductively coupled plasma mass spectrometry*, Anal. Chim. Acta, **245**, 83-88, 1991.

150. J. S. Crains and L. L. Smith, *Enhanced measurement of long-lived actinides by inductively-coupled plasma mass spectrometry*, J. Radioanal. Nucl. Chem, Articles, **194**, 133-139, 1995.

151. E. J. Wyse and D. R. Fisher, *Radionuclide bioassay by inductively-coupled plasma mass spectrometry (ICP/MS)*, Rad. Prot. Dosim., **55**, 199-206, 1994.

152. C. K. Kim, Y. Tagaku, M. Yamamoto, H. Kawamura, K. Shiraishi, Y. Igarashi, S. Igarashi, H. Takayama and N. Ikeda, *Determination of ^{237}Np in environmental samples using inductively coupled plasma-mass spectrometry*, J. Radioanal. Nucl. Chem., **132**, 131, 1989.

153. C. K. Kim, S. Morita, R. Seki, Y. Takaku, N. Ikeda and D. J. Assinder, *Distribution and behaviour of ^{99}Tc, ^{237}Np, $^{239,240}Pu$ and ^{241}Am in the coastal and estuarine sediments of the irish sea*, J. Radioanal. Nucl. Chem., **156**, 201-213, 1992.

154. S. Nicholson, T. W. Sanders and L. M. Blaine, *The determination of low levels of ^{99}Tc in environmental samples by inductively-coupled plasma mass spectrometry*, Sci. Tot. Environm., **130-131**, 275-284, 1993.

155. R. J. Cox, C. J. Pickford and M. Thomson, *Determination of Iodine-129 in vegetable samples by inductively-coupled plasma mass spectrometry*, J. Anal. Atom. Spectrom., **7**, 635-640, 1992.

156. K. E. Jarvis, A. L. Gray and R. S. Houk, *Handbook of inductively coupled plasma mass spectrometry*, Blackie and Sons Ltd, Great Britain, 1992.

157. S. H. Tan and G. Horlick, *Background spectral features in inductively coupled plasma mass spectrometry*, Applied Spectrom., **40**, 445-460, 1986.

158. H. Kawaguchi, T. Tanaka and A. Mizuike, *Continuum background in inductively coupled plasma mass spectrometry*, Spectrochim. Acta, **43B**, 955-962, 1987.

159. E. H. Evans and J. J. Giglio, *Interferences in inductively coupled plasma mass spectrometry, a review*, J. Anal. Atomic Spectrom., **8**, 1–18, 1993.

160. J. I. G. Alonso, D. Thoby-Schutzendorff, B. Giovanonne and L. Koch, *Performance characteristics of a glove box Inductively Coupled Plasma-Mass Spectrometer for the analysis of nuclear materials*, J. Anal. Atom. Spectrom., **8**, 673–679, 1993.

161. O. T. Farmer III, M. R. Smith, E. J. Wyse and D. W. Koppenaal, *Separation and detection of radionuclides by IC/ICP-MS*, 1994 Winter Conference on Plasma Spectrochemistry, San Diego, January 10–15, 1994.

162. J. I. G. Alonso, F. Sena, P. Arbore, M. Betti and L. Koch, *Determination of fission products and actinides in spent nuclear fuels by isotopic dilution-ion chromatography-ICPMS*, 1994 Winter Conference on Plasma Spectrochemistry, San Diego, January 10–15, 1994.

163. R. J. Rosenberg and R. Zilliacus, *The use of quadrupole inductively coupled plasma-mass spectrometry for the measurement of actinides*, International Workshop on the status of measurement techniques for the identification of nuclear signatures, IRMM Geel, 25–27 February, 1997.

164. M. Hollenbach, J. Grohs and S. Mamich, *Determination of radionuclides in soils by ICP-MS using flow-injection concentration and ultrasonic nebulization*, 1994 Winter Conference on Plasma Spectrochemistry, San Diego, January 10–15, 1994.

165. R. Feng, J. Ludden and H. Abercrombie, *Analysis of Pb, Th and U isotopes by laserprobe-inductively coupled plasma-mass spectrometry: sources of error and time-dependent signal variation with impliction for zircon geochronology*, 1994 Winter Conference on Plasma Spectrochemistry, San Diego, January 10–15, 1994.

166. C. K. Kim, R. Seki, S. Morita, S. Yamasaki, A. Tsumura, Y. Takaku, Y. Igarashi and M. Yamamoto, *Application of a high-resolution inductively coupled plasma-mass spectrometer to the measurement of long-lived radionuclides*, J. Anal. Atom. Spectrom., **6**, 205–209, 1991.

167. R. Hearn and H. Wildner, *Isotope ratios of actinide elements using High Resolution ICP-MS*, 2nd ASTM Symposium on Applications of ICP-MS to Radionuclide Determinations at Pittcon '98, New Orleans, March 1–5, 1998.

168. J. Toole, *Sensitive analytical methodology for environmental samples in support of Safeguards*, In Proceedings of Workshop on Science and Modern Technology for Safeguards, Arona, Italy, 28–31 October 1996, 59–63, 1997.

169. J. Toole, I. Adsley, R. Hearn, H. Wildner, N. Montgomery, I. Croudace, P. Warwick and R. Taylor, *Status of analytical techniques for the measurement of uranium isotopic signatures*, Proceedings of the Workshop on the Status of Measurement Techniques for the Identification of Nuclear Signatures, IRMM Geel, Belgium, 25–27 February, 1997, 49–58, 1997.

170. J. H. Chen, R. L. Edwards and G. J. Wasserburg, *^{238}U, ^{234}U and ^{232}Th in seawater*, Earth and Planet. Sci. Lett., **80**, 241–251, 1986.

171. J. L. Banner, G. J. Wassrburg, J. H. Chen and C. H. Moore, *^{234}U-^{238}U-^{230}Th-^{232}Th systematics in saline groundwaters from central Missouri*, Earth Planet. Sci. Lett., **101**, 296–312, 1990.

172. K. O. Buesseler and J. E. Halverson, *The mass spectrometric determination of fallout ^{239}Pu and ^{240}Pu in marine samples*, J. Environ. Rad., **5**, 425-444, 1987.

173. A. McCormick, *Thermal ionisation mass spectrometry for small sample analysis of uranium and plutonium*, Appl. Radiat. Isot., **43**, 271-278, 1992.

174. W. R. Kelly and F. D. Fassett, *Determination of picogram quantities of uranium in biological tissues by isotope dilution thermal ionisation mass spectrometry with ion counting detection*, Anal. Chem., **55**, 1040-1044, 1983.

175. W. McCarthy and T. M. Nicholls, *Mass spectrometric analysis of plutonium in soils near Sellafield*, J. Env. Radioact., **12**, 1-12, 1990.

176. R. L. Walker, R. E. Eby, C. A. Pritchard and J. A. Carter, *Simultaneous uranium and plutonium isotopic analysis from a single resin bead - a simplified chemical technique for assaying spent reactor fuels*, Anal. Letters, **7 (8&9)**, 563-574, 1974.

177. J. D. Fassett and W. R.Kelly, *Interlaboratory isotopic ratio measurement of nanogram quantities of uranium and plutonium on resin beads by thermal ionisation mass spectrometry*, Anal. Chem., **56**, 550-556, 1984.

178. S. K. Aggarwal, P. M. Shah, R. K. Duggal and H. C. Jain, *Experimental evaluation of ^{239}Pu, ^{238}Pu and ^{233}U spikes for determining plutonium concentration by thermal ionization mass spectrometry and alpha spectrometry*, J. Radioanal. Nucl. Chem., **148**, 309-317, 1991.

179. H. M. Shihomatsu and S. S. Iyer, *Application of two-tracer isotope dilution mass spectrometry in the determination of uranium in geological samples*, Anal. Chim. Acta, **228**, 333-335, 1990.

180. E. L. Callis and R. M. Abernathey, *High-precision isotopic analysis of uranium and plutonium by total sample volatilisation and signal integration*, Int. J. Mass Spectrom. Ion Process., **103**, 93-105, 1991.

181. A. S. Cohen and R. K. O'Nions, *Precise determination of femtogram quantities of radium by thermal ionisation mass spectrometry*, Anal. Chem., **63**, 2705-2708, 1991.

182. A. M. Volpe, J. A. Olivares and M. T. Murrell, *Determination of radium isotope ratios and abundances in geologic samples by thermal ionisation mass spectrometry*, Anal. Chem., **63**, 913-916, 1991.

183. J. H. Chen, R. L. Edwards and G. J. Wasserburg, *Mass spectrometry and applications to uranium-series disequilibrium*, In Uranium Series Disequilibrium Applications to Earth, Marine and Environmental Sciences 2nd Edn., Eds M. Ivanovich and R. S. Harmon, Oxford Science Publications, 174-206, 1992.

184. A. E. Litherland, *Fundamentals of accelerator mass spectrometry*, Phil. Trans. Roy. Soc. Lond., **A323**, 5-21, 1987.

185. R. Middleton, *A review of ion sources for accelerator mass spectrometry*, Nucl. Instr. Meth., **233**, 193-199, 1984.

186. W. Henning, *Accelerator mass spectrometry of heavy elements ^{36}Cl to ^{205}Pb*, Phil. Trans. Roy. Soc. Lond., **A323**, 87-99, 1987.

187. H. E. Gore, *Tandem accelerator mass spectrometry measurements of ^{36}Cl, ^{129}I and osmium isotopes in diverse natural samples*, Phil. Trans. Roy. Soc. Lond., **A323**, 103-119, 1987.

188. L. K. Fifield, D. Fink, S. Sie and C. Tuniz (eds), *Proceedings of 6th International conference on accelerator mass spectrometry*, Canberra, Sydney, 28 September-1 October, 1994, Nucl. Instr. Meth. in Phys. Res., in press.

189. K. W. Allen, *Accelerator mass spectrometry (AMS) of heavy elements*, Nucl. Instr. Meth. Phys. Res., **B35**, 273-283, 1988.

190. T. M. Beasley, D. Elmore, P. W. Kubik and P. Sharma, *Chlorine-36 releases from the Savannah River site nuclear fuel reprocessing facilities*, Ground Water, **30**, 539-543, 1992.

191. L.K. Fifield, A.P. Clacher, K. Morris, S.J. King, R.G. Cresswell, J.P. Day and F.R. Livens, *Accelerator mass spectrometry of the planetary elements*, Nucl. Instr. & Meth. in Phys. Res., **B123**, 400-404, 1997,

192. W. Compston, I. S. Williams and C. Meyer, *U-Pb geochronology of zircons from lunar Breccia 73217 using a sensitive high mass-resolution ion microprobe*, J. Geophys. Res., Supp. **89**, B525-534, 1984.

193. A. Zindler, J. L. Rubenstone, J. England, B. Bourdon, L. Reisberg, B. Hamelin, V. Salters, S. Weavers, W.-X. Li and F. Marcantonio, *SIMS measurements of $^{230}Th/^{232}Th$ ratios in rocks*, Abstracts, 7th International conference on geochronology, cosmochronology and isotope geology, Geol. Soc. Australia, **27**, 116, 1990.

194. A. G. Adriaens, J. D. Fassett, W. R. Kelly, D. S. Simons and F. C. Adams, *Determination of uranium and thorium concentrations in soils: comparison of isotope dilution-secondary ion mass spectrometry and isotope dilution-thermal ionisation mass spectrometry*, Anal. Chem., **64**, 2945-2950, 1992.

195. M. Towrie, S. L. T. Drysdale, R. Jennings, A. P. Land, K. W. D. Ledingham, P. T. McCombes, R. P. Singhal and M. H. C. Smyth, *Trace analysis using a commercial resonant ionisation mass spectrometer*, Int. J. Mass Spectrom. Ion Process., **96**, 309-320, 1990.

196. J. D. Fassett and J. C. Travis, *Analytical applications of resonance ionisation mass spectrometry*, Spectrochim. Acta, **43B**, 1409-1422, 1988.

197. N. Trautmann, *Ultratrace analysis of technetium*, Radiochim. Acta, **63**, 37-43, 1993.

198. D. L. Donohue and J. P. Young, *Detection of plutonium by resonance ionisation mass spectrometry*, Anal. Chem., **55**, 378, 1983.

199. D. L. Donohue, D. H. Smith, J. P. Young, H. S. McKown and C. A. Pritchard, *Isotopic analysis of uranium and plutonium mixtures by resonance ionisation mass spectrometry*, Anal. Chem., **56**, 379, 1984.

200. Z.B. Alfassi, Ed., Activation Analysis, Boca Raton, CRC Press, 1989.

201. S. Amiel, Ed., Nondestructive Activation Analysis, Amsterdam, Elsevier, 1981.

202. H.A. Das, A. Faanhof and H.A. van der Sloot, Environmental Radioanalysis, Elsevier, Amsterdam, 1989.

203. H.A. Das, A. Faanhof and H.A. van der Sloot, *Radioanalysis in Geochemistry* Amsterdam, Elsevier, 1989.

204. W.D. Ehmann and D.E. Vance, *Radiochemistry and Nuclear Methods of Analysis,* John Wiley, New York, 1991.

205. K. Heydorn, *Neutron Activation Analysis for Clinical Trace Elements Research,* Vols I and II, Boca Raton, CRC Press, 1984.

206. S.J. Parry, Activation Spectrometry in Chemical Analysis, John Wiley, New York, 1991.

207. Guide to the expression of uncertainty in measurement, ISO, Geneva, Switzerland 1993. (IBSN 92-67-10188-9).

208. Quantifying uncertainty in analytical measurement, Eurachem, 1995.

209. The expression of uncertainty and confidence in measurement, M3003, United Kingdom Accreditation Service, 1997.

210. Guide to the expression of uncertainties in testing, NIS 80, United Kingdom Accreditation Service, 1994.

211. The expression of uncertainty in radiological measurements, B0825, United Kingdom Accreditation Service, 1990.

212. J. C. Miller and J.N. Miller, Statistics for analytical chemistry, 2nd edition, John Wiley & Sons, 1988.

213. H.R. Neave, Elementary statistics tables, Routledge, 1981.

214. R. D. Evans, The Atomic Nucleus, Krieger, New York, 1982.

215. J.C. Lochamy, *The minimum detectable activity concept,* NBS Special Publication 4566, 169, National Bureau of Standards, Gaithersberg, Maryland, 1976.

216. L.A. Currie, *Limits for qualitative detection and quantitative detection. Application to Radiochemistry,* Anal. Chem., **40(3)**, 586-593, 1968.

217. T. J. Summerling and S.C. Darby, *Statistical aspects of the interpretation of counting experiments designed to detect low levels of radioactivity,* National Radiological Protection Board Report, NRPB-R113, 1981.

218. D.A. Chambers, S.S. Dubose and E.L. Sensitaffar, *Detection limits concepts: foundations myths and utilisation,* Health Physics, **63(3)**, 338-340, 1992.

219. L.A. Currie, Lower limits of detection: definition and elaboration of a proposed Standards, NURCG/CR-407, 1984.

220. V. T. Bowen and H. L. Volchok, *Spiked sample standards: their uses and disadvantages in analytical quality control,* Environm. Int., **3**, 365-376, 1980.

221. C. W. Sill and S. David, *Solid standards for quality control in radiochemical analysis,* Radioact. Radiochem., **6**, 28-39, 1995.

222. L.H. Keith, W. Crummett W, J. Deegan, Jr., R.A. Libby, J.K. Taylor and G. Wentler, *Principles of Environmental Analysis*, Anal. Chem., **55**, 2210-2218, 1983.

223. L.H. Keith, Dynamics, Exposure and Hazard Assessment of Toxic Chemicals, Ed., R. Haque, Ann Arbor Science Publishers, pp 41-45, 1980.

224. State of the Art Review of Radioactivity Monitoring Programmes in the United Kingdom, Department of the Environment, Central Directorate on Environmental Pollution, Pollution Report No.17, 1983.

225. The Assurance of Quality in Environmental Radionuclide Analysis, A Report by the Quality Assurance Sub-Group to the Radioactivity Research and Environmental Monitoring Committee, HMSO Publication, 1989. ISBN 0 11 752242 2.

226. R.J. Mesley, W.D. Pocklington and R.F. Walker. *Analytical Quality Assurance: a review*, Analyst, **116**, 975-990, 1991.

227. D. Wood and M. Jessep, *Analytical Quality at the Environment Agency*, VAM Bulletin, Issue 15, pp21-22, 1996.

228. B. King, *Never Mind the Quality - Look at the Paperwork*, VAM Bulletin, Issue 10, pp3-4, 1993.

229. S.F. Platt, *Establishing One Quality Assurance System to Meet the Requirements of ISO 9001, NAMAS and GLP*, VAM Bulletin, Issue 9, pp7-10, 1993.

230. General Criteria of Competence for Calibration and Testing Laboratories, NAMAS Accreditation Standard M10, UKAS, 1989.

231. Regulations to be met by Calibration and Testing Laboratories, NAMAS Regulations, M11, UKAS, 1989.

232. NAMAS, The Quality Manual, Guidance for Preparation, M16, UKAS, 1992.

233. Accreditation for Chemical Laboratories, Eurachem GD No. 1, Edition 1, NIS 45, UKAS, 1993.

234. The Expression of Uncertainty in Radiological Measurements, NIS 0825, UKAS, 1990.

235. Quality Management and Quality System Elements, Part 1, Guidelines, BS EN ISO 9004-1, 1994.

236. Quality Management and Quality Assurance Standards-Part 1, Guidelines for selection and use, EN ISO 9000-1, 1994.

237. The Statutory Instruments 1997, No.654, Health and Safety Executive, The Good Laboratory Practice Regulations, 1997.

238. Good Laboratory Practice and the Role of Quality Assurance, Advisory Leaflet Number 3, Department of Health, London, 1991.

239. HSE Statement on the Approval of Dosimetry Services, Health and Safety Executive, Bootle, Merseyside, UK.

CHAPTER 4   PRODUCTION OF RADIONUCLIDES

GEOFF LONGWORTH AND MARTIN FINLAN

4.1   INTRODUCTION

Artificially produced radionuclides have many and varied applications in which they are used as sources of either alpha or beta particles, gamma radiation or neutrons (see Chapter 5). Production of such radionuclides has been either from the bombardment of suitable targets with neutrons or charged particles or by extraction from fission products. The starting points for this field were the construction of the first cyclotron by Lawrence and Livingstone in 1932 and the operation of the first experimental nuclear reactor by Fermi in 1942. Nuclear reactors in particular are still widely used to provide radionuclides for nuclear medicine [1,2].

In the UK in the 1940's, the Isotope Division at the Atomic Energy Research Establishment at Harwell and the Radiochemical Centre at Amersham were set up to produce radionuclides for use in industry and medicine. Production of radionuclides by what is now Nycomed Amersham plc has grown from about 170 radionuclides and 1000 labelled compounds in 1966 [3] to some 12000 radionuclide-based products in 1996 [4]. The 1990s have been heralded as the decade of molecular nuclear medicine [5] aided by developments in molecular radiopharmaceuticals labelled with short-lived cyclotron-produced radionuclides [6].

In this chapter the main production routes will be briefly discussed together with the precautions necessary because of safety and purity considerations. An overview of the synthesis of radiolabelled compounds is also included. For a fuller treatment the reader is directed to the proceedings of the International Symposia on the Synthesis and Applications of Isotopes and Isotopically Labelled Compounds, see, for example, [7].

4.2   PRODUCTION ROUTES

In this section the main production routes are discussed including the use of neutron, proton and charged particle-induced reactions and of naturally occurring radionuclides and fission products.

In the main, radionuclides are produced by the interaction of a target nucleus with neutrons or charged particles such as protons, deuterons, alphas or ^{3}He. The most commonly used particles for the production of longer lived nuclides are however neutrons and protons because of the larger cross-sections. These and other charged particles are also used for the production of radionuclides with shorter half-lives, often local to their use.

4.2.1 Radionuclides produced by neutron bombardment

Neutron irradiations are generally performed in nuclear reactors and involve the immersion of the primary nuclide in the thermal neutron or fast neutron fluxes. The most common reaction is neutron capture in which a neutron is captured by the nucleus followed by the emission of gamma radiation, represented by A(n,γ)B where A and B represent the target and product radionuclides respectively. Useful neutron fluxes in reactors range from 10^{14} – 10^{15} n.cm^{-2}.s^{-1} which, in conjunction with the associated gamma fluxes, produce heat in the targets in the range of 0.4 to 40 watts g^{-1}. This heat is produced throughout the volume of the target and associated containers and has to be dissipated at a temperature which maintains the target and container integrity. This is the main problem associated with this type of radionuclide production. Double encapsulation is employed for safety reasons and helium gas is introduced to transfer the heat to an outer envelope which is often water cooled aluminium.

Another problem results from the high activity of the product, for example, ^{60}Co, but more often from the incidental production of (usually) short lived radionuclides. The latter problem can sometimes be resolved by a cooling off period, if feasible, otherwise thick lead, steel or concrete is used to shield the source while it is transported from the reactor to the processing facilities. If the transport is over relatively short distances, so-called 'rabbits' are used, using a remotely controlled conveyor belt or pneumatic tube device to remove the target from the reactor to the processing station.

Proton energies at 600 MeV or more have been used in **spallation** reactions where the target, usually a heavy element such as lead or rubidium, takes in the proton and emits a large number of products including protons and neutrons as well as radionuclides in the mass range of A $\cong$ 20-200 via reactions such A(p,pxn)B where x may be up to 5-6. **Spallation** proton sources have been used which produce fast neutron fluxes in excess of 10^{14} n.cm^{-2}.s^{-1}, for example, at the Los Alamos Meson Physics facility (LAMPF) [8,9], at the 500 MeV proton accelerator ISIS at the Rutherford Appleton Laboratory near Harwell, UK, and at the PSI 590MeV accelerator at Zurich, Switzerland. These have been used to produce radionuclides for medical research such as ^{77}Br, ^{82}Sr, ^{75}Se, ^{67}Ga, ^{62}Zn and ^{67}Cu [8,9].

Most of the radionuclides mentioned in this chapter have half-lives long enough for world wide distribution from major producers such as Nycomed Amersham plc. Radionuclides with much shorter half-lives can be distributed using the **radioisotope generator** concept to provide sources of, for example, ^{99m}Tc or ^{188}Re activity at appropriate times at the customer's premises (see Section 4.2.1.3).

4.2.1.1 Yields and specific activities

It is clearly important to be able to calculate the yield of a given reaction or the specific radioactivity of the product radionuclide either in a real situation or in a feasibility study. This requires knowledge of the reaction cross-section both for neutron irradiation of the target and of the product radionuclides. The activity is given by [3]:

$$\text{Activity} = \frac{n_0 \sigma_1 \phi \lambda_1}{\lambda_1 + \sigma_2 \phi - \sigma_1 \phi} \left(e^{-\sigma_1 \phi t} - e^{-(\lambda_1 + \sigma_2 \phi)t} \right)$$

where n_0 is the original number of target nuclides present, σ_1 and σ_2 are the cross-sections of the target and product nuclides, λ_1 is the decay constant of the target nuclide, ϕ is the neutron flux and t is the irradiation time.

For short irradiations at low fluxes, when only a few per cent of the target nuclides are transformed and the neutron cross-section for the product nuclide is small, this activity reduces to the simpler form:

$$\text{Activity} = \sigma \phi n_0 \left(1 - e^{-\lambda t} \right)$$

This is identical to equations 1.12 and 3.1 since $n_0 = N_0wq/A$ where N_0 is Avogadro's number (6.022×10^{23} g per g atom), w is the mass of the target element (g), A is the atomic mass of the target element and q is the isotopic abundance of the nuclide of interest in the target element.

The specific radioactivity in becquerels per gram of target nuclide (S) may be approximated to:

$$S \cong \frac{0.6\sigma\phi}{A}\left(1 - e^{-0.693t/t_{1/2}}\right)$$

where ϕ the effective neutron flux, is in neutrons cm^{-2} s^{-1}, σ the target activation cross-section, is in barns and $t_{1/2}$ is the half-life of the product radionuclide. For long irradiation times t, the specific radioactivity S will saturate at a value S_{sat}:

$$S_{sat} \cong \frac{0.6\sigma\phi}{A}$$

For an irradiation time equal to two half-lives $S/S_{sat} = 0.75$ and for three half-lives $S/S_{sat} = 0.87$. Thus, there is little to be gained from a longer irradiation. Use of the more exact equation does not result in a saturation value for the specific radioactivity. In such situations the specific radioactivity goes through a maximum value as a function of irradiation time.

4.2.1.2 (n,γ) reactions

Thermal neutron reactions generally have high neutron capture cross-sections, for example, the reaction ^{59}Co (n, γ)^{60}Co has a capture cross-section of 43 barns. ^{60}Co ($t_{1/2} = 5.272$y) is a widely used gamma source with applications in radiography (Section 5.2.3), sterilisation (Section 5.2.5), hydrology (Section 5.3.4) and in external beam therapy (Section 5.5.8.1).

Other examples are ^{23}Na(n,γ)^{24}Na with a cross-section of 0.53b [10] and ^{81}Br(n,γ)^{82}Br with a cross-section of 3.2b [10]. Both of these radionuclides are used in hydrological tracer studies (Section 5.3.4). Not all thermal neutron reactions have a high cross-section however. The cross-section for the reaction ^{88}Sr (n,γ)^{89}Sr is only ~6 mbarns. ^{89}Sr is mainly a beta emitter ($t_{1/2} = 50.52$d) and is extensively used to relieve the pain of metastased prostate cancer.

Fast neutron flux reaction cross-sections are usually small - of the order of millibarns, where a neutron enters the nucleus followed by emission of either a proton or an alpha particle. The cross-section for the ^{33}S(n,p)^{33}P reaction is somewhat higher at 76 mbarns where enriched ^{33}S is neutron irradiated to produce the soft beta emitter ^{33}P ($t_{1/2} = 25.4$d) which is a useful label for the auto-radiography of oligonucleotide electrophoretic gel analysis.

Another example of single neutron capture is in the production of ^{186}Re used to label a monoclonal antibody in **radioimmunotherapy** in order to deliver a therapeutic dose to a cancerous tumour (see Section 5.5.8.3 and [11]). It is produced by neutron capture on an isotopically enriched ^{185}Re target:

^{185}Re + n → ^{186}Re + γ   or ^{185}Re(n, γ)^{186}Re where ^{186}Re decays to ^{186}Os by β- decay (β_{max} = 1.075MeV) with a half-life of 3.78d.

Some reactions proceed in two stages, for example, ^{124}Xe (n, γ)^{125}Xe with a cross-section of 169 barns, which is followed by decay of the ^{125}Xe by beta emission with a half-life of 18 hours to give the desired ^{125}I product. This is used to treat prostate cancer via implantation as so-called seeds in brachytherapy (see Section 5.5.8.2).

The product of a single neutron capture process is a radionuclide of the same element as the target which therefore cannot be chemically separated from the target. This limits the specific radioactivity (Bq g^{-1}) obtainable, although it may not be serious if the activation cross-section is high. The recoiling nuclide may have sufficient energy in some compounds to be able to change its chemical state with respect to that of the target nuclide - the Szilard Chalmers reaction. This allows the production of high specific activities by allowing separation of the product nuclide but the quantities involved are sufficiently small for it to have been rarely used in production.

An approach which provides so-called 'carrier-free' radionuclides is to use an (n,γ) reaction to produce a radionuclide (parent) which then decays by beta decay to give a daughter radionuclide which can be chemically separated from its parent, such as ^{125}I as mentioned above. Another example is ^{111}Ag, a beta emitter, which may be attached to therapeutic agents. ^{111}Ag can be separated by anion exchange chromatography from its parent ^{111}Pd produced in the reactor:

$$^{110}\text{Pd(n,}\gamma)^{111}\text{Pd} \qquad ^{111}\text{Pd}(\beta\text{-})\rightarrow^{111}\text{Ag}$$

A further example is:

$$^{198}\text{Pt(n,}\gamma)^{199}\text{Pt} \qquad ^{199}\text{Pt}(\beta\text{-})\rightarrow^{199}\text{Au} \qquad t_{1/2} = 3.14\text{d}$$

where carrier-free ^{199}Au is produced for attachment to antibodies.

An example of a double neutron capture is the production of ^{188}W by irradiation of ^{186}W in which two neutrons are absorbed in succession to create the product. ^{188}W has a half-life of 69.4d and decays by β- emission to produce ^{188}Re which in turn decays by β- emission with a half-life of 16.98h. The ^{188}W $\rightarrow$ ^{188}Re combination is used as a radioisotope generator (see Sections 5.5.7.1 and 4.2.1.3) in nuclear medicine for tumour therapy using ^{188}Re labelled antibodies [12-14].

^{241}Am, the most commonly used alpha emitter in smoke detectors (see Section 5.2.4) is produced from the reactions ^{239}Pu(n, γ)^{240}Pu(n, γ)^{241}Pu. ^{241}Pu then decays by beta emission with a half-life of 14.4y to ^{241}Am.

4.2.1.3 Production of radioisotope generators

A radioisotope generator provides a means of obtaining short-lived radionuclides at places far away from nuclear reactors or cyclotrons. It consists of a longer-lived parent radionuclide which decays to a shorter-lived daughter, which can be removed ('milked') from the system for use as a tracer, for example, in a hospital. The parent radionuclide is usually carried on a column of ion exchange resin and the short lived daughter is eluted using a suitable solvent. After each elution the system is left for several daughter half-lives until its activity has reached near saturation, ready for the next elution. The first functioning ^{99m}Tc generators date from the 1950's [15,16].

The very important radionuclide, ^{99m}Tc, is used to label about 80% of radiopharmaceuticals used in clinics [17,18] and is usually provided in the form of a radioisotope generator (see also Section 5.5.7.1). ^{99m}Tc is formed from the beta decay of ^{99}Mo which may be produced by neutron irradiation of ^{98}Mo (Figure 4.1). The reaction cross-section is however low, 0.13 barn, so that the specific radioactivity obtainable is low [17].

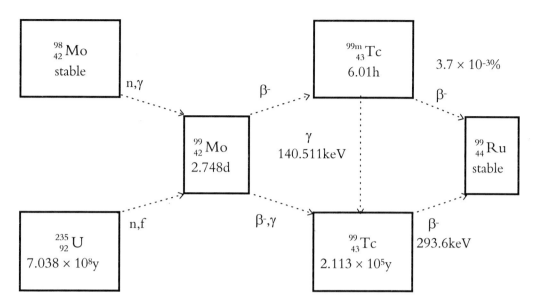

Figure 4.1:   Formation and decay of ^{99}Mo and ^{99m}Tc, after [17].

The preferred production route leading to higher specific activities is via fission of ^{235}U with thermal neutrons. However the process requires separation of ^{99}Mo from the other fission products. ^{99}Mo decays to an isomeric state of ^{99m}Tc by beta decay with a half-life of $t_{1/2}$ of 2.748d and a branching fraction of 87.2%. This state then decays to ^{99g}Tc with the emission of an 140.51keV gamma ray, with a half-life of 6.01h.

Once the unwanted fission products have been removed, ^{99m}Tc is separated from ^{99}Mo on an anion exchange column based on acidic aluminium oxide, the so-called generator column [17]. ^{99}Mo is held on the top of the column while ^{99m}Tc is eluted using a sodium chloride solution. After elution ^{99m}Tc is regenerated on the column by the decay of ^{99}Mo and after 24h its activity will reach 88.2% of that of ^{99}Mo and it may be eluted again. Figure 4.2 indicates how the process can be used to supply successive amounts of ^{99m}Tc activity [19].

Another generator is based on the ^{188}W/^{188}Re combination. Irradiation of ^{186}W leads to the formation of ^{188}W by double neutron capture, which β-decays to ^{188}Re with a half-life of 69.4d. ^{188}Re decays with a half-life of 16.98h by beta decay either to the ground state of ^{188}Os (branching fraction 80%) or to the first excited state of ^{188}Os with a branching fraction of 20% (Figure 4.3). This excited state then decays to the ground state with the emission of a gamma ray at 155.04keV. The relatively long half-life of the parent ^{188}W makes this a convenient source of ^{188}Re via an alumina-based anion generator with a long shelf-life [20].

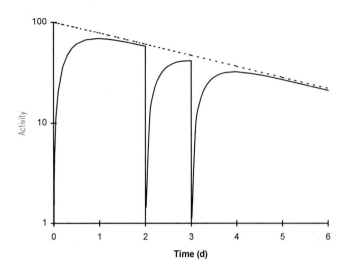

Figure 4.2: Production of ^{99m}Tc activity (in arbitrary units) as a function of time from a ^{99}Mo/^{99m}Tc generator with elutions at 2 and 3 days, after [17].

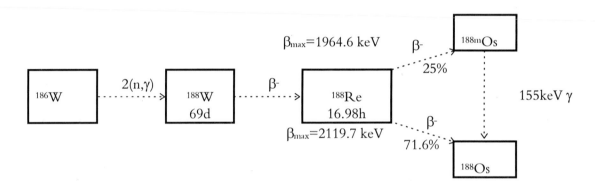

Figure 4.3: Formation and decay of ^{188}W and ^{188}Re.

4.2.2 Accelerator produced radionuclides

In general, neutron deficient radionuclides cannot be produced in nuclear reactors and use is made of charged particle reactions involving protons, deuterons or alpha particles, typically in a cyclotron. Historically, many radionuclides have been produced in particle accelerators whose main function is in physics research which determines the operational conditions. The growth of medical applications of radionuclides has led to the installation of purpose-built cyclotrons in several hospitals and in particular, there has been a significant increase in the use of small cyclotrons dedicated to the production of the required short-lived radionuclides.

A **cyclotron** may be used to accelerate ions to high energies (tens of MeV) by the repeated application of accelerating potentials. In its simplest form, the particles from an ion source move in circles in a constant magnetic field within two hollow metal 'dees'. These form part of a radiofrequency oscillator within a vacuum chamber, which itself is situated between the poles of an electromagnet. The condition for resonant acceleration is that the half-period of the applied radiofrequency field should be equal to the time needed for the ions to make half a revolution in the static magnetic field. The accelerated ions are then allowed to hit a prepared target to induce the required nuclear reaction.

122

Charged particle reactions usually produce a radionuclide which is chemically different from the parent and hence can lead to high specific activities. They do however have their own drawbacks. The reaction cross-sections are usually low, rarely exceeding one barn. The targets are normally thin layers of an expensive separated nuclide coated on a water cooled copper backing. The heat fluxes can exceed 12 kW.cm^{-2} for beam fluxes of 10^{16} p.cm^{-2}.s^{-1}.

The most commonly used reactions are (p,n) reactions with cross-sections in the range 3-400 mbarn for proton energies of about 20 MeV, for example, ^{109}Ag(p,n)^{109}Cd, used to provide a soft X-ray source.

^{56}Co which is used, for example, in the measurement of wear in steel components using **Thin Layer Activation** (see Section 5.3.3) is produced using the reaction ^{56}Fe(p,n) ^{56}Co using protons with energies above about 6 MeV.

The cross-sections for proton reactions on isotopically enriched targets are sufficiently high for the realistic production of short-lived radionuclides for **Positron Emission Tomography (PET)** (see also Section 5.5.7). These include, for example, ^{15}O (t$_{1/2}$ = 2.037m) and ^{18}F (t$_{1/2}$ = 1.828h). Here the requirement is for rapid transport and chemistry for labelling. Current levels of about 50 μa are acceptable. Examples of the reactions used are ^{14}N(p,α)^{11}C, ^{16}O(p,α)^{13}N, ^{13}C(p,n)^{13}N, ^{15}N(p,n)^{15}O, ^{14}N(d,n)^{15}O and ^{18}O(p,n)^{18}F [21,22]. A high yield of, for example, ^{18}F relies on careful design of the ^{18}O target [23].

The choice of cyclotron used will depend upon the range of radionuclides to be produced. Small proton-only cyclotrons designed to produce 11 MeV protons at a high beam current of 50μa with small isotopically enriched targets, can be operated with modular shielding in the hospital environment to produce the short-lived radionuclides for PET [21]. Use of a variable energy proton (30MeV) and deuteron (15MeV) cyclotron is preferred for ^{201}Tl, ^{67}Ga, ^{111}In and ^{123}I as well as ^{124}I, ^{67}Cu and ^{203}Pb [24].

The use of an internal target in a cyclotron either for isotope production or as a neutron source has the limitation that maintenance can be severely hampered by contamination. Machines were developed to provide a sizeable external current at Hammersmith Hospital [25] and at Amersham International (now Nycomed Amersham plc). The Hammersmith cyclotron was designed to provide an external beam of about 200μA of 15MeV deuterons or 50μa of 30MeV alpha particles [25]. The Amersham machine produced an external beam of 200μa of 30 MeV protons. This was achieved by helium jet cooling of both the vacuum window and the irradiated target face, in conjunction with water cooling of the target backing. High currents are needed for the production of the approximately three day half-life diagnostic radionuclides such as ^{201}Tl, ^{67}Ga, ^{111}In, ^{67}Cu. They are also required in the production of radionuclides with shorter half-lives such as ^{123}I (t$_{1/2}$ = 13.2h), used now for brain imaging in the diagnosis of Parkinson's disease.

4.2.3 Naturally occurring and artificial radionuclides

A source of radionuclides used, for example, as alpha or gamma standards has been the natural decay series originating with ^{238}U, ^{235}U and ^{232}Th. In addition, the fission of either ^{235}U or ^{239}Pu in a nuclear power reactor provides a range of fission products (see Section 1.7.3). Clearly the task of separating individual fission products is complex but the principles of the separation process are similar to those used in the radiochemical separation of particular radionuclides prior to their measurement (see Chapter 3). Longer lived fission products such as ^{85}Kr, ^{90}Sr and ^{137}Cs, of interest in industrial applications (see Table 5.1), are produced in this way. Shorter lived fission products such as ^{89}Sr, ^{99}Mo, ^{132}I and ^{140}Ba may be produced from irradiation of uranium in a reactor.

4.3 PRODUCTION CONSIDERATIONS

In this section some of the steps involved in the production of radionuclides are discussed including the choice of target material and chemical processing as well as testing and measurement.

4.3.1 Choice of target

The choice of a particular reaction to produce a given radionuclide will be governed by the reaction cross-section, the specific radioactivity required, the cost and availability of separated radionuclides, the need for chemical processing after irradiation as well as by safety considerations [3]. Irradiation of the target involves the generation of heat so that the target needs to be cooled and the irradiation in a nuclear reactor must not produce corrosive substances and have such a high cross-section that the control of the reactor is affected. The target for neutron irradiation in a reactor is normally sealed in a quartz ampoule which is contained in an aluminium container or rabbit. The use of the inner container both prevents any interaction between the target and aluminium and, in the case of small powdered targets, serves as a safety precaution.

The target material either for neutron or charged particle bombardment should be as pure both chemically and isotopically as is practicable in order to minimise the production of unwanted radionuclides. The chemical form of the target material is important and the required target nuclide is usually in the form of the element, oxide or a simple chemical compound. Thus, in the production of ^{24}Na, the preferred target is sodium carbonate which does not give rise to undesirable radionuclides as is the case with sodium chloride through the reactions ^{35}Cl(n,γ)^{36}Cl, ^{35}Cl(n,p)^{35}S and ^{35}Cl(n,α)^{32}S [10]. In a neutron irradiation it is usually impossible to avoid the production of all unwanted radionuclides and following irradiation it is usual to allow any short-lived radioactivity in the target to decay, particularly that due to irradiation of the aluminium container.

4.3.2 Chemical processing

In some instances it is possible to irradiate a given target to produce the required radionuclide which can be used directly without the need for chemical processing, for example ^{192}Ir, used in radiography (see Section 5.2.3), which has a high activation cross-section ($\cong$ 400 barns). In the remainder of cases it is necessary to process the irradiated target in order to isolate the required radionuclide. The methods used follow the familiar lines of radionuclide separation based on a combination of filtration, distillation, adsorption/co-precipitation and exchange chromatography, albeit frequently on very small masses (See Chapter 3). A summary of such methods is given in [3].

4.3.3 Source containment

Sealed radionuclide sources may contain the radioactive material in many forms, examples being metal foil, powder, wire, gas, pellets, ceramic, glass, anodised plate and plastic. Design of a suitable sealed source is based on a number of factors such as those in the following list based on that given in [3].

1.   The source capsule must contain the radioactive material securely while allowing the radiation to escape through an appropriate window.

2. The radiation emitted must have the desired characteristics. Relevant factors include the self absorption of low energy gamma radiation leading to loss of intensity in the gamma ray peaks and the broadening and reduction in alpha particle peaks due to the source being too thick.

3. The chemical and physical form of the radioactive material should not disperse easily if the capsule is fractured.

4. The source capsule should be the correct shape for purpose and manufactured to close tolerances.

5. Each source should be marked where possible so that it is easily identifiable.

A more detailed discussion is given in [3] but additional requirements in designs today are:

The need to consider the waste or disposal implications

Transport and packaging requirements

Working life of the source.

As relevant today as in reference [3] written in 1966, is the need for 'an early and detailed consultation between user and manufacturer' in determining requirements.

4.3.4 Testing, measurement and Quality Control (QC)

A manufacturer of sealed radiation sources should design any source so that the chances of failure leading to contamination are small. Source designs are validated by prototype testing or assessment and typically the design's performance is considered under elevated temperature, pressure, impact, vibration and puncture. The International Organization for Standardization (ISO) has produced a system for the classification of sealed radioactive sources based on performance specifications and tests (ISO 2919-198(E)). Other tests may be carried out as appropriate. Individual sources are leak and contamination tested by a variety of means including wiping, immersion and helium leak testing (see ISO 9978-1992(E)). In addition, manufacturing and design organisations should have a formal Quality System in place such as ISO 9001 [26].

Measurement and calibration of sources is carried out using calibrated detectors such as ionisation chambers, high resolution gamma spectrometers, alpha spectrometers and liquid scintillation spectrometers (see Chapters 2 and 3).

The quality of a given source needs to be such that the user can be satisfied that it is fit for purpose. This could cover, for example, the purity and specific radioactivity of the source and the structural integrity of the source holder. Reference sources and standardised solutions should be fully traceable to standards held in National Laboratories such as the National Physical Laboratory (NPL), UK and the National Institute of Standards and Technology (NIST), U.S.A. An analytical laboratory attached to a radionuclide manufacturer should be accredited to national standards. Thus, BS EN ISO 9000 registration ensures that an analytical facility has the necessary systems and procedures in place in order to deliver assured contractual requirements to their customers. The United Kingdom Accreditation Service (UKAS) was established by the UK government through the Department of Trade and Industry (DTI) to ensure that analytical testing conforms to defined professional standards (see Section 3.13.3).

The International Atomic Energy Agency (IAEA) has established the basic criteria for the quality control of cyclotron-produced radiopharmaceuticals [27].

4.4 SYNTHESIS OF ISOTOPICALLY LABELLED COMPOUNDS

The use of labelled compounds has changed over the years and there is currently a far greater emphasis on applications closely involved with drug and medical research. The specific use to which the labelled compound is applied dictates the characteristics of the label; the radionuclide, the position within the molecule and the ratio of radioactivity to natural element (the specific radioactivity). Labelled compounds are used to trace the way in which the compound interacts within a particular environment. The radioactive label is an efficient means of detecting the compound, or products of subsequent reactions, through the course of an experiment or other investigation.

Many of the studies undertaken often involve complex biochemical reactions. Most of the compounds used in these studies are covalent organic molecules labelled with an appropriate radionuclide. As an organic molecule, the elements most likely to be available for radioactive labelling are carbon, hydrogen, oxygen, nitrogen, sulphur and phosphorus. ^{14}C, tritium (^{3}H), ^{32}S, ^{35}S, ^{32}P and ^{33}P are used extensively in the production of labelled organic molecules. Although iodine is rarely found naturally associated with organic compounds, it can be used to iodinate peptides and proteins via an amino acid adduct. ^{131}I has been used in the past but ^{125}I and ^{123}I are the preferred radionuclides because of their more convenient emissions.

Only a brief summary of the main synthetic routes is given. More detailed information is available in appropriate conference proceedings [7] and in the Journal of Labelled Compounds and Radiopharmaceuticals [28].

Radioactively-labelled compounds have been synthesised for particular applications. Thus, nucleotide triphosphates are available labelled with ^{32}P, ^{33}P, ^{14}C and tritium for DNA and RNA studies. Proteins and amino acids can be studied using amino acids labelled with ^{14}C, tritium and ^{35}S, and receptor ligands labelled with ^{125}I can be used to investigate cell membrane interactions. In 1991 it was stated that essentially any organic compound can be labelled with a radionuclide for radiotracer studies [29].

The fundamental questions [29] to be asked before the synthesis of a labelled compound are:

- which radionuclide should be employed?

- which position will the radionuclide occupy?

- what specific radioactivity is required?

and the choices made will be critical to the success of the work.

A labelled compound should be chemically and radioactively pure with the label in a stable position with the required specific radioactivity. High specific radioactivity has become increasingly important in biochemical and molecular biological techniques. It is essential that the labelled compound is biologically active. Many systems used in research may be inhibited by chemicals in the formulation or inactivated by the lack of stereo specificity in complex proteins. The quality of a synthesised compound must ensure its compatibility with the system in which it is to be used.

The main routes to labelled compounds are via chemical synthesis, biosynthesis and isotopic exchange reactions. Often a combination of two or more of the techniques is employed.

Classical organic synthesis is employed in the production of ^{14}C labelled compounds. The starting point for often complex organic molecules is a simple compound such as barium carbonate, carbon dioxide, methane, potassium cyanide or formic acid [29,30]. The synthesis is generally carried out on a small scale and special techniques have been developed to manipulate as little as milligram quantities of material. Where possible, purification of intermediate steps is used to ensure the best possible purity of final product. Otherwise, modern purification procedures such as High Performance Liquid Chromatography (HPLC) on increasingly more refined columns is used to produce pure final products. Similar conventional syntheses have been used for compounds labelled with ^{35}S and ^{32}P although in practice the difficult radiological problems of handling ^{32}P virtually exclude this type of synthesis.

Biochemical synthesis is used to produce ^{14}C in naturally occurring compounds by 'isotope farming' in which plants are grown in a 'greenhouse' within a $^{14}CO_2$ atmosphere. The plant tissue is extracted and the compounds separated and purified by chromatographic techniques. Yields and specific activities are very low. Higher specific activities may be obtained by growing algae or isolated plant leaves in almost 100% isotopically pure $^{14}CO_2$ [31]. The growth in Molecular Biology has led to the availability of enzymes that facilitate the specific transfer of chemical groups to defined positions on molecules. Enzyme conversions are used extensively in the production of nucleotides labelled with ^{32}P, ^{33}P and ^{35}S.

Generally, replacement of hydrogen by tritium in an organic molecule is easier than carbon substitution, but it can have its own drawbacks. Direct isotopic exchange has been used to freely label compounds with tritium using homogeneous or heterogeneous catalysts but at the same time it is more readily lost. The use of this technique is limited by the side reactions that may occur and the unpredictable nature of the labelling. More precise labelling can be achieved using traditional organic reactions such as substitution of halogens with tritium and the reduction of unsaturated bonds using tritium gas. In these instances the tritium is more firmly bound and not readily lost. The ability to use tritium NMR techniques to identify the position of labelling [32] and the use of more sophisticated purification methods has greatly improved the availability of pure defined compounds. Homogeneous catalysts such as rhodium or ruthenium have been used to achieve a greater predictability. Use of tritiated water as the tritium source [33] will give limited specific radioactivity but exchange systems using carrier free tritium gas are used to obtain the highest specific activities [34].

^{125}I is an important isotope for studies involving proteins and peptides. For many years ^{125}I has been the isotope of choice for radioimmunoassay. More recently its use in receptor assays has been more important. Most compounds for these applications, which include a growing list of human and animal growth factors, do not contain iodine naturally. Techniques have been developed whereby the iodine is incorporated into a tyrosine residue which is attached to the peptide/protein. The significant change in molecular weight and polarity allows separation of the iodinated material from the non-radioactive starting material thus achieving a compound at maximum specific radioactivity.

Stability of labelled compounds is important and decomposition may occur as a result of the formulation in which the compound is supplied, for example, hydrolysis. Decomposition may also occur by the effect of radiation emitted as a result of radioactive decay. This may take place either directly on the molecule or by a secondary interaction in which the primary radiation produces, for example, free radicals which then interact with the molecule of interest [35]. Decomposition of labelled compounds may be restricted by reducing the specific radioactivity or by low temperature storage [3]. Care must be taken with compounds labelled with tritium at high specific radioactivity and stored in aqueous solutions since these will show increased decomposition when frozen. Dissolution of the labelled compound in a suitable solvent such as toluene, ethanol or water may also inhibit radiation-induced decomposition as the solvent absorbs the radiation energy [29]. The effect of free radicals may be reduced by the addition of 'radical scavengers' such as ethanol, tertiary amines, pyridine or dicarboxylic acids [29].

ACKNOWLEDGEMENTS

The authors are grateful to several many members of staff at Nycomed Amersham plc (formerly Amersham International) including Gareth Beynon, Dave Hunt, Ed Lorch, Neil Rowley and Barry Senior for their comments, suggestions and contributions to this chapter in their fields of expertise. In addition they would like to thank Steve Waters, MRC Cyclotron Unit (Hammersmith Hospital) and Richard Yelland and Richard Garlick, Safeguard International for valuable comments and assistance.

REFERENCES

1. F.F. Knapp. Jr., S. Mirzadeh and A. L. Beets, *Reactor production and processing of therapeutic radioisotopes for applications in nuclear medicine*, J. Radioanal. and Nucl. Chem. Articles, **205(1)**, 93-100, 1996.

2. S. Mirzadeh, R.E. Schenter, A.P. Callahan and F.F. Knapp, Jr., Technical Memorandum 12010, Oak Ridge National Laboratory, 1992.

3. The Radiochemical Manual, Second Edition, Ed. B. J. Wilson, The Radiochemical Centre, Amersham, 1966.

4. B. L. Eyre, *Industrial uses of radiation*, in Becquerel's legacy: a century of radioactivity, Ed. M. C. O'Riordan, Radiation Protection dosimetry, **68**, Nos. 1/2 1996.

5. R.C. Reba, Ed. *Proceedings of a workshop on molecular nuclear medicine*, 23-24 January 1992, US Department of Energy, Washington DC, Conf-9201137, 1992.

6. G.Stocklin and V.W. Pike, Radiopharmaceuticals for positron emission tomography, methodological aspects, Developments in Nuclear Medicine, Volume 24, Ed. P. Cox Sr., Kluwer Academic Publ., Dordrecht, 1993.

7. Synthesis and applications of isotopically labelled compounds 1991, Proceedings of Fourth International Symposium, Toronto, Canada, September 1991, Eds. E. Buncel and G. W. Kabalka, Elsevier, 1992.

8. P.M. Grant, D.A. Miller, J.S. Gilmore and H O'Brien, *Medium-Energy Spallation Cross-Sections. 1. RbBr Irradiation with 800 MeV Protons*, Int. J. Appl. Radiat. Isot., **33**, 415-417, 1982.

9. K.E.Thomas, *Strontium-82 production at Los Alamos National Laboratory*, Int. J. Appl. Radiat. Isot., **38**, 175-180, 1987.

10. International Atomic Energy Agency, Vienna, Guidebook on radioisotope tracers in industry, IAEA, 1990.

11. H.R. Maxon, L.E. Schroder, V.S. Hertzberg, S.R. Thomas, E.E. Englaro, R. Samaratunga, H. Smith, J.S. Moulton, C.C. Williams, G.J. Ehrhardt, *Rhenium-186(Sn)HEDP for treatment of painful osseous metastases: results of a double-blind crossover comparison with placebo*, J. Nucl. Med., **32(10)**, 1877-1881, 1991.

12. G.L. Griffiths, D.M. Goldenberg, A.L. Jones and H.J. Hansen, *Radiolabelling of monoclonal antibodies and fragments with technetium and rhenium*, Bioconjugate Chem., **3**, 91-99, 1992.

13. J.-L. Vanderheyden, A.R. Fritzberg, J.N. Rao, S. Kasina, A. Srinivasan, J.M. Reno and A.C. Morgan Jr., *Rhenium labeling of antibodies for radioimmunotherapy*, J. Nucl. Med., **28**, 465, 1987.

14. G.L. Griffiths, F.F. Knapp Jr., A.P. Callahan, C.-H. Chang, H.J. Hansen and D.M. Goldenberg, *Direct labelling of monoclonal antibodies with generator-produced rhenium-188 or radioimmunotherapy*, Cancer Research, **51**, 4594-4602, 1991.

15. W.D. Tucker, M.W. Greene, A.J. Weiss, A.P. Murrenhoff, *Methods of preparation of some carrier-free radioisotopes, involving sorption on alumina*, (BNL 3746) Trans Am. Nucl. Soc., **1**, 160-161, 1958.

16. P. Richards, W.D. Tucker and S.C. Srivastava, *Technetium-99m: an historical perspective*, Int. J. Appl. Radiat. Isot., **33**, 793-799, 1982.

17. K. Schwochau, *Technetium radiopharmaceuticals-fundamentals, synthesis, structure and development*, Angew. Chem. Int. Ed. Engl., **33**, 2258-2267, 1994.

18. D. T. Drummond, J. P. Larabie and I. C. Trevena, *Production and supply of molybdenum-99 with reactors in North America and Europe current status and future prospects*, Synthesis and Applications of Isotopically Labelled Compounds 1994, John Wiley and Sons, 1995.

19. G. B. Saha, Fundamentals of Nuclear Pharmacy, 2nd. Edition, Springer, Berlin, 1984.

20. H. Kamioki, S. Mirzadeh, R. M. Lambrecht, R. Knapp, Jr. and K. Dadachova, *$^{188}W \rightarrow ^{188}Re$ generator for biomedical applications*, Radiochimica Acta, **65,** 39-46, 1994.

21. M. J. Adam and T. J. Ruth, *Production of radionuclides for clinical PET applications*, in Synthesis and applications of isotopically labelled compounds 1991, Proceedings of Fourth International Symposium, Toronto, Canada, September 1991, Eds. E. Buncel and G. W. Kabalka, pp 165-170, Elsevier, 1992.

22. S.M. Qaim, J.C. Clark, C. Crouzel, M. Guillaume, H.J. Helmeke, B. Nebeling, V.W. Pike and G. Stocklin, *PET Radionuclide production*, in Radiopharmaceuticals for positron emission tomography, methodological aspects, Developments in Nuclear Medicine, ed. G. Stocklin and V.W. Pike, Kluwer Academic Publ., Dordrecht, **24**, 1-43, 1993.

23. A.D. Roberts, L. C. Daniel and R. J. Nickles, *A high power target for the production of [^{18}F] fluoride*, Nucl. Instr. Meth., in Phys. Res., **B99,** 797-799, 1995.

24. R. M. Lambrecht, A. Katsifis, M. Kassiou and S. Smith, *Progress in radiopharmaceutical development in the Australasia region*, ANZ Nuclear Medicine, 22-25 March 1995.

25. J.W. Gallop, D.D. Vonberg, R.J. Post, W.B. Powell, J. Sharp and P.J. Waterton, *A cyclotron for medical research*, Proc. I.E.E., **104**, 452-466, 1957.

26. BS EN ISO 9001: 1994 Model for quality assurance in design, development, production, installation and servicing.

27. H. Vera-Ruiz, C.S. Marcus, V.W. Pike, H.H. Coenen, I.S. Fowler, G.I. Meyer, P.H. Cox, W. Varlburg, R. Cantineau, F. Helus and R.M. Lambrecht, *Report of an International Atomic Energy Agency's Advisory Group Meeting on Quality control of cyclotron-produced radiopharmaceuticals*, Nuc. Med. Biol., **17**, 445-456, 1990.

28. Journal of Labelled Compounds and Pharmaceuticals, John Wiley & Sons.

29. E. A. Evans, *Fifty years of radiochemical tracers*, in Synthesis and applications of isotopically labelled compounds 1991, Proceedings of Fourth International Symposium, Toronto, Canada, September 1991, Eds. E. Buncel and G. W. Kabalka, Elsevier, 1992.

30. R. R. Muccino, Organic Syntheses with Carbon-14, John Wiley & Sons, 1983.

31. J. R. Catch, Carbon-14 Compounds, Butterworths, London, 1966.

32. E. A. Evans, D. C. Warrell, J. A. Elvidge and J. R. Jones, Handbook of tritium NMR spectroscopy and applications, John Wiley & Sons, 1985.

33. D. Hesk, J. R. Jones and W. J. S. Lockley, *Regiospecific tritium labeling on aromatic acids, amines and heterocyclics using homogeneous rhodium trichloride and ruthenium acetylacetonate catalysts*, J. Lab. Comp. Radiopharm., **28**, 1427-1436, 1990.

34. J. R. Heys, *A new homogeneous catalytic approach for specific exchange of isotopic hydrogen gas with substrates in solution*, in Synthesis and applications of isotopically labelled compounds 1991, Proceedings of Fourth International Symposium. Toronto, Canada, September 1991, Eds. E. Buncel and G. W. Kabalka, Elsevier, 1992.

35. R. J. Bayley and H. Weigel, *Self-decomposition of compounds labelled with radioactive isotopes*, Nature, **188**, 384-387, 1960.

CHAPTER 5
INDUSTRIAL, ENVIRONMENTAL AND MEDICAL APPLICATIONS OF RADIONUCLIDES

GEOFF LONGWORTH AND JOE TOOLE

5.1 INTRODUCTION

The aims of this chapter are to discuss the main types of applications in industry, in environmental studies and in medicine and the life sciences and to provide some general guidance in the choice of radionuclide for a particular application. Although the bulk of the discussion will concern the use of artificial radionuclides some applications will be included in which natural radionuclides are used, for example, as natural analogues for those present in radioactive waste repositories, in environmental studies and in the coal industry. The enormous impact of the use of radionuclides in the life sciences and in medicine are discussed in Section 5.5.

Radionuclides are used in, for example, the chemical, paper, printing, petroleum, cement, metallurgical, electronics, automotive and mining industries as well as in medicine, environmental pollution studies, food technology, space technology and forensic investigations. These applications have led to greater industrial productivity, higher quality, improved health and safety and pollution control. In industrial applications, recent emphasis has been placed on safety applications, for example, such as the use of smoke detectors based on ^{241}Am, the use of static controllers to reduce the risk of fires, explosions and electric shocks, and the use of electron capture detectors to detect nerve gas. It is estimated that of the order of 10^8 smoke detectors incorporating small alpha sources have been sold with a consequent increase in domestic and industrial safety [1].

The number of nuclear control gauges used to measure density, thickness and moisture has grown from 125 in Australia in 1961 to over 12,000 in 1990, with an estimated increase in productivity of more than US$50 million per year [2]. About 40,000 medical procedures involving radionuclides are used each day in the United States [3] and there is an ever-growing market for biochemical applications, and radiolabelling of DNA and new pharmaceuticals. The International Atomic Energy Agency (IAEA) has played a major role in helping Member States to introduce radionuclide applications into their own industries through co-operative research and technical assistance programmes and has published guidebooks and technical reports covering the use of such nuclear techniques [4-6]. Short reviews of industrial applications are also available in the literature [1,7 and 8].

The radionuclides used in these applications are usually produced either in nuclear reactors or in particle accelerators. They may be either in the form of a sealed source in a suitable host material or as an unsealed source or radioactive tracer which is then used as a label to follow a given process under study. The principles behind the production of such sources are described in Chapter 4.

A discussion of the types of radiation detector used is given in Chapter 2 while radiological safety considerations are given in Chapter 6.

5.2   THE USE OF SEALED SOURCES IN INDUSTRY

The basic method behind all applications of sealed sources is to direct the radiation at the object to be measured or altered by the radiation. In the former case the radiation transmitted or scattered is measured in a detector and the data used to determine some property of the object.

The advantages of the use of sealed radionuclides are:

1.   they are non-invasive;

2.   they pose less of a radiological hazard than radiotracers;

3.   they may be used to examine materials or processes inside closed vessels;

4.   the use of differing radiations and differing energies provides a flexibility in solving diverse problems;

5.   due to the physical method, the measurement involves no mechanically moving parts, subject to wear;

6.   the measurement is independent of pressure and temperature;

7.   the instrumentation can be made very reliable and the life of the sealed source is usually determined by its design life and the radionuclide half-life.

Many of these advantages over conventional techniques are shared by radiotracers (see Section 5.3).

5.2.1 Process Control Instrumentation

Radionuclides are used in process control instrumentation, sometimes known as industrial radionuclide gauging, which forms the basis of a broad range of techniques including the measurement of thickness, weight, density, concentration, moisture content, level detection as well as measurements of flow, mixing efficiency and leak detection. These techniques are used in a wide range of industries including the production of paper, textiles, metals, plastics, chemicals and glass products and the coal and oil industries. In general, the instrumentation provides a rapid, on-line and non-destructive and sensitive measurement. Although this area represents a mature technology, there is a steady demand for process control instrumentation.

A large proportion of these applications concern measurements of thickness either of the product or of a coating layer on the product, using one of the following techniques, beta transmission or backscattering, gamma transmission or backscattering, XRF (**X-ray Fluorescence**) or neutron backscattering (Figure 5.1). The most popular techniques are beta transmission for thin samples and beta backscattering for measuring a sample from one side. In the transmission geometry, the radiation from the source is attenuated by the material and the resulting count rate measured on a radiation detector. Integration and amplification of the output is then used to produce a signal which may be used to control the production process and to alter the thickness to the required value, for example, the production of steel plate in a rolling mill. The availability of different types of radiation energies from about 10keV to 6MeV means that a variety of materials and thicknesses can be measured (Table 5.1) ranging from paper and plastic to steel sheets. Gamma ray transmission may be used to measure the mass flow on a moving belt with the advantage over conventional weighing systems that there are no mechanical parts, subject to wear and tear.

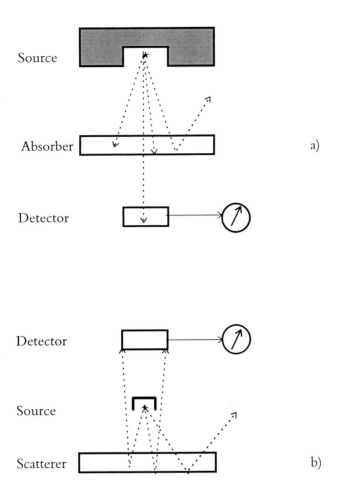

Figure 5.1:   **Schematics of thickness measurements using a. transmission geometry and b. backscattering geometry.**

Beta sources

Transmission
Materials: Paper, textiles, plastics, rubber and thin metal sheet
Thickness: 1-1000mg.cm^{-2}

Backscattering
Materials   Paper, coatings on substrates of different density/atomic number
Thickness   <100μm

Radionuclide	^{63}Ni	^{14}C	^{147}Pm	^{85}Kr	^{204}Tl	^{90}Sr/Y	^{106}Ru/Rh
Energy (keV) (β_{max})	65.9	156.5	224.1	687.4	763.4	2279.2	3541
Half-life (y)	99	5730	2.62	10.73	3.79	28.64	1.01

Gamma sources

Transmission
Materials: metal sheet, plastics, glass and rubber
Thickness: <100 mm steel

Backscattering
Materials   light alloys, plastics, glass and rubber, ash in coal
Thickness $\cong$ 1-30 mm plastic or glass

Radionuclide	^{238}Pu	^{109}Cd	^{241}Am	^{137}Cs	^{60}Co
Energy (keV)	12-17	22.16	59.54	661.66	1173.24, 1332.50
Half-life (y)	87.7	1.27	432.7	30.17	5.27

The basic equation governing the use of gamma transmission (and beta transmission) techniques is the following:

$$I = I_0 \exp(-\mu\rho t)$$

where a narrow beam of intensity I_0 is incident on a material of thickness t and density ρ and μ is the mass absorption coefficient (see also equation 2.2). For a given gamma ray energy, μ is constant and for energies between about 300 keV and 3 MeV, where Compton scattering predominates (see Section 2.1.4), the influence of chemical composition of the absorber is generally negligible.

Such a narrow geometry is usually not achieved in practice and for a diverging geometry the effect of scattering in the absorber may be approximated by the use of an effective mass absorption coefficient μ_{eff} such that the transmitted intensity I is given by:

$$I = I_0 \exp\left(-\mu_{eff}\rho t\right)$$

and μ_{eff} is measured by calibration. Clearly the method may be used either to determine density for a constant thickness or thickness for a constant density. In addition relative changes in either or both quantities can be measured.

Gamma-ray transmission techniques are employed for density gauging of slurries in coal cleaning operations. Conveyor-mounted dual energy gamma-ray transmission systems are used for on-line measurements of the ash content of coal [9]. This is a sophisticated technique which relies on the different interaction processes at two gamma energies and the difference in elemental composition between coal and ash.

A novel use of gamma transmission techniques in the coal industry is the use of the natural gamma activity in the strata overlying coal seams to determine the thickness of a coal seam. Extensive use is made of the differing concentrations of the naturally occurring radionuclides ^{238}U (+ daughters), ^{232}Th (+ daughters) and ^{40}K in the coal and in the adjoining sedimentary shale strata [10]. Typically the activity in the sedimentary shales is an order of magnitude greater than in the coal itself. Thus the overlying strata is treated as a gamma source and the roof coal as a gamma absorber whose thickness can be measured. The technique is used to delineate coal seams during borehole logging operations, as well as steering coal cutters by measuring the gamma flux penetrating the coal roof during the actual mining operation.

The use of gamma transmission to study the contents of vessels is limited to vessels which are small enough to allow a source of acceptable strength to be used. This limitation is overcome with the use of either gamma backscattering or neutron backscattering. The backscattered intensity is a complex function of the sample thickness and density as well as the counting geometry.

Neutron backscattering techniques are used to measure the amount of moisture during on-line processing of bulk materials, such as coke, sand, concrete or wood chips [11]. Neutron measurement techniques are used for moisture content determination (thermal neutron flux distribution) and for neutron capture prompt gamma activation analysis of coal - this again leads principally to a determination of ash content, but also enables pollutants such as sulphur (with relevance to acid rain) to be quantified [12].

5.2.2 Nuclear Borehole logging

Borehole logging involves the recording of both geophysical and geochemical information as a function of depth in a borehole. To do this, a probe carrying the appropriate measuring equipment is lowered into the borehole. The measured parameters include electrical conductivity, acoustic properties, temperature and radioactivity. The term nuclear borehole logging has been used to refer to applications involving measurements of radioactivity.

Borehole logging provides an alternative to an analysis of core material extracted from the borehole with the advantages of [13]:

- the volume sampled is undisturbed and is typically an order of magnitude greater than that available from cores;

- the reduction in the need for expensive drilling of many boreholes;

- provision of information in the case of poor core recovery;

- provision of data from holes drilled for other purposes;

- avoidance of delays due to sampling and laboratory analysis and

- continuous logging enabling efficient re-sampling.

The properties of rock formations below the surface such as the density or average atomic number can be measured using gamma ray backscattering. Pore sizes in rock formations can be assessed using neutron scattering. Analysis of the interactions between gamma rays and neutrons and rock can lead to a rapid elemental analysis of the rock. Measurements may be made of either the radiation produced following irradiation of the rock with either gamma rays or neutrons (active system) (Figure 5.2) or of the natural radioactivity of the rock (passive system).

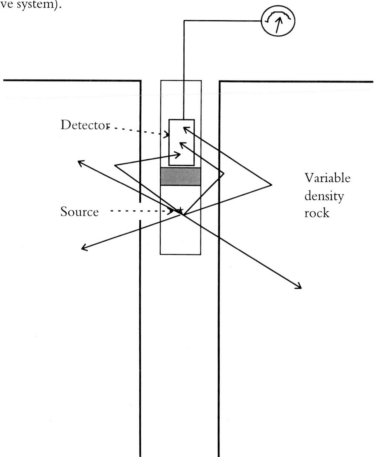

Figure 5.2:   **Schematic diagram of nuclear borehole probe.**

In an active system, the exciting radiation is usually either high energy gamma rays (γ-γ logging) or fast neutrons (neutron-γ or neutron-neutron logging). In γ-γ logging the principal interaction between the high energy gamma radiation (between 0.3 and 3.0 MeV) from the source and the surrounding rock or coal is by Compton scattering (see Chapter 2), which is essentially independent of chemical composition. A gamma ray detector will respond to the electron density of the surrounding medium n_e, where

$$n_e = \rho \cdot N_0 \cdot \sum_i p_i \cdot \left(Z_i / A_i \right)$$

and ρ is the medium bulk density, N_0 is Avogadro's number (6.022×10^{23} atoms per gram atom) and Z_i, A_i and p_i are the atomic number, atomic weight and weight content of element i in the medium. The values of Z_i/A_i for silicon, calcium, magnesium, aluminium and oxygen are approximately 0.5 [12], so that for these elements $n_e \propto \rho$. Thus the probe can be used to detect the interface between, for example, coal and sandstone, due to their differing densities.

Fast neutrons from a source within the probe will rapidly lose energy in collisions mainly with hydrogen and other light atoms and their energies will be reduced to **epithermal** energies (0.5eV–1keV) and then thermal energies ($\cong 0.025$eV). Such **thermal neutrons** may be detected in a BF$_3$ detector whose response will be a measure of the moisture content of soil or of the volume hydrogen content of reservoir rocks. Typical sources are the spontaneous fission radionuclide ^{252}Cf or the composite α-n source ^{241}Am/Be with outputs of typically 10^6 neutrons/sec.

Prompt gamma rays following thermal neutron capture and from fast neutron interactions have energies above 2MeV. It has been demonstrated that virtually all the elements in coal may be detected in a gamma ray spectrum [12]. Such an elemental analysis gives an early and rapid indication of the value of a coal deposit in the exploration stage.

In the passive system, natural radiation from either natural series decay radionuclides (see Chapter 1) or ^{40}K are detected either in a total gamma measurement (γ logging) or by measurement of individual gamma rays (γ spectral logging). These techniques are of wide interest in uranium exploration as well as in coal and oil exploration.

5.2.3 Radiography

The use of X-rays in **radiography** for medical diagnosis is well known. A later application was their use in industry as a non-destructive tool to examine welds and to search for flaws in engineered structures such as aeroplanes, ships, pressure vessels and bridges. Field portable X-ray equipment is available with either panoramic or directional tubeheads with focal spots down to a few mm at voltages up to 300kV.

The use of projected images combined with image processing has led to sharper images with enhanced signal-to noise ratios and to the availability of cross-sectional views of objects using computer tomography.

The use of gamma radiography with sealed sources has the advantages of greater portability and in applications where access is restricted, but the disadvantage that the range of energies available is more limited. The main radionuclides used are ^{60}Co (1173keV and 1333 keV) and ^{192}Ir (316.5keV and 468 keV) for which the optimum thicknesses of steel sections are approximately 50–150mm and 12–62mm respectively [1].

Neutron radiography using neutrons from a reactor, a **spallation** source (see Section 4.2.1) or from a neutron source such as ^{252}Cf may be used for specialist applications [14]. Although most metals are transparent to neutrons, thermal neutrons can be absorbed in elements with high neutron cross-sections and may be used in neutron resonance radiography to locate such elements.

5.2.4 Alarms

Instrumentation based on a radioactive source/detector combination has been used to operate an alarm when, for example, the level of liquid in a vessel exceeded preset limits. In one geometry the radioactive source and detector are placed on opposite sides of a vessel containing a given material. Radiation from the source is attenuated by the material and the resulting count-rate in the detector depends upon the presence or absence of the material. The measured count-rate may be converted to an electrical signal to sound an alarm, for example, when the vessel is either full or empty.

By far the most common application in alarm sensing is the smoke detector based on the ionisation produced in a small air chamber due to alpha particles emitted by an ^{241}Am source. Under normal conditions ionised air molecules flow freely to a detector electrode to form a small ionisation current. When smoke particles enter the chamber the ionisation current is reduced which operates an alarm at a predetermined level. Such ionisation devices are particularly sensitive to the early stages of a fire. The particle range detected is about 10^{-4} - 10 μm which extends considerably below the lower limit for light scattering devices of 0.3 μm.

Detection of hazards such as explosives, poisons and chemical agents is possible with the use of electron capture detectors. Such detectors employ a radioactive source, such as ^{63}Ni, ^{55}Fe or tritium to provide a source of electrons leading to a steady leakage current. They rely on the compound to be detected having an appreciable electron affinity. When the compound absorbs electrons, the subsequent change in electric current is detected.

5.2.5 Radiation processing

There are many applications of radiation processing covering sterilisation of medical equipment, food irradiation, radiation cross-linking of insulation wire, production of high-temperature resistant SiC fibre, curing of surface coatings, cleaning of flue gases and waste water sterilisation [1,2].

Commercial production of cross-linked polyethylene for insulation of wire and cable using radiation processing has been in operation since the 1950s. Examples of materials produced using radiation processing include cured surface coatings, automobile tyres, contact lenses and disposable nappies [2]. Advantages are achieved in terms of economies in production and a wide range of processing temperatures and environmental protection. For example, the use of electron beams or ultraviolet light to produce cured surface coatings has eliminated the need for organic solvents which were evaporated in thermal curing to produce polymer films. This has resulted in the elimination of the environmental hazard caused by the emission of large quantities of organic solvents.

Radiation sterilisation of medical products is carried out using either ^{60}Co sources (source strengths of 4×10^{15}- 2×10^{17} Bq) or 5-10 MeV electrons. Most irradiation plants are capable of handling both food and medical products. There is an upper limit of 5MeV to the energy of radiation permitted in food irradiation in the United States due to the photoneutron threshold reactions in hydrogen, oxygen and carbon which produce appreciable activation of the food above this energy [1].

Pilot electron beam plants have been set up to remove flue gases (SO_2 and NO_x) from coal-burning power stations, municipal waste incinerators and traffic tunnels in order to reduce the risk of pollution of the environment by acid rain [2].

5.2.6 Static elimination

A major problem in many industries is the build up of electrostatic charges on insulating surfaces with the risk of discharge leading to electric shocks, fires or explosions. Examples are the use of flammable solvents with metallic inks in the printing industry and the use of plastic or injection moulding where the static build up on mouldings attracts dust particles leading to blemishes on the surface of the product.

The residual surface charge may be discharged with the use of a practically pure alpha emitting source such as [210]Po. Ionisation of the air molecules by the alpha particles takes place up to about 3cm from the source and the resulting positive and negative ions serve to neutralise the static surface charge by providing a discharge path to earth.

In addition to the safety aspects of this application, static eliminators are used to increase the quality of finished manufactured products, for example, in paper production and in any application which generates static electricity through moving webs or belts. Another important quality-related application is in automobile paint spraying.

5.2.7 Heat and light sources

Sealed sources may also be used to power heat and light sources. Applications of radionuclide power sources has concentrated on space technology and on the artificial heart programme. There are six such power systems on the Moon and two on Mars while the success of the Pioneer, Voyager and Galileo missions has relied on their use to supply electrical power and heat for the instruments and stabilising thrusters [3]. Thermal energy released in the decay of radionuclides such as [238]Pu and [90]Sr (see Chapter 8) is converted into electricity typically using thermoelectric conversion (the Seebeck effect). Radionuclide thermoelectric generators have been considered to represent the safest and economical approach to the supply of power in remote regions when compared with, for example, propane fuelled thermoelectric generators, batteries, fuel cells and landlines [15]. Light sources consist of either phosphors activated by beta particles from, for example, ^{3}H, or they utilise the ionisation produced by beta particles from [85]Kr.

5.2.8 Analytical measurements

Measurements of radionuclide concentration are often used to infer elemental or chemical composition, for example, in the use of **Inductively Coupled Plasma–Mass Spectrometry** (ICP-MS), X-Ray Fluorescence (XRF), **neutron activation** and **Mössbauer** spectroscopies. These techniques are mentioned briefly here, a more detailed comparison of techniques for elemental analysis is given in [16] while the principles and applications of Mössbauer spectroscopy can be found, for example, in [17-22].

In ICP-MS the analyte solution is sprayed into the inductively coupled plasma where it is vaporised, atomised and ionised before being injected into a quadrupole mass spectrometer. Here all isotopes are separated and measured in terms of their mass/atomic number. This provides a rapid multi-isotope analysis. The disadvantages are the presence of isobaric overlap of signals from other isotopes and species and sensitivity of signal at higher matrix concentrations. It is restricted to the measurement of solutions with low salt concentrations.

XRF relies on the production and measurement of characteristic X-rays excited by a source of X-rays or gamma rays either from an X-ray tube or from a radionuclide source. Examples of such sources are [55]Fe (6keV), [109]Cd (22keV), [241]Am (60keV), [57]Co (122 and 136keV), where the excitation energies are given in parentheses. Choice of a particular source depends upon the elemental mass range of interest. XRF is again a technique for multi-element analysis which is well-suited to solid samples but suffers from self-absorption effects of the measured X-rays which gives rise to particle size effects and strong matrix effects.

The neutron activation technique [23-25] consists of the production of a convenient gamma-emitting radionuclide by neutron irradiation in a nuclear reactor and measurement of the gamma ray spectrum using a high resolution solid state detector (see Chapter 2). This technique is discussed in more detail in Chapter 3. It has a high potential sensitivity for about two thirds of all elements and a very large linear range. It is a non-destructive method of bulk analysis and has the advantage of being well suited to solids. There are few matrix effects and it can be applied to a variety of materials, including samples as diverse as soils, plastics, pharmaceuticals, crops, biological tissue, air particulates and coal. The main disadvantage is that the analyst must have access to a nuclear reactor and radionuclides with short half lives must be measured on site before they decay. Samples analysed for radionuclides with longer half lives may be taken back to the analyst's laboratory for radiochemical separations and/or counting but will benefit from a decay period of days or even weeks to reduce shorter-lived interferences.

Mössbauer spectroscopy may be used to determine the chemical composition of a solid sample which contains a Mössbauer nuclide such as ^{57}Fe [17,18]. A Mössbauer nuclide is one whose nuclear energy level scheme contains a first excited state which decays to the ground state by emission of a low energy gamma ray (10-50keV). If such a nuclide is incorporated into a suitable crystalline lattice then there is a finite probability that the gamma ray will be emitted with the full energy of the transition with no nuclear recoil effects (see Chapter 1 for related discussion of recoil following alpha emission). This gamma ray may be resonantly absorbed in a sample containing the same nuclide, for example, ^{57}Fe whose relative abundance is about 2%. Each chemical compound has a unique Mössbauer absorption spectrum due to the interactions of the nucleus with its surrounding electrons, which determine its chemical behaviour. Analysis of the spectrum may be used to identify and quantify, for example, all iron-containing compounds in a sample, as well as providing information about valence states and magnetic properties. The Mössbauer source, ^{57}Fe, is produced by the decay of ^{57}Co by electron capture. Mössbauer spectroscopy has the advantage of being very sensitive and non-destructive but it clearly limited to compounds containing a suitable Mössbauer nuclide, of which 5-10 are used regularly [18-22].

5.3 RADIOTRACER TECHNOLOGY

The advantages of radioactive tracers are [5]:

1. identity of chemical and physical properties of all isotopes of a given element;

2. radiation is specific to tracer and not affected by interference from other materials except background;

3. high sensitivity for low concentrations of radionuclide;

4. large number of radionuclides to fit most situations, with a wide range of energies and half-lives;

5. radioactivity is essentially independent of pressure, temperature, physical and chemical state and can be used under extreme conditions, for example, high pressure, high temperature and corrosive atmospheres;

142

6.   radiotracers do not affect the system and can be used in non-destructive techniques.

5.3.1 Selection of radiotracer

Radiotracers are used to follow the behaviour of a certain element, compound, chemical reaction or fluid flow etc. In some situations the radiotracer must be chemically identical with the traced material, for example, substitution of $^{14}CO_2$ for CO_2 or $(^3HH)_2O$ for H_2O. In other cases this condition need not be met provided the tracer obeys other necessary conditions, for example, ^{82}Br is used to measure flow in surface or groundwaters under the assumption that it behaves conservatively and does not interact with solid phases.

Since the activity of the radiotracer used is kept to a minimum for radiological safety reasons it is necessary to minimise unwanted losses of radiotracer from the system, for example, due to adsorption on vessel walls or precipitation from solution. Such losses result in smaller amounts of activity for detection with consequent increase in measuring uncertainty. These effects can be reduced by adding an inactive carrier in addition to the radiotracer, for example, stable ^{197}Au in addition to active ^{198}Au. In the case of a ^{82}Br tracer used to detect movement of surface or groundwaters, a carrier may not be needed due to the presence of sufficient chloride in the water. In this and related situations, allowance must be made for dilution of the tracer within the system so as to be able to measure the tracer activity or concentration to the required precision.

In general, the lower limit to the activity of radiotracer used is set by the measurement precision required and the upper limit by radiological safety considerations. Injection of the tracer into the system may be either in a single or a continuous process. Similarly, measurement of the tracer may either be on samples extracted at given times or be continuous and on-line. The detector used will vary depending on the radiation to be detected and on whether a simple count rate measurement is sufficient. In the latter case a scintillation probe (see Section 2.2.2) and ratemeter may be used for gamma radiation possibly coupled to a chart-recorder. The other extreme would be a multichannel system in which several energies are measured in order to extract the maximum amount of information from the system (see Section 2.2.5). The measured signal may be used to control the working of a process, for example, the efficiency in which two or more materials are mixed.

5.3.2 Use of radionuclides in the oil industry

Radiotracers such as ^3H, ^{82}Br and ^{131}I are used in oil field production to measure the flow profiles in injection and production wells and to optimise oil recovery. Production zones can be marked with radionuclides in order to locate them at some time in the future. The applications in the oil refining industry are similar to those in other industries which deal with measurements of flow rates, levels and densities in containers. Leak detection in buried pipelines is a standard technique using added tracers.

In order to increase the oil yield from a production well which may have decreased due to a decrease in hydrostatic pressure, fluids (such as water) or gas are injected into the field to force increased amounts of oil to the production well. It is clearly desirable to be able to trace the behaviour and extent of these floods. The extent of the flooded zone will depend on the importance of channelling which can reduce the overall extent. The reservoir behaviour will be determined by the number and arrangement of production wells. The effect of channelling can be reduced by injecting emulsion to block the channelling. Such studies may be complemented by laboratory studies on representative rock samples.

Radioactive tracers, such as tritium are more sensitive and cheaper to use than chemical tracers. The choice of tracer depends upon having a long enough half-life to match the timescale of the study, which is typically several months to years, as well as on the chemical form of the tracer [5]. Since clays usually carry a negative surface charge, the use of metallic cations, for example, cobalt or iron is inhibited by their strong adsorption on the clay. Few radioactive elemental anions are available, so it is necessary to use anionic complexes [5]. The uniqueness of gamma tracers has led to the use of dual tracers where the oil and aqueous phases are separately labelled. The oil phase is labelled with ferrocene, labelled with ^{59}Fe ($t_{1/2}$ = 44.50 days, E_γ= 1099.3keV), while the aqueous phase is labelled with potassium cobalt cyanide containing ^{58}Co ($t_{1/2}$ = 70.86 days, E_γ= 810.77keV) [26].

In one such water flood study, tritiated water containing about 2.2×10^{11}Bq of tritium was injected as a pulse into the injection well and water samples collected from two production wells about 400m away [5]. The tracer was detected in one of the production wells within a week and the peak concentration was reached after two weeks (Figure 5.3). The effectiveness of emulsion treatment was studied by injecting emulsion for several days followed by tritiated water (3.7×10^{11}Bq) and a ^{60}Co labelled cyanide complex (1.1×10^9Bq), followed by further water flooding. The ^{60}Co tracer was used to distinguish additional tritiated water from the first and second injections. The recovery curves for the tritiated water and ^{60}Co injections were very similar (Figure 5.3).

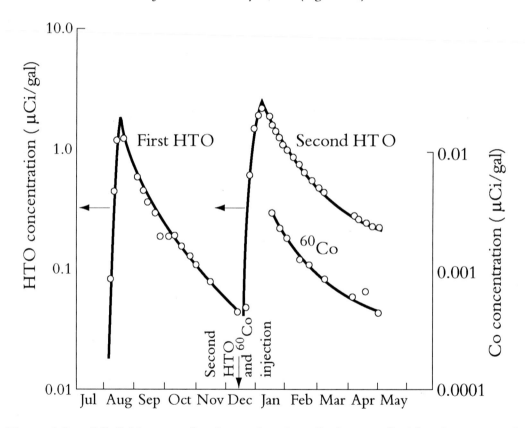

Figure 5.3: **Oil field water flood test showing discharge of tritiated water and ^{60}Co radiotracer from production well, after [5]. Adapted from Guidebook on radioactive tracers in industry, IAEA, by permission of the International Atomic Energy Agency, Vienna.**

Figure 5.4 illustrates the spread of tritiated water in a water flood tracer study of oil flow in an Oklahoma reservoir [27]. The initial flow was expected to be fracture flow in the fractured limestone which had a low porosity and permeability. The measurements suggested rapid water movement initially in a north east direction, as expected with indications of a second unexpected fracture orientation to the north west.

Flow Patterns

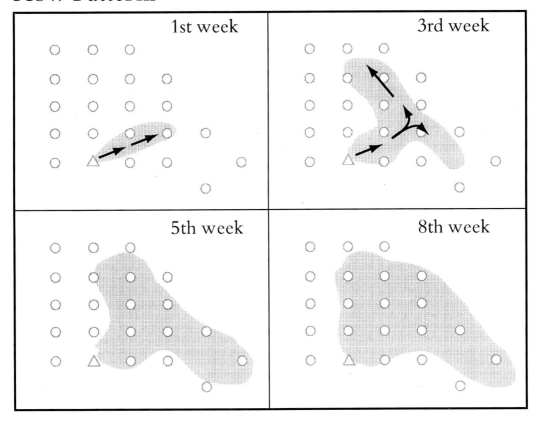

Figure 5.4: **Breakthrough of tritiated water in water flood tracer study of fracture orientation and rate of flow in Oklahoma oil field, after [27].**

5.3.3 Use of radionuclides in the automotive industry

An important example of radiotracers in the automotive industry is the use of **Thin Layer Activation** (TLA) [28,29] in which a beam of high energy ions from an accelerator is used to produce radionuclides in the near surface layers (to a depth of 10-100µm) of an object which is then subjected to wear. The removal of surface material during wear can be accurately measured by either measuring the change in radioactivity of the object or by measuring the radioactivity of the wear debris.

The advantages of this method are that it is non-intrusive and it is an on-line measurement so that wear measurements can be made on a system in a real situation. A high level of sensitivity in the wear measurement arises from the high sensitivity achievable in radioactivity measurements using gamma active radionuclides (see Table 5.2).

Table 5.2: Radionuclides generated from typical material elements in TLA using stated ion beams, after [29].

Element	Radionuclide(s)	Principal gamma ray energy (keV)	Half-life (days)	Ion beam
Iron	^{56}Co	846.75	77.26	protons
	^{57}Co	122.06	271.79	deuterons
Copper	^{65}Zn	1115.55	244.26	protons
Titanium	^{48}V	983.5	15.97	protons
Nickel	^{56}Co+^{58}Co	846.75 + 810.78	77.26+70.86	deuterons
Chromium	^{51}Cr	320.08	27.71	protons

Typical applications include measurements of wear in cutting tools and in automobile engine components (Figure 5.5). In the biomedical area, the wear rate of orthopaedic hip joint replacements has been improved in simulator tests [28].

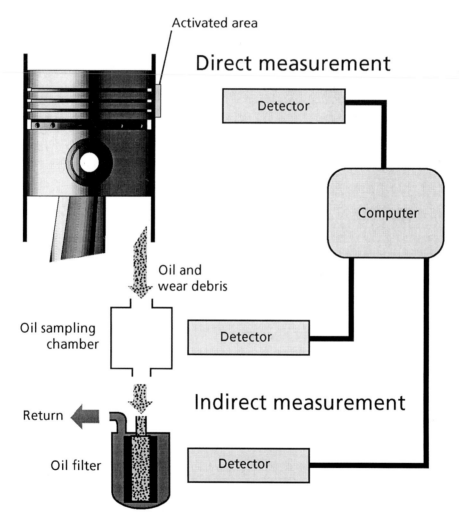

Figure 5.5: Measurement of wear using Thin Layer Activation (TLA) in automobile engines by direct measurement from loss of component activity and by indirect measurement of wear debris activity in the fluid environment.

In a somewhat different application of TLA, the corrosion-erosion rate at a given surface may be measured. A limitation here is the requirement that material must be removed from the surface for the measurement to be meaningful which need not be the case in static environments. In a fluid environment the amount removed from the surface will depend upon the flow rate so that care must be taken in the interpretation of the measured changes in activity. Measurements of corrosion-erosion have been made on the debris produced both in small-scale laboratory loops [30] and in water cooling plant and reactor boilers [29].

5.3.4 Use of radionuclides in hydrology

Radionuclides have been used in the study of the Earth's water cycle [31,32]. They may be injected into surface or groundwaters or used to label sediments and are used to measure some aspect of each medium, such as the flow rate, or sedimentation rate or permeability of the underlying rock. The tracer may be either an environmental radionuclide or an anthropogenic radionuclide such as ^{3}H and ^{85}Kr from nuclear weapons tests, or an artificial radionuclide. In the first and second cases the tracer is passive and forms part of the fluid under study while in the third case an artificial tracer is introduced in order to measure a given fluid property and its behaviour must be physically and chemically compatible with the fluid.

The main requirements of a radiotracer in hydrology are that it should not interact chemically or physically with the rock, it should have a convenient half-life and preferably should be able to be measured *in situ*. Tritium fulfils the first two of these criteria but not the third due to the relatively low β energy (β_{max} of 18.57keV) which requires a measurement in the laboratory. A list of radiotracers used in groundwater studies is given in Table 5.3.

Table 5.3: Common radiotracers used in hydrology studies, after [31].

Radionuclide	Half-life	Principal gamma energies (keV)	Chemical form
^{24}Na	14.965h	1368.63, 2754.03	$NaHCO_3$
^{82}Br	1.472d	554.35, 776.52, 1317.48	KBr, NH_4Br
^{198}Au	2.694d	411.80	$HAuCl_4$, $AuCl_3$
^{131}I	8.04d	364.48, 636.97	NaI, KI
^{51}Cr	27.71d	320.08	$CrCl_3$, EDTA
^{103}Ru	39.26d	497.08, 610.33	$RuCl_3$
^{58}Co	70.86d	810.78	$Co(CN)_6^{3-}$
^{46}Sc	83.79d	889.28, 1120.55	$ScCl_3$
^{153}Gd	240.5d	103.18	EDTA
^{57}Co	271.79d	122.06	$Co(CN)_6^{3-}$
^{134}Cs	2.0652y	604.71, 795.91	$CsCl$
^{60}Co	5.2718y	1173.24, 1332.50	$Co(CN)_6^{3-}$
^{3}H	12.33y	18.57(β_{max})	HTO

In this list, three of the most common radiotracers are ^{82}Br and ^{131}I used as bromide or iodide to measure water flows and flow rates and an anionic tracer such as ^{51}Cr EDTA which is used since it is less likely to be sorbed on to mineral surfaces than the cationic form.

Scandium-loaded glass beads can be matched in ranges of sizes to sediment particles and can be irradiated to produce a [46]Sc tracer, suitable for tracing the movements of sediments. Alternatively the sediment may be coated, for example, with [198]Au although the measured activity will be proportional to the total surface area of the particles rather than to their total mass. Radiotracers may be injected into a confined region of a borehole using an inflatable packer in order to measure either the flow up and down the borehole or out of the borehole. Measurement of the concentration as a function of time may be used to measure the properties of the surrounding matrix, such as the location of fractures in metamorphic rocks. Alternatively the tracer concentration may be measured in a second pumped borehole in order to measure the permeability of the matrix.

5.4 MEASUREMENTS USING COSMOGENIC AND PRIMORDIAL RADIONUCLIDES

5.4.1 Measurements using natural series radionuclides

A frequent situation occurs in the three natural decay series originating with [238]U, [232]Th and [235]U such that the half-life of a given daughter radionuclide is much less than that of its parent radionuclide, for example, [234]U and [238]U or [230]Th and [234]U. It was stated in Section 1.3 that after the parent radionuclide has decayed for several half-lives, the activities of the daughter and parent radionuclides become and remain equal, corresponding to secular equilibrium. The daughter/parent activity ratio therefore becomes one. This takes no account of the differing chemical properties of the daughter and parent radioelement. Since there are 10-11 elements involved in each decay series there is scope for large differences in their chemical properties. The daughter radionuclides produced, for example, by a uranium mineralisation will be transported by the groundwater to an extent depending on the radioelement solubility. Thus the original [238]U is much more soluble in oxidising groundwaters than [234]Th and [230]Th. Such behaviour may lead to a physical separation of parent and daughter and a state of disequilibrium, such that the daughter/parent activity ratio is no longer equal to one [33-36].

Disequilibrium may also occur between two isotopes of the same element, for example [238]U and [234]U due in this case to recoil of the intermediate nuclide [234]Th during α decay (see Section 1.4.1). This recoil may be sufficiently energetic for the recoiling nucleus in the near surface layers of a rock either to be transferred to the surrounding groundwater or to create sufficient radiation damage in the lattice that it may then be easily leached by the groundwater. [234]Th then decays to the very short-lived [234]Pa daughter ($t_{1/2} = 6.78$h) which decays to [234]U. This results in a small excess in the number of [234]U radionuclides over [238]U radionuclides in the groundwater and an [234]U/[238]U activity ratio which is greater than one. It is important to remember that only a small difference in the numbers of [238]U and [234]U radionuclides is needed to produce a relatively large difference in activities due to the widely differing decay constants (see Chapter 1).

Uranium series disequilibrium measurements of daughter/parent activity ratios in rocks and groundwaters may be used to study the long term migration of actinides through geological formations [33-36]. Such measurements are used to study rock/water interactions occurring over periods of time of up to several million years which are of interest in the underground disposal of radioactive waste [33,34,35,37,38]. The value of such a natural analogue approach is that processes may be studied over timescales and distances that are not attainable in the laboratory [34,37].

Apart from this application in radioactive waste disposal studies, uranium series studies are used in a wide range of environmental sciences including archaeology, volcanology, palaeoclimatology and exploration geology [33].

148

5.4.2 Age determination using radionuclides

The basis of such dating techniques consists in the measurement of either the ingrowth of a daughter radionuclide from zero activity or the decay of an **unsupported radionuclide**. The range of accessible dates covers about 5 half-lives of this radionuclide and covers tens of years for tritium ($t_{1/2}$ =12.33y), for example, in groundwaters, about a century for [210]Pb ($t_{1/2}$ =22.3 y), used in dating recent sediments [39], up to tens of thousands of years for [14]C ($t_{1/2}$ = 5730y) in organic material in archaeology and going back to the age of the earth ($\cong$5 × 10^9 y) in [40]K - [40]Ar, and [87]Rb - [87]Sr studies in rocks [40].

An example of nuclear dating in the natural decay series concerns the [230]Th/[234]U dating of carbonate minerals such as calcites ($CaCO_3$) either formed from groundwater in rock fractures or as speleothems in caves. It is assumed that uranium but not thorium is incorporated into the calcite at formation due to the very low solubility of thorium in these waters. Thus the original [230]Th concentration will be zero but will increase due to the decay of its parent [234]U at a rate given by the [230]Th half-life (7.54×10^4y).

In order to determine the age of a calcite it is necessary to measure the [230]Th/[234]U and [234]U/[238]U activity ratios and to use the following expression:

$$\frac{^{230}Th}{^{234}U} = \frac{^{238}U}{^{234}U}\left(1 - e^{-\lambda_0 t}\right) + \left(1 - \frac{^{238}U}{^{234}U}\right)\left(\frac{\lambda_0}{\lambda_0 - \lambda_4}\right)\left(1 - e^{-(\lambda_0 - \lambda_4)t}\right)$$

where t is the age and λ_0 and λ_4 are the decay constants for [230]Th and [234]U. The graphical solution to this equation is illustrated in Figure 5.6. Determination of an accurate age depends upon the absence of significant uranium-bearing impurities and on the assumption that the system has remained closed to any inward or outward radionuclide movement [33,41].

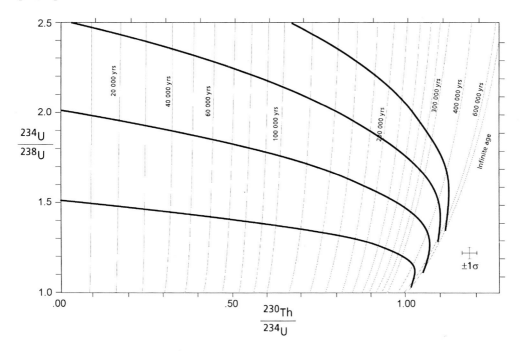

Figure 5.6: **Graphical solution to [230]Th-[234]U dating equation [41]. Reprinted from Nuclear Instruments and Methods in Physical Research, Volume 223, T.L. Ku and Z.C. Liang, pp423-432, Copyright (1992), with permission from Elsevier Science.**

The most well-known dating technique is that of **radiocarbon** [14]C dating [42,43] based on a measurement of residual [14]C. The dominant production route is via the [14]N(n,p)[14]C reaction in the atmosphere between cosmic ray-produced neutrons and [14]N. It is assumed that the production rate has been constant and that equilibrium exists such that the production and decay rates are balanced. The half-life of ^{14}C is sufficiently long (5730y) to allow equilibrium to be reached between ^{14}C in the various reservoirs such as the atmosphere, the oceans and the exchangeable carbon in natural materials [44] (see Figure 5.7). Metabolic processes within living organisms maintain an equilibrium between the ^{14}C concentration in the organism and that in the atmosphere, such that all living material has a ^{14}C concentration of about 227Bq/kg carbon. Since this exchange ceases on the death of the organism and the ^{14}C decays by beta emission at a fixed rate given by the half-life ($t_{1/2}$ = 5730y), measurement of the ^{14}C activity at a later time may be used to determine the date of death or more generally the date of isolation of a material from the atmosphere. It is assumed that the only loss of ^{14}C from the material is via its decay.

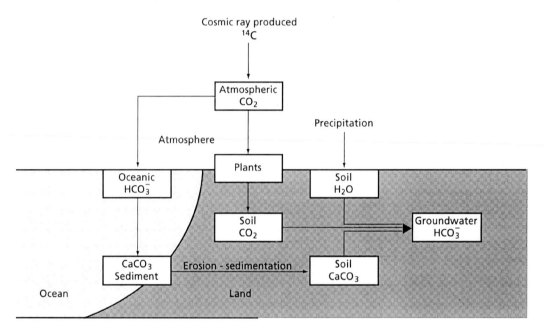

Figure 5.7: **The main components of the carbon cycle in nature illustrating the production, distribution and exchange of ^{14}C, after [44]. Reproduced with permission of the author.**

The age (t) is given by the equation (see Chapter 1):

$$A_t = A_0 \exp\left(\frac{-\ln(2)t}{t_{1/2}}\right)$$

where A_t is the present-day ^{14}C activity and A_0 is the activity at the time the material was isolated from the atmosphere. A_0 is usually taken as the activity of a contemporary standard such as NBS oxalic acid [43].

There are two main corrections usually applied to a measured radiocarbon age. The first is due to isotopic fractionation in metabolic processes which lead to a small deficit in ^{14}C with respect to stable [12]C. This may be corrected by making use of measurements of the stable carbon isotope ratio ^{13}C/[12]C.

The variation of $^{13}C/^{12}C$ isotopic ratios in carbon-containing materials is illustrated in Figure 5.8 [45]. The ratio is expressed as a factor δ in parts per thousand $(\%o)$.

$$\delta(\%o) = \left(\frac{^{13}C\big/_{12}C_{\text{SAMPLE}}}{^{13}C\big/_{12}C_{\text{STANDARD}}} - 1 \right) 1000$$

where the standard is usually taken as a calcium carbonate belemnite from the Peedee Formation (PDB).

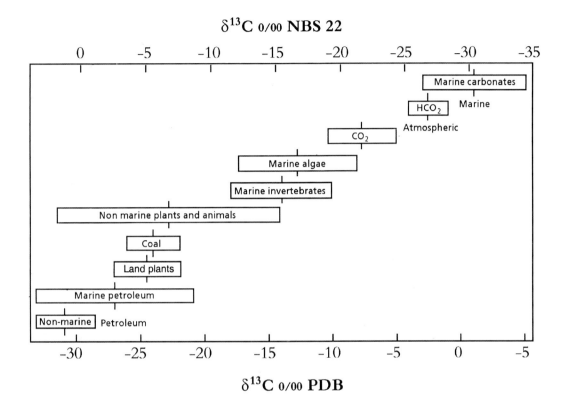

Figure 5.8: **Variation in $^{13}C/^{12}C$ ratios in natural materials expressed as $\delta^{13}C$ (0/00) with respect to PDB standard, after [45]. Reproduced from Principles of Geochemistry, B. Mason and C.B. Moore, with permission from John Wiley & Sons.**

The other main correction is for small changes in the cosmic ray intensity over long periods of time. Here the 'radiocarbon ages' may be corrected to 'calendar ages' using tree ring dating of ancient trees, mainly Bristlecone pines, which is possible to about 6700 B.C. [43].

Radiocarbon dating has also been used to determine the 'age' of groundwaters or more precisely the time since the last recharge. Any such estimate will be a mean value for the distribution of ages over all the water molecules present. A given groundwater sample will in general have a complex history due to dispersion and diffusion as well as rock/water interactions which may result in chemical and isotopic exchange of carbon. Thus, interpretation of the ^{14}C data requires an understanding of the evolution of the groundwater. In studies of groundwater samples from a borehole, allowance must be taken for the presence of organic carbon in the drilling fluids which will correspond to 'modern' ^{14}C.

5.5 MEDICAL USE OF RADIONUCLIDES

5.5.1 Introduction

According to a Nuclear Medicine Survey [46] in the UK, a total of 430,000 administrations of radiopharmaceuticals were carried out in about 296 sites where *in vivo* nuclear medicine was undertaken. The total figure was broken down as follows (Table 5.4):

Table 5.4: Radiopharmaceutical administrations in the UK (1989/90).

Procedure type	Estimated no. of administrations
Diagnostic, imaging	382,700
Diagnostic, non-imaging	34,400
Therapeutic	12,900
Total	430,000

From the survey responses, the most frequently performed procedures were listed and from this the usage of radionuclides could be calculated, regardless of radiopharmaceutical. ^{99m}Tc was by far the most frequently used radionuclide (Table 5.5).

Table 5.5: Frequency of use of radionuclides in UK nuclear medicine.

Radionuclide	Estimated no. of procedures	% of total procedures
Tc-99m	301,500	70.1
Kr-81m	16,400	3.8
I-131	12,500	2.9
Tl-201	12,300	2.9
Cr-51	11,700	2.7
Xe-133	10,900	2.5
Co-57	4,700	1.1
others	~60,000	13.9

The 'others' category in Table 5.5 contains a wide range of radionuclides.

This section provides reference information on radionuclides used for medical applications in the UK, and many others available or becoming available. Up-to-date information on the nuclear decay properties of radionuclides and dose-related information for individual radiopharmaceuticals is given.

The radiation doses from radioactivity used for medical and clinical research purposes present a special case of external and internal irradiation, and the basis for absorbed dose calculations is given here rather than in Chapter 6.

An indication of the wide range of applications of radiopharmaceuticals, sealed sources and nuclide generators available to the nuclear medical community is presented together with examples of their use in diagnostic and therapeutic procedures, supported by references.

The relevant legislation specific to the use of radioactivity in nuclear medicine facilities and other hospital departments is summarised as is that covering the use of radioactivity for medical research purposes and clinical trials. This complements the wider discussion on the legislative aspects of radioactivity use given in Chapter 7.

5.5.2 Nuclear decay data

Data on the radioactive half-life, radiation type, particle and photon energies and branching fractions for a wide range of radionuclides used in Nuclear Medicine and clinical research are incorporated in the Nuclear Data Table in Chapter 8 of this Manual. Included are important parent radionuclides used as generators for short-lived daughter products (e.g ^{99}Mo for ^{99m}Tc, ^{81}Rb for ^{81m}Kr, ^{113}Sn for ^{113m}In). Where different, the data in this Table should be used in preference to its equivalent in the MIRD (Medical Internal Radiation Dose) Data Tables [47] and ICRP 38 [48] as they are based on the latest reviews. The MIRD Radionuclide Data and Decay Schemes [47] present information on the energies and intensities of radiations emitted by 242 radionuclides, selected on the basis of their relevance to diagnostic and therapeutic nuclear medicine. ICRP 38 contains nuclear data for 812 radionuclides. The availability of these data in unabridged form and of the associated beta spectra, both in electronic form, has been described by Eckerman *et al* [49].

Table 5.6 lists the main radionuclides used in medicine, together with some of their uses for clinical diagnosis and treatment. Nuclear data for all of these radionuclides can be found in Chapter 8. Note that the list of radionuclides is constantly evolving.

Table 5.6:   **Some uses of radionuclides in diagnosis and treatment.**

Nuclide	Some Applications/Uses
Ag–109m	DI
Au–198	Brachytherapy
C–11	DI (PET)
C–14	In-vitro
Cd–109	DI
Cf–252	Brachytherapy (neutrons)
Co–57	In-vitro, in-vivo
Co–58	In-vivo
Co–60	Brachytherapy, beam therapy
Cr–51	Bone cancer, in-vivo
Cs–129	DI
Cs–137	Brachytherapy, beam therapy
Cu–62	DI (PET)
Cu–64	DI (PET)
Cu–67	DI, RIT
Dy–165	Arthritis therapy
F–18	DI (PET)
Fe–59	In-vivo
Ga–67	DI, radiotherapy
Ga–68	DI (PET)
Ga–70	DI
Gd–153	DI, Bone densitometry
H–3	In-vitro
Ho–166	Arthritis therapy, RIT, Bone cancer therapy
I–123	DI
I–125	In-vitro, brachytherapy, Bone densitometry
I–131	In-vitro, RIT, Bone cancer therapy, DI
In–111	DI, cancer therapy
In–113m	DI
Ir–191m	DI
Ir–192	Brachytherapy
Kr–81m	DI, in-vivo
N–13	DI (PET)
O–15	DI (PET
Os–191	DI
P–32	In-vitro, cancer therapy, RIT
P–33	In-vitro
Pd–103	Brachytherapy

Nuclide	Some Applications/Uses
Ra-226	External beam therapy
Re-186	RIT, bone cancer therapy
Re-188	RIT, Arthritis therapy
S-35	In-vitro
Se-75	DI, in-vitro
Sm-145	RIT, brachytherapy
Sm-153	Bone cancer therapy, DI, RIT
Sn-117m	DI, bone cancer therapy
Sr-89	Bone cancer therapy
Sr-90	Brachytherapy
Ta-182	Brachytherapy
Tc-99m	DI
TI-207	DI
W-188	RIT, bone cancer therapy
Xe-127	DI
Xe-133	DI, in-vivo
Xe-133m	Bone cancer therapy
Y-90	Arthritis therapy

Abbreviations:

DI   Diagnostic Imaging
PET   Positron Emission Tomography
RIT   Radioimmunotherapy

5.5.3 Absorbed Radiation Dose from radiopharmaceuticals

The estimate of absorbed radiation dose from internal emitters provides the information required to assess the radiation risk associated with the administration of radiopharmaceuticals for medical applications. The principal efforts in this direction have come from the International Commission on Radiological Protection (ICRP), the International Commission on Radiation Units and Measurement (ICRU), the National Council on Radiation Protection and Measurements (NCRP) and, in particular, the Medical Internal Radiation Dose (MIRD) Committee of the U.S. Society of Nuclear Medicine.

The MIRD method of radiation absorbed dose calculations began to evolve around 1968 and has been published as a series of pamphlets [50 - 59], and a series of Dose Estimate Reports, each covering a different radiopharmaceutical, were published in the Journal of Nuclear Medicine [60-74]. A primer explaining the MIRD method in more detail was published by the Committee in 1988 [75] and this also reproduces the series of Dose Estimate Reports with revisions made by the MIRD Committee covering SI units, editorial changes and rearrangements of dose estimate tables. The computations of radiation absorbed doses by the MIRD schema adopt a systematic approach to combining the biologic distribution data and radiopharmaceutical clearance data with the physical properties of the radionuclides. These are suitable for β and γ decay when the distribution of radionuclides in the body is relatively homogeneous throughout volumes of the order of a few grams or more. Because absorbed dose from internally-distributed radionuclides is never completely uniform, the MIRD equations give the average absorbed dose to a volume of tissue. Dose assessment methods to cope with high-LET emitters (alpha and EC decay) have also been developed [76] - see Section 5.5.4. Some of the difficulties associated with the MIRD schema have been outlined in a paper given at a U.S. conference on the dosimetry of administered radionuclides [77].

In its simpler form, the equation for the mean dose to a target organ per unit administered activity of radiopharmaceutical is:

$$D/A_0 = \tilde{A}S$$

where   D = mean dose
      A_0 = administered activity
      $\tilde{A}$ = cumulated activity = $\int A(t)dt$
      S = dose to target organ from unit cumulated activity

For **Reference Man**, the 'S' values have been tabulated for many source organs paired with various target organs, for many important radionuclides [58]. For internal photon sources, 'S' values have been calculated for **Reference Woman** and other age groups [78].

For the more usual and more complex situation, where several types of radiation are emitted by the radiopharmaceutical and several source organs contribute to the dose in the target organ, the equation for calculating the absorbed dose may be written in various forms depending on available information. An example is shown below [79]:

$$D\ (r_k \leftarrow r_h) = A_h\ \Sigma\ \Delta_i\ \phi_i\ (r_k \leftarrow r_h)\ /\ m_k$$

where $D\ (r_k \leftarrow r_h)$ is the mean absorbed dose in a target region r_k from activity in a
      source region r_h
      A_h is the cumulated activity (time integral of activity over time interval of interest)
      in the source
      Δ_i is the mean energy emitted by a radionuclide per nuclear transition
      $\phi_i\ (r_k \leftarrow r_h)$ is the absorbed fraction (fraction of energy emitted in region r_h that
      is absorbed in region r_k)
      m_k is the mass of the target r_k

The total mean absorbed dose in a target region is calculated by summing the doses from all source regions to the target.

The MIRD Primer [75] gives eight examples of dose calculations, commencing with a simple problem and progressing to more complex situations.

The relevant ICRU report, 'Methods of Assessment of Absorbed Dose in Clinical Use of Radionuclides' [80], sets out the basic concepts and formulae of internal dosimetry. It gives an appraisal of the methods for obtaining biological data, ranging from animal distributions through scanning methods. Six examples of dose calculations of increasing complexity are explained in an Appendix.

The NCRP have also undertaken reviews of internal radiation dosimetry as a result of medical uses of radionuclides [81,82], and have published other reports related to other aspects of radiological protection in nuclear medicine [83-87].

A number of publications by the ICRP provide radiological protection guidance in the field of nuclear medicine [88-94]. ICRP publication 52 [88] provides guidance on good clinical practice in the diagnostic, therapeutic and research uses of radiopharmaceuticals. Advice is given for nuclear medicine physicians, radiopharmacists, medical physicists and others on factors which influence the absorbed doses to patients from different types of nuclear medicine examinations. Recommendations were extended to protection of the patient's family, of more importance in radiotherapy than in diagnosis. Absorbed doses to the most highly exposed organs are listed and the effective dose equivalents (mSv/MBq) for adults are calculated for selected radiopharmaceuticals. Useful guidance on radiopharmaceutical laboratory design, Quality Control (both equipment and radiopharmaceutical) and record keeping are also given.

ICRP publication 53 [89] gives methods for selecting tissues and organs for dose calculations, for choosing appropriate metabolic models and biokinetic data and for calculating absorbed doses. Absorbed doses for organs, effective dose equivalents for adults, 15-, 10-, 5- and 1-year olds and biokinetic data are given for some 120 radiopharmaceuticals.

In 1991, in ICRP publication 60 [90], the ICRP introduced the quantity 'effective dose' to replace the term 'effective dose equivalent', taking account of new tissue weighting factors. Along with other changes, this change led to the publication of ICRP 62 [91], an addendum to ICRP 53. This Addendum contains the effective doses per unit administered activity for adults for all 120 radiopharmaceuticals given in ICRP 53 and for six new radiopharmaceuticals. These data are reproduced in Table 5.7.

In 1994, the ICRP published a summary of the then current principles for protection of the patient in nuclear medicine [92]. This document summarises the information given in ICRP 52 and further updates the summary with the later information in ICRP publications 53, 60 and 62, particularly on the latest health effects and the updated system of radiological protection in ICRP 60. Arising from this are the latest data, for 36 radiopharmaceuticals, on absorbed dose (mGy) for the 3 most irradiated organs and the effective dose (mSv/MBq) for adults - see Table 5.8.

There is some overlap in Tables 5.7 and 5.8 in that both give effective doses for radiopharmaceuticals. However, the number of radiopharmaceuticals covered in Table 5.7 is more extensive but does not provide doses to the most irradiated organs. Conversely, Table 5.8 lists fewer radiopharmaceuticals but does provides doses to the most irradiated organs and to conceptus. The Tables are therefore complementary. Permission from ICRP to reproduce these is gratefully acknowledged.

ICRP Committee 3 will be publishing dosimetric information and advice on several new radiopharmaceuticals in 1998 [93]:

^{11}C	[methyl-^{11}C]thymidine
^{11}C	[2-^{11}C]thymidine
^{14}C	labelled urea
^{15}O	water
^{99m}Tc	human immunoglobulin
^{99m}Tc	Tetrofosmin
^{99m}Tc	Technegas
^{99m}Tc	Pertechnegas
^{99m}Tc	ethylene cysteinate
^{99m}Tc	ethylene dicystein
^{99m}Tc	Q12-Furifosmin
^{111}In	Octreotide
^{111}In	human immunoglobulin

Table 5.7: Effective doses to adults per unit administered activity for radiopharmaceuticals (compilation of data from ICRP 62).

Radionuclide	Chemical species	Effective dose, E (mSv/MBq)
^{3}H	water	1.5E-02
^{3}H	neutral fat and free fatty acids	2.2E-01
^{3}H	Inulin	9.4E-04
^{11}C	CO (single inhalation, 20s breath hold)	4.8E-03
^{11}C	CO (continuous inhalation for 1 hour)	3.2E-03
^{11}C	CO_2 (single inhalation, 20s breath hold)	1.6E-03
^{11}C	CO_2 (continuous inhalation for 1 hour)	1.0E-03
^{11}C	COHb-labelled erythrocytes	5.0E-03
^{11}C	Spiperone	5.3E-03
^{14}C	neutral fat and free fatty acids	2.1E+00
^{14}C	Inulin	8.2E-03
^{13}N	Nitrogen gas (single inhalation, 20s breath hold)	3.8E-04
^{13}N	Nitrogen gas (continuous inhalation for 1 hour)	4.3E-04
^{13}N	Nitrogen gas in solution	4.1E-04
^{13}N	Ammonia	2.0E-03
^{13}N	l-glutamate	3.9E-03
^{15}O	CO (single inhalation, 20s breath hold)	8.0E-04
^{15}O	CO (continuous inhalation for 1 hour)	5.5E-04
^{15}O	CO_2 (single inhalation, 20s breath hold)	5.1E-04
^{15}O	CO_2 (continuous inhalation for 1 hour)	3.8E-04
^{15}O	Oxygen gas (single inhalation, 20s breath hold)	3.7E-04
^{15}O	Oxygen gas (continuous inhalation for 1 hour)	4.0E-04
^{18}F	fluoride	2.4E-02
^{18}F	2-fluoro-2-deoxy-d-glucose (FDG)	2.0E-02
^{22}Na	sodium (intravenous or oral)	2.6E+00
^{24}Na	sodium	3.2E-01
^{24}Na	sodium (oral administration)	3.6E-01
^{28}Mg	magnesium	7.2E-01
^{32}P	phosphate	2.4E+00
^{33}P	phosphate	6.6E-01
^{35}S	sulphate	9.0E-02
^{34m}Cl	chloride	1.4E-02
^{36}Cl	chloride	6.7E-01
^{38}Cl	chloride	1.4E-02
^{38}K	potassium	1.9E-02
^{42}K	potassium	2.8E-01
^{42}K	potassium (oral administration)	3.4E-01
^{43}K	potassium	2.0E-01
^{43}K	potassium (oral administration)	2.2E-01
^{45}Ca	calcium	3.1E+00
^{45}Ca	calcium (oral administration)	1.8E+00
^{47}Ca	calcium	1.2E+00
^{47}Ca	calcium (oral administration)	1.8E+00
^{46}Sc	Sc-labelled non-absorbable markers (fluids)	1.6E+00
^{46}Sc	Sc-labelled non-absorbable markers (solids)	1.7E+00
^{47}Sc	Sc-labelled non-absorbable markers (fluids)	4.7E-01
^{47}Sc	Sc-labelled non-absorbable markers (solids)	7.6E-01
^{51}Cr	chromium III chloride	6.8E-02
^{51}Cr	chromium EDTA	2.1E-03

Table 5.7 (continued)

Radionuclide	Chemical species	Effective dose, E (mSv/MBq)
^{51}Cr	chromium EDTA (oral administration)	4.4E-02
^{51}Cr	Cr-labelled platelets (thrombocytes)	1.4E-01
^{51}Cr	Cr-labelled erythrocytes	1.7E-01
^{51}Cr	Cr-labelled denatured erythrocytes	1.8E-01
^{51}Cr	Cr-labelled white blood cells (leukocytes)	1.2E-01
^{51}Cr	Cr-labelled non-absorbable markers (fluids)	4.3E-02
^{51}Cr	Cr-labelled non-absorbable markers (solids)	4.5E-02
^{52}Fe	iron	1.1E+00
^{52}Fe	iron (oral administration)	7.1E-01
^{55}Fe	iron	4.0E+00
^{55}Fe	iron (oral administration)	4.2E-01
^{59}Fe	iron	1.0E+01
^{59}Fe	iron (oral administration)	2.0E+00
^{57}Co	Co-labelled bleomycin	4.7E-02
^{57}Co	vitamin B12 (intravenous injection, with no carrier)	4.4E+00
^{58}Co	vitamin B12 (intravenous injection, with no carrier)	8.2E+00
^{57}Co	vitamin B12 (intravenous injection, with carrier)	4.6E-01
^{58}Co	vitamin B12 (intravenous injection, with carrier)	8.9E-01
^{57}Co	vitamin B12 (oral administration with flushing)	2.1E+00
^{58}Co	vitamin B12 (oral administration with flushing)	4.0E+00
^{57}Co	vitamin B12 (oral administration without flushing)	3.1E+00
^{58}Co	vitamin B12 (oral administration without flushing)	5.9E+00
^{64}Cu	copper	3.6E-02
^{67}Cu	copper	1.5E-01
^{62}Zn	zinc	3.5E-01
^{65}Zn	zinc	8.4E+00
^{69m}Zn	zinc	1.4E-01
^{66}Ga	gallium citrate	3.2E-01
^{67}Ga	gallium citrate	1.1E-01
^{68}Ga	gallium citrate	2.0E-02
^{72}Ga	gallium citrate	3.4E-01
^{68}Ga	Ga-EDTA	4.0E-02
^{72}As	arsenate, arsenite	3.6E-01
^{74}As	arsenate, arsenite	5.1E-01
^{76}As	arsenate, arsenite	2.8E-01
^{75}Se	selenite	2.6E+00
^{75}Se	selenomethylcholesterol	1.5E+00
^{75}Se	1-selenomethionine	2.5E+00
^{75}Se	selenium-labelled bile acid (SeHCAT)	6.6E-01
^{76}Br	bromide	2.8E-01
^{77}Br	bromide	7.7E-02
^{82}Br	bromide	4.0E-01
^{77}Br	bromospiperone	8.5E-02
^{81m}Kr	krypton	9.5E-04
^{81}Rb	rubidium	2.8E-02
^{82}Rb	rubidium	3.4E-03
^{84}Rb	rubidium	2.8E+00
^{86}Rb	rubidium	3.0E+00
^{81}Rb	Rb-labelled denatured erythrocytes	1.4E-01
^{85}Sr	strontium	7.9E-01

Table 5.7 (continued)

Radionuclide	Chemical species	Effective dose, E (mSv/MBq)
^{87m}Sr	strontium	6.4E-03
^{89}Sr	strontium	3.1E+00
^{99m}Tc	Tc-labelled albumin (HSA)	6.1E-03
^{99m}Tc	Tc-labelled citrate complex	6.1E-03
^{99m}Tc	Tc-labelled large colloids	9.2E-03
^{99m}Tc	Tc-labelled small colloids	9.7E-03
^{99m}Tc	Tc-DMSA	8.7E-03
^{99m}Tc	Tc-DTPA	5.2E-03
^{99m}Tc	Tc-labelled plasmin	7.3E-03
^{99m}Tc	Tc-gluconate, glucoheptonate	5.4E-03
^{99m}Tc	Tc-penicillamine	7.3E-03
^{99m}Tc	pertechnetate	1.2E-02
^{99m}Tc	pertechnetate (blocking agent given)	4.7E-03
^{99m}Tc	pertechnetate (oral administration, no blocking)	1.4E-02
^{99m}Tc	Tc-labelled IDA derivatives	1.5E-02
^{99m}Tc	Tc-labelled fibrinogen	6.2E-03
^{99m}Tc	Tc-labelled erythrocytes	6.6E-03
^{99m}Tc	Tc-HMPAO (Ceretec)	9.3E-03
^{99m}Tc	Mercaptoacetyltriglycine (MAG3, normal renal function)	7.3E-03
^{99m}Tc	Mercaptoacetyltriglycine (MAG3, abnormal renal function)	6.3E-03
^{99m}Tc	Mercaptoacetyltriglycine (MAG3, acute unilateral renal blockage)	1.1E-02
^{99m}Tc	methyl oxy-isobutyl-isonitrile (MIBI, resting subject)	8.5E-03
^{99m}Tc	methyl oxy-isobutyl-isonitrile (MIBI, after exercise)	7.5E-03
^{99m}Tc	Tc-labelled denatured erythrocytes	1.9E-02
^{99m}Tc	Tc-labelled phosphates and phosphonates	5.8E-03
^{99m}Tc	Tc-labelled aerosols (fast clearance substances)	6.1E-03
^{99m}Tc	Tc-labelled aerosols (slow clearance substances)	1.4E-02
^{99m}Tc	Tc-labelled heparin	5.5E-03
^{99m}Tc	Tc-labelled macroaggregated albumin	1.1E-02
^{99m}Tc	Tc-labelled non-absorbable markers (fluids)	2.0E-02
^{99m}Tc	Tc-labelled non-absorbable markers (solids)	2.2E-02
^{99m}Tc	Tc-labelled albumin microspheres	1.0E-02
^{99m}Tc	Tc-labelled platelets (thrombocytes)	1.2E-02
^{99m}Tc	Tc-labelled white blood cells (leukocytes)	1.1E-02
^{111}In	Indium	2.1E-01
^{113m}In	Indium	1.0E-02
^{113m}In	Indium hydroxide (colloidal)	1.1E-02
^{111}In	In-DTPA	2.1E-02
^{113m}In	In-DTPA	1.1E-02
^{111}In	In aerosols (substances with fast clearance)	2.5E-02
^{111}In	In aerosols (substances with slow clearance)	2.4E-01
^{113m}In	In aerosols (substances with fast clearance)	1.6E-02
^{113m}In	In aerosols (substances with slow clearance)	2.5E-02
^{111}In	In-labelled non-absorbable markers (fluids)	3.1E-01
^{111}In	In-labelled non-absorbable markers (solids)	3.2E-01
^{113m}In	In-labelled non-absorbable markers (fluids)	2.0E-02

Table 5.7 (continued)

Radionuclide	Chemical species	Effective dose, E (mSv/MBq)
[113m]In	In-labelled non-absorbable markers (solids)	2.9E-02
[111]In	In-labelled platelets (thrombocytes)	3.9E-01
[111]In	In-labelled white blood cells (leukocytes)	3.6E-01
[111]In	In-labelled bleomycin	1.0E-01
[123]I	Iodide (thyroid blocked, uptake 0%)	1.1E-02
[123]I	Iodide (thyroid uptake 35%)	2.2E-01
[124]I	Iodide (thyroid blocked, uptake 0%)	9.5E-02
[124]I	Iodide (thyroid uptake 35%)	1.5E+01
[125]I	Iodide (thyroid blocked, uptake 0%)	9.1E-03
[125]I	Iodide (thyroid uptake 35%)	1.4E+01
[131]I	Iodide (thyroid blocked, uptake 0%)	6.1E-02
[131]I	Iodide (thyroid uptake 35%)	2.4E+01
[123]I	Iodoamphetamine (IMP)	2.7E-02
[123]I	Iodine-labelled fibrinogen	2.0E-02
[125]I	Iodine-labelled fibrinogen	8.0E-02
[131]I	Iodine-labelled fibrinogen	4.2E-01
[123]I	Iodine-labelled albumin (HSA)	2.0E-02
[125]I	Iodine-labelled albumin (HSA)	2.2E-01
[131]I	Iodine-labelled albumin (HSA)	6.4E-01
[131]I	Iodine-labelled macroaggregared albumin (MAA)	4.5E-01
[125]I	Iodine-labelled non-absorbable markers (fluids)	1.7E-01
[125]I	Iodine-labelled non-absorbable markers (solids)	1.7E-01
[131]I	Iodine-labelled non-absorbable markers (fluids)	1.2E+00
[131]I	Iodine-labelled non-absorbable markers (solids)	1.2E+00
[123]I	Iodine-labelled microaggregared albumin (MIAA)	1.8E-02
[131]I	Iodine-labelled microaggregared albumin (MIAA)	2.2E-01
[123]I	Hippuran	1.2E-02
[125]I	Hippuran	7.7E-03
[131]I	Hippuran	5.3E-02
[131]I	Iodo-antipyrine	6.7E-02
[125]I	Iodo-antipyrine	1.0E-02
[125]I	Iothalamate	7.2E-03
[131]I	Iodomethyl-19-norcholesterol (NP 59)	1.8E+00
[125]I	Iodinated polyvinylpyrrolidone (PVP)	6.5E-01
[131]I	Iodinated polyvinylpyrrolidone (PVP)	6.0E-01
[125]I	Thyroxine (T4)	1.0E-01
[131]I	Thyroxine (T4)	4.4E-01
[125]I	Triiodothyronine (T3)	4.7E-02
[131]I	Triiodothyronine (T3)	3.0E-01
[125]I	Reverse triiodothyronine (rT3)	3.7E-02
[131]I	Reverse triiodothyronine (rT3)	2.5E-01
[125]I	Diiodothyronine	3.6E-02
[131]I	Diiodothyronine	2.5E-01
[123]I	Metaiodobenzylguanidine (MIBG)	1.4E-02
[131]I	Metaiodobenzylguanidine (MIBG)	1.4E-01
[123]I	Sodium Rose Bengal	5.9E-02
[131]I	Sodium Rose Bengal	1.1E+00
[127]Xe	Xenon gas (single inhalation or i.v. inj.,30s breath hold)	1.3E-04

Table 5.7 (continued)

Radionuclide	Chemical species	Effective dose, E (mSv/MBq)
^{133}Xe	Xenon gas (single inhalation or i.v. inj.,30s breath hold)	1.8E-04
^{127}Xe	Xenon gas (rebreathing for 5 min)	7.1E-04
^{127}Xe	Xenon gas (rebreathing for 10 min)	1.1E-03
^{133}Xe	Xenon gas (rebreathing for 5 min)	7.3E-04
^{133}Xe	Xenon gas (rebreathing for 10 min)	1.1E-03
^{129}Cs	caesium	4.9E-02
^{130}Cs	caesium	3.4E-03
^{131}Cs	caesium	5.0E-02
^{134m}Cs	caesium	6.7E-03
^{131}Ba	barium	5.0E-01
^{133m}Ba	barium	4.7E-01
^{135m}Ba	barium	3.4E-01
^{131}Ba	Ba-labelled non-absorbable markers (fluids)	4.9E-01
^{131}Ba	Ba-labelled non-absorbable markers (solids)	5.1E-01
^{140}La	La-DTPA	1.5E-01
^{169}Yb	Yb-DTPA	3.6E-02
^{198}Au	Gold colloid	1.1E+00
^{197}Hg	Mercury chloride	1.4E-01
^{197}Hg	Bromo-mercuri-hydroxypropane (BMHP)	1.4E-01
^{197}Hg	Chlormerodrin	8.7E-02
^{203}Hg	Chlormerodrin	1.1E+00
^{201}Tl	thallium	2.3E-01

Table 5.8: Absorbed dose (mGy) and effective dose (mSv) per unit administered activity (MBq) in normal adults.

Function of organ examined	Radio-nuclide	Pharmaceutical	Most highly irradiated organs			Conceptus (mGy/MBq)	Effective Dose (mSv/MBq)
			Organ 1 (mGy/MBq)	Organ 2 (mGy/MBq)	Organ 3 (mGy/MBq)		
Bone	^{99m}Tc	phosphate/ phosphonate	6.3×10^{-2} (bone surface)	5.0×10^{-2} (bladder)	9.6×10^{-3} (red marrow)	6.1×10^{-3}	5.8×10^{-3}
Renal (normal renal function)	^{51}Cr	EDTA	2.3×10^{-2} (bladder)	2.8×10^{-3} (uterus)	1.8×10^{-3} (kidneys)	2.8×10^{-3}	2.1×10^{-3}
	^{123}I	hippurate	2.0×10^{-1} (bladder)	1.7×10^{-2} (uterus)	7.3×10^{-3} (lower large intestine)	1.7×10^{-2}	1.2×10^{-2}
	^{131}I	hippurate	9.6×10^{-1} (bladder)	3.5×10^{-2} (uterus)	3.0×10^{-2} (kidneys)	3.5×10^{-2}	5.3×10^{-2}
	^{99m}Tc	DTPA	6.5×10^{-2} (bladder)	7.9×10^{-3} (uterus)	4.4×10^{-3} (kidneys)	7.9×10^{-3}	5.2×10^{-3}
	^{99m}Tc	DMSA	1.7×10^{-1} (kidneys)	1.9×10^{-2} (bladder)	1.3×10^{-2} (adrenals spleen)	4.6×10^{-2}	8.7×10^{-3}
	^{99m}Tc	MAG$_3$	1.1×10^{-1} (bladder)	1.2×10^{-2} (uterus)	5.7×10^{-3} (lower large intestine)	1.2×10^{-2}	7.3×10^{-3}
Thyroid	^{99m}Tc	pertechnetate (no blocking)	6.2×10^{-2} (upper large intestine)	2.9×10^{-2} (stomach)	2.3×10^{-2} (thyroid)	8.1×10^{-3}	1.2×10^{-2}
	^{131}I	iodide (35% uptake)	5.0×10^{-2} (thyroid)	4.6×10^{-1} (stomach)	4.0×10^{-1} (bladder)	5.0×10^{-2}	24
	^{123}I	iodide (35% uptake)	4.5 (thyroid)	6.8×10^{-2} (stomach)	6.0×10^{-2} (bladder)	1.4×10^{-2}	2.2×10^{-1}
Liver (& gall bladder)	^{99m}Tc	colloid (large)	7.7×10^{-2} (spleen)	7.4×10^{-2} (liver)	1.2×10^{-2} (pancreas)	1.9×10^{-3}	9.2×10^{-3}
	^{99m}Tc	colloid (small)	7.7×10^{-2} (spleen)	7.4×10^{-2} (liver)	1.5×10^{-2} (red marrow)	1.8×10^{-3}	9.7×10^{-3}
	^{99m}Tc	HIDA	1.1×10^{-1} (gall bladder)	9.2×10^{-2} (upper large intestine)	6.2×10^{-2} (lower large intestine)	1.3×10^{-2}	1.5×10^{-2}
	^{57}Co	B$_{12}$ (no carrier)	5.1×10 (liver)	5.4 (adrenals, pancreas)	5.0 (kidneys)	1.8	4.4
Brain	^{99m}Tc	pertechnetate (blocked thyroid)	3.2×10^{-2} (bladder)	6.6×10^{-3} (uterus)	4.7×10^{-3} (kidneys, ovaries)	6.6×10^{-3}	4.7×10^{-3}
	^{99m}Tc	gluconate/ glucoheptonate	5.6×10^{-2} (bladder)	4.9×10^{-2} (kidneys)	7.7×10^{-3} uterus)	7.7×10^{-3}	5.4×10^{-3}
	^{99m}Tc	HMPAO	3.4×10^{-2} (kidneys)	2.6×10^{-2} (thyroid)	2.3×10^{-2} (bladder)	6.6×10^{-3}	9.3×10^{-3}
	^{18}F	FDG	1.7×10^{-1} (bladder)	6.5×10^{-2} (heart)	2.6×10^{-2} brain)	2.0×10^{-2}	2.0×10^{-2}
Lung	^{99m}Tc	MAA	6.7×10^{-2} (lungs)	1.6×10^{-2} (liver)	1.0×10^{-2} (bladder)	2.4×10^{-3}	1.1×10^{-2}
	^{99m}Tc	aerosol (fast clearance)	4.7×10^{-2} (bladder)	1.7×10^{-2} (lungs)	5.9×10^{-3} (uterus)	5.9×10^{-3}	6.1×10^{-3}
	^{99m}Tc	aerosol (slow clearance)	9.3×10^{-2} (lungs)	1.3×10^{-2} (bladder)	6.4×10^{-2} (breasts)	1.7×10^{-3}	1.4×10^{-2}
	^{133}Xe	gas, 5 min. (re-breathing)	1.1×10^{-3} (lungs)	8.4×10^{-4} (red marrow)	8.3×10^{-4} (breasts)	7.4×10^{-4}	7.3×10^{-4}
	^{133}Xe	gas, 30 s 1 breath	7.7×10^{-4} (lungs)	1.2×10^{-4} (bone surfaces, red marrow, breasts)	1.1×10^{-4} (small and large intestines, liver, ancreas, spleen, uterus)	1.1×10^{-4}	1.8×10^{-4}
	^{81m}Kr	gas	2.1×10^{-4} (lungs)	4.6×10^{-6} (breasts)	3.5×10^{-6} (pancreas)	1.3×10^{-7}	9.5×10^{-4}

163

Table 5.8 (continued)

Function of organ examined	Radio-nuclide	Pharmaceutical	Most highly irradiated organs			Conceptus (mGy/MBq)	Effective Dose (mSv/MBq)
			Organ 1 (mGy/MBq)	Organ 2 (mGy/MBq)	Organ 3 (mGy/MBq)		
Heart	^{201}Tl	thallous ion	5.6×10^{-1} (testes)	5.4×10^{-1} (kidneys)	3.6×10^{-1} (lower large intestine)	5.0×10^{-2}	2.3×10^{-1}
	^{99m}Tc	RBC	2.3×10^{-2} (heart)	1.5×10^{-2} (spleen)	1.4×10^{-2} (lungs)	4.7×10^{-3}	6.6×10^{-3}
Abscess	^{111}In	white cells	5.5 (spleen)	7.1×10^{-1} (liver)	6.9×10^{-1} (red marrow)	1.2×10^{-1}	3.6×10^{-1}
	^{67}Ga	citrate	5.9×10^{-1} (bone surfaces)	2.0×10^{-1} (lower large intestine)	1.9×10^{-1} (red marrow)	7.9×10^{-2}	1.1×10^{-1}
Thrombi	^{125}I	fibrinogen (thyroid totally blocked)	3.2×10^{-1} (heart)	2.4×10^{-1} (spleen)	2.3×10^{-1} (lungs)	5.5×10^{-2}	8.0×10^{-2}
	^{111}In	platelets	7.5 (spleen)	7.3×10^{-1} (liver)	6.6×10^{-1} (pancreas)	9.5×10^{-2}	3.9×10^{-1}
	^{51}Cr	platelets	2.6 (spleen)	3.0×10^{-1} (liver)	1.9×10^{-1} (red marrow)	2.8×10^{-2}	1.4×10^{-1}
Pancreas	^{75}Se	methionine	6.2 (liver)	5.3 (kidneys)	3.9 (spleen)	2.6	2.5
Adrenals	^{75}Se	methyl cholesterol	5.1 (adrenals)	2.0 (liver)	1.8 (small intestine, pancreas, uterus, red marrow)	1.8	1.5
	^{131}I	MIBG	8.3×10^{-1} (liver)	5.9×10^{-1} (bladder)	4.9×10^{-1} (spleen)	8.0×10^{-2}	1.4×10^{-1}
Spleen	^{51}Cr	RBC denatured	5.6 (spleen)	3.0×10^{-1} (pancreas)	1.7×10^{-1} (liver)	1.3×10^{-2}	1.8×10^{-1}
GIT	^{99m}Tc	pertechnetate (oral, no blocking agent)	7.4×10^{-2} (upper large intestine)	5.0×10^{-2} (stomach)	3.0×10^{-2} (small intestine)	8.7×10^{-3}	1.4×10^{-2}

Two further ICRP publications are relevant to radiological protection in medicine. ICRP 57 [94] deals with the protection of workers in medicine and dentistry, and also covers handling, storage, use and disposal of unsealed radionuclides in hospitals and medical research establishments. ICRP 73 [95], entitled 'Radiological Protection and Safety in Medicine' was published in March 1996 and provides an extension of the recommendations in ICRP 60, clarifying how its recommendations should be applied to medicine, where the exposure to the patient is deliberate. In ICRP 73 the Commission recommends the use of 'diagnostic reference levels' (DRL's) for patients, and in nuclear medicine the quantity which applies will usually be the administered activity. The diagnostic reference level will be intended for use as a simple test for identifying situations where the levels of patient dose or administered activity are unusually high. A local review of procedures or equipment is called for if the relevant DRLs are consistently exceeded.

In the UK, the National Radiological Protection Board (NRPB) has provided guidance on the acceptability and applicability for the UK of the ICRP recommendations [96]. The NRPB, together with the Health and Safety Executive and UK Government departments, have also published guidance notes for the protection of persons against ionising radiations arising from medical and dental use [97], and a Board Statement on diagnostic medical exposures during pregnancy [98]. A concise training booklet to assist in the training of those personnel involved in administration of radiation for diagnostic or therapeutic purposes has been produced by the Royal Postgraduate Medical School, London [99].

In biomedical research there are a variety of research objectives for which radioactive tracers find application in human studies. The ethical and procedural aspects of the use of volunteers in the fields of medicine and human radiobiology have been addressed in ICRP 62 [91]. In the UK, the Administration of Radioactive Substances Advisory Committee (ARSAC) details in its Guidance Notes [100] the requirements for obtaining the necessary certificates for administering radioactive substances to volunteers for the purpose of diagnosis, therapy or research. This publication is due for re-issue in 1998. These Regulations do not apply to nuclear-powered pacemakers nor to the irradiation of persons by ionising radiations from X-ray or teletherapy machines, but they do apply to brachytherapy with sealed sources. Other publications dealing with the ethical side of such volunteer studies are listed in the Reference Section [101-104].

5.5.4 Dosimetry of Auger electrons

Auger emitters give off a cascade of low-energy electron (see Section 1.4.2.3), the total energy of which is deposited within tens of nanometres. The local dose is therefore very high and the biological effects can be as severe as those of alpha particles. Examples of Auger emitters used in nuclear medicine are ^{67}Ga, ^{99m}Tc, ^{111}In, ^{123}I, ^{125}I and ^{201}Tl. The problem of Auger electron doses will only arise where a proportion of the radiopharmaceutical is closely bound to DNA.

Methods to calculate the absorbed dose from Auger electron emitters at the DNA, cellular, multicellular and organ levels are described in the Third Report of the AAPM (American Association of Physics and Medicine) Nuclear Medicine Task Group No. 6 [105]. This report contains 120 references.

The radiation spectra provided by MIRD[47] and by the ICRP [48] are not adequate for Auger emitters and Auger electron spectra have been calculated using Monte Carlo techniques [106-110].

Following the formalism of the ICRP [90], the equivalent dose for Auger emitters in organ or tissue T ($H_{T,R,Auger}$), modified to accommodate its dependence on the subcellular distribution of Auger emitters, is given by [105]:

$$H_{T,R_{Auger}} = \left(1 + f_0\left(\omega_{R_{Auger}} - 1\right)\right) \sum_{R_{Auger}} D_{T,R_{other}}$$

where f_0 is the fraction of organ or tissue activity that is bound to DNA

$\omega_{R_{Auger}}$ is the radiation weighting factor for Auger electrons only (excludes all other radiations)

$D_{T,R_{other}}$ is the mean absorbed dose from other radiations

For Auger electrons emitted from radionuclides bound to DNA, the Task Group recommends the use of radiation weighting factors of 10 for deterministic effects and 20 for stochastic effects, but cautioned that the dose equivalents calculated with these weighting factors must be modulated by experimentally-determined subcellular distributions.

Although the physical aspects of calculating doses to tissues from Auger electrons are becoming well developed, there is only limited information on cellular distribution of specific radionuclides. It will be some time before sufficient data will be available for refining Auger dosimetry calculations, and the ICRP Committee 2 is keeping the work under review [111].

5.5.5 Legislation in patient protection

Directive 84/466/Euratom [112] of the Council of the European Communities was the driving legislation for the production of regulations in the UK concerning the radiation protection of patients. In the UK these regulations were introduced as the Ionising Radiation (Protection of Persons Undergoing Medical Examination or Treatment) Regulations 1988 [113], sometimes called the POPUMET Regulations, and in Northern Ireland as the Ionising Radiation (Protection of Patients) Regulations (Northern Ireland) 1988 [114]. Directive 84/466/Euratom is now superseded by Directive 97/43, in which the scope is far wider in terms of patient protection. This new Directive has to be implemented in the year 2000 and so new UK Regulations are being produced to replace the POPUMET Regulations.

The Medicines (Administration of Radioactive Substances) Regulations 1978 [115] are concerned with the protection of the patient during the clinical or research use of radioactive substances. The Medicines (Radioactive Substances) Order 1978 [116] brings within the regulations interstitial and intercavitary appliances, surface applicators, neutron generating apparatus and other substances as if they were medical products.

The legislation governing radiation protection in medicine has been usefully summarised by Hufton [117] and by Roberts [118]. European legislation as it affects radiopharmaceuticals has been reviewed by Cox and Meyer [119]. This review included Good Manufacturing Practice for short-lived generator- or cyclotron-produced radionuclides defined by the European Commission for Proprietary Medical Products [120,121].

Practical advice on minimisation of doses to patients and workers is given in references [122-125].

5.5.6 Quality standards in nuclear medicine and radiotherapy

The British Nuclear Medicine Society has produced checklists [126] to provide guidance on aspects of a nuclear medicine service that should be considered when drawing up standards for a radiopharmacy. Further guidance has been given in ICRP 52 [88] and in the Guidance notes [97].

The different areas where standards are necessary are listed and discussed by Hesslewood in his paper on radiopharmacy standards [127]. He discusses:

- facilities (for preparation of radiopharmaceutical, blood-labelling, storage);

- documentation (written procedures, record keeping);

- radiopharmaceuticals (product quality, purity with respect to radionuclide, radiochemical, chemical, biodistribution, particle size, pH, sterility, apyrogenicity);

- monitoring (of the product and the environment);

- reporting (of defective products).

Quality control of radionuclide calibrators and nuclear medicine instruments are covered in references [128] and [129] respectively.

More detailed information on standards are available elsewhere [130-139].

5.5.7 Uses of radionuclides in nuclear medicine

Radionuclides have been used in Medicine for over 50 years. They are used in human diagnostic procedures (imaging and non-imaging) and for therapeutic purposes.

Radiopharmaceuticals are usually, but not always, administered by intravenous injection, and there are over a hundred radiopharmaceuticals (e.g. see lists in [89] and [91]) which have been or are being used. A radionuclide used for clinical diagnosis should produce the clinical information with the minimum of radiation exposure to the patient.

Radiopharmaceuticals consist of a radioactive label and a non-radioactive component. The latter may assume various forms such as:

- an ion (e.g. ^{201}Tl-chloride);

- a more complex compound (e.g. ^{51}Cr-EDTA);

- radionuclide of an element naturally occurring in the body (e.g. ^{123}I as iodide, ^{15}O as oxygen);

- radionuclide of an element naturally-occurring in the body (e.g. ^{75}Se-selenomethionine as an analogue of methionine);

- a radiolabelled biological component (e.g. leukocytes - patient specific, monoclonal antibody - manufactured).

Most medicine investigations involve gamma camera imaging of the distribution of the radiopharmaceutical, but sometimes non-imaging procedures using probes and whole-body counting systems are of value. Positron emission tomography (PET) scanners consist of rings of detectors around the patient; when an administered positron emitter decays in the body, the coincident gamma rays are detected in opposite detectors and, with computer assistance, allows accurate quantification of the positioning and uptake of the PET radionuclide.

A useful summary of nuclear medicine procedures has recently been given by McKillop [140], while Bennett [141] discusses the uses of reactor-produced radionuclides in the medical market.

No information is provided here on the radiopharmaceutical products and kits available – the radiopharmacist, medical physicist or other responsible persons should consult product specifications or monographs provided by the supplier which should give details on composition, preparation, administered activity, quality control procedures, purity, shelf life, dosimetry data, storage conditions, contraindications, side-effects and other parameters.

Given the wide application of radionuclides in medicine, only a few select examples of their application in diagnostic and therapeutic procedures can be given here. An encyclopaedic compilation of applications of nuclear medicine in the clinical and research environment, running to 114 chapters, is given in reference [142].

5.5.7.1 Uses in diagnostic imaging

^{99m}Tc is the most widely used radionuclide for diagnostic imaging. The low patient dose, optimum gamma energy, ease of preparation from a ^{99}Mo generator and acceptably short half-life have favoured its use. In addition, Tc can be readily reduced and incorporated with many different pharmaceuticals. Other radionuclides used include ^{201}Tl, ^{111}In, ^{67}Ga, ^{51}Cr, ^{131}I, ^{81m}Kr and ^{18}F. Some specific applications are outlined below.

The d,l diastereoisomer of hexamethylpropyleneamineoxine (HMPAO) labelled with ^{99m}Tc is a lipophilic complex which rapidly crosses the intact blood-brain barrier and is retained in the brain for an extended period, making detailed tomographic studies of regional cerebral blood flow possible. Abnormal cerebral blood flow following e.g stroke, Alzheimer's disease and dementia can be diagnosed.

The same radiopharmaceutical ^{99m}Tc- HMPAO is used to label mixed leucocytes separated from the patient's blood. The labelled leucocytes are reinjected where the cells migrate to areas where there is acute infection or active inflammation. These areas show up as 'hot spots' on the gamma camera images. ^{111}In-labelled granulocytes are also used for similar purposes.

The use of radiopharmaceuticals in the evaluation of gastrointestinal function has been reviewed by Frier and Perkins [143]. Test meals have been radiolabelled with radiopharmaceuticals of ^{99m}Tc, ^{51}Cr, ^{129}Cs, ^{111}In and ^{131}I.

As an example of a gaseous radionuclide in clinical use, ^{81m}Kr may be used for ventilation lung scans. The radionuclide is eluted from a ^{81}Rb generator for use as required. The half-life of ^{81}Rb is only 4.576 hours, so reasonable access to a cyclotron for its production and column preparation is required. The gas is inhaled via a nasal catheter and the gamma images provide a picture of the regional ventilation in the lungs. ^{133}Xe and ^{127}Xe have also been used as alternatives.

As an example of use of a PET radionuclide, [^{18}F]-2 deoxy-2-fluoro-D-glucose (FDG) is used predominantly in the study of cerebral and myocardial metabolism. In the brain, FDG undergoes carrier-mediated uptake as a glucose analogue and serves as a substrate for hexokinase. Due to the structural differences from the parent molecule (glucose), FDG is metabolically trapped in the cell because phosphorylation cannot proceed past the C-1 carbon [144]. FDG has also been evaluated for uses in **oncology** [145].

5.5.7.2 Uses in diagnostic non-imaging / *in vitro* studies

^{14}C is used to study the absorption and metabolism of various substances by the oral administration of ^{14}C-labelled glychocolic acid (for bacterial overgrowth in the gut), ^{14}C-labelled triolein (for fat malabsorption), ^{14}C-labelled aminopyrine (for hepatic function) and, most commonly, ^{14}C-urea (for H-pylori detection). In each case, the exhaled CO_2 is collected over a set period of time, measured and the total activity exhaled over the relevant period is compared to the total administered activity.

An example of a dual-tracer test is the Schilling test for the study of malabsorption of vitamin B_{12} [146-148]. The patient is given one capsule containing ^{58}Co-labelled cyanocobalamin (vitamin B12) and a second capsule containing ^{57}Co bound to human gastric juice, then a flushing injection of cyanocobalamin intramuscularly to flush the labelled vitamin from the bloodstream. The measured ratio of $^{57}Co/^{58}Co$ in a 24-hour urine sample can lead to diagnosis of mild or intestinal malabsorption of the vitamin, or pernicious anaemia.

5.5.7.3 Bone densitometry

This is a common technique using ^{125}I and ^{153}Gd sealed sources to determine the calcium content in bones by differentiated absorption of the photon energies. It is commonly used in the diagnosis of osteoporosis in women, particularly those in the post-menopausal stage of life.

5.5.8 Uses of radionuclides in treatment

For therapeutic purposes, the radiation exposure is the aim of the treatment but it should be no more than that necessary for the required effect – the radioactivity should be localised at the site of interest, either as an unsealed radiopharmaceutical or sealed (e.g. brachytherapy) source, with the gamma or particulate radiation delivering most of the dose in the immediate surrounding tissue. The radiopharmaceutical should clear by decay and biological removal, the brachytherapy source usually by physical removal.

5.5.8.1 External beam therapy

A variety of clinical radiation generators are used for beam therapy, including X-ray tubes, linear accelerators, heavy particle beams and teletherapy devices which use sealed radionuclide sources. Radionuclide gamma ray sources which have been used are ^{226}Ra, ^{137}Cs and ^{60}Co. ^{60}Co units are by far the most common, and are the only ones available commercially, with air **kerma** outputs typically 1-2 Gy min^{-1} at 1 metre e.g. see [149] and [150]. In the UK at least, the trend is away from use of teletherapy equipment using ^{60}Co and/or ^{137}Cs sources. Linear accelerators are now the preferred option, with only a few radionuclide-based machines now present in UK hospitals.

5.5.8.2 Brachytherapy

Brachytherapy is the practice of emplacing small sealed sources of radionuclides within or on the body, in or near a cancerous tumour for its irradiation [151,152]. The sources are available as wires (for example, ^{192}Ir), needles or tubes (for example ^{137}Cs) seeds (for example, ^{125}I) or discs (for example, ^{90}Sr). Sources are either placed into the tumour itself (interstitial) or into a body cavity (intracavity). Surface applicators, for example, onto the eye, are also available.

The radioactive implants are placed into the tumour (interstitial) remotely following the surgical emplacement of a catheter or applicator ('remote afterloading'). Ir-192 wire is commonly the source emplaced for the irradiation treatment [153-157], but ^{137}Cs pellets are also important.

Intracavity treatments for gynaecological brachytherapy, also loaded remotely, are temporary and frequently use ^{137}Cs as beads or tubes [158-160].

Permanent interstitial implants are usually in the form of ^{125}I seeds [161-165]. The ^{125}I is absorbed on anion exchange resin spheres which are contained within a welded titanium capsule. The dose distribution around each seed is anisotropic and often a number of seeds are implanted to achieve a relatively uniform dose to the tumour.

Other radionuclides which have been used for brachytherapy are ^{198}Au, ^{103}Pd, ^{182}Ta, ^{252}Cf (as neutron source), ^{226}Ra (historically) and ^{145}Sm (proposed) [142].

5.5.8.3 Radiotherapy

Radioiodine therapy with ^{131}I is one of the major treatments for hyperthyroidism [166] and is increasingly used even in younger patients. Thyrotoxicosis is also treatable with ^{131}I – the size of the gland is first estimated from an image following administration of tracer amount of ^{131}I, then the therapeutic dose, usually given orally as Na^{131}I, is delivered at typically 4 MBq per gram of thyroid.

^{89}Sr as strontium chloride is used to provide partial or complete pain relief to patients with bone metastases secondary to prostatic carcinoma at the stage of hormone therapy failure. Typically 150 MBq of ^{89}SrCl$_2$ as aqueous solution is injected intravenously. It acts as a calcium analogue with selective uptake at sites of increased bone metabolism, with consequent minimal beta irradiation of healthy tissue. Other radionuclides used for bone cancer pain relief are ^{186}Re and ^{153}Sm while ^{117m}Sn, ^{188}W, ^{166}Ho have been proposed [142].

Radioimmunotherapy involves the delivery of a therapeutic dose to a cancerous tumour by labelling a cell-killing radionuclide onto a monoclonal antibody whose uptake is very strong in the tumour. Ideally, the half-life of the radionuclide should be similar to the uptake and residence times of the antibody. This type of therapy is relatively new and developing. Currently used radionuclides are:

^{32}P, ^{67}Cu, ^{186}Re

and others proposed for use are:

^{188}W/^{188}Re, ^{33}P, ^{166}Ho, ^{153}Sm, ^{145}Sm [142]

5.5.9 Radioprotection research

As well as clinical trials run for radiopharmaceuticals, which form part of a multi-stage process prior to introduction of new diagnostic and therapeutic procedures, other trials are run to provide information on the human metabolism of radioactive and stable elements for radioprotection research.

A wide range of volunteer studies have been carried out and some of these are listed in Table 5.9.

Table 5.9: Summary of some radioprotection research studies.

Oral administration	Radionuclide	Foodstuff	Reference
	^{137}Cs	mutton	[167]
	^{74}As	fish	[168]
	^{115m}Cd	crab	[169]
	^{203}Pb	aqueous chloride	[170]
Intravenous administration	Radionuclide	medium	Reference
	^{133}Ba	saline	[171]
	^{45,47}Ca, ^{85}Sr	saline	[172]
	^{237}Pu	Pu(IV) citrate	[173]
	^{237}Pu	Pu(IV) citrate	[174]
	^{26}Al	citrate	[175]
	^{26}Al, ^{67}Ga	citrate	[176]

Information on biological half-life, uptake factor, distribution, renal clearance and excretion are obtained from such studies.

ACKNOWLEDGEMENTS

The authors are indebted to Susan Parry (Centre for Environmental Technology, Imperial College at Silwood Park) for the sub-section on neutron activation analysis and to Ian Adsley (AEA Technology plc) for a contribution on applications in the coal industry. They are grateful to Ed Lorch and Mark Shilton (Nycomed Amersham plc) and to Mike Angus (Safeguard International) for valuable comments on the sections on industrial applications of radionuclides. Phil Dendy (Addenbrook's Hospital, Cambridge) Graham Hart (Bradford Royal Infirmary), Nigel Williams and colleagues of the Institute of Physics and Engineering in Medicine (Radionuclide SIG) and Steve Waters (MRC Cyclotron Unit, Hammersmith Hospital) are thanked for their valuable comments on the medical applications sections.

REFERENCES

1. R. G. Bennett, *Markets for reactor-produced non-fission radioisotopes*, Idaho National Engineering Laboratory Report, INEL-95/0048, 1995.

2. S. Machi and R. Iyer, *Nuclear and radiation applications in industry: Tools for innovation*, IAEA Bulletin **1**, 1-6, 1994.

3. G. L. Tingey, G.P. Dix and E.J Wahlquist, *Contributions and future of radioisotopes in medical, industrial and space applications*, American Nuclear Society winter meeting November 1990.

4. International Atomic Energy Agency, Vienna, Industrial applications of radioisotopes and radiation technology, IAEA,1982.

5. International Atomic Energy Agency, Vienna, Guidebook on radioisotope tracers in industry, IAEA,1990.

6. International Atomic Energy Agency, Vienna, Applications of isotopes and radiation in conservation of the environment, IAEA,1992.

7. B. L. Eyre, *Industrial applications of radiation*, in Becquerel's legacy: A century of radioactivity, Radiat. Prot. dosim., **68**(1/2), 63-72, 1996.

8. E. Lorch, *Industrial and analytical applications of radioisotope radiation sources*, J. Radioanal. Chem., **48**, 209-212, 1979.

9. G. J. Lyman and R. J. Chesher, On-stream analysis for ash in coal slurries, Paper C-1, in Preprints, 5th. Int. Conf. Coal Reseach, Düsseldorf, FRG, 1-5 September 1980, Essen, FRG, Steinkohlenbergbauverein, **2**, 145-163 1980.

10. J. S. Wykes, I. Adsley, L. R. Cooper and G. M. Croke, *Natural γ-radiation: a steering guide in coal seams*, in Nuclear Geophysics: a selection of papers on applications of nuclear techniques in minerals exploration, mining and process control, Ed. C. G. Clayton, Intl, J. Appl. Radiation and Isotopes, **34(1)**, 23-36, 1983.

11. N. Küper, *Benefits of the use of radioisotopes in industrial gauging and control*, in Industrial applications of radioisotopes and radiation technology, 379-391, IAEA,1982.

12. C.G. Clayton and M.R. Wormald, *Coal analysis by nuclear methods*, in Nuclear Geophysics: a selection of papers on applications of nuclear techniques in minerals exploration, mining and process control, Ed. C. G. Clayton, Intl, J. Appl. Radiation and Isotopes, **34(1)**, 3-22, 1983.

13. P.G. Killeen, *Borehole logging for uranium*, in Nuclear Geophysics: a selection of papers on applications of nuclear techniques in minerals exploration, mining and process control, Ed. C. G. Clayton, Intl, J. of Appl. Radiation and Isotopes, **34(1)**, 1-476, 1983.

14. M. T. Hutchings and C. G. Windsor, Industrial applications, Methods of Exptl. Phys., (Academic Press, New York) **23**, 405, 1987.

15. T. R. Lamp and B.D. Donovan, *Unattended power sources for remote, harsh environments*, AIAA Report, AIAA-94-4206-CP, 1994.

16. B. Sansoni, *Nuclear and nuclear related analytical techniques*, in International Atomic Energy Agency, Vienna, Applications of isotopes and radiation in conservation of the environment, IAEA, pp17-41, 1992.

17. T.E. Cranshaw, B.W. Dale, G. Longworth and C.E. Johnson, Mössbauer spectroscopy and its applications, Cambridge University Press, 1985.

18. N. N. Greenwood and T. C. Gibb, Mössbauer spectroscopy, Chapman and Hall, London, 1971.

19. G. Longworth, *Instrumentation for Mössbauer spectroscopy*, chapter in advances in Mössbauer spectroscopy: applications to research in physics, chemistry and biology, Elsevier, 1983.

20. G. Longworth, *The use of Mössbauer spectroscopy in non-destructice testing,* N.D.T. International, October 1977, 241-246, 1977.

21. G. Longworth, *The use of Mössbauer spectroscopy in Materials Science*, in Treatise on Materials Science and Technology, Academic Press, **19A**, 107-150, 1980.

22. G. Longworth and M.S. Tite, *Mössbauer and magnetic susceptibility studies of iron oxides from soils from archaeological sites*, Archaeometry, **19**, 3-13, 1977.

23. Z. B. Alfassi, (ed.) *Activation Analysis*, Boca Raton, CRC Press, 1989.

24. W. D. Ehmann and D. E.Vance, *Radiochemistry and Nuclear Methods of Analysis,* John Wiley, New York, 1991.

25. S. J. Parry, *Activation Spectrometry in Chemical Analysis,* New York, John Wiley, 1991.

26. Russell Sims, AEA Technology plc., Private Communication 1997.

27. Russell Sims, AEA Technology plc., as quoted in [7].

28. T. W. Conlon, *Nuclear physics for Materials Technology : accelerator-based methods*, Contemporary Physics, **26**, 521, 1985.

29. J. Asher, Wear measurements using thin layer activation (TLA), Chapter 2 in Surface activation: a practical approach, Scandinavian Scientific Press, to be published, 1997.

30. J. Asher, M. J. Bennett, R. W. M. Hawes, J. B. Price, A. T. Tuson, D. J. Savage and S. Sugden, *Thin layer activation: a technique for monitoring material loss during high temperature surface degradation processes*, Mats. Sci. and Eng., 88, 143, 1987.

31. G. V. Evans, *Tracer techniques in hydrology*, in Nuclear Geophysics: a selection of papers on applications of nuclear techniques in minerals exploration, mining and process control, Ed. C. G. Clayton, Intl, J. Appl. Radiation and Isotopes, **34(1)**, 451-475, 1983.

32. International Atomic Energy Agency, Vienna, Isotope Techniques in Ground Water Hydrology, Vol 1, IAEA, 1974.

33. M. Ivanovich and R.S. Harmon, *Uranium series disequilibrium: Application to earth, marine and environmental sciences*, 2nd Edition, Clarendon Press, Oxford 1992.

34. G. Longworth, C.E. Linklater, S.E. Hasler, A.E. Milodowski and E.K. Hyslop, *Interpretation of uranium series measurements on Sellafield rocks and groundwaters*, Nirex Science Report S/97/004 United Kingdom Nirex Limited 1997.

35. J.I. Kim, B. Delalowitz, P. Zeh, T. Probst, X. Lin, U. Erlicher, C. Schauer, M. Ivanovich, G. Longworth, S.E. Hasler, M. Gardiner, P. Fritz, D. Klotz, D. Lazik, M. Wolf, S. Geyer, J.L. Alexander, D. Read and J. B. Thomas, *Colloid migration in groundwaters: geochemical interactions of radionuclides with natural colloids*, Final Report, Contract No. FI2W/CT91/0084, European Commisssion Report, EUR 16754EN, 1996.

36. J.K. Osmond and J.B. Cowart, *The theory and uses of natural uranium isotope variations in hydrology*, Atomic Energy Reviews, **14** ,621-679, 1976.

37. W. M. Miller, W. R. Alexander, N. A. Chapman, I. G. McKinley and J. A. T. Smellie, Natural analogue studies in the geological disposal of radioactive wastes, Elsevier, Studies in Environmental Science 57, 1994.

38. M. Ivanovich, J. H. Tellam, G. Longworth and J.J. Monaghan, *Rock/water interaction timescales involving U and Th isotopes in a Permo-Triassic sandstone*, Radiochim. Acta., **58/59**, 423-432, 1992.

39. J.R.L. Allen, J.E. Rae, G. Longworth, S.E. Hasler and M. Ivanovich, *A comparison of the 210Pb dating technique with three other independent dating methods in an oxic estuarine salt-marsh sequence*, Estuaries, **16(3B)**, 670-677, 1993.

40. G. Faure, Principles of Isotope Geology, 2nd edition, John Wiley & Sons, 1987.

41. T.L. Ku and Z.C. Liang, *The dating of impure carbonates with decay-series isotopes*, Nuclear Instr. and Meth. in Phys. Res., 223, 563-571 1984.

42. M. J. Aitken, Physics and archaeology, Second edition, Clarendon Press, Oxford,1974.

43. R. E. Taylor, Radiocarbon dating, an archaeological perspective, Academic Press, 1987.

44. W. G. Mook, Carbon-14 in hydrogeological studies, in Handbook of environmental isotope geochemistry, Eds. P. Fritz and J. Ch. Fontes, Volume 1, the terrestial environment, A, Elsevier, 1980.

45. B. Mason and C.B. Moore, Principles of geochemistry, John Wiley and Sons, 1982.

46. A.T Elliott and R.A. Shields, *UK nuclear medicine survey, 1989/90,* Nuclear Medicine Communications, **14**, 360-364, 1993.

47. D. A. Weber, K. F. Eckerman, L. T. Dillman and J. C. Ryman, *MIRD: Radionuclide Data and Decay Schemes*, Society of Nuclear Medicine, New York, 1989.

48. ICRP, *Radionuclide transformations*, ICRP Publication 38, International Commission on Radiological Protection, Pergamon, Oxford, 1983.

49. K. F. Eckerman, R. J. Westfall, J. C. Ryman and M. Cristy, *Availability of nuclear decay data in electronic form, including beta spectra not previously published*, Health Phys., **67** (4), 1994.

50. R. Loevinger and M. Berman, *A revised schema for calculating the absorbed dose from biologically distributed radionuclides.* MIRD Pamphlet No.1 (Rev), Society of Nuclear Medicine, New York, 1976.

51. M. J. Berger, *Energy deposition in water by photons from point isotropic sources*, MIRD Pamphlet No. 2, J. Nucl. Med, **10**, Suppl. No. 1, 1968.

52. G. L. Brownell, W. H. Ellet and A. R. Reddy, *Absorbed fractions for photon dosimetry*, MIRD Pamphlet No. 3, J. Nucl. Med., Suppl. No. 1, 1968.

53. W. S. Snyder, M. R. Ford and G. G. Warner, *Estimates of specific absorbed fractions for photon sources uniformly distributed in various organs of a heterogeneous phantom*, MIRD Pamphlet No. 5 (revised), Society of Nuclear Medicine, New York, 1978.

54. M. J. Berger, *Distribution of absorbed dose around point sources of electrons and beta particles in water and other media*, MIRD Pamphlet No. 7, J. Nucl. Med.,**12**, Suppl. No. 5, 1971.

55. W. H. Ellet and R. M. Humes, *Absorbed fractions for small volumes containing photon-emitting radioactivity*, MIRD Pamphlet No. 8, J. Nucl. Med. Suppl. No. 5, 1971.

56. K. A. Lathrop, R. E. Johnstone, M. Blau and E. Q. Rothschild, *Radiation dose to humans from ^{75}Se-L-selenomethionine*, MIRD Pamphlet No. 9, J. Nucl. Med. Suppl. No. 6, 1972.

57. L. T. Dillman and F. C. Von der Lage, *Radionuclide decay schemes and nuclear parameters for use in radiation-dose estimation*, MIRD Pamphlet No. 10, Society of Nuclear Medicine, New York, 1975.

58. W. S. Snyder, M. R. Ford, G. G. Warner and S. B. Watson, *'S', Absorbed dose per unit cumulated activity for selected radionuclides and organs*, MIRD Pamphlet No. 11, Society of Nuclear Medicine, New York, 1975.

59. M. Berman, *Kinetic models for absorbed dose calculations*, MIRD Pamphlet No. 12, Society of Nuclear Medicine, New York, 1977.

60. MIRD Dose Estimate Report No. 1, *Summary of current radiation dose estimates to humans from ^{75}Se-L-selenomethionine*, J. Nucl. Med., **14**, 49-50, 1973.

61. MIRD Dose Estimate Report No. 2, *Summary of current radiation dose estimates to humans from* ^{66}Ga, ^{67}Ga, ^{68}Ga *and* ^{72}Ga-*citrate*, J. Nucl. Med, **14**, 755-756, 1973.

62. MIRD Dose Estimate Report No. 3, *Summary of current radiation dose estimates to humans with various liver conditions from* ^{99m}Tc-*sulphur colloid*, J. Nucl. Med, **16**, 108, 1975.

63. MIRD Dose Estimate Report No.4, *Summary of current radiation dose estimates to humans with various liver conditions from* ^{198}Au-*colloidal gold*. Nucl. Med., **16**, 173-174, 1975.

64. MIRD Dose Estimate Report No.5, *Summary of current radiation dose estimates to humans from* ^{123}I, ^{124}I, ^{125}I, ^{126}I, ^{130}I, ^{131}I, ^{132}I *as sodium iodide*, J. Nucl. Med, **16**, 857-860, 1975.

65. MIRD Dose Estimate Report No.6, *Summary of current radiation dose estimates to humans from* ^{197}Hg *and* ^{203}Hg-*labelled chlormerodrin*, J. Nucl. Med., **16**, 1095-1098, 1975.

66. MIRD Dose Estimate Report No.7, *Summary of current radiation dose estimates to humans from* ^{123}I, ^{124}I, ^{126}I, ^{130}I, ^{131} *as sodium Rose Bengal*, J. Nucl. Med., **16**, 1214-1217, 1975.

67. MIRD Dose Estimate Report No.8, *Summary of current radiation dose estimates to normal humans from 99mTc as sodium pertechnetate*, J. Nucl. Med., **17**, 74-77, 1976.

68. MIRD Dose Estimate Report No.9, *Estimates of radiation absorbed doses from radioxenons in lung imaging*, J. Nucl. Med., **21**, 459-465, 1980.

69. MIRD Dose Estimate Report No.10, *Radiation absorbed dose from albumin microspheres labeled with* ^{99m}Tc, J. Nucl. Med., **23**, 915-917, 1982.

70. MIRD Dose Estimate Report No.11, *Radiation absorbed doses from* ^{52}Fe, ^{55}Fe *and* ^{59}Fe *used to study ferrokinetics*, J. Nucl. Med., **24**, 339-348, 1983.

71. MIRD Dose Estimate Report No.12, *Radiation absorbed dose from Tc-99m diethylenetriaminepentaacetic acid*, J. Nucl. Med., 25, 503-505, 1984.

72. MIRD Dose Estimate Report No.13, *Radiation absorbed dose from technetium-99m labelled bone imaging agents*, J. Nucl. Med, 30, 1117-1122, 1989.

73. MIRD Dose Estimate Report No.14, *Radiation absorbed dose from technetium-99m labelled red blood cells*, J. Nucl. Med., 31, 378-380, 1990.

74. MIRD Dose Estimate Report No.15, *Radiation absorbed dose for radioindium-labelled autologous platelets*, J. Nucl. Med., 33, 777-780, 1992.

75. R. Loevinger, T. F. Budinger and E. E. Watson, *MIRD Primer for absorbed dose calculations*, Society of Nuclear Medicine, New York, 1988.

76. A. I. Kassis, K. S. Sastry and S. J. Adelstein, *Intracellular localisation of Auger electron emitter: biophysical dosimetry*, Radiat. Prot. Dosim., **13**, 233-236, 1985.

77.   D. A. Weber, *Biologic data, models and dosimetric methods for internal emitters, In Dosimetry of Administered Radionuclides*, Eds S. J. Adelstein and A. I. Kassis, pp 58-88, American College of Nuclear Physicians, Washington, 1989.

78.   M. Cristy and K. F. Eckerman, *Specific absorbed fractions of energy at various ages from internal photon sources*, ORNL/TM-8381, vols **1-7**, 1987.

79.   E. E. Watson, M. G. Stabin and J. A. Siegel, *MIRD formulation*, J. Med. Phys, **20**, 511-514, 1993.

80.   International Commission on Radiation Units and Measurements, ICRU Report 32: *Methods of assessment of absorbed dose in clinical use of radionuclides*, 1979.

81.   NCRP. *Nuclear Medicine: Factors influencing the choice and use of radionuclides in diagnosis and therapy*, NCRP Report No. 70. National Council on Radiation Protection and Measurements, Bethesda, Maryland, 1982.

82.   NCRP. *The experimental basis for absorbed-dose calculations in medical uses of radionuclides*, NCRP Report No. 83. National Council on Radiation Protection and Measurements, Bethesda, Maryland, 1985.

83.   NCRP. *Precautions in the management of patients who have received therapeutic amounts of radionuclides*, NCRP Report No. 37.. National Council on Radiation Protection and Measurements, Washington DC, 1970.

84.   NCRP. *Protection against radiation from brachytherapy sources*, NCRP Report No. 40. National Council on Radiation Protection and Measurements, Washington DC,.1972.

85.   NCRP. *Radiation protection for medical and allied health personnel*. NCRP Report No. 48. National Council on Radiation Protection and Measurements, Washington DC, 1976.

86.   NCRP. *Structural shielding design and evaluation for medical use of X-rays and gamma-rays of energies up to 10 MeV*. NCRP Report No. 49. National Council on Radiation Protection and Measurements, Washington DC, 1976.

87.   NCRP. *Medical radiation exposure of pregnant and potentially pregnant women*. NCRP Report No. 54. National Council on Radiation Protection and Measurements, Washington DC, 1977.

88.   ICRP. *Protection of the patient in nuclear Medicine*, ICRP Publication 52, Annals ICRP, **17 (4),** 1987.

89.   ICRP. *Radiation dose to patients from radiopharmaceuticals*, ICRP Publication 53, Annals ICRP, **18 (1-4),** 1987.

90.   ICRP. *1990 Recommendations of the Internal Commission on Radiological Protection*, ICRP Publication 60, Annals ICRP, **21 (1-3)**, 1991.

91.   ICRP. *Radiological protection in biomedical research (includes Addendum 1 to Publication 53 - Radiation dose to patients from radiopharmaceuticals)*, ICRP Publication 62, Annals ICRP, **22 (3)**, 1991.

92. ICRP. *Dose coefficients for intakes of radionuclides by workers (includes Summary of the current ICRP Principles for Protection of the Patient in Nuclear Medicine)*, ICRP Publication 68, Annals ICRP, **24 (4)**, 1994.

93. NRPB Radiological Protection Bulletin, No. 197, 18-22, January 1998.

94. ICRP. *Radiological protection of the worker in medicine and dentistry*, ICRP Publication 57, Annals ICRP, **20 (3)**, 1989.

95. ICRP. *Radiological protection and safety in medicine*, ICRP Publication 73, Annals ICRP, **26 (2)**, 1996.

96. NRPB. *Occupational, public and medical exposure*, Documents of the NRPB, **4 (2)**, 1993.

97. NRPB. *Guidance notes for the protection of persons against ionising radiations arising from medical and dental use*, HMSO (ISBN 0 85951 299 1), 1988.

98. NRPB. *Board statement on diagnostic medical exposures to ionising radiation during pregnancy*, Documents of the NRPB, **4 (4)**, 1993.

99. R. Wooton (ed), *Radiation protection of patients*, Cambridge University Press (ISBN 0 521 42669 3), 1993.

100. ARSAC. *Notes for guidance on the administration of radioactive substances to persons for purposes of diagnosis, treatment or research*, 1993.

101. MRC. *Responsibility in investigations on human subjects*, Medical Research Council Report, pp 21-25, 1962-63.

102. WHO. *Use of radiation and radionuclides on human beings for medical research, training and non-medical purposes*. Report of a WHO Expert Committee. Technical Report Series 611, WHO Geneva, 1977.

103. *Guidelines on the practice of ethics committees in medical research*, Royal College of Physicians, London, 1984.

104. *Irradiation of human subjects for medical research*, British Institute of Radiology Bulletin, **1 (2)**, 1975.

105. J. L. Humm, R. W. Howell and D. V. Rao, *Dosimetry of Auger-emitting radionuclides: Report No. 3 of AAPM Nuclear Medicine task Group No, 6*, Med. Phys., **21**, 1901-1915, 1994.

106. D. E. Charlton and J. Booz, *A Monte Carlo treatment of the decay of I-125*, Radiat. Res., **87**, 10-23, 1981.

107. J. L. Humm, *The analysis of Auger electrons released following the decay of radioisotopes and photoelectric interactions and their contribution to energy deposition*, PhD Thesis, Polytechnic of the South Bank, London, 1983.

108. R. W. Howell, K. S. R. Sastry, H. Z. Hill and D. V. Rao, *Cis-platinum-193m: Its microdosimetry and potential for chemo-Auger combination therapy of cancer*, In Proceedings of Fourth International Radiopharmaceutical Dosimetry Symposium, Eds A. T. Schlafke-Stelson and E. E. Watson, National Technical Information Service, Springfield, VA, 1986.

109. E. Pomplun, J. Booz and D. E. Charlton, *A Monte Carlo simulation of Auger cascades*, Radiat. Res., **111**, 533-552, 1987.

110. D. V. Rao, K. S. R. Sastry, H. E. Grimmond, R. W. Howell, G. F. Govelitz, V. K. Lanka and V. B. Mylavarapu, *Cytotoxicity of some indium radiopharmaceuticals in mouse testes*, J. Nucl. Med., **29**, 375-384, 1988.

111. NRPB, Radiological Protection Bulletin, No. 172, 1995.

112. EC Directive 84/466/Euratom, Official J. of European Communities, **27**, 1984.

113. *Ionizing Radiation (Protection of Persons Undergoing Medical Examination or Treatment) Regulations*, 1988 (HMSO, London).

114. *Ionizing Radiation (Protection of Patients) Regulations (Northern Ireland)*, 1988, (HMSO, Northern Ireland).

115. *The Medicines (Administration of Radioactive Substances) Regulations 1978*, SI 1978 No 1006.

116. *The Medicines (Radioactive Substances) Order 1978*, SI 1978 No 1004.

117. A. P. Hufton, *Protection of the general public and workers in medicine: implementation of the CEC directives in the UK*. In Medical Radiation Protection Practice Within the EEC, Eds M. Fitzgerald and J.-M. Courades, British Institute of Radiology, London, 1991.

118. P. J. Roberts, *UK Patient protection legislation*. In Medical Radiation Protection Practice Within the EEC, Eds M. Fitzgerald and J.-M. Courades, British Institute of Radiology, London, 1991.

119. P. H. Cox and G. J. Meyer, *Pharmaceuticals 1994, Nil desperandum*. Europ. J. Nucl. Med., 22 (6), 1995.

120. *Guide to good pharmaceutical manufacturing practice*, HMSO London (ISBN 0 11 320832 4).

121. *Guide to good manufacturing practice*. In Netherlands Pharmacopoeia, 9th edn, incorporating the European Pharmacopoeia, 2nd Edition. 519-559.

122. T. J. Godden, *Therapeutic uses of unsealed radionuclides*, In: Radiation Protection in Nuclear Medicine and Pathology, Institute of Physical Sciences in Medicine Report No. 63, 1991.

123. E. D. Williams, *Imaging and other diagnostic and research in vivo procedures*, In: Radiation Protection in Nuclear Medicine and Pathology, Institute of Physical Sciences in Medicine Report No. 63, 1991.

124. K. J. Langan, H. N. Wagner and J. W. Buchanan, *Design concepts of a nuclear medicine department*, J. Nucl. Med., **20**, 1093-4, 1979.

125. L. K. Harding, S. Hesslewood, S. K. Ghose and W. H. Thomson, *The value of syringe shields in a nuclear medicine department*, Nucl. Med. Commun., **6**, 449-454, 1985.

126. E. D. Williams, L. K. Harding and J. H. McKillop, *Checklists for quality assurance and audit in nuclear medicine*, Nucl. Med. Commun., **10**, 595-599, 1989.

127. S. R. Hesslewood, *Radiopharmacy standards*, In Quality Standards in Nuclear Medicine, The Institute of Physical Sciences in Medicine Report No. 65, Eds G. C. Hart and A. H. Smith, pp85-98, 1992.

128. A. Parkin, J. P. Sephton, E. G. A. Aird, J. Hannan, A. E. Simpson and M. J. Woods, *Protocol for establishing and maintaining the calibration of medical radionuclide calibrators and their quality control*, Proceedings of the joint IPSM/BIR Meeting on Quality Standards in Nuclear Medicine, BIR, London, February 1992. Institute of Physical Sciences in Medicine Report No. 65, 60-77, 1992.

129. Hospital physicists Association, *Quality control of nuclear medicine instrumentation* (CRS 38), HPA London, 1983.

130. *Guidance notes for hospitals on the premises and environment for the preparation of radiopharmaceuticals*, HMSO London, 1982.

131. R. M. Abra, N. D. S. Ball and P. W. Horton, *An evaluation of some radiopharmaceutical transfer techniques*, J. Clin. Hosp. Pharm., **5**, 3-9, 1980.

132. Health Equipment Information. *An evaluation of the AMERCARE containment cabinet*, 25-29, DHSS London, 1987.

133. C. R. Lazarus, *Techniques for dispensing of radiopharmaceuticals*, In Textbook of Radiopharmacy Theory and practice, Ed C. B. Sampson, 85-99, Gordon and Breach, New York, 1990.

134. C. R. Lazarus, *Design of hospital radiopharmacy laboratories*, In Textbook of Radiopharmacy Theory and practice, Ed C. B. Sampson, 163-176, Gordon and Breach, New York, 1990.

135. *Hospital Radiopharmacy Theory and Practice*, Eds M. Frier, J. G. Hardy, S. R. Hesslewood and R Lawrence, Institute of Physical Sciences in Medicine, York, 1988.

136. *Health Service use of Ionising Radiations*, Health Circular HC(89)18, Department of Health, London, 1989.

137. S. Brown and M. H. Baker, *The sterility testing of dispensed radiopharmaceuticals*, Nucl. Med. Commun., **7**, 327-336, 1986.

138. *Reporting Accidents with and Defects in Medicinal products; Buildings and Plant: and Other Medical and non-Medical Equipment and Supplies*, Health Circular HC(88)51, Department of Health, London, 1988.

139. World Health Organisation, *Quality Assurance in nuclear medicine*, WHO, Geneva, 1982.

140. J. H. McKillop, *Nuclear Medicine*, Rad. Prot. Dosim., **68** (1/2), 1996.

141. R. G. Bennett, *Markets for reactor-produced non-fission radioisotopes*, Idaho National Engineering Laboratory report INEL-95/0048, 1995.

142. I. P. C. Murray and P. J. Ell (eds), *Nuclear medicine in clinical diagnosis and treatment*, Vols 1 and 2, Churchill Livingstone, 1994.

143. M. Frier and A. C. Perkins, *Radiopharmaceuticals and the gastrointestinal tract*, Eur. J. Nucl. Med., **21**, 1234-1242, 1994.

144. T. J. McCarthy, S. W. Schwarz and M. J. Welch, *Nuclear medicine and positron emission tomography: an overview*, J. Chem. Education, **71**, 830-836, 1994.

145. C. S. Brock, S. R. Meikle and P. Price. *Does fluorine-18 fluorodeoxyglucose metabolic imaging of tumours benefit oncology?* Eur. J. Nucl. Med., **24**, 691- 705, 1997.

146. R. F. Schilling, *Intrinsic factor studies II*, J. Lab and Clin. Med., **42**, 860, 1953.

147. J. H. Katz, J. Dimase and R. M. Donaldson, *Simultaneous administration of gastric-juice bound and free radioactive cyanocobalamin: rapid procedure for diferentiating between intrinsic factor deficiency and other causes of vitamin B₁₂ malabsorption*, J. Lab. and Clin. Med., **61**, 266-271, 1963.

148. H. I. Atrah and R. J. L. Davidson, *A survey and critical evaluation of a dual isotope (Dicopac) vitamin B12 absorption test*, Eur. J. Nucl. Med., **15**, 57-60, 1989.

149. IAEA, *Co-60 teletherapy: a compendium of international practice*, IAEA Vienna, 1984.

150. ICRU, *Specification of high activity gamma ray sources*, International Commission on Radiation Units and Measurements, ICRU Report 18, Washington DC, 1970.

151. R. Sauer, *Interventional radiation therapy techniques - Brachytherapy*, Springer-Verlag, Berlin, 1991.

152. N. G. Trott, *Radionuclides in brachytherapy: Radium and after*, Br. J. Radiol., **21**, 1987.

153. R. Rozan, *et al, Interstitial Iridium-192 for bladder cancer, a multicentre survey: 205 patients*, Int. J. Rad. Onc. Biol. Phys., **24**, 469-477, 1992.

154. J. L. Habrand *et al, Twenty years experienceof interstitial iridium brachytherapy in the management of soft tissue sarcomas*, Int. J. Rad. Onc. Biol. Phys., **20**, 405-411, 1991.

155. J. E. Bello, C. Oyarzun, F. Abrath and J. Sole, *Study of the characteristics of Iridium-192 wire used in interstitial implants*, Radiol., **145**, 224-225, 1982.

156. I. S. Fentiman, C. Poole, D. Tong, P. J. Winter, H. M. Mayles, P. Turner, M. A. Chaudary and R. D. Rubens, *Iridium implant treatment without external radiotherapy for operable breast cancer*, Eur. J. Cancer (England), **27**, 447-450, 1991.

157. E. F. Thomson, F. Afshar and P. N. Plowman, *Paediatric brachytherapy - brain implantation*, Br. J. Radiol., **626**, 223-229, 1989.

158. M. Hareyama, M. Nishio, A. Saito, Y. Kagami, K. Asano, A. Oouchi, N. Narimatsu, Y. Somekawa, S. Sanbe and K. Morita, *Results of Cs needle interstitial implantation for carcinoma of the oral tongue,* Int. J. Rad. Oncol. Biol. Phys., **25**, 29-34, 1993.

159. L. Krishnan *et al, Dosimetric analysis in Brachytherapy of carcinoma of the cervix,* Int. J. Rad. Onc. Biol. Phys.,**18**, 965-970, 1990.

160. F. Ellis and C. B. G. Taylor, *The Amersham Caesium-137 afterloading system for gynaecological brachytherapy,* Amersham publication S/1/82, 1982.

161. R. Nath, A. S. Meigoni and A. Mellillo, *Some treatment planning considerations for Pd-103 and I-125 permanent interstitial implants,* Int. J. Rad. Onc. Biol. Phys., **22**, 1131-1138, 1992.

162. G. S. Burns and D. E. Raeside, *The accuracy of single-seed dose superposition for I-125 implants,* Med. Phys., **16**, 627-631, 1989.

163. S. C. Sharma, *Procedures for radioactive Iodine-125 seed implants,* Med. Dosim., **13**, 171-172, 1988.

164. L. L. Anderson, H. M. Kuan and I. Y. Ding, *Modern interstitial and intracavitary radiation cancer management,* Ed. F. W. George III, Masson, New York, 9-15, 1981.

165. S. Packer, S. Stoller, M. L. Lesser, F. S. Mandel and P. T. Finger, *Long term results of iodine-125 irradiation of uveal melanoma,* Opthamol., **99**, 767-773, 1992.

166. S. E. M. Clarke, *Radionuclide therapy of the thyroid,* Eur. J. Nucl. Med., **18**, 984-991, 1991.

167. R. J. Talbot, D. Newton, A. J. Warner, B. Walters and J. C. Sherlock, *Human uptake of ^{137}Cs in mutton,* Health Phys., **64**, 600-604, 1993.

168. R. M. Brown, D. Newton, C. J. Pickford and J. C. Sherlock, *Human metabolism of arsenobetaine ingested with fish,* Hum. Experim. Toxicol., **9**, 41-46, 1990.

169. D. Newton, P. Johnston, A. E. Lally, R. J. Pentreath and D. J. Swift, *The uptake by man of cadmium ingested in crab meat,* Human Toxicol., **3**, 23-28, 1984.

170. D. Newton, C. J. Pickford, A, C, Chamberlain, J. C. Sherlock and J. S. Hislop, *Elevation of lead in human blood from its controlled ingestion in beer,* Human Experim. Toxicol., **11**, 3-9, 1992.

171. D. Newton, G. E. Harrison, C. Kang and A. J. Warner, *Metabolism of injected barium in six healthy men,* Health Phys., **61**, 191-201, 1991.

172. D. Newton, G. E. Harrison, J. Rundo, C. Kang and A. J. Warner, *Metabolism of Ca and Sr in late adult life,* Health Phys., **59**, 433-442, 1990.

173. R. J. Talbot and D. Newton, *Blood retention and renal clearance of ^{237}Pu in man,* In Health Effects of Internally Deposited Radionuclides, Eds G. van Kaick, A. Karaoglou and A. M. Kellerer,, Proceedings of an International Seminar, Heidelberg, Germany, 18-21 April 1994.

174. A. J. Warner, R. J. Talbot and D. Newton, *Deposition of plutonium in human testes*, Rad. Prot. Dosim., **55**, 61-63, 1994.

175. R. J. Talbot, D. Newton, N. D. Priest, J. G. Austin and J. P. Day, *Inter-subject variability in the metabolism of aluminium following intravenous injection as citrate*, Human Experim. Toxicol., **14**, 595-599, 1995.

176. N. D. Priest, D. Newton, J. P. Day, R. J. Talbot and A. J. Warner, *Human metabolism of aluminium-26 and gallium-67 injected as citrates*, Human Experim. Toxicol., **14**, 287-293, 1995.

CHAPTER 6   RADIOLOGICAL PROTECTION

RICHARD BULL

6.1   INTRODUCTION

Ionising radiations can produce a variety of harmful effects in living organisms and their offspring [1]. Effects in humans characterised by an increase in severity of effect with increasing dose were known as **non–stochastic** [2], but are now referred to as **deterministic** effects [3]. Such effects include skin burns, clinically significant depression in the blood cell production by the bone marrow and formation of cataracts in the lens of the eye. Effects for which the probability of occurrence increases with increasing dose are known as **stochastic** effects [2]. Such effects show no apparent dose threshold and include the induction of cancers and **hereditary** effects (also known as **genetic effects)** in the descendants of the exposed individual.

The purpose of radiological protection is to prevent the occurrence of deterministic effects and to keep the probability of stochastic effects within acceptable limits.

This Chapter gives a brief description of radiological protection, with special reference to the radiochemical laboratory. Although current legislation is based on **ICRP** 26 [2], new regulations based on ICRP 60 [3] are imminent. This Chapter is, therefore, based on ICRP 60 quantities and recommendations. A short appendix on the ICRP 26 system is included.

6.2   DOSIMETRIC QUANTITIES & UNITS

A number of quantities are currently in use in radiological protection. Only the more frequently used quantities are described here.

The **absorbed dose** is defined as the energy absorbed per unit mass of irradiated material. The S.I. unit of absorbed dose is the **gray** (Gy) which is equal to one joule per kilogram. The biological effect of densely ionising radiations such as alpha particles is much greater than that of the same dose of radiations such as gamma rays which produce more widely spaced ionisation events. To allow for this difference a further quantity called **equivalent dose** is used. The S.I. unit of equivalent dose is the **sievert** (Sv). This quantity is defined as the product of absorbed dose and a radiation weighting factor, w_R which allows for the increased biological effectiveness of densely ionising radiations. These radiation weighting factors are listed in Table 6.1.

Different tissues and organs have different probabilities of suffering stochastic effects from a given equivalent dose. Therefore, when considering non-uniform irradiation of the body, it is necessary to combine the equivalent doses to various tissues in a manner which reflects these differences in tissue sensitivity. This is done by the use of **tissue weighting factors**, w_T which represent the relative contribution of the organ or tissue T to the total harm (or detriment, in ICRP terminology) resulting from uniform irradiation of the body. [3]. These are given in Table 6.2. The **effective dose** E is defined as the equivalent dose weighted over all irradiated tissues, so that

$$E = \sum_T w_T H_T \qquad (6.1)$$

where H_T is the equivalent dose received by tissue or organ T.

The equivalent doses to organs, resulting from intake of radionuclides, will be acquired over a considerable time period after intake. For the purposes of internal dosimetry it is useful to define the committed equivalent dose, $H_T(\tau)$ to an organ or tissue T. This is given by

$$H_T(\tau) = \int_{t_0}^{t_0+\tau} H_T(t)dt \qquad (6.2)$$

where $H_T(\tau)$ is the time-varying equivalent dose to T and τ is the integration period in years, following intake. If not specified, τ is taken to be 50 yr. for adults and 70 yr. for children. A tissue-weighted average of this quantity can be formed, which is called the **committed effective dose**, $E(\tau)$.

Table 6.1: Radiation weighting factors [1]

Type and energy range [2]		Radiation weighting factor w_R
Photons, all energies		1
Electrons and muons, all energies[2]		1
Neutrons, energy	< 10 keV	5
	10 keV to 100 keV	10
	>100 keV to 2 MeV	20
	> 2 MeV to 20 MeV	10
	> 20 MeV	5
Protons, other than recoil protons, energy >2 MeV		5
Alpha particles, fission fragments, heavy nuclei		20

[1] All values relate to the radiation incident on the body or, for internal sources, emitted from the source.

[2] Excluding Auger electrons emitted from radionuclides bound to DNA.

From ICRP 60 [3]. Adapted by permission of the International Commission on Radiological Protection.

Table 6.2: Tissue weighting factors[1]

Tissue or Organ	Tissue weighting factor, w_T
Gonads	0.20
Bone marrow (red)	0.12
Colon	0.12
Lung	0.12
Stomach	0.12
Bladder	0.05
Breast	0.05
Liver	0.05
Oesophagus	0.05
Thyroid	0.05
Skin	0.01
Bone surface	0.01
Remainder	0.05[2,3]

[1] The values have been developed from a reference population of equal numbers of both sexes and a wide range of ages. In the definition of effective dose they apply to workers, to the whole population and to either sex.

[2] For purposes of calculation, the remainder is composed of the following additional tissues and organs: adrenals, brain, upper large intestine, small intestine, kidney, muscle, pancreas, spleen, thymus and uterus. The list includes organs which are likely to be selectively irradiated. Some organs in the list are known to be susceptible to cancer induction. If other tissues and organs subsequently become identified as having a significant risk of induced cancer they will then be included either with a specific w_T or in this additional list constituting the remainder. The latter may also include other tissues or organs selectively irradiated.

[3] In those exceptional cases in which a single one of the remainder tissues or organs receives an equivalent dose in excess of the highest dose in any of the twelve organs for which a weighting factor is specified, a weighting factor of 0.025 should be applied to that tissue or organ and a weighting factor of 0.025 to the average dose in the rest of the remainder as defined above.

From, ICRP 60 [3]. Adapted by permission of the International Commission on Radiological Protection.

6.3 ICRP RECOMMENDATIONS

In ICRP 60 [3], practices are defined as those activities which increase the overall exposure to radiation. The system of protection in the case of practices is based on the following three principles.

a)   No practice involving exposures to radiation should be adopted unless it produces sufficient benefit to the exposed individuals or to society to offset the radiation detriment it causes. This principle is termed the justification of a practice.

b)   In relation to any particular source within a practice, the magnitude of individual doses, the number of people exposed and the likelihood of incurring exposures, should all be kept as low as reasonably achievable, economic and social factors being taken into account. This procedure should be constrained by restrictions on the doses to individuals (dose constraints) or to the risks to individuals in the case of potential exposures (risk constraints), to limit the inequity likely to result from the inherent economic and social judgements. This principle is termed the optimisation of protection.

c) The exposure of individuals resulting from the combination of all the relevant practices should be subject to dose limits, or to some control of risk in the case of potential exposures. These are aimed at ensuring that no individual is exposed to radiation risks that are judged to be unacceptable from these practices in any normal circumstances. This is the principle of dose and risk limitation. ICRP 60 **dose limits** are given in Table 6.3.

Table 6.3: ICRP 60 dose limits

Recommended dose limits[1]

Application	Dose Limit	
	Occupational	Public
Effective dose	20 mSv per year averaged over defined periods of 5 years[2]	1 mSv in a year[3]
Annual equivalent dose in		
the lens of the eye	150 mSv	15 mSv
the skin[4]	500 mSv	50 mSv
the hands and feet	500 mSv	–

[1] The limits apply to the sum of the relevant doses from external exposure in the specified period and the 50-year committed dose (to age 70 years for children) from intakes in the same period.

[2] With the further provision that the effective dose should not exceed 50 mSv in any single year. Additional restrictions apply to the occupational exposure of pregnant women. The proposed revisions to the Ionising Radiations Regulations include an option for a 20 mSv limit per year with no averaging [7].

[3] In special circumstances, a higher value of effective dose could be allowed in a single year, provided that the average over 5 years does not exceed 1 mSv per year.

[4] The limitation on the effective dose provides sufficient protection for the skin against stochastic effects. An additional limit is needed for localised exposures in order to prevent deterministic effects.

From ICRP 60 [3]. Adapted by permission of the International Commission on Radiological Protection.

6.4 UK LEGISLATION: THE IONISING RADIATIONS REGULATIONS (IRRs)

The Ionising Radiations Regulations [4] were published in 1985 and provide the current fundamental regulatory framework for radiation work in the Great Britain[1] (see also Section 7.1.3). These regulations are detailed and comprehensive, only their general outline can be described here.

The regulations define the responsibilities of employer and employee. Every employer must take all necessary steps to restrict, as far as reasonably achievable, the radiation exposure of his employees and other persons. The HSE must be notified at least 28 days before commencement of work with ionising radiations. Persons who are likely to receive a dose which exceeds three tenths of any dose limit must be designated as classified persons. Controlled areas are areas in which doses of ionising radiation are likely to exceed three-tenths of any dose limit for employees aged 18 years or over. A supervised area is any area (which is not designated as a controlled area) in which any person is likely to receive a dose which exceeds one tenth of any dose limit. Controlled areas can also be designated in relation to internal radiation (see below). Workers in a controlled area are required to follow well established procedures. In a supervised area, special procedures are not normally needed but the situation is kept under review.

Where any employee is exposed to an instantaneous dose rate of 7.5 μSv h^{-1} or the employer has designated a controlled area which persons enter, that employer shall appoint one or more radiation protection advisers (RPAs) to advise on the observance of the regulations. Employers must ensure that all RPAs can satisfy the Health & Safety Executive (HSE) as to their qualifications and experience. Employers must set down in writing local rules to enable work to be carried out in compliance with the regulations. Suitable employees will be appointed as radiation protection supervisors to secure compliance with the requirements of the regulations, in work with ionising radiations. Employers must ensure that employees receive adequate information, instruction and training concerning work with ionising radiations.

Classified workers (and any other workers whom the HSE deem to be in need of protection) should receive adequate dosimetry and medical surveillance. For the purpose of providing dosimetry (including maintenance of dose records) the employer shall obtain the services of an approved dosimetry service (ADS). The HSE publishes detailed requirements [5] for the approval of dosimetry services (RADS) and guidance on how these requirements can be met.

Employers shall, whenever reasonably practicable, ensure that radioactive substances in the workplace are sealed sources. Proper provision must be made for the accounting and storage of radioactive substances.

The employer must provide properly maintained equipment for monitoring radiation levels and records of monitoring results must be kept.

Further sections of the regulations concern the assessment of hazards arising from foreseeable accidents or occurrences, contingency plans to deal with such incidents and investigation and notification of over-exposure to employees. An Approved Code of Practice [6] has been published which gives guidance on ways of complying with legal requirements.

---

[1] an equivalent set of regulations apply in Northern Ireland [4]

Schedule 1 of the IRRs gives dose limits. These are based on those given in ICRP 26 and state that employees aged 18 years or over shall not exceed whole body doses of 50 mSv nor doses to individual organs or tissues (except the lens of the eye) of 500 mSv. The dose limit for the lens of the eye is 150 mSv. The dose limit to the abdomen of women of reproductive capacity is 13 mSv in any consecutive three month interval. The dose limit to the abdomen of a pregnant woman is 10 mSv during the declared term of pregnancy. In the light of the revisions to dose limits contained in ICRP 60 [3], the HSE has published an Approved Code of Practice, Part 4 [6] as additional guidance on restriction of exposure. It recommends that the occupational exposure to workers be so controlled as not to exceed an average dose of 15 mSv per year. Employers should investigate cases where an employee reaches a cumulative total of 75 mSv or more within any five consecutive calendar years.

Schedule 2 of the regulations gives an extensive list of radionuclides along with air concentrations, surface contaminations and total concentrations such that, if they are exceeded in any area, it must be designated a controlled area. The employer shall not undertake any work which involves quantities of any nuclides in excess of levels given in column 6 of Schedule 2, unless he has made an assessment of the radiation hazard that could arise from such work and sent a report to the HSE. Employers shall notify the HSE if a quantity of any nuclide in excess of levels in column 7 of Schedule 2 has been released or spilled, except where such a release has been authorised. Where an employer believes that a quantity of radioactive substance in excess of the activities given in column 2 of Schedule 2 has been lost or stolen, the HSE must be notified forthwith.

Because of lack of space it is not possible to summarise all of the legal requirements here. Anyone in Great Britain contemplating work with radionuclides should familiarise themselves with the detailed contents of the Ionising Radiations Regulations. The Health and Safety Commission has issued a consultative document which gives details of revised Ionising Radiations Regulations and Approved Code of Practice [7]. These regulations incorporate a 20 mSv annual dose limit, although an option to allow averaging over 5 years is under discussion.

6.5 PROTECTION AGAINST EXTERNAL RADIATION

The external radiation hazard arises from sources of radiation outside the body. Alpha particles have a range of only a few tens of microns in tissue (or a few centimetres of air) and will not usually penetrate the outer layers of the skin. They will not, therefore, be discussed further in this section. Gamma and X-ray photons, beta particles and neutrons can all pose an external radiation hazard.

The general principles to be used in minimising the exposure to a source of radiation are:

a)   minimise the amount of radionuclide to be used in any operation;

b)   minimise the exposure time;

c)   maximise the distance from the radiation source and

d)   place shielding between the individual and the radiation source.

The scope for putting these principles into practice will, of course, depend on the type of work being performed.

6.5.1 Dose rates from radiation sources

For a source emitting S particles (or photons) per second, the number of particles or photons crossing unit area per unit time at distance r is given by

$$f = \frac{S}{4\pi r^2} \qquad (6.3)$$

where f is the **fluence rate** (or flux) of particles. For a constant fluence rate the fluence of particles or photons is simply given by the product of fluence rate and exposure time. The dose or equivalent dose delivered by a given fluence will depend on the type and energy of the particles or photons. For photons and neutrons the effective dose per unit fluence is shown, as a function of energy, in Figures 6.1 and 6.2. The conversion factors from electron fluence to effective dose are shown in Table 6.4.

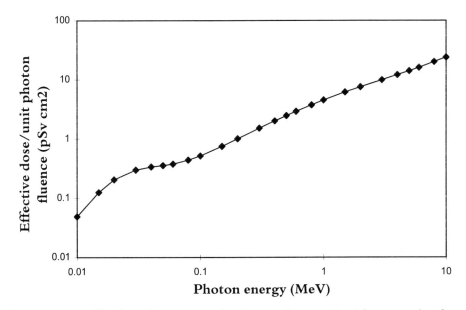

Figure 6.1: **Effective dose per unit photon fluence incident on the front of the body. Data from ICRP 74 [8]. Adapted with permission from the International Commission on Radiological Protection.**

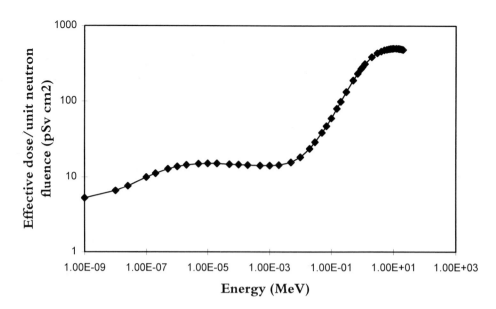

Figure 6.2: Effective dose per unit neutron fluence incident on the front of the body. Data from ICRP 74 [8]. Adapted with permission from the International Commission on Radiological Protection.

Table 6.4: Effective dose per unit electron fluence incident on the front of the body.

Electron energy (MeV)	Effective dose per unit fluence (pSv cm²)
0.1	0.1
0.4	1.0
0.6	1.5
1.0	2.7
1.5	5.9
2.0	11.0
4.0	44.0
10.0	131.0

N.B. For energies <1 MeV, the effective dose is dominated by the dose to the skin. From ICRP 74 [8]. Adapted with permission from the International Commission on Radiological Protection.

Doses from exposure to point sources can be estimated by calculating fluences and then using the conversion factors given in Figures 6.1, 6.2 and Table 6.4. However, some simple formulae are available which allow dose rates to be estimated directly from the source strength and distance.

The equivalent dose rate from an unshielded point gamma source of strength S MBq is given by the approximation [9]:

$$\dot{H} \cong \frac{SE}{6r^2} \qquad (6.4)$$

192

where $\dot{H}$ is the equivalent-dose rate in $\mu Sv\ h^{-1}$, E is the gamma energy per disintegration in MeV and r is the distance from the source in metres. Equation 5 gives a reasonable estimate of dose rate, provided that r is large compared with the dimensions of the source and that E is greater than ~0.1 MeV. Table 6.5 gives the equivalent-dose rate at 1m from 1MBq sources of various radionuclides.

Table 6.5: Equivalent dose rates at 1 m from gamma emitters

Nuclide	Dose rate in air ($\mu Sv\ h^{-1}$) at 1m from 1 MBq
^{72}As	0.25
^{74}As	0.11
^{76}As	0.060
^{198}Au	0.059
^{140}Ba+	0.32
^{82}Br	0.37
^{58}Co	0.14
^{60}Co	0.32
^{137}Cs#	0.083
^{59}Fe	0.15
^{131}I	0.055
^{132}I	0.32
^{192}Ir	0.12
^{42}K	0.034
^{52}Mn	0.46
^{54}Mn	0.12
^{22}Na	0.30
^{24}Na	0.46
^{226}Ra★	0.23
^{124}Sb	0.25
^{182}Ta	0.16
^{65}Zn	0.077

+ ^{140}Ba in equilibrium with ^{140}La

^{137}Cs in equilibrium with ^{137}Ba

★ ^{226}Ra in equilibrium with daughter products

For a point source of S MBq of β-particles, a rough estimate of the equivalent-dose rate in $\mu Sv\ h^{-1}$ at 0.1m is:

$$\dot{H} \cong 850S \qquad (6.5)$$

If the source dimensions are small, this formula can be scaled to other distances using the inverse square law. The equivalent-dose rate is only weakly dependent on the β-particle energy.

Neutron equivalent-dose rates are best estimated from a fluence calculation and the conversion factors at Figure 6.2.

Whilst equivalent-dose calculations of the type described above are often useful, they should not replace measurements of dose rate.

6.5.2 Radiation shielding

(i) Beta-particles

Energy loss for electrons and positrons is a more-or-less continuous process in which energy is given up to orbital electrons of the stopping medium. Therefore, unlike gamma rays, electrons and positrons have a well defined range. The electrons or positrons emitted in β-decay have a spectrum of energies up to a maximum, β_{max}. The mean β-energy is roughly 1/3 β_{max}. Most β-emitters yield maximum energies of a few MeV or less. For energies less than 2.5 MeV, the range of a β-particle of energy E is given empirically by:

$$R = 412E^{1.265-0.0954\ln E} \qquad (6.6)$$

where E is in MeV and the range is expressed as mass-thickness in mg cm^{-2}. In calculating shields for β-emitters, the maximum energy β_{max} should be used in this formula. A useful nomogram for the absorption of β-particles is given in Figure 6.3.

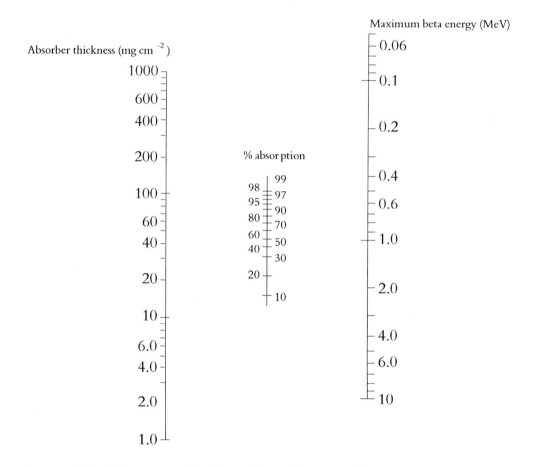

Figure 6.3: Nomogram for absorption of beta particles.
For example, to find the percentage absorption of beta particles of maximum energy 1 MeV by a shield of thickness 100 mg cm^{-2}, draw a straight line connecting 100 mg cm^{-2} and 1 MeV. This intersects the absorption line at 80%.

194

A complication in shielding β-particles is that the slowing electrons or positrons emit **bremsstrahlung** (see Chapter 2). A rough estimate of the fraction, f, of beta energy converted into photons is [10]:

$$f \cong 3.5 \times 10^{-4} Z \beta_{max} \qquad (6.7)$$

where again β_{max} is in MeV and Z is the atomic number of the absorber. Production of bremsstrahlung can be reduced by using a low-Z shield such as Perspex or aluminium. A shield of 1cm of Perspex would completely absorb all β-particles up to 2 MeV in energy.

A further complication is encountered in the case of positrons. When these are annihilated in the stopping medium, 511 keV gamma rays are emitted (see Chapters 1 and 2). The first few centimetres or so of the shield will, therefore, be a source of gamma rays which will need to be shielded using the principles described in the next section.

(ii)   Gamma and X-rays

The attenuation of a narrow beam of gamma or X-rays is given by:

$$I = I_0 e^{-\mu t} \qquad (6.8)$$

where I_0 is the initial fluence rate, I is the fluence rate after passing through a thickness t and μ is the linear attenuation coefficient of the attenuating medium (see also Chapter 2, Section 1). In the case of broad or uncollimated beams (see Figure 6.4), photons which undergo scattering can still reach the detector, so that the gamma fluence declines less rapidly than indicated by equation 6.8. This phenomenon is known as **build-up**. The fluence which is present after the beam has passed through a shield of thickness t is increased by a factor B, known as the build-up factor. This factor is a function of the composition and thickness of the shield and the gamma energy. Tabulations of calculated build-up factors are given in many books on shielding (see, for example, Price, Horton and Spinney [11], Jaeger [12] and Blizzard and Abbott [13]).

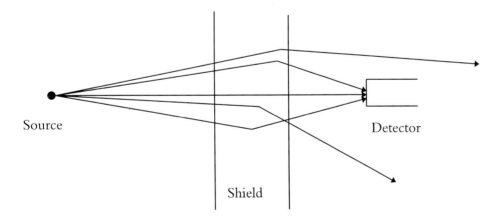

Figure 6.4: Build-up caused by scattering towards the detector.

Materials with high atomic number and high density provide the best shields for electromagnetic radiation, although lighter materials such as concrete are often used for cheapness and convenience. Table 6.6 gives the linear attenuation coefficients for a number of materials at various gamma energies.

The accurate calculation of gamma transmission through thick shields can be performed using large computer codes such as RANKERN [14]. However, whilst such calculations are essential in the case of reactor shields, they are rarely necessary for shielding of radionuclide sources. Simpler codes which can be run on a personal computer [15] are now available. Rough estimates of shielding requirements can be made using Figure 6.5 a–d. These figures show the fraction by which the gamma dose rate from a point source at 1m is reduced by various thicknesses of concrete, iron, lead and uranium.

Concrete

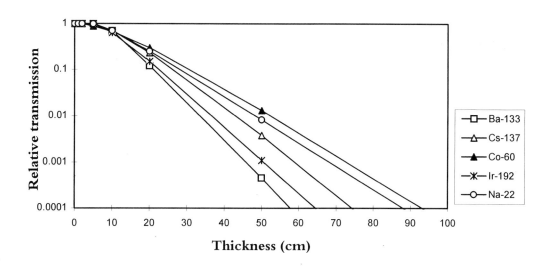

Figure 6.5a: Relative transmission of gamma rays through concrete.

Iron

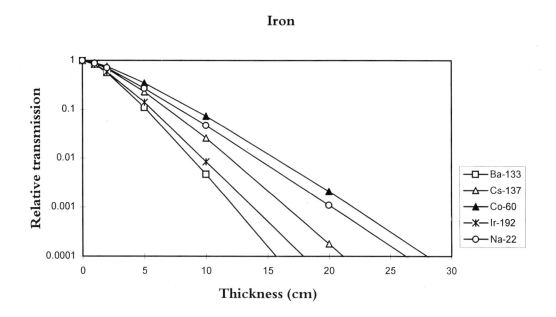

Figure 6.5b: Relative transmission of gamma rays through iron.

Lead

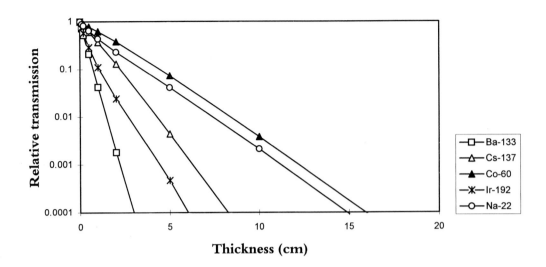

Figure 6.5c: Relative transmission of gamma rays through lead.

Uranium

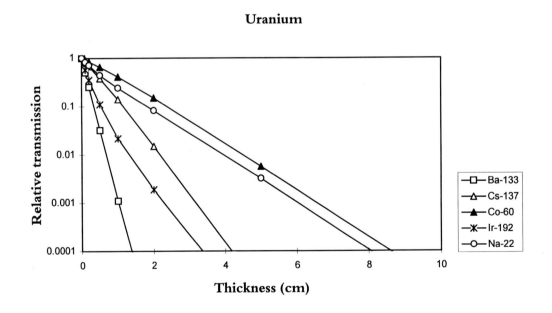

Figure 6.5d: Relative transmission of gamma rays through uranium.

Table 6.6: Linear attenuation coefficients for some shielding materials at various gamma energies.

Linear Attenuation Coefficients in cm^{-1}

Material	Gamma Energy (MeV)					
	0.1	0.2	0.5	0.66	1	2
Water	0.165	0.136	0.097	0.086	0.071	0.049
Aluminium	0.425	0.321	0.227	0.202	0.166	0.117
Concrete ($\rho = 2.35$ gm cm^{-3})	0.392	0.291	0.205	0.182	0.147	0.105
Iron	2.31	0.952	0.564	0.510	0.416	0.298
Lead	61.6	10.9	1.74	1.23	0.790	0.522

(iii)   Neutrons

In the radiochemical laboratory the most likely source of neutrons will be the radionuclide ^{252}Cf, which undergoes spontaneous fission. Various (α,n) sources, such as listed in Table 6.7, may also be present.

Table 6.7: Characteristics of some (α,n) neutron sources

Source	Half-life	Average Neutron Energy (MeV)	Yield n s^{-1}MBq^{-1}
Am + Be	432y	4.4	66
Ra + Be	1600y	5	459
Ra + B	1600y	3	184
^{210}Po + Be	138d	4	81
^{210}Po + B	138d	2.5	24
^{210}Po + F	138d	1.4	11
^{210}Po + Li	138d	0.42	2.4
^{239}Pu + Be	24,000y	4	27

Data adapted from[10], H. Cember, Introduction to Health Physics (© McGraw-Hill Companies Inc, 1983), with permission from The McGraw-Hill Companies Inc.

Neutron shielding is a complex subject which can only be discussed briefly here. Neutron interactions with matter are described in Chapter 2. A neutron shield will usually contain a large proportion of light elements, most often in the form of hydrogenous materials. These will reduce neutron energies via elastic scattering. There is some advantage in including a heavy element such as lead, barium or iron in a shield as these elements can reduce energies to ~1 MeV via inelastic scattering. They will also be useful in attenuating the gamma rays which are always associated with neutron fluences. However, the inelastic scattering process itself produces further gamma rays. Once slowed to thermal energies, neutrons can be captured by hydrogen nuclei. Boron is a useful addition to shield materials – in the form of borated concrete or plastics – as it will absorb slow neutrons without the emission of energetic gamma rays.

As with photon shielding, there are computer codes available for neutron attenuation calculations [16–17]. However, for broad beams of neutrons incident on thick shields, rough calculations of the reduction of equivalent dose rate can be made by assuming exponential attenuation of the neutron beam. The attenuation lengths for 3 MeV neutrons in various materials are given in Table 6.8. It must be emphasised that any shield for a neutron source must be checked by thorough monitoring of the residual neutron and gamma ray fields.

More detailed discussion of neutron attenuation can be found in books on radiation shielding [11–13].

Table 6.8: Attenuation lengths for 3MeV neutrons

Material	Attenuation length (cm)
Concrete	15
Paraffin	8
Polyethylene	8
Water	9

6.5.3 Monitoring for external radiations

The principles behind the usual radiation dosimetry devices have been discussed briefly in Chapter 2. In this section the range of application of some methods of dosimetry and environmental monitoring is described.

6.5.3.1 Area monitoring

Area monitoring is usually carried out with devices which give dose rate information in real time, although passive dosemeters may be used in some cases. Area monitoring is used to determine the characteristics of the radiation field in a workplace. Information on the radiation quality and on spatial and temporal variations must be obtained. This information is used to classify the working conditions in a given area. Continued monitoring is essential to ensure that radiation levels remain within prescribed limits. A dose limit of 20 mSv in a year of 2000 working hours will be reached if the dose rate is 10 μSv h^{-1}. A demarcation between controlled and supervised areas of 6 mSv yr^{-1} corresponds to a dose rate of 3 μSv h^{-1}. Clearly, any dose rate meter to be used for area monitoring must have a sensitivity such that dose rates of the order of 1 μSv h^{-1} can be measured accurately.

A number of devices can be used to detect gamma rays and higher energy X-rays (see Chapter 2). Geiger counters are simple and robust and because they produce large voltage pulses require little ancillary electronics. However, they give no information on the energy of the incident gamma photons. Gas-filled proportional counters can be used for spectrometry, however all gas-filled instruments suffer from the drawback that they have a low efficiency for the detection of gamma rays. Higher efficiencies can be achieved with solid–state devices such as scintillation detectors. Scintillators such as sodium iodide are available as large crystals (of ~15cm diameter or larger) with correspondingly high detection efficiencies.

Spectrometry with moderate energy resolution can be performed with scintillation detectors. Solid state ionisation devices such as the lithium-drifted germanium (Ge (Li)) detector or the intrinsic germanium detectors are not usually available with such large crystals as the scintillators, but are capable of much higher energy resolution (typically, better than ~1%). These crystals require cooling to liquid-nitrogen temperatures and are not often used for routine measurements. They can be useful for characterising the radiation field in a workplace.

A knowledge of just the photon flux gives little indication of the dose rate, because the dose rate per unit flux varies strongly with energy (see Figure 6.1). Ideally, a dose rate meter should give a response which is proportional to dose rate, irrespective of the photon energy spectrum. An ion-current chamber has an approximately flat dose response for energies ≥ 100 keV. Other instruments such as Geiger-Müller and scintillation counters can be fitted with compensation devices so as to yield an approximately dosimetric response over a wide energy band. Such instruments are used as the basis for modern survey instruments, to measure dose rates down to ~μSv h^{-1} or less. Thin-window devices can measure β and low-energy X-radiation as well as gamma radiation.

Neutron monitoring presents more difficulty, because of the many orders of magnitude over which neutron energies may vary.

Thermal neutrons can be detected via the reaction ^{10}B(n,α)^{7}Li. Devices are available in which boron is used as a lining in an ion chamber or BF$_3$ gas is used as a filling for a proportional counter. Dose rates of a few μSv h^{-1} are readily measurable because of the high cross-section (~4000 barns at thermal energies) of the (n,α) reaction.

BF$_3$ proportional counters which are sensitive to fast neutrons are also available. These are surrounded by a moderator such as polythene to slow down the fast neutrons via elastic collisions. Proportional counters filled with a hydrogenous gas such as methane can be used to detect neutrons of energy ≥ 0.5 MeV via recoil protons produced in the gas.

An ideal neutron dosemeter would have a response which mimics the dose equivalent versus neutron energy curve (see Figure 6.2) from thermal energies up to ~10 MeV. One such device was designed by Andersson and Braun [18] and consists of a BF$_3$ counter surrounded by a cadmium shield and a polyethylene moderator. The Leake [19] survey instrument has an 8 inch (20.3 cm) moderator sphere and a perforated cadmium shield surrounding a ^{3}He counter to produce an approximately dose equivalent response. This device uses the reaction ^{3}He (n, p) ^{3}H. Similar features are incorporated into most modern neutron monitors, which can measure dose equivalent rates down to ~1 μSv h^{-1}.

6.5.3.2 Personal dosemeters

Personal dosimetry is important because spatial and temporal variations in workplace dose rates make it difficult to construct a worker's dose from survey results. The dose measured by a personal dosemeter is entered on a worker's dose record and forms part of the dose (with doses from internal monitoring) used for legal and regulatory purposes.

The **film badge** (photographic emulsion) has long formed the basis for most personal dosimetry. Personal Monitoring film consists of a double emulsion. A fast emulsion on one side allows γ doses from about 100 μSv to 50 mSv to be measured. If a dose in excess of 50 mSv has been received, the fast emulsion can be stripped off and the slow emulsion used to measure doses up to 10 Gy. Several filters are incorporated in the film badge holder, so that beta, gamma, X-ray and thermal neutron doses can be measured. More details of the properties and use of film badges can be found in [10, 20].

Film badges are now being superseded by **thermoluminescence dosimeters (TLDs)**. These have the advantage that the response is proportional to the dose absorbed by the phosphor. Provided that the phosphor has a similar effective atomic number to human tissue, the response will be approximately proportional to tissue dose. The most widely-used phosphor is lithium fluoride (LiF) doped with Ti and Mg. This has a good energy response and can detect doses down to ~40 μSv. Phosphors such as CaF_2 and $CaSO_4$ have higher sensitivities than LiF and can record doses down to a few μSv. However, they over-respond at low photon energies, although this can be corrected to some extent, by placing the phosphor behind a lead shield. Commercial TLD systems are now available with automated readers capable of handling a hundred or more TLD badges per hour. Thermoluminescence dosimetry is discussed at length in the monograph by McKinlay [21].

Film badges and TLDs are passive devices which are worn for a fixed period and then processed to give a measure of dose. Where large variations of dose rate, in either space or time, are present, it is useful for workers to wear some sort of direct-reading device. One such dosemeter is a **quartz fibre electrometer (QFE)**, which gives a continuous visual indication of accumulated gamma dose. As the dosemeter is exposed to radiation the quartz fibre is discharged and the reduced deflection of the fibre can be viewed via a microscope lens [20]. QFEs with a full scale deflection corresponding to 1mSv are available.

Electronic personal dosemeters are now available. The most recent designs are based on solid state detectors and incorporate microprocessors and memory for storage of dosimetry data. One such device is described by Marshall et al., [22]. These dosemeters are versatile and can be used for both direct reading of acquired dose as well as providing the longer-term personal dose measurement. At present, unit costs are still rather high.

Where neutron fields are present, special types of personal dosemeters are required. Some film badges incorporate a cadmium shield, allowing thermal neutrons to be detected via the (n,γ) reaction. Li-bearing TLDs will also detect thermal neutrons via the reaction ^{6}Li (n,α)^{3}H.

Fast neutrons can be detected via proton recoil tracks in special nuclear emulsions. These can only detect neutrons with energies above 0.5 MeV. The sensitivity depends on the area of emulsion scanned, but dose equivalents down to ~200 μSv are measurable. **Track-etch detectors** can also detect fast neutrons via recoil reactions. The polymer CR-39 will record proton recoil tracks resulting from neutrons with energies down to ~0.2 MeV. These can be enlarged, using electrochemical etching, for ease of scanning [23]. Track-etch plastics have the advantage of being insensitive to gamma radiation.

TLDs can be used to measure doses from neutrons with energies up to tens of keV via the albedo mechanism. Fast and intermediate energy neutrons incident on the human body are slowed down by means of elastic collisions with hydrogen nuclei in the body. These albedo neutrons are then detected by a neutron sensitive TLD which is shielded from direct irradiation by field neutrons. A neutron-insensitive TLD element must also be worn so that the gamma-induced contribution to the TL signal can be allowed for. Personal neutron dosimetry is an active area of research. A good review of work up to the mid-1980s can be found in IAEA Technical Report 252 [24].

All of the above-mentioned dosemeters are worn on the trunk so that they give an estimate of body dose. When work is being performed on radiochemicals, particularly where short-range radiations are being emitted, it is advisable to use extremity dosemeters. A sachet of TLD powder can be worn as a finger badge to measure dose to the fingers.

6.6 PROTECTION AGAINST INTERNAL RADIATIONS

6.6.1 Introduction

In workplaces where unsealed sources are present, it is possible for workers to take material into the body, inadvertently. If this material emits alpha or beta particles, it is possible for a considerable internal radiation dose to be acquired, even where the external hazard is small. There are three main routes by which radioactive material may enter the body.

(i)   Inhalation of airborne contamination
(ii)   Ingestion
(iii) Entry via the undamaged skin (absorption) or, more usually, via a wound.

Once radionuclides enter the body they can be retained there for weeks, months or even years and dose to body organs and tissues can accumulate throughout this period. The dose to any organ or tissue, integrated over 50 yr. for adults, is the committed equivalent dose $H_T(50)$ which was introduced in Section 6.2. The tissue-weighted average is the committed effective dose, $E(50)$. The **annual limit on intake** (denoted I_L or more usually, **ALI**) is given, for ICRP 60 dose limits, by $0.02/e(50)$ Bq where 0.02 is the annual effective dose limit in Sv and $e(50)$ is the dose coefficient or the committed effective dose arising from an intake of 1 Bq of a radionuclide. ALIs recommended by the ICRP have undergone several revisions in recent years. Table 6.9 gives ALIs and dose coefficients for a number of radionuclides, based on the latest biokinetic and lung modelling [25]. An extensive compilation of dose coefficients for workers is given in ICRP 68 [25].

The main objective of internal radiation protection must be to ensure that intakes of any nuclide are kept as low as is reasonably practicable. Where internal and external exposures occur together, a combined measure of exposure called the compliance index is used. If the annual limit of intake for nuclide j is ALI_j and the external dose limit is E_{lim} then the compliance index is given by:

$$CI = \frac{E_{ext}}{E_{lim}} + \sum_j \frac{I_j}{ALI_j} \qquad (6.9)$$

where I_j is the intake of nuclide j and E_{ext} is the external effective dose. It is necessary to ensure that $CI < 1$ for any year of working.

Table 6.9a Dose coefficients and Annual Limits of Intake.

(i) Inhalation

Nuclide	Lung type★★	e_{inh} (50) (1 µm AMAD) (Sv/Bq)	ALI ★ (Bq)
Tritiated Water		1.8E-15	1E13
Co-58	M	1.5E-9	1E7
	S	2.0E-9	1E7
Co-60	M	9.6E-9	2E6
	S	2.9E-8	7E5
Sr-89	F	1.0E-9	2E7
	S	7.5E-9	3E6
Sr-90	F	2.4E-8	8E5
	S	1.5E-7	1E5
Y-90	M	1.4E-9	1E7
	S	1.5E-9	1E7
Zr-95	F	2.5E-9	8E6
	M	4.5E-9	4E6
	S	5.5E-9	4E6
Tc-99m	F	1.2E-11	2E9
	M	1.9E-11	1E9
Ru-106	F	8.0E-9	3E6
	M	2.6E-8	8E5
	S	6.2E-8	3E5
I-131	F	7.6E-9	3E6
Cs-134	F	6.8E-9	3E6
Cs-137	F	4.8E-9	4E6
Pm-147	M	4.7E-9	4E6
	S	4.6E-9	4E6
Eu-152	M	3.9E-8	5E5
Po-210	F	6.0E-7	3E4
	M	3.0E-6	7E3
Ra-226	M	1.6E-5	1E3
Th-228	M	3.1E-5	600
	S	3.9E-5	500
Th-232	M	4.2E-5	500
	S	2.3E-5	900
U-234	F	5.5E-7	4E4
	M	3.1E-6	6E3
	S	8.5E-6	2E3
U-235	F	5.1E-7	4E4
	M	2.8E-6	7E3
	S	7.7E-6	3E3
U-238	F	4.9E-7	4E4
	M	2.6E-6	8E3
	S	7.3E-6	3E3

Table 6.9a (Contd)

Nuclide	Lung type** –	e_{inh} (50) (1 μm AMAD) (Sv/Bq)	ALI * (Bq)
Tritiated Water		1.8E–15	1E13
Pu–238	M	4.3E–5	500
	S	1.5E–5	1000
Pu–239	M	4.7E–5	400
	S	1.5E–5	1000
Am–241	M	3.9E–5	500
Cf–252	M	1.8E–5	1000

* ALI calculated from $20 \times 10^{-3}/e_{inh}(50)$ and rounded to one significant figure.

** Lung type refers to rate of clearance from the lung. See Section 6.6.3.

Data adapted from ICRP 68 [25] with permission from the International Commission on Radiological Protection.

Table 6.9: a. Dose coefficients and annual limits of intake.

(ii) Ingestion

Nuclide	f_1^*	$e_{ing}(50)$ (Sv Bq^{-1})	ALI (Bq)
Tritiated Water	1.0	1.8E–11	1E9
Co-58	0.1	7.4E–10	3E7
	0.05	7.0E–10	3E7
Co-60	0.1	3.4E–9	6E6
	0.05	2.5E–9	8E6
Sr-89	0.3	2.6E–9	8E6
	0.01	2.3E–9	9E6
Sr-90	0.3	2.8E–8	7E5
	0.01	2.8E–9	7E6
Y-90	1E–4	2.7E–9	7E6
Zr-95	0.002	8.8E–10	2E7
Tc-99m	0.8	2.2E–11	9E8
Ru-106	0.05	7.0E–9	3E6
I-131	1.0	2.2E–8	9E5
Cs-134	1.0	1.9E–8	1E6
Cs-137	1.0	1.3E–8	2E6
Pm-147	5E–4	2.6E–10	8E7
Eu-152	5E–4	1.4E–9	1E7
Po-210	0.1	2.4E–7	8E4
Ra-226	0.2	2.8E–7	7E4
Th-228	5E–4	7.0E–8	3E6
	2E–4	3.5E–8	6E5
Th-232	5E–4	2.2E–7	9E4
	2E–4	9.2E–8	2E5
U-234	0.02	4.9E–8	4E5
	0.002	8.3E–9	2E6
U-235	0.02	4.6E–8	4E5
	0.002	8.3E–9	2E6
U-238	0.02	4.4E–8	5E5
	0.002	7.6E–9	3E6
Pu-238	5E–4	2.3E–7	9E4
	1.E–5	8.8E–9	4E5
	1E–4	4.9E–8	4E5
Pu-239	5E–4	2.5E–7	8E4
	1E–5	9.0E–9	2E6
	1E–4	5.3E–8	4E5
Am-241	5E–4	2.0E–7	1E5
Cf-252	5E–4	9.0E–8	2E5

$\star$ f_1 is the fraction of material taken up by the bloodstream from the gut.
Data adapted from ICRP 68 [25] with permission from the International Commission on Radiological Protection.

Table 6.9: b. Effective dose coefficients for some gases.

Gas	$e_{inh}(50)$ Sv Bq^{-1}
Tritium	1.8E-15
Tritiated Water	1.8E-11
Organically bound Tritium	4.1E-11
C-14 Vapour	5.8E-10
S-35 Vapour	1.2E-10
I-126 Vapour	2.6E-08
I-131 Vapour	2.0E-8
Ar-41	5.3E-9
Kr-85	2.2E-11

Adapted from ICRP 68 [25] with permission from the International Commission on Radiological Protection.

6.6.2 Control of contamination

In order to minimise intakes of radionuclides it is necessary to achieve levels of surface and airborne contamination within the workplace which are as low as reasonably practicable. Before outlining the procedures needed to achieve this, some secondary limiting quantities need to be defined.

6.6.2.1 Derived limits

If a worker breathes at a rate R m^3 h^{-1} in an air concentration of C Bq m^{-3} of a given radionuclide, the rate of intake of activity is RC Bq h^{-1}. In a standard working year of 2000 h, the total intake I would be given by:

$$I = 2000 \, RC$$

The **derived air concentration** (DAC) is that value of C, for the nuclide in question, such that I becomes equal to one ALI (ALI for intake via inhalation) when a worker is exposed for 2000 hr. So 1 DAC = ALI/2000R. The ICRP, in its data for reference man [26] gives a standard breathing rate of 1.2 m^3 h^{-1} so that, for any nuclide, 1 DAC = ALI/2400. Some DACs are listed in Table 6.10. These are based on the dose coefficients of ICRP 68 [25].

The levels of surface contamination which can be tolerated will depend on the radiotoxicity of the nuclide. The derived limits (DL) of surface contamination are set so that the amount resuspended does not cause the DAC to be exceeded, the amount ingested does not cause the ingestion ALI to be exceeded and the external dose from surfaces does not exceed the dose limits. Also, levels on the skin should not lead to the limit of skin dose being exceeded. Schedule 2 of the Ionising Radiations Regulations [4] gives derived limits on air concentrations and surface contamination for an extensive list of radionuclides. An area must be designated as a controlled area if these limits are exceeded, or likely to be exceeded. For example, if work on ^{241}Am is being carried out, a controlled area must be designated if the air concentration exceeds 0.02 Bq m^{-3} or the surface contamination exceeds 6 Bq cm^{-2}. Contamination levels shall be determined by averaging over an area not exceeding 1000 cm^2 for floors, walls or ceiling and 300 cm^2 for other surfaces. The surface contamination levels are set with ingestion of radioactivity as the route of exposure. An area is designated as a upervised area in relation to internal radiation if the air concentration or the contamination level exceeds one third of the values specified for a controlled area.

Table 6.10: Derived Air Concentrations

Nuclide	Lung Type	DAC Bq m^{-3}
Trit. Water	–	4E9
Co-58	M	4E3
	S	4E3
Co-60	M	800
	S	300
Sr-89	F	8E3
	S	1E3
Sr-90	F	300
	S	40
Y-90	M	4E3
	S	4E3
Zr-95	F	3E3
	M	2E3
	S	2E3
Tc-99m	F	8E5
	M	4E5
Ru-106	F	1E3
	M	300
	S	100
I-131	F	1E3
Cs-134	F	1E3
Cs-137	F	2E3
Pm-147	M	2E3
	S	2E3
Eu-152	M	200
Po-210	F	12
	M	3
Ra-226	M	0.4
Th-228	M	0.3
	S	0.2
Th-232	M	0.2
	S	0.4
U-234	F	20
	M	3
	S	0.8
U-235	F	20
	M	3
	S	1
U-238	F	20
	M	3
	S	1

Table 6.10 (Contd)

Derived air concentrations

Nuclide	Lung Type	DAC Bq m³
Pu–239	M	0.2
	S	0.4
Am–241	M	0.2
Cf-252	M	0.4

DACs based on ALIs given in Table 6.9 and rounded to one significant figure.

6.6.2.2 Principles of contamination control

The basic principles for protecting against internal radiation are as follows:

(i)   the minimum amount of activity which is necessary for any job should be used;

(ii)   where a job could be performed with a variety of radionuclides, the radiotoxicities should be taken into account in relation to the amounts required;

(iii)   adequate containment should be provided for radioactive materials;

(iv)   a high standard of cleanliness should be maintained;

(v)   correct procedures should be followed for the use of protective clothing, washing and monitoring facilities.

6.6.2.3 Controlled areas for radiochemical work

In areas where unsealed radioactive sources are present it is important that surfaces should be easily cleaned. The floor should be covered with an impervious surface such as a continuous sheet of PVC or linoleum. Walls and ceilings should be smooth and painted with a hard gloss or waterproof vinyl emulsion to facilitate cleaning. Wooden surfaces should be covered with plastic laminate material or painted with a high quality polyurethane gloss paint. Working surfaces should be smooth, hard and non-absorbent and have heat and chemical resistant properties.

Dedicated areas of bench should be set aside for radioactive work and plastic or metal trays used to minimise the spread of contamination arising from spills. Volatile radioactive materials or those which may produce radioactive aerosols should not be used in the open laboratory. Relatively low levels of activity can be handled in a fume cupboard. For higher levels of activity or where highly radiotoxic materials are being used, a glove box may be required. Fume cupboards are maintained at a pressure slightly below that of the outside laboratory so that ventilation air flows into the fume cupboard. This ventilation flow should be checked with an anemometer. The air discharged from both fume cupboards and glove boxes should pass through high-efficiency filters to remove particulates.

Sinks for the disposal of radioactive aqueous waste should be constructed of a suitable material such as stainless steel (though special precautions may be needed with some chemicals such as phosphate ions which can bind strongly onto stainless steel). Drainage system materials should be chosen to minimise the build-up of contamination on surfaces.

The laboratory should be provided with adequate waste disposal bins and decontamination facilities. A designated hand-wash basin should be provided.

Warning notices should be displayed at the entrance to active areas, showing the classification and the nature of the radiation hazard. A barrier should separate active from non-active areas. Protective clothing will be necessary in a contaminated area. This may range from a laboratory coat with gloves and overshoes, where contamination levels are low, to a full protective suit with mask and air supply, where there are high levels of airborne contamination. There should be provision for storage of personal clothing on the non-active side of the barrier. Change areas should have washing facilities and monitoring equipment (see Section 6.6.2.4).

Strict house rules will need to be imposed on staff working in radiochemical laboratories. For example, there must be no eating, drinking or smoking. Cuts or other skin breaks must be covered with waterproof dressing before the laboratory is entered. Disposable tissues must be used instead of handkerchiefs. Staff leaving a contaminated area must remove protective clothing, wash and then check for contamination. Items such as tools and laboratory equipment must be cleared by Health Physics surveyors before being removed from the active area.

The Environment Agency has issued valuable guidance on standards for radiochemical laboratories [27]. Further details on the design of facilities for working with unsealed sources and the requirements for safe handling of such material are given in [28, 29] and in Health Physics texts by Martin and Harbison [9], Cember [10] and Kathren [31]. A useful compendium of radiological protection data for a wide range of radionuclides has recently been published [32].

6.6.2.4 Monitoring equipment

Surface contamination with β/γ emitters can be detected using a thin-window Geiger-counter. Alpha-emitting contaminants can be detected using a scintillator covered with a very thin layer of aluminium-coated plastic.

The degree to which contamination is fixed to a surface can be determined with a wipe test. An area of suspected contamination is wiped with a filter paper. This is then taken to a low-level counting area for counting under a suitable detector in a standard geometry. Some assumption must be made concerning the percentage of the contamination picked up by the wipe. An assumption of 10% pick-up is often used.

Airborne particulate contamination is monitored using various air sampling devices. A volume of air is drawn through a filter paper. At the end of the sampling period, the filter paper is removed and counted. From the number of counts obtained, the efficiency of the detector and the volume of air sampled, the airborne concentration of activity can be calculated. Air sampling is discussed further in Section 6.6.4.

The results of surface contamination or air monitoring will be activities per unit area or per unit volume. In order to convert these to units of a DL or a DAC it is necessary to know the identity of the contaminant. If the detector used to count the activity is capable of energy spectrometry, the radionuclides present may be determined directly. Otherwise, some assumptions must be made based on a knowledge of the work carried out in the area.

Contamination monitoring is described in more detail by Cember [10] and in an IAEA Technical Report [33].

6.6.2.5 Treatment of contaminated personnel

Accidents can occur, even in the best regulated laboratories. For example, contaminated wounds can be sustained through breakage of glassware in fume cupboard operations or a glove-box leak can expose the user to airborne radioactivity. A wound will usually be apparent at the time it occurs. Other contamination incidents should be revealed through workplace air sampling or through monitoring of staff, for example when leaving the active area.

Once the extent and location of the contamination has been determined, protective clothing should be removed and the affected area washed thoroughly. Washing with soap and water may be sufficient but in some cases the use of decontamination agents or gentle brushing may be required. The affected areas should be re-monitored after each washing stage, to check on the progress of the cleansing process.

Contaminated wounds should be allowed to bleed freely and washed with water. The wound should be monitored to check on the removal of activity. Medical assistance should be obtained, unless the wound is very slight. If a contaminated glass shard is embedded in the wound then minor surgery may be necessary. If a significant intake of radiotoxic nuclides such as actinides has occurred, certain chemicals known as chelating agents can be administered, to increase the rate of excretion of contaminants [34,35]. Since these compounds are themselves somewhat toxic, medical advice must be sought before using them.

Whilst decontamination of personnel must always be of primary importance, consideration should also be given to the eventual assessment of doses received via contamination incidents. Excretion monitoring should be started as soon as possible after any contamination incident. In some cases, in-vivo monitoring may also be useful. Monitoring programmes and dose assessment are discussed in Section 6.6.4 and also in ICRP 54 [36], Cember [10] and Martin & Harbison [9], give useful information on practical measures for control of contamination.

6.6.3 Internal dosimetry

Radioactivity can enter the body via the lungs, gut or the skin. From these entry routes, radionuclides can be taken up by various body organs and tissues. The equivalent doses delivered to these organs and tissues will depend upon both the length of time for which the nuclide is retained in the organ (which itself depends upon the **biological half-life** of the compound) and the type and energy of radiation it emits. The sites at which radionuclides become concentrated depend on the chemical element involved. For example, iodine isotopes are concentrated in the thyroid, whereas plutonium tends to accumulate in the bone and liver.

Biokinetic models to describe the behaviour of various elements in the body were described in ICRP 30 [37]. On the basis of these models, dose equivalents per unit intake were calculated and tabulated in the various supplements to ICRP 30 [38]. More recent tabulations of effective dose coefficients are given in ICRP 68 [25] based on new metabolic models and a new model for the lung [39]. Some of these dose coefficients and associated annual limits of intake are listed in Table 6.9.

The initial deposition of particulates in the lung depends on the particle size. Absorption from the lung into the bloodstream depends on the chemical form of the particulate. In the new lung model, described in ICRP 66 [39], compounds are assigned to an **inhalation type** F, M or S accordingly as absorption to blood proceeds mostly in a few minutes (F), a few months (M) or many years (S). The effective dose coefficients for the various compounds of radionuclide will depend on the lung types to which the compounds are assigned. For example, oxides of plutonium are assigned to type S whereas most other plutonium compounds are assigned to type M.

6.6.4 Monitoring for intakes of radionuclides

Workplace air sampling has already been mentioned. Where the risk of release of airborne particulates is high, workers can be equipped with personal air samplers (PAS). These consist of a robust, battery-operated pump, connected to a small sampling head which is positioned as close as possible to the worker's breathing zone.

In many cases of intake, particularly if the ALI of a radionuclide is low or the nuclide is difficult to detect, **biological sampling** may be used. When activity is taken into the body, some of this material will be excreted in urine and faeces over a period of days, months or even years after intake. Urine or faecal samples are provided in labelled bottles located at the nearest toilets to the workplace. When filled, the bottles are collected and analysed at a bioassay laboratory using methods described in Chapter 3.

When the activities in excretion samples have been measured, intakes are assessed by comparing these levels with excretion rates calculated using biokinetic models. ICRP 54 [36] gives some model excretion curves (based on the older, ICRP 30 models) and valuable information about monitoring regimes. The programme LUDEP [40], which can be run on a personal computer, allows both dose coefficients and excretion curves to be calculated and incorporates the ICRP 66[39] lung model.

Gamma-emitting nuclides can be detected by means of a **whole-body monitor**. This consists of an array of scintillation counters (see Chapter 2) which can measure the gamma rays emitted from the nuclides retained in the body. The intake is calculated by comparing the retained activity with model calculations [36, 40]. Individual organs can also be monitored. For example, exposure to ^{125}I or ^{131}I can be monitored by measuring gamma activity in the thyroid.

6.7 RECORD KEEPING

(i)   Personnel records

The radiation dose records of any classified person must be retained for 50 years after the last entry. ICRP [36] recommend that recording levels be set at one tenth of the pro-rata dose limit for the monitoring period. However, a lower recording level can be set, if required.

The health record of all medical examinations performed on an employee must be kept for 50 years after the last entry.

(ii)   Survey records

The results of surveys of dose rates in the workplace and contamination levels must be recorded. These records should include the position and time of the measurement, the result and the identity of the instrument used to make the measurement. Survey records must be kept for a minimum of 2 years.

The results of tests and calibrations of survey instruments must be kept for 2 years.

(iii) Source records

Radiation source records shall include the following information:

a) the radionuclide and its activity on a specified date, with any reference mark to identify a sealed source. For unsealed materials, the compound in which it is incorporated, together with any special label, should be recorded;

b) the date of receipt and details of from whom the source was received;

c) the place of storage or use;

d) the date and manner of disposal and

e) the results of any leak tests performed on sources and other articles containing radioactive substances.

These records must be kept for 2 years from the date of disposal or transfer. Leak test results must be retained for 3 years.

6.8 WASTE DISPOSAL

Low-level aqueous liquid waste can be disposed of down the sink provided that this is designated and labelled for such a purpose and that an authorisation under the Radioactive Substances Act (see Chapter 7) is in place. The surround of the sink should allow easy cleaning and decontamination. After waste is poured down the sink it should be flushed with large quantities of clean water.

More highly active liquids can be stored in hold-up tanks to allow short-lived nuclides to decay. Treatment with ion-exchange or chemical processing may allow the activity to be converted into a solid waste for storage or disposal.

Small amounts of gaseous activity from fume cupboards etc., can be vented to the atmosphere provided that care is taken to avoid recirculation into the building. Active dusts may need to be removed from the discharge by filtration. Some gaseous activities, such as radioiodine can be removed from the air stream by adsorption systems.

Solid wastes can be stored to allow short-lived radionuclides to decay. Low level wastes may be disposed of to an authorised tip or via a specialist waste disposal service.

Legislation concerning waste storage and disposal is described in Chapter 7. More details of the practicalities of waste disposal are given in radiological protection texts such as Cember [10] and Martin and Harbison [9].

6.9 PACKAGING AND TRANSPORT OF RADIOACTIVE MATERIALS

The IAEA transport regulations [41] form the basis for most national regulations concerning transport and packaging.

Limits are placed on the equivalent dose rate at the surface of the package and at 1m from the centre of the package. These limits depend on the mode of transport to be used. Furthermore, categories of packaging are defined according to the degree of containment they provide. Type A packages are designed to retain the integrity of containment and shielding under normal conditions of transport. Type B packages must withstand the effects of a transport accident. Small quantities of activity may be sent in an excepted package.

A type A package might consist of a lead shield in a metal can packed in a cardboard box or expanded polystyrene casing. Large sources of penetrating radiations may be contained within a heavy lead shield inside a steel drum. Further details of types of packaging are provided by Nycomed Amersham plc [42]. Details of the regulations concerning transport and packaging are given in Chapter 7 and [41].

ACKNOWLEDGEMENTS

This chapter has benefited from reviews by Dr R Birch, AEA Technology plc, Mr I Adsley, AEA Technology plc, Dr M C Thorne, AEA Technology plc, Mr J A B Gibson, Radiation Dosimetry Consultant, Mr C Ellis, AEA Technology plc and Dr J Gill and Dr D Smith, HSE and also members of the ad hoc working party from DTI's Measurement Advisory Committee (MAC). The author thanks Pat Collis for her careful typing of this chapter.

REFERENCES

1. D. Sumner, T. Wheldon and W. Watson, Radiation Risks, The Tarragon Press, Glasgow, 1992.

2. ICRP, Recommendations of the International Commission on Radiological Protection, ICRP Publication 26, Annals of the ICRP 1 (30), Pergamon Press, Oxford, 1977.

3. ICRP, Recommendations of the International Commission on Radiological Protection, ICRP Publication 60, Annals of the ICRP **21**, (1-3), Pergamon Press, Oxford, 1991.

4. HSE, The Ionising Radiations Regulations 1985, HMSO, London, No. 1333, 1985. Radiation work in Northern Ireland is covered by The Ionising Radiations Regulations (Northern Ireland) 1985 - Statutory Rules of Northern Ireland, 1985, No. 273.

5. HSE, Requirements for the Approval of Dosimetry Services under the Ionising Radiations Regulations 1985, Parts 1-3, Revised 1996.

6. Health and Safety Commission. Approved Code of Practice, Parts 1 and 2: The protection of persons against ionising radiation arising from any work activity, The Ionising Radiations Regulations 1985, HMSO 1985. Part 3: Exposure to radon, HMSO 1988. Part 4: Dose limitation - restriction of exposure. Additional guidance on regulation 6 of the Ionising Radiations Regulations 1985, HMSO 1991.

7. Health and Safety Commission. Proposals for revised Ionising Radiations Regulations and Approved Code of Practice, Consultative Document, 1998.

8. ICRP, Conversion Coefficients for use in Radiological Protection Against External Radiation, ICRP Publication 74, Annals of the ICRP, **26**, Nos. 3-4, Pergamon Press, Oxford, 1996.

9. A. Martin, and S.A. Harbison, An Introduction to Radiation Protection, 4th Edition, Chapman & Hall Medical, London, 1996.

10. H. Cember, Introduction to Health Physics 2nd Ed., Pergamon Press, New York, 1983.

11. B.T. Price, C.C. Horton and K.T. Spinney, Radiation Shielding, Pergamon Press, Oxford, 1957.

12. R.G. Jaeger, (Ed.), Engineering Compendium on Radiation Shielding, Vols. I & II, Springer-Verlag, New York, 1968.

13. E.P. Blizzard, and L.S. Abbot, Reactor Handbook, Vol. IIIB, Shielding, Interscience, New York, 1962.

14. RANKERN: A Point Kernel Program for Gamma-Ray Transport Solutions. User Guide for Version 14A, ANSWERS/RANKERN (95) 03, 1995.

15. MICROSHIELD, Version 3, Grove Engineering Inc., Rockville, MD, 1987.

16. J. Briemeister, (Ed.) MCNP-A, A General Monte-Carlo Code for Neutron and Photon Transport, Report: LA 7396-M, Rev. 2, (Los Alamos), 1991.

17. T.P. Wilcox, MORSE-L, A Special Version of the MORSE program designed for Neutron, Gamma and Coupled Neutron–Gamma Penetration Problems VCID-16680, 1972.

18. I.O. Andersson, and J.A Braun, *Neutron Rem Counter,* Aktiebolaget Atomenergi, Studsvik Rep-132, 1964.

19. J.W. Leake, *An Improved Spherical Dose - Equivalent Neutron Detector*, Nucl. Instrum. Methods, **63,** 329-332, 1968.

20. IAEA, Personnel Dosimetry Systems for External Radiation Exposures, IAEA Technical Report, 109, Vienna, 1970.

21. A.F. McKinlay, Thermoluminescence Dosimetry, Adam Hilger, Bristol, 1981.

22. T.O. Marshall, D.T. Bartlett, P.H. Burgess, C.S. Cranston, D.J. Higginbottom and K.W. Sutton, The development of an Electronic Dosimeter, in: Occupational Radiation Protection, Proc. BNES Conf., BNES, London, 1991.

23. L. Tommasino and C. Armellini, *A New Etching Technique for Damage Track Detectors*, Radiat. Effects, **20,** 253-255, 1973.

24. IAEA, Neutron Monitoring for Radiological Protection, IAEA Technical Report 252, Vienna, 1985.

25. ICRP, Dose Coefficients for Intakes of Radionuclides by Workers. ICRP Publication 68, Annals of the ICRP, **24,** 4, Elsevier Science Ltd., Oxford, 1994.

26. ICRP, Reference Man: Anatomical, Physiological and Metabolic Characteristics, ICRP Publication 23, Pergamon Press, Oxford, 1975.

27. Environment Agency, Guidance on Standards for Radiochemical Laboratories in Non-Nuclear Premises, Radioactive Substances Developments Group Environment Agency, 1997.

28. IAEA, A Basic Toxicity Classification for Radionuclides, Technical Reports Series No.15, Vienna.

29. ICRP, The Handling, Storage, Use and Disposal and Unsealed Radionuclides in Hospitals and Medical Research Establishments, ICRP Publication 25, Annals of ICRP, **1,** 2, Pergamon Press, Oxford, 1977.

30. IAEA, Design of and Equipment for Hot Laboratories, IAEA Proceedings Series STI/PUB/436, Vienna, 1976.

31. R.L. Kathren, Radiation Protection, Adam Hilger Ltd., Bristol, 1985.

32. D. Delacroix, J.P. Guerre, P. Leblanc and C. Hickman, Radionuclide and Radiation Protection Data Handbook 1998, Rad. Prot. Dosim., **76**, Nos. 1-2, 1998.

33. IAEA. Monitoring of Radioactive Contamination on Surfaces, Technical Report Series No. 120, IAEA, Vienna, 1970.

34. M.H. Bhattacharyya, B.D. Breitenstein, H. Metivier, B.A. Muggenburg, G.N. Stradling, and V. Volf, Guidebook for the Treatment of Accidental Internal Radionuclide Contamination of Workers, Eds. G.B. Gerber and R.G. Thomas, Rad. Prot. Dosim., **41**, 1, 1992.

35. G.N. Stradling, *Recent Progress in Decorporation of Plutonium, Americium and Thorium*, Rad. Prot. Dosim., **53**, 1-4, 297-304, 1994.

36. ICRP, Individual Monitoring for Intakes of Radionuclides by Workers: Design and Interpretation, ICRP Publication 54, Annals of the ICRP, **19**, 1-3, Pergamon Press, Oxford, 1988.

37. ICRP, Limits for Intakes of Radionuclides by Workers. ICRP Publication 30, Part 1, Annals of ICRP, **2**, 3-4; 1979; Part 2, Annals of ICRP, **4,** 3-4 1980; Part 3, Annals of ICRP, **6,** 2-3, 1981 and Part 4, Annals of ICRP, **19**, 4 1988; Pergamon Press, Oxford.

38. Ibid, Supplement to Part 1; Annals of ICRP, 3, 1-4, 1979; Supplement to Part 2, Annals of ICRP, **5,** 1980; Supplements A and B to Part 3 Annals of ICRP, **7** and **8**, 1981, Pergamon Press, Oxford.

39. ICRP, Human Respiratory Tract Model for Radiological Protection, ICRP Publication 66, Annals of the ICRP, **24**, 1-4, Elservier Science Ltd., Oxford, 1994.

40. N.S. Jarvis, A. Birchall, A.C. James, M.R. Bailey and M.D. Dorrian, Ludep 2.0, Personal Computer Program for Calculating Internal Doses using ICRP Publication 66 Respiratory Tract Model, NRPB SR 287, 1996.

41. IAEA Regulations for the Safe Transport of Radioactive Material, 1985 Edition (As Amended 1990), Safety Series No.6, IAEA, Vienna, 1990.

42. Amersham International Radiopharmaceuticals and Medical Radiation Sources: General Information, Amersham International plc., 1997.

APPENDIX   ICRP 26

The recommendations of ICRP 60 [3] were used as the basis for Chapter 6. However, ICRP 26 [2] dose limits and terminology still appear in much of the literature published prior to 1991. A few notes on these older recommendations are given here.

The **dose equivalent** is defined as the product of absorbed dose and quality factor, where the **quality factors** Q allow for the increased biological effectiveness of highly ionising radiations. Q values are listed in Table A1. Clearly the dose equivalent corresponds to the equivalent dose of ICRP 60. The effective dose equivalent is defined in the same way as effective dose in ICRP 60, but the tissue weighting factors are different – see Table A2. The committed dose equivalent is the integral of the dose rate to an organ or tissue over the 50 yr following intake. It is therefore essentially the same as the committed equivalent dose of ICRP 60.

The most significant change between ICRP 26 and ICRP 60 is in the dose limits. In ICRP 26, the limit on effective dose equivalent is 50 mSv per year, for radiation workers. The dose equivalent limit to all individual tissues or organs is 500 mSv per year, with the exception of the lens of the eye, for which the limit is 300 mSv. Note that in the Ionising Radiations Regulations [4] the dose limit for the lens of the eye is set at 150 mSv.

Table A1: Quality factors recommended in ICRP 26.

Radiations	$\overline{Q}$
X-rays, γ-rays and electrons	1
Neutrons, protons and singly-charged particles with rest mass greater than one atomic mass unit of unknown energy	10
α-particles and multiply-charged particles (and particles of unknown charge), of unknown energy	20

From ICRP 26 [2]. Adapted with permission from the International Commission on Radiological Protection.

Table A2: Tissue weighting factors, w_T, recommended in ICRP 26.

Tissue	w_T
Gonads	0.25
Breast	0.15
Red bone marrow	0.12
Lung	0.12
Thyroid	0.03
Bone surfaces	0.03
Remainder	0.30

From ICRP 26 [2], adapted with permission from the International Commission on Radiological Protection.

CHAPTER 7
LEGISLATION, LICENSING, TRANSPORT AND WASTE DISPOSAL RELEVANT TO RADIOACTIVE SUBSTANCES

SUSAN SCRIVENS

7.0   INTRODUCTION

The legislation of most immediate consequence to the user of radionuclides emanates from National Statutes passed by Government. However, before detailing the various National Acts of Parliament it is useful to understand the basis for the regulations and their place in the larger picture, namely that of an International context.

The International Commission on Radiological Protection (ICRP) is the primary international body making recommendations on standards and practices in radiological protection. The United Nations via its Scientific Committee on Effects of Atomic Radiation (**UNSCEAR**) is the primary international body which carries out scientific reviews on ionising radiation levels and biological effects.

The International Atomic Energy Agency (IAEA) is an autonomous inter-governmental organisation also founded by the United Nations General Assembly and is the main vehicle by which the UN translates ICRP recommendations into the form of international standards. Its purpose since 1957 is to support research and development in the peaceful uses of nuclear power. As a part of that commitment the IAEA has established a basic safety philosophy for radioactive waste management. A great many publications are produced by the IAEA and are classified into various types, for example Safety Series, Technical Reports, TECDOCS and Proceedings Series. An individual description of each of these types of documents and their uses is beyond the scope of this chapter, however, the reader will find a very good overview of the IAEA's activity in this field in the IAEA Source Book, Radioactive Waste Management [1].

The role of the IAEA publications under the Radioactive Waste Safety Standards Programme (**RADWASS**) are advisory. However, negotiations have begun on a legally binding IAEA agreement entitled 'Convention on the Safety of Radioactive Waste Management' [2].

These International Agencies represent the collective opinion of Governments on radioactive waste. The Nuclear Energy Agency (**NEA**), a part of the Organisation for Economic Co-operation and Development (**OECD**), is publishing 'The Environmental and Ethical Basis of Geological Disposal of Long-Lived Radioactive Wastes'. Similarly the International Commission for Radiological Protection (ICRP), has given recommendations on safe disposal practices. In 1990, ICRP 60 recommended a reduced dose limit of 1mSv yr^{-1} for members of the public, which has had to be incorporated by National Governments when considering waste disposal strategies. The Euratom Directive 96/29 [3] implements ICRP 60 recommendations and is the basis for new UK regulations.

The International Agencies provide recommendations based on the collective opinions and information supplied by the Member States. These recommendations are translated into regulations, procedures and practices by National Governments. However, in the case of the European Community there is an additional statutory Treaty establishing 'The European Atomic Energy Community' (Euratom).

The Euratom Basic Safety Directive is implemented in the United Kingdom by National Statutes. Responsibility for regulation and control of radioactive waste management is shared by the Government, the Regulators and the Producers of the waste. The Government passes Acts and Statutes in accordance with its own policy and international agreements; the Regulating Bodies ensure the implementation of the policy; and the User must manage the waste in accordance with the regulation.

A number of national bodies exist for provision of advice and research to the Government.

The Radioactive Waste Management Advisory Committee (**RWMAC**) is an independent body of experts, drawn from a wide range of backgrounds including nuclear, academic, medical, research and lay interests. It was established in 1978 in response to a recommendation in the 'Flowers Report' [4] and is a source of independent advice to the Secretaries of State for the Environment on matters of civil radioactive waste management.

The Advisory Committee on the Safety of Nuclear Installations (**ACSNI**) was set up in 1977 to advise the Health and Safety Commission (HSC) and, where appropriate, Secretaries of State, on major issues affecting the safety of nuclear installations. It is made up of an independent Chairman and 12 members appointed by the HSC, together with a number of members nominated by the Confederation of British Industry (CBI) and the Trades Union Congress (TUC). ACSNI is assisted by assessors from the nuclear industry, the Nuclear Installations Inspectorate (**NII**) and observers from Government departments as appropriate.

The Ionising Radiations Advisory Committee (**IRAC**) was established in 1995 by the Health and Safety Commission (HSC) to consider all matters concerning protection against exposure to ionising radiations that are relevant to the work of the HSC, and to advise the Commission and its Executive. The work includes monitoring the effectiveness of legislation and monitoring developments in technology.

The National Radiological Protection Board (NRPB) was created by the Radiological Protection Act 1970. The functions of the Board are to give advice, to conduct research, and to provide technical services in the field of protection against both ionising and non–ionising radiations. The Board issues advice in the Documents of the NRPB series.

The Committee on Medical Aspects of Radiation in the Environment (**COMARE**) was set up in 1985 in response to a recommendation in the report of the independent advisory committee chaired by Sir Douglas Black on the possible increased incidence of cancer in West Cumbria. Its terms of reference are to assess and advise the Government on the health effects of natural and man-made radiation in the environment, and to assess the adequacy of the available data in addition to the need for further research. COMARE has provided Statements of Advice on a number of issues.

The Government also takes advice from the regulatory bodies themselves and consults widely on the preliminary conclusions of the review of radioactive waste management policy.

The purpose of this chapter is to provide an overview of the current legislation, and subsequent user obligations and practices associated with the handling of radionuclides. Legal requirements are incorporated from initial user registration/authorisations through to radioactive waste disposal, including transport considerations. Any differences in the implementation of regulations in Scotland and Northern Ireland compared with England and Wales are described. The reader may use this chapter as a guide, but **must** research the subject area for himself or herself to ensure that the responsibilities as a user, waste accumulator or disposer are met in all respects.

7.1 REGULATIONS RELEVANT TO REGISTRATION, AUTHORISATIONS AND HEALTH AND SAFETY, FOR THE PROVISION OF A SMALL RADIOACTIVE FACILITY

7.1.1 The Radioactive Substances Act 1993 (RSA93)

The Radioactive Substances Act 1993 [5] supersedes the 1960 version and consolidates certain enactments relating to radioactive substances. Since 1995, changes have been made to RSA93 to reflect the Environment Act 1995. These mainly concern the Environment Agency replacing Her Majesty's Inspectorate of Pollution (HMIP) as the Regulatory Body concerned with applications, registrations and authorisations under the various sections of RSA93.

In broad terms, RSA93 defines 'radioactive material' as anything, which not being waste, is either wholly or partly a substance containing the specified elements actinium, lead, polonium, protactinium, radium, radon, thorium or uranium, or, a substance possessing radioactivity which is wholly or partly attributable to a process of nuclear fission or other process of subjecting a substance to bombardment by neutrons or to ionising radiations.

'Radioactive Waste' is defined as waste consisting wholly or partly of a substance or article which, if it were not waste, would be radioactive material, or, which has been contaminated in the course of production, keeping or use of radioactive material.

The sections in RSA93 of principal concern to most small users are:

- Section 7 requiring registration of users of radioactive material.

- Section 10 requiring registration of mobile radioactive apparatus.

- Sections 13 and 14 requiring authorisation to dispose and accumulate radioactive waste.

- Section 19 requiring the display of certificates of registration or authorisation on the user premises.

- Section 20 requiring retention and production of site or disposal records.

- Section 21 concerning enforcement notices for failure to comply with any limitation or condition subject to the registration or authorisation.

- Section 26 giving the user the right to appeal on decisions from the appropriate Agency on most issues concerned with registrations, authorisations and notices, and

- Section 27 dictating the procedure for such appeals.

To provide a full review of RSA93 is outside the scope of this chapter and therefore the reader is referred to the Act itself or to the Regulatory Bodies for further information. Guidance and contact details are given in the following section:

7.1.2 Regulatory Bodies, Charging Scheme and Guidance

The Environment Agency delivers a service to its customers, with the emphasis on authority and accountability at the local level.

The Environment Agency Head Office is responsible for overall policy and relationships with national bodies including Government:

The Environment Agency Head Office
Rio House
Waterside Drive
Aztec West
Almondsbury
Bristol BS12 4UD

In **England and Wales**, applications relevant to RSA93, and their associated fees and charges are dealt with by the Agency's Regional Offices which, at the time of writing, are situated as follows:

ANGLIAN

Kingfisher House
Goldhay Way
Orton Goldhay
Peterborough
PE2 5ZR

NORTH EAST

Rivers House
21 Park Square South
Leeds
LS1 2QG

NORTH WEST

Richard Fairclough House
Knutsford Road
Warrington
WA4 1HG

MIDLANDS

Sapphire East
550 Streetsbrook Road
Solihull
B91 1QT

SOUTHERN

Guildbourne House
Chatsworth Road
Worthing
West Sussex
BN11 1LD

SOUTH WEST

Manley House
Kestrel Way
Exeter
EX2 7LQ

THAMES

Kings Meadow House
Kings Meadow Road
Reading
RG1 8DQ

WELSH

Rivers House/Plas-yr-Afon
St Mellons Business Park
St Mellons
Cardiff
CF3 0LT

The following application forms and accompanying guidance are available through Environment Agency offices:

RSA 1 (Closed Sources) – used for application for registration under RSA93 section 7 of radioactive substances other than open sources on specified premises.

RSA 1 (Open Sources) – used for application for registration under RSA93 section 7 of radioactive substances other than closed sources on specified premises.

RSA 2 (Mobile Closed Sources) – used for application for registration under RSA93 section 10 for mobile radioactive apparatus in England and Wales for activities involving the testing, measurement or otherwise investigating any of the characteristics of substances or articles, that is, radioactive material, in the form of closed sources moved from site to site for use. Such sources include radiography sources, road density gauges, borehole logging sources and crop yield meters on combine harvesters.

RSA 2 (Environmental Studies) - used for application for registration under RSA93 section 10 for mobile radioactive apparatus for releasing quantities of radioactive material into the environment or introducing such material into organisms which are released into the environment.

RSA 3 – used for the application for authorisation to *accumulate and dispose of radioactive waste* under sections 13 and 14 of RSA93.

In **Scotland**, applications relevant to RSA93 are dealt with by the Scottish Environment Protection Agency (SEPA). The initial contact for anyone applying should be directed to:

Head of Radioactive Policy
SEPA Head Office
Erskine Court
Castle Business Park
Stirling
FK9 4TR

Within **Northern Ireland**, the Industrial Pollution and Radiochemical Inspectorate is the Competent Authority in respect of RSA93. (This forms part of the Environment and Heritage Service which was set up as an agency within the Department of the Environment for Northern Ireland on 1 April 1996). The amendments to RSA93 as a result of the Environment Act 1995 do not apply in Northern Ireland. All disposals of radioactive material are authorised by the Chief Radiochemical Inspector or are exempt from the requirements of the Act and are covered by one of the Exemption Orders made under the Act (discussed further in section 7.2). The Inspectorate is also responsible for implementing legislation relating to the transport of radioactive substances. The contact for the Inspectorate on radioactive matters is:

Chief Radiochemical Inspector
Industrial Pollution and Radiochemical Inspectorate
Environment and Heritage Service
Calvert House,
23 Castle Place
Belfast
BT1 1FY

The Environment Act 1995, section 41, provides for the Environment Agency to recover the costs and expenses incurred by the Agency and by the Ministry of Agriculture, Fisheries and Food (MAFF) in carrying out their functions in relation to the RSA93. (Regulation prior to 1 April 1996 was carried out by Her Majesty's Inspectorate of Pollution (HMIP) with, for nuclear sites, MAFF). The regulatory functions of both of these bodies transferred to the Agency on that date. The Environment Agency Charging Scheme [6] is structured on the basis of the following four bands:-

Band 1 –   British Nuclear Fuels Ltd reprocessing plant, Sellafield.

Band 2 –   Other sites subject to licensing under section 1 of the Nuclear Installations Act 1965 (mainly nuclear power stations).

Band 3 –   Authorisations under sections 13 and 14 of the RSA93 to accumulate or dispose of radioactive waste.

Band 4 – Registrations under section 7 of the RSA93 for keeping and use of radioactive material, or under section 10 for the keeping and use of mobile radioactive apparatus, including use for tracer testing.

Band 3 and 4 charges are based on a system of flat-rate fees and charges for Applications, Subsistence, Variation and Supplementary.

There is also an associated charging scheme applicable in Northern Ireland [7].

7.1.3 The Ionising Radiation Regulations 1985 (IRR *1985*)

The primary aim of the Ionising Radiation Regulations 1985 [8] and the Health and Safety Ionising Radiation Regulations (Northern Ireland) 1985 [9], is to introduce conditions whereby doses of ionising radiation can be maintained at an acceptable level. Users must register with the Health and Safety Executive and comply with the conditions of the Regulations. The Regulations are extensive and account for the health and safety aspects in all uses/applications of radionuclides. For the purposes of providing general information, the scope of the Regulations is presented in this section. However, readers intending to work with ionising radiation must familiarise themselves with the detail of the Regulations.

IRR's 1985 are based on Directives 80/836/Euratom and 84/467/Euratom which have been superseded by Directive 96/29/Euratom. The new Directive takes into account the recommendations of ICRP 60. Draft Regulations to replace IRR's 1985 have already been produced for public comment and the final version will be implemented by the year 2000. The key changes are the use of the new ICRP concepts of practices and intervention, a lower principal dose limit, a mandatory requirement for 'prior authorisation' of certain activities, explicit treatment of natural radiation sources and explicit treatment of 'intervention' which includes emergency preparedness. The Outside Workers Regulations of 1993 are also likely to be incorporated within the new IRR's. In the meantime, the 1985 IRR's are the relevant legislation.

The IRR's 1985 contain the fundamental requirements needed to control exposure to radiation. Details of acceptable methods of meeting those requirements are given in the supporting Approved Code of Practice [10]. In each case compliance with a Regulation may be achieved by a method other than described in the Code to account for the latest practices adopted through advancing knowledge.

Radiation protection is based on three general principles, that is, every practice resulting in exposure to ionising radiation shall be justified by the advantages it produces; all exposures shall be kept as low as reasonably achievable; and the sum of doses and committed doses received shall not exceed certain limits. The Regulations ensure that the necessary steps are taken to comply with these basic principles including the setting of limits on the amount of dose to be received in any calendar year by various categories of person: workers, trainees, members of the public and women of reproductive capacity. They also impose duties on people not to cause those limits to be exceeded.

In order to facilitate the control of doses to people, the Regulations require controlled and supervised areas to be identified where certain criteria are met (as described in Schedule 6 to the Regulations). Where a person enters a controlled area he or she must be designated a classified person unless entering under a written system of work designed to ensure that he or she cannot receive a significant dose.

The Regulations require specially appointed doctors to undertake medical surveillance on workers who are to be classified and on classified persons in order to assess their fitness. A review of medical findings is also catered for. Furthermore there has to be a system for regular assessment of doses received by classified persons and dosimetry services approved by the Health and Safety Executive must be used for this purpose. Individual records must be kept of medical findings and assessed doses. There are specific requirements to provide appropriate safety devices, warning signals, handling tools, etc, to leak-test radioactive sources, to provide protective equipment and clothing and to test them, to monitor radiation and contamination levels, to store radioactive substances safely, to design, construct and maintain buildings, fittings and equipment so as to minimise contamination, and to make contingency arrangements for dealing with foreseeable but unintended incidents. In addition, undertakings holding large quantities of radioactive substances will need to make a survey of potential hazards and prepare a report, a copy of which should be sent to the Executive.

There is a requirement for users to notify the Executive in the event of a release or loss of radioactive substances, and when someone has received an excessive dose of radiation. Local investigations of excessive doses will have to be made and reports kept.

It is also important that any equipment, device or other article used in connection with ionising radiation affords optimum radiation protection. There are associated duties on designers, manufacturers, importers, suppliers, erectors and installers.

The provision of information on potential hazards and the instruction and training of people involved with ionising radiation are an essential part of radiation protection, and are required in the Regulations. Additionally there are requirements to formulate local rules covering all radiation protection arrangements and to provide supervision of work. The latter requirement will normally necessitate the appointment by management of a Radiation Protection Supervisor whose responsibilities should be clearly defined. The Regulations also require Radiation Protection Advisers to be appointed wherever expert advice is needed and for appointments to be notified to the Executive.

Special considerations apply to medical exposures. Doses received by patients undergoing diagnosis or treatment involving the use of ionising radiation are not taken into account in determining compliance with dose limits.

For specific guidance on the use of ionising radiations in educational establishments and associated health and safety management the reader is referred to the Department of Education Science publication [11], and to the Committee of Vice-Chancellors and Principals of the Universities of the UK 'Code of Practice' [12].

7.2 EXEMPTION ORDERS

Exemptions from the requirements of the Radioactive Substances Act 1993 (update of the 1960 version) exist in the form of Exemption Orders.

Descriptions of Exemption Orders are difficult to generalise but a broad description of the concepts and types of restrictions are as follows:

KEEPING AND USE

Usually a limit on total quantity - by mass as in Uranium or Thorium usage; by number of items as in smoke detectors; storage in transit; by activity or specific activity; substances of low specific activity.

DISPOSAL

Usually restricted on quantity (by weight or activity) and route (by activity, need for authorisation).

The powers to make Exemption Orders are held by the Secretaries of State for the Environment. They may grant exemptions from the need to be registered under section 7 and 10 of RSA93 for the keeping and use of radioactive materials and mobile radioactive apparatus, and from the need to be authorised under sections 13 and 14 of RSA93 for the accumulation and disposal of radioactive waste.

The Radioactive Substances (RAS) Division of DoE's Directorate of Pollution Control and Wastes is responsible for formulating Exemption Orders on behalf of the Secretaries of State. The Regulatory Bodies (see Section 7.1.2) advise the RAS Division on the regulatory and technical (including radiological) aspects of Exemption Orders.

7.2.1 Exemption orders applicable in Scotland, England and Wales

The twenty Exemption Orders applicable in Scotland, England and Wales are listed in the references to this chapter [13-32]. Some of them date back as far as 1962 and refer to exemption from registration under various sections of the Radioactive Active Substances Act 1960. It is imperative that the reader ensures relevant exemptions are still current before operating under the prescribed conditions.

Exemption Orders are specific to particular radionuclides, activity level, intended use, sample type, or facility, as appropriate. To provide a full description of each Exemption Order would constitute a chapter in itself. Instead, the general scope of exemptions is described to assist the reader in assessing whether exemption from registration is likely for certain radioactive materials or applications. It must be emphasised that the reader should obtain and be confident that he or she fully understands the relevant Exemption Order(s) to ensure compliance with all conditions. It is prudent to seek advice from the Regulators for whom contact details (depending on location within the UK) have been provided in Section 7.1.2.

The scope of Exemption Orders covers the following:

Articles containing lead in common use excluding that arising from refining or extraction of radium or uranium, from a process in which the proportion of lead-210 or polonium-210 is artificially increased, or from a radon source.

Specific uses and disposal of limited quantities of prepared compounds of either uranium or thorium from which each of the radioactive decay products has been substantially removed in the course of preparation.

The keeping, use and disposal of limited quantities of commonplace radioactive materials containing natural thorium and natural uranium, that is, incandescent mantles, heat-resisting thoria ware, substances/articles containing less than 4% by weight of natural thorium including hardener alloy for the production of magnesium alloy, or a mixture of these materials.

The keeping, use and disposal of limited quantities of geological specimens containing uranium or thorium for demonstration, investigation or sale.

The use and disposal of certain substances and articles of limited radioactivity which are derived from phosphatic ores or which contain the rare earth elements or titanium, yttrium, zirconium, niobium or hafnium.

The use and disposal of limited quantities of closed sources containing any radionuclides, and also open sources which contain beta/gamma emitting radionuclides other than strontium-90, in certain schools, teacher training colleges and institutions for further education which are approved by the Department of Education.

The accumulation and disposal of waste closed sources either by return to the manufacturer or by sending them to a person who is specifically authorised under the Act to dispose of such sources.

The keeping, use and disposal, other than by the manufacturer, of electronic valves which contain only one radionuclide and not more than limited activity of certain radionuclides, that is, cobalt-60, nickel-63, caesium-137, thorium, thallium-204, radium-226, uranium, carbon-14, chlorine-36, promethium-147, krypton-85 and tritium. Valves containing more than one of the fore-mentioned radionuclides at limited radioactivity are also exempt.

The keeping, use and restricted disposal of smoke detectors.

The keeping, use and restricted disposal of instruments, illuminants and similar devices containing tritium gas in robust sealed containers.

The keeping, use and disposal of radioactive luminous instruments and indicators containing no radionuclides other than limited quantities of promethium-147 or tritium or decay products, and satisfying specific criteria with respect to physical properties.

The keeping, use and restricted disposal (except for exhibition purposes or on the manufacturer's premises) of closed sources which either are incorporated in or accompany instruments (including mobile radioactive apparatus) designed for testing, measuring or investigating the characteristics of substances and articles. The closed sources referred to are electrodeposited, containing either nickel-63 or iron-55, and tritium foil sources.

The keeping, use and disposal of substances of low activity, for example, solid radioactive material, other than a closed source, which is substantially insoluble in water, the activity of which does not exceed 0.4 Becquerels per gram of mass.

The keeping, use and restricted disposal of certain solid or liquid radioactive materials for use in hospitals for the purposes of medical diagnosis, treatment of patients or supply to another hospital.

The keeping and use of radioactive material containing precipitated phosphate (and not containing uranium other than natural uranium, and certain other radionuclides) for the purposes of application to soil for cultivation, the production of a mixture for such application, or sale for either of these purposes.

The keeping of radioactive material contained in a package, or packaged in transit, but restricted on dose rate at or near its surface, and on the radionuclides and activity of its contents.

The keeping or use of a homogeneous source, sealed source of limited activity, an open source (not being dry powder) containing only certain radionuclides, or equipment which is radioactive material (incorporating one of these sources), for the purpose of demonstrating its characteristics or uses at exhibitions.

7.2.2 Statutory rules and orders of Northern Ireland

A full list of the eighteen Exemption Orders currently in force in Northern Ireland is provided in the references to this chapter [33-50]. Although they apply to Northern Ireland only, they are equivalent to the Great Britain Exemption Orders except for subtle differences in four of them.

These are:

- The Radioactive Substances (Precipitated Phosphate) Exemption Order (Northern Ireland) [40];

- The Radioactive Substances (Smoke Detectors) Exemption Order (Northern Ireland) [44];

- The Radioactive Substances (Substances of Low Activity) Exemption Order (Northern Ireland) [48]; and

- The Radioactive Substances (Hospitals) Exemption Order (Northern Ireland) [49].

The reader who requires further detail is advised to review the Exemption Orders referenced.

7.3 WASTE ACCUMULATION, STORAGE AND DISPOSAL

This section gives an overview of the current legislation and practices associated with waste accumulation, storage and disposal of radioactive waste. To reiterate, the reader may use this information as a guide, but <u>must</u> research the subject area to ensure that his or her responsibilities as a waste accumulator and disposer are fully met. Changes in legislation and local licence conditions must be fulfilled by the responsible officer when accumulating and disposing of radioactive waste.

It should also be borne in mind when considering the disposal of radioactive waste that the conventional physical and chemical hazards of the waste must also be addressed.

Finally, consideration of waste accumulation and disposal should not be approached as a last minute detail or a bridge to be crossed when reached, instead it should be considered from the onset. The choice of radionuclide for an application can greatly affect the ease or difficulty of disposal and ultimately the final cost borne by the user. Similarly, consideration of the final waste form arising from a particular project should be a part of the project planning phase. Immediate aqueous disposal may be preferred to accumulation as a solid waste prior to disposal or *vice versa*. Simple treatments of waste, for example, dissolution of solids or precipitation of active species from solution can assist the user in the management of the waste. As in all things, prevention is better than cure and by the application of some simple rules and especially the application of forward planning, the volumes of waste produced in the use of radionuclides can be greatly reduced. Segregation of certain waste from active waste, such as non–active and very low active waste which can be disposed of via conventional routes, prevents cross contamination and limits the quantity of radioactive waste disposed. Project planning can avoid complications such as the production of mixed wastes, that is, both hazardous and radioactive, as well as ensuring all working procedures are written to minimise waste volumes and simplify disposal routes.

The quality assurance requirement for solid waste disposal can have exacting demands concerning the history of the sample and radionuclide content. To avoid unnecessary complications, expensive confirmation analyses and to take advantage of the exemption limits on particular radionuclides, it is important to maintain detailed and accurate records and to keep wastes segregated during the accumulation and storage period prior to final disposal. It is also necessary to ensure that all users are aware of the planned disposal route and the record keeping system.

7.3.1 National regulation

As already discussed, the Radioactive Substances Act 1993 [5] gives the responsibility for the regulation of radioactive waste to the Environment Agency (EA) in England and Wales, to the Scottish Environment Protection Agency (SEPA) in Scotland, and to the Industrial Pollution and Radiochemical Inspectorate in Northern Ireland.

Much of the documentation produced with regard to radioactive waste management is concerned with control and disposal of very large amounts of radioactive waste as produced by the nuclear power industry. These documents are rightly concerned with the problems of a national repository for **high** and **intermediate level wastes (HLW and ILW)**, limitation of discharges into the environment and protection of the public from unauthorised disposal of radioactive material.

For the small user of radioactive materials the prospects of finding a way through the labyrinth of legislation may seem rather daunting and a recent publication by RWMAC entitled Review of Problems Encountered by Small Users of Radioactive Substances [51] has expressed the need for 'streamlining' of the procedures for small users.

The immediate need for all users, is to comply with the requirements of the IRR's 85 [8] and RSA93 (see Section 7.1). Information is available to the small user through official documents such as Approved Codes of Practice and specialised publications [52-54] as well as commercially held courses by the suppliers of radioactive materials. Ultimately the user is responsible to the regulator and therefore it is to the advantage of any small user to consult with the local EA Inspector at the planning stage of any intended changes or additions to existing authorised procedures.

Under the conditions of the Radioactive Substances Act 1993, Section 13, an authorisation is required for the disposal of any radioactive waste arising from a permanent or mobile facility. The accumulation of radioactive waste on the premises, with the intention of future disposal, also requires authorisation under the Act.

Application for registration and authorisation should be made to the EA (see Section 7.1). A system of fees and charges are made for these services. Details of these charges can be obtained from the EA document 'Fees and Charges for Radioactive Substances Act Regulations' which can be obtained from a local EA office.

Under the 1993 Act it is an offence to:

a) dispose or accumulate radioactive waste other than in accordance with the conditions specified in the authorisation granted to the premises and to

b) dispose of radioactive waste arisings from a mobile facility other than in accordance with the authorisation granted for the provision of services supplied by the mobile apparatus.

Penalties for offences under the Act can be fines, imprisonment or both. Exemptions from these conditions exist in the form of Exemption Orders. A full listing of Exemption Orders is provided in the references to this chapter [13-50], and further detail is given in Section 7.2. The reader must ensure that any of the listed exemptions are still current before assuming they may operate under the prescribed conditions.

7.3.2 Disposal

Disposal of very low level radioactive wastes less than 0.37 Bq g^{-1} does not require authorisation under the 1993 Radioactive Substances Act and can be disposed of as 'free release' to the domestic refuse stream. Small amounts of solid waste can be authorised for disposal with ordinary waste, provided the activity does not exceed 370 kBq in 0.1 m^3 and 37 kBq per article and provided it does not contain either alpha emitters or strontium-90. Radioactive waste consisting of only weak beta emitters and/or carbon-14 and/or tritium but no alpha emitters or strontium-90, can have an increased disposal limit of 3.7 MBq in 0.1 m^3.

Solid waste unsuitable for disposal, as described above, may be disposed of via a specialist contractor such as Safeguard International [55] who supply a full disposal service. Authorisation for such a waste stream must be agreed with the EA and must be a condition of the authorisation for the premises.

Disposal of liquid radioactive waste is regulated by the EA authorisation for the premises. Where liquid activities are low enough, disposal may be directly to the sewer without prior collection or monitoring. Records must be kept and made available for inspection by the EA. Records should include total quantities of radionuclides involved and the means and date of disposal. Normally only a designated sink with a sealed drain running to the sewer is used. The establishment's Radiation Safety Officer is responsible for overseeing the installation/designation of this sink.

Non-aqueous liquids (organic solvents) may be disposed of in several ways. Again authorisation is required and will be a part of the premises radioactive disposal conditions. The waste may be removed by a specialist contractor (eg Safeguard International) where radionuclide concentrations are less than 3.7 Bq cm^{-3}. Alternatively small quantities of solvent may be evaporated on the owner's premises provided this can be carried out safely and does not create a problem with concentrated residues. Incineration on the owner's premises where such a facility exists may be used as a disposal option. However, all conventional Health and Safety Regulations must be adhered to as well as those pertaining to radioactive authorisations.

Normal laboratory work involves the use of fume cupboards and/or glove boxes which are used to protect workers from radioactive gas, vapours or dusts. All such airborne discharges require authorisation which will usually specify a limit on the quantity of activity and nuclide type which may be discharged in a given period. Records must be kept of all discharges. Where higher levels of airborne activity are expected then further precautions such as HEPA filters may be specified.

7.3.3 Special wastes

In the UK the Hazardous Waste Directive (91/689/EEC) is now implemented through the 1996 Special Waste Regulations [56]. Similarly, the requirements of the Directives on the Classification, Packaging and Labelling of Dangerous Substances (67/584/EEC) and Preparations (83/467/EEC) are implemented in this country through the 1994 CHIP2 (Chemicals, Hazard Information and Packaging for Supply) Regulations, as amended in 1996 and 1997.

The link between Special Waste and CHIP2 is included in Schedule 2 Part IV of the SWR (Special Waste Regulations, 1996) [57]. This regulation correlates the classifications of hazardous substances in the waste to those listed in the ASL (Approved Supply List), or if they are not listed, to classifications derived in line with methods given in the 'Approved Guide' – both of which documents are prepared under the CHIP2 Regulations.

Official guidance in the Department of the Environment Circular 6/96 recognises the difficulties inherent in sampling and analysing wastes which are often heterogeneous and may be bulky and difficult to handle. However, it emphasises that waste producers should, wherever possible, assess waste by analysis of its components rather than by direct testing for hazardous properties.

The Environment Agency has indicated that Waste Management Paper 23 will be published early in 1998 and this will contain practical guidance on sampling strategies, sampling methods, management of analytical data and appropriate test methods. This Paper also includes more detailed guidelines for assessment of the hazard categories. The Agency has produced a series of Technical Assessment Guidance notes which consider specific waste streams and advise on the circumstances under which these will become Special Wastes. The Agency has also drawn up internal guidance notes on Legal Interpretation and Policy, one of which clarifies the situation for producers of very small quantities of Special Wastes.

Radioactive wastes fall into the categorisation of Special Wastes if, in addition to their radioactive content, they contain one of the 14 specified hazards. Small producers should be familiar with the regulations and procedures as discussed above.

7.4 TRANSPORT, PACKAGING AND SHIELDING

7.4.1 Regulations overview

The transport of radioactive material is subject to a number of statutory requirements specifically pertaining to its radioactive content. The material for transport is still subject to regulations covering conventional physical and chemical hazards [57] and so these transport criteria must also be met. The specific regulations to be complied with by the consignor depend on the physical and chemical form, radioactive content, the amount of material, the type of transport to be used and whether or not the package must cross national boundaries.

The quantity and complexity of the regulations, international and national, and local rules governing this area are too extensive to give detailed examples in this chapter. Instead the reader will be introduced to the structure of the legislation, be made aware of his or her responsibility in transporting radioactive materials, given a full set of references for further detailed information and be provided with a summary of the regulations applying to the UK. More information is provided in Section 6.9.

Responsibilities: The consignor who is transporting radioactive material is responsible for ensuring that:

a) dose limits at the surface and 1 metre from the package are not exceeded;
b) the packaging is of the correct type eg Type A, Type B or Excepted packages;
c) the package is correctly labelled and
d) the documentation complies with all the relevant legislation.

The carrier has the responsibility to ensure that the package is correctly loaded and transported in accordance with all relevant legislation.

Legislation: In 1961 the IAEA issued 'Regulations for the Safe Transport of Radioactive Material', Safety Series No. 6 [58]. Safety Series No. 6 has become the basis world-wide on which national and international regulations are formulated. The International Civil Aviation Organisation (ICAO) and the International Maritime Organization (IMO) which have binding safety conditions have modelled their regulations on Safety Series No. 6. This is also true of the International Air Transport Association and the applicable roads, rail and inland waterway regulations within Europe.

In recognition of the need to maintain the regulations abreast of technical innovation and radiation protection principles, the IAEA regularly issue revisions to the transport regulations. The latest was in 1986, however, in September 1996 the IAEA approved a draft revision for publication and recommended it to the Member States. Any changes accepted by the Member States will be reflected by changes in their own national regulations as well as changes to international practices. Safety Series No. 6 is not a stand alone document and is supported by a number of other IAEA publications covering planning, quality assurance, air transport, emergency response and other topics. A list of publications is given in the references [59-65]. Reference [63] is a hypertext software guide to IAEA Safety Series Nos 6, 7, 37 and 80. Entire text is cross referenced and it has an additional facility to add notes.

European legislation is contained within the Euratom directives which are translated into national law by Government Acts. Relevant Euratom directives are given in references [66,67].

Translation of the IAEA Safety Series No 6 is found in 'The Radioactive Material (Road Transport Great Britain) Regulations 1996' [68]. These regulations cover definitions of excepted packages, categories of active materials, types of packages, labelling requirements, determination of the transport index (TI), and specify the QA requirements and supplies tables for the calculation of allowable activities for each radionuclide in each of the package types. Many other requirements such as driver training and Tests for Packages are also given in the regulations [69].

Additional requirements for sea and air shipments are found in the codes, agreements and Notices relating to Merchant Shipping [70-73]. Regulations for air transport are found in the IATA Dangerous Goods Regulation, ICAO Regulations and the Air Navigation Regulation [74-76]. Rail transport is covered in the UK by reference [77]. Additional requirements and information for road transport are found in references [78-81]. In Northern Ireland the relevant road regulations which apply are as referenced [82-87].

Further requirements are raised by the transport of radioactive materials over country borders. This is covered in the Transfrontier Shipment Regulations [88,89]. In some cases it may be necessary to consult the Department of Trade and Industry (DTI) regarding Export Control [90] and also the Customs and Excise Authorities [91,92].

The small user can find guidance from specialist publications such as those produced by AURPO (Association of University Radiation Protection Officers), HCB (Hazardous Cargo Bulletin), Safeguard International (now out of print) and the NRPB [55, 93-95].

The Post Office in the UK is not licensed to carry any radioactive materials but specialist carriers are available for transport of these materials, for example, Securicor Omega Express (Radiac). This carrier complies with UK regulations regarding the transport of radioactive wastes.

7.4.2 Summary

Before attempting to ship radioactive material the consignor must first designate the appropriate category for his shipment. These categories are given in the 1996 regulations [68]. Requirements for excepted packages are given in Schedule 3, industrial packages types IP 1 to 3 in Schedule 9, Type A packages in Schedule 11 and type B packages in Schedules 12 and 13.

The consignor must then ensure the package type, labelling and documentation are all in accordance with the regulatory requirement, remembering the additional needs for the individual form of transport, rail, road, air or sea, or the combined needs if the shipment will use more than one form of transport before arriving at its intended destination.

The requirements for transporting radioactive material can be complicated and care should be taken to consult the relevant publications as referenced in this section. It is also useful to contact service suppliers (packaging suppliers, courier services, shipping companies) who can give advice to the user on the specialist service they supply. For small users the specialist advice groups are especially useful. Above all, the consignor must remember that it is his/her responsibility to see that all current regulations are obeyed.

7.5 NUCLEAR MATERIALS

7.5.1 Background to the relevant legislation

The UK is subject to Euratom safeguards in connection with the Treaty on the Non-Proliferation of Nuclear Weapons. The UK Government, via the Department of Trade and Industry (DTI), requires relevant establishments to maintain a system of accountancy and control of all nuclear materials subject to international safeguards.

The Commission Regulation (EURATOM) No 3227/76 of 19 October 1976 [96] concerns the application of the provisions on Euratom safeguards, and codifies all relevant safeguard regulations in a single text. This became essential in view of the increasing quantities of nuclear materials produced. For example, some installations are liable to be involved in the production cycle for defence needs and as such require specific safeguard procedures.

It was necessary to bring up to date and define the nature and the extent of the requirements of the Treaty in order to ensure the effectiveness of safeguards. This was done in the light of experience gained, particularly with regard to the transportation of, or commerce in these materials. One of the undertakings of an Agreement (5 April 1973) between Member States and the International Atomic Energy Agency (IAEA) concerning the implementation of the Treaty, was to establish particular procedures for the application of safeguards based on the most modern developments in the field.

7.5.2 Definition of nuclear materials and relevance to the small user

The term 'Nuclear Materials' refers to any *ore, source or special fissile material* as defined in Part VI of the Commission Regulation (EURATOM) No 3227/76, 1976.

> 'Special Fissile Materials' means plutonium-239; uranium-233; uranium enriched in uranium-235 or uranium-233 (that is, uranium in which the ratio of U-235 or U-233 to U-238 is greater than occurs in nature); and any substance containing one or more of the foregoing isotopes. 'Special Fissile Materials' does not, however, include source materials, ores or ore waste.

> 'Source Materials' means uranium containing the mixture of isotopes occurring in nature; uranium whose content in uranium-235 is less than the normal, thorium and any of the foregoing in the form of metal, alloy, chemical compound or concentrate. The words 'Source Materials' are not to be taken to include ores or ore waste.

> 'Ores' means any ore containing average concentration of substances (as specified by the appointed Council acting on the Commission proposal) from which the source materials defined above may be obtained by the appropriate chemical and physical processing.

As such, the 'small user' is not often concerned with the handling, transport and accountancy of nuclear materials. Furthermore, under Part II, Article 22, of the Commission Regulation, installations holding only small quantities (which are kept in the same state for long periods) can request, in accordance with the form set out in Annex VIII, that the Commission exempt the following materials from declaration, provided that they are not processed or stored together with non-exempted nuclear materials:

- special fissile materials which are used in quantities of the order of a gram or less and sensing components in instruments;

- plutonium with an isotopic concentration of plutonium-238 in excess of 80% by activity;

- nuclear materials which are used exclusively in non-nuclear activities.

For the 'larger user', a useful publication entitled 'The Law of Nuclear Installations and Radioactive Substances' [97] is comprehensive and complementary to this chapter.

7.5.3 An overview - Commission Regulation (EURATOM) No 3227/76, 1976

For the purpose of providing information to all user categories, an overview of the Commission Regulation is presented below. It is notable that the Annexes to this Regulation form an integral part.

Part I comprises 'Basic Technical Characteristics and Particular Safeguard Provisions'.
Under *Declaration of the Technical Characteristics,* Article 1 requires any person or organisation setting up or operating an installation for the production, separation or other use of source materials or special fissile materials, or for the processing of irradiated nuclear fuels, to declare to the Commission the basic technical characteristics of the installation. For this purpose a questionnaire is provided in Annex I to the Regulation document. Such

declaration is also required of any person or organisation responsible for the storage of these materials. Article 2 requires that these basic technical characteristics must be declared at least 45 days before the first consignment of nuclear material is due to be received.

Under *Programme of Activities,* Article 6 requires the person or organisation to inform the Commission annually of an outline programme of activities drawn up in accordance with the 'particular safety provisions' (see below). The first communication (on the basis of the guidelines given in Annex X of the Regulation document) must be made at the same time as the declaration on basic technical characteristics.

Under *Particular Safeguard Provisions*, Article 7, the Commission are empowered to specify the procedures by which the person or organisation concerned shall meet the requirements in relation to safeguards imposed on them. Among others these procedures will include designation of the material balance areas, procedures for keeping records of nuclear materials and for drawing up reports; the frequency of and procedures for drawing up physical inventories for accounting purposes; containment and surveillance measures and sampling by the plant operator solely for safeguard purposes. The 'particular safeguard provisions' also lay down the content of subsequent communications as well as the conditions requiring advance notification of shipments and receipts of nuclear material. The Commission will reimburse the person or organisation concerned for the cost of those special services associated with the 'particular safeguard provisions'.

Part II comprises the 'Accounting System' (Articles 9 - 23 inclusive). This lays down a requirement to maintain a system of accounting for, and control of, nuclear materials. This system must include accounting and operating records and, in particular, information on the quantities, nature, form and composition of these materials. Also required are details on their location, the particular safeguarding obligation, their intended use, and the shipper or recipient when the materials are transferred. The system of measurements on which the records are based must comply with the most recent international standards or will be equivalent in quality to those standards. Where appropriate, notifications must be expressed in kilograms for source materials and in grams for special fissile materials.

The 'accounting system' is extensive to say the least, hence the informed reader is referred to the Regulation document itself. In general terms, the 'accounting system' encompasses accounting records, operating records, special reports, initial inventories, inventory change reports, material balance reports and physical inventory listings.

It should be noted that this Regulation does not apply to holders of finished products used for non-nuclear purposes which incorporate nuclear materials that are virtually irrecoverable.

Part III concerns 'Transfers: Imports/Exports'. Article 24 requires the person or organisation exporting source or special fissile materials to a Member or non-Member State to notify the Commission of every such export at least 8 working days prior to preparation of materials for shipment. Such notification and detailed information must be given in accordance with the form set out in Annex V to the Regulation document. However, advance notification is required only where the consignment exceeds one effective kilogram, or where the 'particular safety provisions' so specify in the case of installations habitually transferring large total quantities of materials to the same State, even though no single consignment exceeds one effective kilogram.

Article 25 refers to the import of nuclear materials and requires notification to the Commission as far in advance as possible of the expected arrival date, and no later than the date of receipt and 5 working days before the material is unpacked. Such notification and detailed information must be given in accordance with the form set out in Annex VI to the Regulation document.

Part IV accounts for 'Specific Provisions' relevant to Ore Producers, Carriers and Intermediaries. Articles 29-31 refer to the record keeping and notification requirements for Ore Producers, in accordance with the form set out in Annex VII of the Regulation document.

Articles 32-33 refer to Carrier obligations to accept or hand over nuclear materials only against a duly signed and dated receipt stating the names of the parties concerned, the quantities carried, and the nature, form and composition of the materials.

Article 34 requires that every Intermediary (authorized agents, brokers, business agents) taking part in the conclusion of any contract for the supply of nuclear materials, must keep all documents relating to the transactions for at least one year after the expiry of the contract.

Part V accounts for 'Specific Provisions Applicable in the Territories of Member States which are Nuclear Weapon States'.

Part VI, 'Final Provisions' mainly provides definitions for certain terms relevant to the Regulation. One of particular interest to the reader is likely to be the definition of an 'Effective Kilogram'. This is a special unit used in safeguarding nuclear materials. The quantity in effective kilograms is obtained by taking:
for plutonium, its weight in kilograms;
for uranium with an enrichment of 0.01 (1%) and above, its weight in kilograms multiplied by the square of its enrichment;
for uranium with an enrichment below 0.01 (1%) and above 0.005 (0.5%), its weight in kilograms multiplied by 0.0001 and
for depleted uranium with an enrichment of 0.005 (0.5%) or below, and for thorium, its weight in kilograms multiplied by 0.00005.

7.5.4 The United Kingdom Atomic Energy Authority (UKAEA) System of Accountancy for Nuclear Materials

Sites which are managed by the UKAEA (for example, Harwell in Oxfordshire or Winfrith in Dorset) are licensed by the Nuclear Installations Inspectorate (NII) to use, store and transport nuclear materials. An outline of their approach to this is presented as an example of the operational needs for these activities.

The UKAEA approach to establishing and maintaining a system of accountancy and control for all nuclear materials subject to international safeguards, is through implementation of specific UKAEA Corporate Safety Instructions (CSI). This involves complying with the requirements laid down in the current editions of the UKAEA Nuclear Material Accounting and Control Manual and any procedures issued for ensuring compliance with that manual. The CSI [98] which accounts for nuclear material on and consigned from UKAEA sites, references others which are also relevant.

In summary, Nuclear Materials Controllers appointed by the Safety Directorate for operating an accountancy and safeguards system in respect of nuclear materials, receive information from UKAEA Responsible Managers. The Responsible Managers are responsible for accounting for all nuclear materials brought on to, used, or stored in facilities under their control. This includes responsibility for:

preparing and obtaining approval for safety cases, all movements of nuclear materials and obtaining a statement on their safeguards status from the consignor or consignee (as appropriate);

safe storage when not in use in operations, in accordance with the requirements of the safety case and its associated operating rules and instructions;

keeping records of the material in their plant and of consignments from their plant for a period of 30 years from the date of receipt or despatch and

packaging/transporting the material when required in accordance with the relevant UKAEA Quality Assurance Programme.

ACKNOWLEDGEMENTS

The author wishes to thank everybody who has contributed to this chapter by virtue of providing valuable information and documentation. In particular I would like to thank George Elder, Bradtec Ltd. (The University of the West of England, Bristol) Colin Davies (The Matthew Project, Bristol) Trevor Moseley (the Association of University Radiation Protection Officers (AURPO), University of Sheffield) Robert Larmour (Industrial Pollution & Radiochemical Inspectorate, Belfast, Northern Ireland) Mike Angus (Safeguard International Ltd.) and Kevin Butter (AEA Technology plc) are thanked for valuable comments on the chapter.

REFERENCES

1. Radioactive Waste Management: an IAEA source book. ISBN: 920102892X.

2. Review of Radioactive Waste Management Policy, Final Conclusions, July 1995. ISBN 0-10-129192-2.

3. Euratom Directive 96/29 – Basic Safety Standards.

4. Flowers Report, House of Commons Publication Office.

5. Radioactive Substances Act 1993, Chapter 12, ISBN 0 11 057333 1.

6. Environment Agency Charging Scheme for Radioactive Substances Act Regulation, 1997-98.

7. The Radioactive Substances (Fees and Charges) Scheme (Northern Ireland).

8. The Ionising Radiation Regulations 1985 (IRR's 1985), SI 1985 No 1333.

9. SI 1985 No. 273, Health and Safety Ionising Radiations Regulations (Northern Ireland) 1985.

10. The Protection of Persons against Ionising Radiation Arising from Any Work Activity, Approved Code of Practice – HSE/C.

11. The use of Ionising Radiation in Educational Establishments in England and Wales.1992 DES Publication.

12. Code of Practice for University Health and Safety Management, May 1995 – (Committee of Vice Chancellors and Principals of the Universities of the UK) CVCP Publication, ISBN: 0 948890525.

13. SI 1962 No. 2645, The Radioactive Substances (Exhibitions) Exemption Order 1962.

14. SI 1962 No. 2648, The Radioactive Substances (Phosphatic Substances, Rare Earths etc.) Exemption Order 1962.

15. SI 1962 No. 2646, The Radioactive Substances (Storage in Transit) Exemption Order 1962.

16. SI 1962 No. 2649, The Radioactive Substances (Lead) Exemption Order 1962.

17. SI 1962 No. 2710, The Radioactive Substances (Uranium and Thorium) Exemption Order 1962.

18. SI 1962 No. 2711, The Radioactive Substances (Prepared Uranium and Thorium Compounds) Exemption Order 1962.

19. SI 1962 No. 2712, The Radioactive Substances (Geological Specimens) Exemption Order 1962.

20. SI 1963 No. 1831, The Radioactive Substances (Waste Closed Sources) Exemption Order 1963.

21. SI 1963 No. 1832, The Radioactive Substances (Schools etc.) Exemption Order 1963.

22. SI 1963 No. 1836, The Radioactive Substances (Precipitated Phosphate) Exemption Order 1963.

23. SI 1967 No. 1797, The Radioactive Substances (Electronic Valves) Exemption Order 1967.

24. SI 1980 No. 953, The Radioactive Substances (Smoke Detectors) Exemption Order 1980.

25. SI 1991 No. 477, The Radioactive Substances (Smoke Detectors) Exemption (Amendment) Order 1991.

26. SI 1985 No. 1047, The Radioactive Substances (Gaseous Tritium Light Devices) Exemption Order 1985.

27. SI 1985 No. 1048, The Radioactive Substances (Luminous Articles) Exemption Order 1985.

28. SI 1985 No. 1049, The Radioactive Substances (Testing Instruments) Exemption Order 1985.

29. SI 1986 No. 1002, The Radioactive Substances (Substances of Low Activity) Exemption Order 1986.

30. SI 1992 No. 647, The Radioactive Substances (Substances of Low Activity) Exemption (Amendment) Order 1992.

31. SI 1990 No. 2512, The Radioactive Substances (Hospitals) Exemption Order 1990.

32. SI 1995 No. 2395, The Radioactive Substances (Hospitals) Exemption (Amendment) Order 1995.

33. SI 1962 No. 240, The Radioactive Substances (Lead) Exemption Order (Northern Ireland).

34. SI 1962 No. 242, The Radioactive Substances (Prepared Uranium and Thorium Compounds) Exemption Order (Northern Ireland).

35. SI 1962 No. 244, The Radioactive Substances (Uranium and Thorium) Exemption Order (Northern Ireland).

36. SI 1962 No. 246, The Radioactive Substances (Storage in Transit) Exemption Order (Northern Ireland).

37. SI 1962 No. 248, The Radioactive Substances (Geological Specimens) Exemption Order (Northern Ireland).

38. SI 1962 No. 249, The Radioactive Substances (Phosphatic Substances, Rare Earths, etc.) Exemption Order (Northern Ireland).

39. SI 1962 No. 250, The Radioactive Substances (Exhibitions) Exemption Order (Northern Ireland).

40. SI 1963 No. 218, The Radioactive Substances (Precipitated Phosphate) Exemption Order (Northern Ireland).

41. SI 1963 No. 219, The Radioactive Substances (Schools, etc) Exemption Order (Northern Ireland).

42. SI 1963 No. 222, The Radioactive Substances (Waste Closed Sources) Exemption Order (Northern Ireland).

43. SI 1967 No. 313, The Radioactive Substances (Electronic Valves) Exemption Order (Northern Ireland).

44. SI 1980 No. 304, The Radioactive Substances (Smoke Detectors) Exemption Order (Northern Ireland).

45. SI 1986 No. 10, The Radioactive Substances (Gaseous Tritium Light Devices) Exemption Order, (Northern Ireland).

46. SI 1986 No. 11, The Radioactive Substances (Luminous Articles) Exemption Order (Northern Ireland).

47. SI 1986 No. 12, The Radioactive Substances (Testing Instruments) Exemption Order (Northern Ireland).

48. SI 1990 No. 115, The Radioactive Substances (Substances of Low Activity) Exemption Order (Northern Ireland).

49. SI 1993 No. 54, The Radioactive Substances (Hospitals) Exemption Order (Northern Ireland).

50. SI 1995 No. 297, The Radioactive Substances (Metrication) Exemption Order (Northern Ireland).

51. RWMAC Report - Review of Problems Encountered by Small Users of Radioactive Substances for Better or Worse - The Stationery Office Feb 1996, ISBN: 011 753238X.

52. I S Mclintock, (on behalf of AURPO, The Association of University Radiation ProtectionOfficers),The Management of Radioactive Waste in Laboratories, HHSC Handbook No. 19,1996.ISBN 0-94237-30-9.

53. The Royal Society of Chemistry, Radioactive Waste Group, Burlington House, Piccadilly, London.

54. Croner's Waste Management, Croner Publications Ltd. Croner House, London Road, Kingston-upon-Thames, Surrey, KT2 6SR.

55. Removal and Disposal of Sources (brochure) - Safeguard International Ltd, Culham, Abingdon, Oxfordshire OX14 3EB.

56. Croner Waste Management Magazine, Issue 4, Croner Publications, Winter 1997.

57. Environmental Protection Act 1990: Part II, Special Waste Regulations 1996, Joint Circular from the Department of the Environment, Welsh Office, Scottish Office Agriculture Environment and Fisheries Department, 13th June 1996, Circular 6/96, Department of the Environment, WO21/96 Welsh Office, SOAEFD 13/96 Scottish Office and Fisheries Office Agriculture Environment and Fisheries Department, HMSO.

58. IAEA Safety Standards, Safety Series No. 6 Regulations for the Safe Transport of Radioactive Materials. 1996 Revision.

59. IAEA Safety Series 7 - Explanatory Material for the IAEA Regulations for the Safe Transport of radioactive Material - 1985 Edition (as amended 1990).

60. IAEA Safety Series 37 - Advisory Material for the IAEA Regulations for the Safe Transport of Radioactive Material - 1985 Edition (as amended 1990).

61. IAEA Safety Series 80 - Schedules of Requirements for the Transport of Specified Types of Radioactive Materials Consignments (as amended 1990).

62. IAEA Safety Series 113 - Quality Assurance for the Safe Transport of Radioactive Material (1994), ISBN 920-103-6949.

63. Hypertrans - The Stationery Office, a hypertext software guide to IAEA Safety Series Nos 6, 7, 37 and 80.

64. Richard R Rawl (Head, Transport Safety Unit) IAEA, International Regulations Governing the Safe Transport of Radioactive Material, 1996.

65. UN Recommendations on the Transport of Dangerous Goods (the Orange Book) ninth edition. 1995, ISBN 92 113 9048 6.

66. Council Regulation (Euratom) No. 1493/93, 8 June 1993, Shipments of Radioactive Substances between Member States.

67. ADR Agreement: European Agreement concerning the International Carriage of Dangerous Goods by Road, Volumes I and II, 1997.

68. Atomic Energy and Radioactive Substances. SI 1996 No. 1350. The Radioactive Material(Road Transport) (GB) Regulations 1996. ISBN 011 0547 42 X.

69. The Carriage of Dangerous Goods by Road (Driver Training) Regulations 1996 SI No. 2094.

70. International Maritime Dangerous Goods (IMDG) Code. International Maritime Organisation, 1994, ISBN 92 801 1314 3.

71. Merchant Shipping (Dangerous Goods) Regulations 1981, SI 1747, ISBN 011 0 17 7479.

72. Merchant Shipping (Reporting Requirements) 1995, SI 1995, No. 2498, ISBN 011 053 4778.

73. Merchant Shipping (Dangerous or Noxious Liquid Substances in Bulk). Regulations 1996. SI 1996, No. 3010. ISBN 011-0633-512.

74. The Air Navigation (Dangerous Goods) Regulations 1985, SI 1994 No. 3187. ISBN 011-043-7330.

75. International Civil Aviation Organisation (ICAO) Technical Instructions for the Safe Transport of Dangerous Goods by Air, 1997-1998 Edition.

76. International Air Transport Association (IATA) Dangerous Goods Regulations, 1997.

77. The Packaging, Labelling and Carriage of Radioactive Materials by Rail Regulations 1996, SI No. 2090.

78. G. S. Saggu and I. H. Davies, Procedure for the Transport of Radiopharmaceuticals; South Glamorgan Health Authority Department of Medical Physics and Bioengineering.

79. Department of Transport (DOT) Guide No. 1 to SI 1996, No. 1350.

80. Transport, Movement and Packaging of Radioactive Materials, UKAEA Safety Instruction, Number 85.

81. NIREP: UK Nuclear Industry Road/Rail Emergency Response Plan, UKAEA Document.

82. SI 1986 No 61, The Radioactive Substances (Carriage by Road) (Amendment) Regulations (Northern Ireland), 1986.

83. SI 1983 No. 344, Radioactive Substances (Carriage by Road) Regulations (Northern Ireland).

84. SI 1986 No. 61, Radioactive Substances (Carriage by Road) (Amendment) Regulations (Northern Ireland).

85. SI 1992 No. 234, The Radioactive Material (Road Transport) (Northern Ireland) Order.

86. SI 1992 No. 262, Road Traffic (Training of Drivers of Vehicles Carrying Dangerous Goods)Regulations (Northern Ireland).

87. SI 1993 No. 240, Road Traffic (Training of Drivers of Vehicles Carrying Dangerous Goods) (Amendment) Regulations (Northern Ireland).

88. The Transfrontier Shipment of Radioactive Waste Regulations 1993, SI No. 3031.

89. The International Atomic Energy Agency Code of Practice on the International Transboundary Movement of Radioactive Waste.

90. Security Export Control, Sept 1991, DTI Publication 843/10K/9/91.

91. Customs and Excise, The Export of Goods (Control) Order 1994, SI 1994, No. 1191.

92. Customs and Excise, The Dual Use and Related Goods (Export Control) Regulations 1995, SI 1995, No. 271.

93. T. J. Moseley , Transport of Radioactive Materials by Road, AURPO (Association of University Radiation Protection Officers), Guidance Note No. 6.

94. Hazardous Cargo Bulletin 'Packaging Guide', available from IRR Media.

95. Hughes and Shaw, Accidents and Incidents involving the Transport of Radioactive Materials in the UK from 1958 - 1994, and their Radiological Consequences, NRPB - R282, 1996.

96. Commission Regulation (Euratom) No. 3227/76 of 19 October 1976 concerning the Application of the Provisions on Euratom Safeguards. Published in the official journal of the European Communities Legislation, Vol. 19, No. L363, 31 December 1976.

97 S. Tromans and J. Fitzgerald, The Law of Nuclear Installations and Radioactive Substances, 1st Edition, Sweet and Maxwell, London, 1997.

98. Accounting for Radioactive Material including Nuclear Material and Matter on and Consigned from UKAEA Sites, UKAEA Corporate Safety Instruction, Number 82.

CHAPTER 8
NUCLEAR DATA TABLE

ALAN L. NICHOLS AND EMMA HUNT

8.1 FOREWORD

Nuclear data files have been assembled over many years for direct application in the nuclear power industry, fuel reprocessing, and waste management. These data libraries are updated over regular (and not so regular) time intervals either by international consensus [1-3], or through more localised efforts that are sometimes based on specific industrial needs [4-6]. Comprehensive decay-data and neutron cross-section files are accessible through various communication networks to provide the user with recommended values from international libraries (such as JEF-2.2 (OECD-Nuclear Energy Agency) and US ENDF/B-VI).

A number of groups around the world are actively engaged in the evaluation and compilation of a wide range of nuclear data. A major objective of the data table presented here is to provide the reader with the most reliable nuclear decay data at the time of publication of this Manual (1998). The complexity of the detailed spectral data within the cross-section data files precludes their consideration in such a relatively modest exercise, which is also limited to the prominent decay parameters of the most commonly encountered radionuclides. Nevertheless, a useful dataset has been assembled to cover those nuclides considered as important in the main text.

The following data sources have been used in the compilation:

ENSDF [1,2]
JEF-2.2 [3]
UK Heavy Element and Actinide Decay Data Files [4]
UK Activation-Product Decay Data Files, UKPADD [5,6]
IAEA-TECDOC-619 [7]
NPL Report (RSA(EXT)53) [8]
UK Department of Environment Report, DOE/HMIP/CPR2/41/1/219 [9]

These libraries were chosen as principal data sources because of the well-defined evaluation procedures adopted to derive their recommended decay data. A significant proportion of the radionuclide decay data to be found in the table originates from the UKPADD and UKHEDD files and the NPL report; furthermore, many of these data have subsequently been adopted by the OECD-NEA Data Bank in formulating JEF-2.2. Overall, the dataset represents a consistent library of decay data that can be judged as 'up to date' in 1998.

A large proportion of the recommended half-lives, branching fractions, energies and emission probabilities are derived from a well-defined evaluation procedure [7,10]. The recommended value consists of the weighted average of the published values in which the weights are taken to be the inverse of the squares of the overall uncertainties. A set of data is considered self-consistent if the reduced Chi-squared value is approximately 1.0. When the data in a set are inconsistent, and there are three or more such values, the method of limitation of the relative weight is recommended [11]. The sum of the individual weights is computed; if any one weight contributes over 50% of the total, the corresponding uncertainty is increased so that the contribution to the value of the sum of the weights is less than 50%. The weighted average is then recalculated and adopted if the reduced Chi-squared value for this average is less than 2. If the reduced Chi-squared value is greater than 2, the weighted or unweighted mean is chosen according to whether or not the 1 sigma uncertainty on each mean value includes the other term.

It should be noted that any compilation of nuclear data will become outdated in a fairly short time as our knowledge of various data parameters improve and re-evaluations are made. It is anticipated that the nuclear data table in this manual will be updated on an approximate 5-yearly cycle.

8.2 EXPLANATORY NOTES FOR THE NUCLEAR DATA TABLE

Nuclide

There are many different ways of organising recommended lists of radionuclidic decay data; it was decided to arrange them in alphabetical order by chemical symbol, and by increasing mass number for the same radioelement. Since the table will be referred to by persons from a wide range of disciplines, this arrangement was considered to be suitable for the rapid location of the radionuclide of interest.

When a short-lived daughter grows-in to a longer-lived parent (for example, Ag-109m and Cd-109), a cross-reference is made to the daughter at the parent entry, and to the parent at the daughter entry. The gamma-ray energies are assigned to the appropriate parent or daughter nuclide; thus, readers are advised of in-growing gamma rays in such parent-daughter relationships.

Photon energies are normally defined to the nearest 0.1 to 0.01 keV, although there are some exceptions (for example, energy standards such as Au-198, Ta-182 and Ir-192). Beta-particle transition energies, in particular, are often not known with a high degree of confidence because of significant uncertainties in the total decay energy (Q-value). Alpha-particle energies are mainly based on a recent compilation [12].

Obviously only a small fraction of the approximately 2500 radionuclides (including metastable states) could be incorporated into this type of modest compilation. The selection criteria consisted of an additive process: an initial listing was based on the contents of Chapters 1 to 7 of the manual, supplemented by important nuclides found in key references (see end of each chapter) and by suggestions made by reviewers. A number of primordial nuclides were also included. In a few cases, some additional work was required to improve specific aspects of the nuclear data listed (see final column entitled 'Comments'). A total of 290 radionuclides appear in the table.

Half-life

All half-life values have been converted to days, where necessary, using the definition of a Tropical year (1 Tropical (civil) year = 365.2422 days). Other common units for the half-life have also been included, that is s = seconds, m = minutes, h = hours, y = years.

Exponential notation has been adopted for each unit when the value is ≥1000 or ≤ 0.001, for example,

> 7.952E+03d means 7952 days,
> 2.569E-05y means 0.00002569 years.

Uncertainties in half-life values are presented in the format 1234(x) where x is the uncertainty in the last figure or figures (limited to two figures of uncertainty), for example,

> 6.13(1)h means 6.13 ± 0.01 hours,
> 0.07613(29)d means 0.07613 ± 0.00029 days.

Combining the exponential notation with the uncertainties gives, for example,

> (5.730(40))E+03y means 5730 ± 40 years,
> (6.438(35))E-03d means 0.006438 ± 0.000035 days.

The provision of half-life data follows consultation of the report by Woods and Munster for calibrant radionuclides [10].

Decay modes

Decay modes are represented as follows:

α Alpha decay
β^- Negatron decay
β^+ Positron decay
EC   Electron capture
IT   Isomeric transition
SF   Spontaneous fission
$\beta^- n$ Beta-particle/delayed neutron

Descriptions of these decay processes are given in Chapter 1 of this manual.

The branching fractions (or ratios) of decays are given where more than one decay type occurs, for example,

> EC 0.913
> IT 0.087

means that 91.3% of the decay from the radionuclide occurs by the electron capture process, while 8.7% occurs by isomeric transition decay i.e. by gamma-ray transition(s).

Decay energies and emission probabilities

The particle energies for α and β decay and photon energies for γ decay are given in kiloelectron volts (keV).

β_{max} Energy represents the maximum beta-particle energy for a beta-particle transition.

All emission probabilities for the various forms of decay are expressed as absolute probabilities of the specific emission per decay i.e. as fractional decay.

For radionuclides containing numerous emissions (whether they be α, β or γ), only the most intense transitions are included. Ten transitions have normally been selected under such circumstances. However, as a consequence of some poorly defined uncertainties and very low emission probabilities, this number may have been reduced in some instances, or increased due to the least intense energies being identical or very similar in magnitude.

In some circumstances, data have not been included in the table because of their poor quality and/or ill-defined uncertainties (for example, Eu-157, Ho-166 and Ra-228). There are also some instances in which the uncertainty in an emission probability is extremely large (for example, 0.035 ± 0.035), and these transitions were not included in the listing.

Emissions that are judged to be 'doublets' are denoted by [D] after the emission energy (for example, transitions in Th-229 and Pa-234 decay).

Reference should be made to the 'Comments' column where additional information may be given (for example, for Pa-234 the beta-particle energy at 1175.2 keV is stated to be an unresolved doublet).

When x-ray emissions are listed, they are denoted by [X] after the emission energy (these specific radionuclides are Ca-41, Cd-109, Fe-55, La-137, Mn-53, Ni-59 and Np-235). These data are not strictly the individual x-ray emissions, but rather the recommended values for the main shell groupings for that radionuclide. The average uncertainties in the x-ray emission probabilities are estimated to be between 5 and 10%.

Positron annihilation radiation (511 keV gamma-ray emission) is denoted by [A] after the emission energy (for example, Bi-207).

Uncertainties in energies and emission probabilities

As described above, the convention for assigning uncertainty values to these parameters is defined in the following examples:

Am-243	α energy 5233.4(12) means 5233.4 ± 1.2 keV
	emission probability 0.106(11) means 0.106 ± 0.011

Ba-140	β_{max} energy 454(10) means 454 ± 10 keV
	emission probability 0.2469(22) means 0.2469 ± 0.0022

Br-82	γ energy 776.517(3) means 776.517 ± 0.003 keV
	emission probability 0.835(15) means 0.835 ± 0.015

8.3 DATA PREFERENCES

The primary data sources were UKHEDD-2.2 [4], UKPADD [5,6], JEF-2.2 [3], NPL [8] and ENSDF [1,2]. Various data preferences were adopted on the basis of data quality and known consistencies in the data files, as specified below:

Emphasis was placed on the ENSDF data for La-138 and Hf-180m [2].

ENSDF data were adopted for the uncertainty of the gamma-ray emission probability for Re-186 and for the beta-particle and gamma-ray emission probabilities of Rh-106 [2].

Uncertainties in the beta-decay data for Ba-146 were taken from ENSDF [2].

Uncertainties in the data of I-130m, Xe-135m, Pr-142 and Tm-171 were adopted from ENSDF [2].

Uncertainties in the gamma-ray data were taken from the NPL report for Br-82, I-124, W-187, Au-195 and Hg-197 [8].

UKPADD data were preferred for Rb-86 and I-132 [5,6].

Emphasis was placed on the DOE/HMIP/CPR2/41/1/219 data for Th-234 [9].

The uncertainty in the emission probability of the annihilation radiation was arbitrarily estimated to be 10%.

8.4   NUCLEAR DECAY CHAINS

The three natural series decay chains (Th-232, U-235 and U-238) and the 4n+1 decay chain are shown in Figures 1.9 and 1.10, and the relevant decay data are included throughout the nuclear data table.

8.5   ELECTRONIC SOURCES OF NUCLEAR DATA

There are several electronic nuclear databases or databanks accessible via the World Wide Web (WWW). Two of direct relevance to the present data compilation are the NEA Data Bank and the National Nuclear Data Cente (NNDC/Brookhaven, USA). At the time of writing, these databases can be accessed as follows:

(a) NNDC

Available databases include ENSDF (evaluated nuclear structure and decay data), atomic masses, NUDAT (nuclear data), CSISRS (experimental nuclear reaction data) and ENDF (evaluated nuclear data files). Links are provided to other sites including the NEA Data Bank (see below).

The NNDC web site is accessed via: http://www.nndc.bnl.gov

Click on the required database and follow appropriate instructions.

(b) NEA Data Bank

To access information on nuclear data via the World Wide Web:

Access the Web site: http://www.nea.fr

Click on the option 'Programmes'.
Click on the option 'The Data Bank'.
Click on the option 'Nuclear Data Services'.

To obtain access to the databases new users are required to register electronically under the option 'Registration', where a password will be provided. Approval to use the data from this source requires this form of registration within the UK. Access to information other than the databases is open to everyone without the need for a password.

ACKNOWLEDGEMENTS

The authors are grateful to Joe Toole, AEA Technology plc, for valuable discussions and to Simon Woods and Mike Woods, NPL, for their useful comments on the contents of the nuclear data table.

REFERENCES

1. M. R. Bhat, *Evaluated Nuclear Structure Data File (ENSDF)*, in Proc Nucl Data for Science and Technology, Editor: S. M. Qaim, pp817-821, Springer-Verlag, Berlin, 1997; also Nuclear Data Sheets, Academic Press Inc., New York.

2. National Nuclear Data Centre, *ENSDF: the Evaluated Nuclear Structure Data File*, Brookhaven National Laboratory Report BNL-NCS-51655, 1987.

3. C. Nordborg and M. Salvatores, *Status of the JEF Evaluated Data Library*, in Proc. Nucl. Data for Science and Technology, Editor, J. K. Dickens, pp680-684, Am. Nucl. Soc. Inc., La Grange Park, 1994.

4. A. L. Nichols, *Heavy Element and Actinide Decay Data: UKHEDD-2 Data Files*, AEA Technology Report AEA-RS-5219, 1991.

5. A. L. Nichols, *Evaluation of Activation Product Decay Data*, Nucl. Instrum. Meth. Phys. Res., **A369**, 516-522, 1996.

6. J. S. Backhouse and A. L. Nichols, *Assessment and Evaluation of Decay Data for Nuclear Reactor Applications*, Conference on Radionuclide Metrology and Its Applications (ICRM97), National Institute of Standards and Technology, Gaithersburg, Maryland, 19-23 May 1997; published in Appl. Radiat. Isot., **49**, 1393-1396, 1998.

7. X-ray and Gamma-ray Standards for Detector Calibration, IAEA-TECDOC-619, IAEA Vienna 1991.

8. D. Smith, and M. J. Woods, *Recommended Nuclear Decay Data*, NPL Report RSA(EXT)53, 1995.

9. I. Adsley, A. L. Nichols and J. Toole, *Decay of Th-234 and Daughter Pa-234m in Secular Equilibrium: Resolution of Observed Anomalies*, UK Department of the Environment Report DOE/HMIP/CPR2/41/1/219, 1996.

10. M. J. Woods and S. Munster, *Evaluation of Half-life Data*, NPL Report RS(EXT)95, 1988.

11. W. L. Zijp, *On the Statistical Evaluation of Inconsistent Measurement Results Illustrated on the Example of the Sr-90 Half-life*, Energieonderzoek Centrum Nederland Report ECN-179, Petten, The Netherlands, 1985.

12. A. Rytz, *Recommended Energy and Intensity Values of Alpha Particles from Radioactive Decay*, Atomic Data and Nuclear Data Tables, **47**, 205-239, 1991.

8.6 NUCLEAR DATA TABLE

Nuclide	Half-life	Decay Modes	α Energy (keV)	α Emission Probability	β$_{max}$ Energy (keV)	β$_{max}$ Emission Probability	γ Energy (keV)	γ Emission Probability	Data Reference	Comments
Ac-225	10.0(1)d	α	5581(3)	0.012(1)			62.9(1)	0.0055(5)	UKHEDD-2.2	
			5608(3)	0.011(1)			73.8(1)	0.0032(3)		
			5637(3)	0.045(3)			87.4(2)	0.0029(3)		
			5682(3)	0.014(2)			99.5(1)	0.0068(7)		
			5723(3)	0.029(5)			99.8(1)	0.017(2)		
			5731(3)	0.100(1)			111.5(5)	0.0032(3)		
			5791(2)	0.086(9)			150(1)	0.0071(8)		
			5793(2)	0.181(20)			157.3(2)	0.0031(3)		
			5804(2)	0.0030(3)			188.0(1)	0.0046(5)		
			5829(2)	0.507(15)			216(1)	0.006(2)		
Ac-227	21.773(3)y	β⁻ 0.9862(1)	4712(4)	0.000043(4)	20.5(22)	0.10(4)	15.2(3)	0.00011(6)	UKHEDD-2.2	
	(7.952(1))E+03d	α 0.0138(1)	4735(4)	0.000012(3)	35.7(21)	0.35(5)	24.5(2)	0.00015(6)		
			4766(3)	0.00023(3)	45(2)	0.54(5)	70(1)	0.00022(8)		
			4782(4)	0.000011(3)			84(1)	0.00022(6)		
			4793(4)	0.000112(12)			87(1)	0.00022(11)		
			4583(3)	0.00051(5)			100(1)	0.00036(6)		
			4870(2)	0.00084(9)			160(1)	0.00019(3)		
			4897(3)	0.000018(4)						
			4938(2)	0.0055(3)						
			4951(2)	0.0065(3)						
Ac-228	6.13(1)h	β⁻			413(8)	0.016(1)	209.264(5)	0.046(20)	UKHEDD-2.2	
	0.2554(4)d				449(7)	0.025(1)	270.272(12)	0.038(13)		
					454(8)	0.016(1)	328.050(9)	0.034(11)		
					491(8)	0.050(1)	338.370(9)	0.12(4)		
					606(8)	0.086(8)	463.073(11)	0.046(11)		
					969(7)	0.034(1)	795.069(135)	0.048(11)		
					1014(7)	0.067(5)	911.316(35)	0.290(4)		
					1115(7)	0.037(6)	964.843(90)	0.055(13)		
					1168(7)	0.40(6)	969.161(34)	0.17(4)		
					1741(7)	0.065(65)	1587.9(4)	0.037(11)		
					2079(7)	0.093(2)				
Ag-108m	418(15)y	EC 0.913(6)					79.14(1)	0.066(5)	UKPADD	
	(1.527(55))E+05d	IT 0.087(6)					433.937(9)	0.905(6)		
							614.28(2)	0.910(6)		
							722.94(2)	0.911(6)		

Nuclide	Half-life	Decay Modes	α Energy (keV)	α Emission Probability	β_{max} Energy (keV)	β_{max} Emission Probability	γ Energy (keV)	γ Emission Probability	Data Reference	Comments
Ag-109m (see also Cd-109 parent)	39.8(2)s (4.606(23))E-04d	IT					88.0341(11)	0.0364(3)	UKPADD	
Ag-110m	249.79(18)d	β⁻ 0.9873(20) IT 0.0127(20)			84(2) 134(2) 168(2) 351(2) 471(2) 530(2) 654(2) 723(2) 932(2)	0.677(9) 0.0041(4) 0.0003(1) 0.0003(1) 0.0006(4) 0.304(3) 0.000018(2) 0.00006(1) 0.0005(1)	657.764(3) 677.618(5) 687.008(9) 706.682(6) 763.941(6) 818.033(12) 884.685(3) 937.496(6) 1384.297(5) 1505.042(6)	0.945(2) 0.105(1) 0.067(3) 0.164(2) 0.227(3) 0.0733(4) 0.747(19) 0.3431(13) 0.2425(9) 0.1302(5)	UKPADD;NPL	
Al-26	(7.2(3))E+05y (2.63(11))E+08d	EC/β⁺					511[A] 1129.6(2) 1808.6(1) 2938(1)	1.64(16) 0.024(2) 0.997(52) 0.027(2)	UKPADD	
Al-28	2.241(3)m (1.556(2))E-03d	β⁻			2864.3(7)	1.00(1)	1778.7(1)	1.00(1)	UKPADD	
Am-241	432.7(5)y (1.5804(18))E+05d	α SF (3.77(8))E-12	5244(2) 5267(3) 5322(1) 5388(1) 5442.90(13) 5470(3) 5485.60(12) 5512(2) 5544.3(3)	0.000017(1) 0.000026(1) 0.00015(5) 0.014(2) 0.128(2) 0.0004(2) 0.852(8) 0.0020(5) 0.0034(5)			26.34(2) 33.19(1) 43.43(3) 55.5(1) 59.536(3) 69.77(3) 98.951(5) 102.966(5) 125.292(10)	0.024(1) 0.0012(1) 0.00071(10) 0.00016(4) 0.359(4) 0.0064(6) 0.00020(1) 0.000196(10) 0.000041(1)	UKHEDD-2.2	
Am-243	(7.370(15))E+03y (2.6918(55))E+06d	α SF (3.7(9))E-11	5178.7(12) 5233.4(12) 5275.7(10) 5318.6(10) 5349.2(10)	0.011(1) 0.106(11) 0.88(8) 0.0012(1) 0.0016(2)			43.533(1) 74.664(1) 86.72(7) 117.72(2)	0.0594(11) 0.674(10) 0.00343(5) 0.0072(6)	UKHEDD-2.2	

Nuclide	Half-life	Decay Modes	α Energy (keV)	α Emission Probability	β_{max} Energy (keV)	β_{max} Emission Probability	γ Energy (keV)	γ Emission Probability	Data Reference	Comments
Ar-41	1.827(7)h 0.07613(29)d	β^-			815(1) 1198(1) 2492.0(8)	0.00052(5) 0.9917(6) 0.0083(6)	1293.7(1) 1677.2(1)	0.9916(6) 0.00052(5)	UKPADD;NPL	
As-76	1.097(3)d	β^-			299.0(18) 313.4(18) 539.9(18) 606.0(18) 1087.9(18) 1181.0(18) 1752.6(18) 1846.4(18) 2409.6(18) 2968.6(18)	0.0064(4) 0.0119(7) 0.0189(12) 0.00066(6) 0.00070(6) 0.0202(12) 0.076(5) 0.0078(6) 0.346(15) 0.51(2)	559.10(5) 563.23(8) 657.03(5) 665.31(7) 1212.72(18) 1216.02(7) 1228.52(8) 1787.67(8) 2096.33(14) 2110.79(15)	0.447(8) 0.0117(5) 0.061(3) 0.0039(3) 0.0163(12) 0.0384(25) 0.0139(7) 0.0033(2) 0.0066(5) 0.0039(3)	JEF 2.2; ENSDF	
At-217	0.0323(4)s (3.738(46))E-07d	α β^- 0.00012(4)	6482(5) 6608(7) 6811(5) 7067(5)	0.0003(1) 0.00005(3) 0.0006(2) 0.999(1)	733(11)	0.00012(4)	261(5) 335(5) 468(7) 596(5)	0.0004(2) 0.0001(1) 0.00005(3) 0.0002(1)	UKHEDD-2.2	
Au-195	186.09(2)d	EC					30.876(6) 98.88(2) 129.757(20) 199.46(4) 211.36(3)	0.0075(6) 0.109(9) 0.0082(5) 0.000086(8) 0.00011(1)	JEF-2.2;NPL	Uncertainties in gamma-ray data from NPL
Au-198	2.6943(8)d	β^-			284.8(6) 960.7(6) 1372.5(6)	0.00985(5) 0.9899(67) 0.00025(5)	411.8044(11) 675.887(2) 1087.691(3)	0.9557(47) 0.00804(7) 0.00159(3)	UKPADD	
Au-199	3.139(7)d	β^-			244.8(20) 294.6(20) 453.0(20)	0.189(6) 0.664(10) 0.147(5)	49.825(7) 158.380(7) 208.200(7)	0.0033(1) 0.369(7) 0.084(3)	JEF-2.2;NPL	

255

Nuclide	Half-life	Decay Modes	α Energy (keV)	α Emission Probability	β_{max} Energy (keV)	β_{max} Emission Probability	γ Energy (keV)	γ Emission Probability	Data Reference	Comments
Ba-133	10.57(4)y (3.861(15))E+03d	EC					53.1587(16)	0.0020(5)	UKPADD	
							79.6139(29)	0.0258(10)		
							80.9982(26)	0.341(8)		
							160.6120(39)	0.00641(11)		
							223.2494(32)	0.00453(8)		
							276.3990(27)	0.0717(10)		
							302.8541(12)	0.1834(27)		
							356.0127(11)	0.621(8)		
							383.8521(23)	0.0891(13)		
Ba-137m (see also Cs-137 parent)	2.553(1)m (1.7729(7))E-03d	IT					661.660(3)	0.901(2)	UKPADD	
Ba-139	1.384(5)h 0.05767(21)d	β^-			549(4)	0.000021(3)	165.864(6)	0.238(26)	JEF-2.2	
					627(4)	0.000026(3)	1090.8(2)	0.000081(8)		
					774(4)	0.000051(6)	1215.5(4)	0.000031(3)		
					834(4)	0.000175(20)	1219.1(4)	0.000039(5)		
					889(4)	0.00287(7)	1254.7(2)	0.00026(3)		
					929(4)	0.000032(5)	1256.7(10)	0.000027(3)		
					1053(4)	0.000108(14)	1310.6(2)	0.000159(15)		
					1091(4)	0.0000427(7)	1370.5(3)	0.000029(3)		
					2144(4)	0.297(4)	1420.5(2)	0.00261(3)		
					2310(4)	0.700(4)	1476.3(3)	0.0000159(3)		
Ba-140 (see also La-140 daughter)	12.74(5)d	β^-			454(10)	0.2469(22)	13.85(5)	0.0120(8)	JEF-2.2	
					567(10)	0.0986(8)	29.97(5)	0.137(4)		
					872(10)	0.0381(12)	118.82(10)	0.00052(6)		
					991(10)	0.39(4)	132.67(8)	0.0020(2)		
					1005(10)	0.23(4)	162.61(2)	0.0627(7)		
							304.85(1)	0.0430(5)		
							423.72(1)	0.0315(5)		
							437.57(2)	0.0193(5)		
							467.57(5)	0.0015(1)		
							537.27(2)	0.244(2)		

Nuclide	Half-life	Decay Modes	α Energy (keV)	α Emission Probability	β_{max} Energy (keV)	β_{max} Emission Probability	γ Energy (keV)	γ Emission Probability	Data Reference	Comments
Ba-146	2.22(7)s (2.569(81))E-05d	β⁻			2500(50) 2560(50) 2590(50) 2760(50) 2840(50) 2850(50) 2970(50) 3150(50) 3320(50) 3380(50) 3660(50)	0.043(4) 0.035(4) 0.033(3) 0.024(2) 0.032(3) 0.031(3) 0.063(6) 0.086(9) 0.092(9) 0.024(2) 0.28(3)	121.2(1) 140.7(1) 175.3(1) 197.0(1) 231.6(1) 251.2(1) 294.9(3) 392.5(1) 429.3(1)	0.142(3) 0.202(6) 0.0480(11) 0.126(4) 0.107(2) 0.196(6) 0.0545(18) 0.062(2) 0.061(2)	JEF-2.2;ENSDF	Uncertainties in beta-decay data from ENSDF
Be-7	53.24(4)d	EC					477.605(3)	0.103(2)	UKPADD;NPL	
Be-10	(1.6(2))E+06y (5.84(73))E+08d	β⁻			555.9(7)	1.00(1)			UKPADD	
Bi-207	31.8(19)y (1.161(69))E+04d	EC/β⁺					511[A] 569.703(2) 897.7(1) 1063.662(4) 1442.2(1) 1770.237(9) 897.7(1) 1063.662(4) 1442.2(1) 1770.237(9)	0.00028(3) 0.9774(4) 0.00128(6) 0.745(2) 0.00131(3) 0.0688(4) 0.00128(6) 0.745(2) 0.00131(3) 0.0688(4)	UKPADD	
Bi-210 (see also Pb-210 parent)	5.013(5)d	β⁻ α (1.3(1))E-06	4648(2) 4686(2)	0.0000080(5) 0.0000050(5)	1161.5(15)	1.00(1)	265.7(2) 304.9(3)	0.0000004(1) 0.0000006(1)	UKHEDD2.2	
Bi-211 (see also Pb-211 parent and Po-211 and Tl-207 daughters)	2.17(4)m (1.507(28))E-03d	α β⁻ 0.00273(4)	6278.8(7) 6623.1(6)	0.164(4) 0.836(4)	584(4)	0.00273(4)	351.0(1)	0.130(4)	UKHEDD-2.2	

257

Nuclide	Half-life	Decay Modes	α Energy (keV)	α Emission Probability	βmax Energy (keV)	βmax Emission Probability	γ Energy (keV)	γ Emission Probability	Data Reference	Comments
Bi-212 (see also Pb-212 parent and Po-212 and Tl-208 daughters)	1.010(1)h 0.042083(42)d	α 0.3594(5) β⁻ 0.6406(5)	5346(2) 5482(1) 5606.8(2) 5625.6(3) 5768.5(2) 6051.13(3) 6090.24(4) 9498.1(2) 10432.2(3) 10551.7(6)	0.000004(2) 0.000054(4) 0.0039(2) 0.000597(7) 0.0062(3) 0.252(1) 0.0967(5) 0.0000024(4) 0.000010(3) 0.000106(3)	440(4) 445(5) 567(4) 625(4) 733(4) 1519(4) 2246(4)	0.0072(6) 0.0013(3) 0.0020(5) 0.0188(5) 0.0142(5) 0.0454(24) 0.5517(22)	39.858(4) 288.08(7) 452.8(1) 727.20(5) 785.378(8) 893.43(9) 952.1(2) 1078.6(6) 1512.66(7) 1620.58(6)	0.0102(5) 0.00314(11) 0.00333(18) 0.0675(11) 0.01094(24) 0.00381(12) 0.0014(1) 0.0063(4) 0.00278(15) 0.0149(4)	UKHEDD-2.2	
Bi-213 (see also Po-213 daughter)	45.59(6)m 0.031660(42)d	β⁻ 0.9784(13) α 0.0216(13)	5549(10) 5870(6)	0.0016(3) 0.020(1)	331(6) 993(6) 1432(5)	0.010(3) 0.308(8) 0.66(4)	292.8(10) 324.0(10) 440.46(50) 808.9(10) 1101.0(10)	0.00429(7) 0.00122(2) 0.261(3) 0.00292(12) 0.005(1)	UKHEDD-2.2	
Bi-214 (see also Pb-214 parent and Po-214 daughter)	19.9(4)m 0.01382(28)d	β⁻ 0.99979(1) α 0.00021(1)	4941(3) 5023(3) 5184(3) 5268(3) 5448(3) 5512(3)	0.00000053(13) 0.00000044(11) 0.0000013(2) 0.0000122(8) 0.000113(6) 0.000082(5)	822(12) 1066(12) 1151(12) 1253(12) 1423(12) 1505(12) 1540(12) 1727(12) 1892(12) 3270(12)	0.029(4) 0.059(3) 0.043(5) 0.027(3) 0.085(9) 0.180(6) 0.182(7) 0.032(5) 0.076(10) 0.161(9)	609.318(20) 768.36(2) 934.05(2) 1120.28(2) 1238.1(1) 1377.65(3) 1407.98(4) 1509.2(1) 1729.60(5) 1764.5(1) 1847.4(1) 2204.1(1)	0.469(40) 0.0497(50) 0.0319(32) 0.155(3) 0.061(6) 0.041(2) 0.0250(30) 0.0220(20) 0.030(3) 0.1625(5) 0.0216(22) 0.0525(25)	UKHEDD-2.2	
Br-77	2.3765(2)d	EC/β⁺					238.98(7) 249.77(7) 281.65(7) 297.23(8) 439.47(6) 511[A] 520.69(6) 578.91(7) 585.48(7) 755.35(7) 817.79(6)	0.231(5) 0.0298(7) 0.0229(5) 0.0416(18) 0.0156(3) 0.0147(18) 0.224(3) 0.0296(7) 0.0157(3) 0.0167(3) 0.0208(5)	JEF-2.2	

Nuclide	Half-life	Decay Modes	α Energy (keV)	α Emission Probability	β_{max} Energy (keV)	β_{max} Emission Probability	γ Energy (keV)	γ Emission Probability	Data Reference	Comments
Br-82	1.472(1)d	β^-			172.8(16)	0.00006(3)	221.480(2)	0.0226(8)	UKPADD;NPL	Uncertainties in gamma-ray data from NPL
					264.4(15)	0.0138(3)	554.348(3)	0.707(14)		
					444.1(15)	0.980(11)	619.107(4)	0.434(9)		
							698.374(4)	0.285(6)		
							776.517(3)	0.835(15)		
							827.827(5)	0.240(5)		
							1007.6(1)	0.0127(3)		
							1044.002(5)	0.272(6)		
							1317.476(6)	0.265(5)		
							1474.884(6)	0.163(3)		
Br-87	55.69(13)s	β^- 0.9748(70)			1870(120)	0.0314(13)	421.74(10)	0.032(3)	JEF-2.2	
	(6.45(2))E-04d	β^-,n 0.0252(70)			2120(120)	0.0321(14)	532.03(7)	0.054(4)		
					2230(120)	0.0232(12)	1360.59(20)	0.034(2)		
					2410(120)	0.0338(22)	1419.717(7)	0.220(15)		
					2650(120)	0.046(3)	1476.06(7)	0.079(6)		
					3570(120)	0.0369(23)	2005.52(7)	0.053(4)		
					3800(120)	0.0524(19)	2071.66(7)	0.023(2)		
					3990(120)	0.056(3)	2997.21(7)	0.023(2)		
					5410(120)	0.059(16)	3917.06(10)	0.020(1)		
					6830(120)	0.182(19)	4180.54(10)	0.040(3)		
							4961.54(15)	0.020(1)		
C-11	20.385(20)m	β^+					511[A]	1.9952(3)	JEF-2.2	
	0.014156(14)d									
C-14	(5.730(40))E+03y	β^-			156.5(1)	1.00(1)			UKPADD;NPL	
	(2.093(15))E+06d									
Ca-41	1.03(4)E+05y	EC					3.3111[X]	0.037(2)	UKPADD	
	(3.76(15))E+07d						3.3138[X]	0.073(4)		
							3.59[X]	0.0131(7)		
Ca-45	162.7(4)d	β^-			244.5(10)	0.000017(5)	12.396(20)	0.00000043(16)	UKPADD	
					256.9(10)	0.999983(5)				

259

Nuclide	Half-life	Decay Modes	α Energy (keV)	α Emission Probability	β_{max} Energy (keV)	β_{max} Emission Probability	γ Energy (keV)	γ Emission Probability	Data Reference	Comments
Ca-47 (see also Sc-47 daughter)	4.538(2)d	β⁻			691(4) 1988(4)	0.82(2) 0.18(2)	41.06(5) 489.2(2) 530.3(2) 766.83(9) 807.9(1) 1297.12(8) 1878.2(7)	0.00064(7) 0.065(4) 0.00095(10) 0.00193(14) 0.065(4) 0.75(2) 0.00029(3)	UKPADD;NPL	
Ca-49	8.72(2)m (6.056(14))E-03d	β⁻			530(4) 775(4) 1196(4) 1751(5) 2184(4) 2896(4)	0.0021(6) 0.0063(6) 0.071(7) 0.0018(6) 0.915(10) 0.0042(13)	855.9(5) 987.6(5) 1144.8(5) 1288.1(5) 1408.9(3) 2228.6(3) 2371.9(4) 3084.4(1) 4071.9(1) 4738.2(2)	0.0013(3) 0.0008(3) 0.0011(3) 0.0007(3) 0.0063(6) 0.0019(5) 0.0049(9) 0.921(9) 0.070(7) 0.0021(6)	UKPADD	
Cd-109 (see also Ag-109m)	1.267(2)y 462.76(73)d	EC					21.99[X] 22.16[X] 24.93[X] 25.46[X]	0.188(9) 0.355(18) 0.097(5) 0.0177(9)	UKPADD	
Cd-115 (see also In-115m daughter)	2.225(2)d	β⁻			158.3(41) 253.2(41) 404.2(42) 581.6(40) 617.1(41) 848.6(40) 1109.5(40)	0.000009(1) 0.00013(2) 0.0000008(3) 0.331(3) 0.033(4) 0.0118(5) 0.624(8)	35.5(1) 231.4(1) 260.9(1) 267.0(1) 328.4(2) 363.9(2) 492.3(1) 527.9(1) 595.4(1) 856.3(1)	0.00421(6) 0.0074(3) 0.0194(3) 0.000094(3) 0.000033(6) 0.000061(6) 0.081(1) 0.275(2) 0.000017(3) 0.000022(1)	UKPADD	

Nuclide	Half-life	Decay Modes	α Energy (keV)	α Emission Probability	β_{max} Energy (keV)	β_{max} Emission Probability	γ Energy (keV)	γ Emission Probability	Data Reference	Comments
Cd-115m	44.6(3)d	β⁻			140.6(46)	0.000007(1)	105.2(1)	0.000044(3)	UKPADD	
					148.2(48)	0.0000007(3)	158.02(6)	0.00019(2)		
					177.9(48)	0.00020(1)	316.2(1)	0.00025(2)		
					208.5(45)	0.0027(1)	484.5(1)	0.0265(29)		
					336.1(45)	0.0092(4)	492.3(1)	0.00090(8)		
					494.1(45)	0.00061(3)	933.78(4)	0.0199(5)		
					692.9(45)	0.0174(2)	1132.57(3)	0.00085(4)		
					1626.7(45)	0.97(2)	1290.59(3)	0.0090(6)		
							1418.25(3)	0.000019(2)		
							1448.78(3)	0.000167(12)		
Ce-139	137.640(23)d	EC					165.857(6)	0.7991(8)	UKPADD	
Ce-141	32.50(1)d	β⁻			436(2)	0.705(7)	145.441(3)	0.484(4)	JEF-2.2	
					580.0(15)	0.295(7)				
Ce-143	1.375(8)d	β⁻			57.3(36)	0.0038(2)	57.365(1)	0.118(17)	JEF-2.2	
					73.0(36)	0.00030(2)	231.56(3)	0.020(3)		
					140.6(36)	0.00100(5)	293.262(21)	0.42(2)		
					294.6(36)	0.00500(25)	350.59(5)	0.034(5)		
					302.1(36)	0.00070(4)	490.36(7)	0.020(3)		
					517.2(36)	0.014(1)	664.55(10)	0.053(8)		
					564.4(36)	0.0040(2)	721.96(11)	0.051(7)		
					733.0(36)	0.120(6)	880.39(13)	0.0092(13)		
					1105.0(36)	0.475(24)	1102.98(18)	0.0037(6)		
					1398.0(36)	0.380(19)				
Ce-144 (see also Pr-144 daughter)	284.9(2)d	β⁻			184.7(20)	0.196(4)	33.568(10)	0.0020(2)	JEF-2.2;NPL	
					238.1(20)	0.039(2)	40.98(10)	0.0257(16)		
					318.2(20)	0.765(5)	53.395(5)	0.00100(8)		
							80.120(5)	0.0136(6)		
							99.961(15)	0.00040(5)		
							133.515(2)	0.1109(20)		
Cf-252	2.645(8)y 966.1(29)d	α SF 0.03092(8)	5616(2)	0.0000006(3)			43.399(25)	0.000150(6)	UKHEDD-2.2	
			5826.4(10)	0.00002(1)			100.2(4)	0.000129(2)		
			5976.7(10)	0.0023(4)			160(10)	0.000006(3)		
			6075.7(5)	0.152(3)						
			6118.3(5)	0.816(3)						

Nuclide	Half-life	Decay Modes	α Energy (keV)	α Emission Probability	β_{max} Energy (keV)	β_{max} Emission Probability	γ Energy (keV)	γ Emission Probability	Data Reference	Comments
Cl-36	(3.02(3))E+05y (1.103(11))E+08d	β⁻ 0.981(2) EC/β⁺ 0.019(2)			709.6(3)	0.981(2)			UKPADD	
Cl-38	37.2(1)m 0.02583(7)d	β⁻			1107(1) 2749(1) 4917(1)	0.325(19) 0.115(3) 0.560(16)	1642.4(2) 2167.5(1) 3809.7(2)	0.325(16) 0.440(16) 0.00025(2)	UKPADD	
Cm-242	162.94(5)d	α SF (6.33(13))E-08	5814(3) 5969(3) 6069.63(12) 6112.92(8)	0.000044(5) 0.00032(2) 0.259(5) 0.740(5)			44.08(3)	0.000325(12)	UKHEDD-2.2	
Cm-243	30(2)y (1.096(73))E+04d	α EC 0.0024(3)	5639(6) 5686(3) 5742.2(10) 5785.1(10) 5876(3) 5992.2(10) 6010(3) 6057(3) 6067(3)	0.0014(1) 0.016(1) 0.106(2) 0.735(10) 0.006(1) 0.065(2) 0.010(1) 0.047(5) 0.014(2)			209.753(2) 228.184(2) 254.41(8) 277.599(2) 285.460(2)	0.0329(10) 0.106(3) 0.0011(1) 0.140(4) 0.0073(2)	UKHEDD-2.2	
Cm-244	18.10(2)y (6.6109(73))E+03d	α SF (1.347(7))E-06	5665.7(2) 5762.84(3) 5804.96(5)	0.000163(7) 0.2300(5) 0.7698(5)			42.824(8)	0.000248(6)	UKHEDD-2.2	
Co-56	77.26(8)d	EC/β⁺					511[A] 846.75(1) 1037.86(2) 1238.29(3) 1360.23(2) 1771.39(2) 2015.22(2) 2034.81(2) 2598.53(2) 3202.06(2) 3253.52(2)	0.39(4) 0.99937(5) 0.1405(7) 0.666(4) 0.0427(1) 0.1553(6) 0.0304(2) 0.0779(4) 0.170(8) 0.0313(5) 0.076(1)	UKPADD	

Nuclide	Half-life	Decay Modes	α Energy (keV)	α Emission Probability	β_{max} Energy (keV)	β_{max} Emission Probability	γ Energy (keV)	γ Emission Probability	Data Reference	Comments
Co-57	271.79(9)d	EC					14.41300(15)	0.097(4)	UKPADD	
							122.062(1)	0.847(1)		
							136.474(1)	0.104(3)		
							339.67(2)	0.000030(7)		
							352.35(1)	0.000019(6)		
							366.76(1)	0.000006(2)		
							570.00(2)	0.000015(2)		
							692.02(2)	0.00158(4)		
							706.43(2)	0.000050(3)		
Co-58	70.86(7)d	EC/β⁺					511[A]	0.30(3)	UKPADD	
							810.775(9)	0.9945(1)		
							863.959(9)	0.0683(20)		
							1674.73(1)	0.00519(9)		
Co-60	5.2718(14)y (1.92548(51))E+03d	β⁻			317.88(12)	0.9989(2)	347.1(1)	0.0000742(44)	UKPADD	
					665.00(14)	0.00001(1)	826.12(1)	0.000076(8)		
					1491.12(12)	0.0011(3)	1173.238(4)	0.99857(22)		
							1332.501(5)	0.99983(6)		
							2158.64(3)	0.0000108(33)		
							2505.76(1)	0.0000000005(3)		
Cr-51	27.706(7)d	EC					320.0842(9)	0.0986(5)	UKPADD	
Cs-129	1.342(8)d	EC					39.578(2)	0.030(4)	UKPADD	
							93.32(1)	0.0067(9)		
							177.04(1)	0.0027(3)		
							266.82(1)	0.0028(3)		
							278.60(1)	0.0134(16)		
							318.18(1)	0.025(3)		
							371.92(1)	0.31(3)		
							411.50(1)	0.226(24)		
							548.96(1)	0.034(4)		
							588.53(1)	0.0060(8)		

Nuclide	Half-life	Decay Modes	α Energy (keV)	α Emission Probability	β_{max} Energy (keV)	β_{max} Emission Probability	γ Energy (keV)	γ Emission Probability	Data Reference	Comments
Cs-134	2.0652(6)y 754.30(22)d	β⁻ EC 0.000003(1)			88.5(4) 415.0(5) 657.8(4)	0.273(1) 0.0252(3) 0.701(3)	242.8(1) 475.45(6) 563.24(2) 569.26(7) 604.71(1) 795.91(4) 801.93(5) 1038.69(6) 1167.94(1) 1365.17(5)	0.00023(3) 0.0149(2) 0.0837(3) 0.1538(7) 0.9763(6) 0.853(8) 0.0871(3) 0.00992(5) 0.0179(9) 0.0303(2)	UKPADD	
Cs-135	(2.4(3))E+06y (8.8(11))E+08d	β⁻			205(5)	1.000			UKPADD	
Cs-136	13.03(7)d	β⁻			175(2) 192(2) 341(2) 408(2) 495(2) 682(2)	0.020(1) 0.0002(1) 0.73(3) 0.12(2) 0.040(15) 0.07(3)	66.9(1) 86.3(1) 153.3(1) 163.9(1) 176.6(1) 273.6(1) 340.5(1) 818.52(2) 1048.1(1) 1235.4(1)	0.048(2) 0.056(4) 0.058(2) 0.041(5) 0.100(4) 0.111(4) 0.46(2) 1.000(3) 0.80(2) 0.198(5)	UKPADD	
Cs-137 (see also Ba-137m daughter)	30.17(16)y (1.1019(58))E+04d	β⁻			511.5(9) 1173.2(9)	0.9460(14) 0.0540(14)			UKPADD	

264

Nuclide	Half-life	Decay Modes	α Energy (keV)	α Emission Probability	β$_{max}$ Energy (keV)	β$_{max}$ Emission Probability	γ Energy (keV)	γ Emission Probability	Data Reference	Comments
Cs-138	32.2(1)m 0.0222361(69)d	β⁻			2343.8(40) 2555.5(40) 2695.4(40) 2751.8(40) 2889.3(40) 2919.4(40) 3027.3(40) 3117.0(40) 3436.3(40) 3899.1(40)	0.0064(4) 0.0159(7) 0.0870(23) 0.0167(8) 0.430(7) 0.0063(4) 0.079(2) 0.130(3) 0.137(7) 0.046(18)	138.10(6) 227.76(6) 408.98(6) 462.800(5) 547.000(5) 871.80(8) 1009.80(8) 1435.90(9) 2218(1) 2639.60(13)	0.0149(8) 0.0151(4) 0.0466(9) 0.307(6) 0.108(2) 0.0511(13) 0.298(6) 0.763(15) 0.152(3) 0.0763(23)	JEF-2.2	
Cs-139	9.27(5)m (6.438(35))E-03d	β⁻			1607(5) 1681(5) 1863(5) 2102(5) 2532(5) 2592(5) 2792(5) 2905(5) 2930(5) 4213(5)	0.0055(23) 0.006(3) 0.014(6) 0.009(4) 0.0044(18) 0.0047(19) 0.0043(18) 0.0026(11) 0.07(3) 0.82(7)	627.24(3) 1283.23(5) 1308.13(6) 1420.66(6) 1620.74(6) 1680.72(6) 1877.45(7) 2110.91(9) 2349.92(6) 2531.84(7)	0.0178(9) 0.083(5) 0.0043(2) 0.0091(5) 0.0048(2) 0.0070(3) 0.0039(2) 0.0076(4) 0.0064(3) 0.0048(3)	JEF-2.2	
Cu-62	9.75(1)m (6.7708(69))E-03d	EC/β⁺					511[A] 875.7(2) 1128.9(2) 1172.9(1) 1718.3(4) 1985.1(4) 2084.8(3) 2097.0(3) 2301.8(1) 3370.3(2)	1.96(20) 0.00154(25) 0.00033(6) 0.0035(4) 0.000027(7) 0.000011(5) 0.000053(17) 0.00030(7) 0.00042(7) 0.000081(4)	UKPADD	
Cu-64	12.702(2)h 0.52925(8)d	EC/β⁺ 0.6114(31) β⁻ 0.3886(31)			578(1)	0.3886(31)	511[A] 1345.79(2)	0.3576(23) 0.00479(14)	UKPADD;NPL	

Nuclide	Half-life	Decay Modes	α Energy (keV)	α Emission Probability	β$_{max}$ Energy (keV)	β$_{max}$ Emission Probability	γ Energy (keV)	γ Emission Probability	Data Reference	Comments
Cu-67	2.578(4)d	β⁻			182(8)	0.011(1)	91.266(5)	0.070(1)	UKPADD;NPL	
					391(8)	0.571(2)	93.311(5)	0.161(2)		
					483(8)	0.218(9)	184.577(10)	0.487(4)		
					576(8)	0.20(2)	208.95(1)	0.00115(5)		
							300.22(1)	0.0080(1)		
							393.53(1)	0.0022(1)		
Dy-165	2.334(6)h	β⁻			205.5(30)	0.00160(16)	94.700(3)	0.0358(25)	JEF-2.2	
	0.09725(25)d				229.3(30)	0.000430(43)	279.763(12)	0.00498(25)		
					289.1(30)	0.0170(17)	361.68(2)	0.0084(4)		
					569.8(30)	0.00058(6)	545.83(2)	0.00162(5)		
					718.3(30)	0.0039(4)	565.72(2)	0.0013(4)		
					794.1(30)	0.00140(14)	575.56(2)	0.00079(2)		
					864.1(30)	0.00050(5)	620.64(2)	0.00097(4)		
					1075.3(30)	0.000160(16)	633.42(2)	0.00568(8)		
					1189.1(30)	0.150(15)	715.33(2)	0.00534(8)		
					1284.1(30)	0.830(83)	1079.63(3)	0.00092(3)		
Er-169	9.3(2)d	β⁻			233(8)	0.00005(1)	8.401(8)	0.00158(18)	JEF-2.2;ENSDF	
					343(8)	0.42(3)	109.77(6)	0.000013(3)		
					352.2(15)	0.58(3)				
Eu-152	13.51(3)y	EC/β⁺ 0.720(2)			179(2)	0.0189(3)	121.7824(4)	0.2837(13)	UKPADD	
	(4.934(11))E+03d	β⁻ 0.280(2)			216(2)	0.0011(1)	244.699(1)	0.0753(4)		
					272(2)	0.00044(6)	344.281(2)	0.2657(11)		
					388(2)	0.0238(3)	443.965(4)	0.0281(5)		
					540(2)	0.00032(6)	778.903(6)	0.1297(6)		
					699(2)	0.1380(3)	867.390(6)	0.4214(25)		
					713(2)	0.0027(2)	964.055(4)	0.1463(6)		
					892(2)	0.0029(2)	1085.842(4)	0.1013(5)		
					1067(2)	0.0090(2)	1112.087(6)	0.1354(6)		
					1478(2)	0.082(2)	1408.022(4)	0.2085(9)		

Nuclide	Half-life	Decay Modes	α Energy (keV)	α Emission Probability	β_{max} Energy (keV)	β_{max} Emission Probability	γ Energy (keV)	γ Emission Probability	Data Reference	Comments
Eu-152m	9.275(9)h 0.38646(38)d	β⁻ 0.72(4) EC/β⁺ 0.28(4)			112(2) 407(2) 553(2) 820(2) 1252(2) 1523(2) 1867.7(18)	0.00080(5) 0.00012(3) 0.016(1) 0.0012(1) 0.00002(1) 0.018(1) 0.68(4)	121.7824(4) 344.2811(19) 562.922(2) 841.582(8) 961.08(5) 963.38(1) 970.39(1) 1314.67(1) 1389.01(1)	0.076(6) 0.0250(13) 0.00226(12) 0.147(4) 0.0022(1) 0.122(5) 0.00595(5) 0.0097(6) 0.0084(4)	UKPADD	
Eu-154	8.593(4)y (3.1385(15))E+03d	β⁻ 0.9998(1) EC 0.0002(1)			249(2) 308(2) 352(2) 571(2) 705(2) 841(2) 973(2) 1153(2) 1598(2) 1846(2)	0.285(2) 0.0084(2) 0.0161(2) 0.361(3) 0.0070(2) 0.174(2) 0.024(3) 0.0031(9) 0.0038(17) 0.105(2)	123.070(4) 247.939(8) 591.81(4) 723.43(8) 756.92(6) 873.24(8) 996.0(2) 1004.57(18) 1274.69(6) 1596.5(1)	0.404(3) 0.0693(6) 0.0497(4) 0.201(2) 0.0452(4) 0.121(1) 0.104(1) 0.179(2) 0.350(1) 0.0179(2)	UKPADD	
Eu-155	4.84(12)y (1.768(44))E+03d	β⁻			106.6(17) 134.7(17) 147.4(17) 166.2(17) 192.7(17) 252.7(17)	0.008(1) 0.12(1) 0.48(3) 0.16(1) 0.10(1) 0.13(1)	26.54(1) 45.2972(13) 60.0100(18) 86.0621(51) 86.5452(33) 105.308(3)	0.0033(2) 0.0135(10) 0.0132(11) 0.0016(2) 0.322(10) 0.214(10)	UKPADD	
Eu-157	15.18(3)h 0.6325(13)d	β⁻			888(6) 929(6) 1299(6)	0.22(1) 0.15(1) 0.48(9)	9.365(12) 54.548(14) 63.929(8) 318.710(8) 370.509(8) 409.135(10) 410.723(9) 474.625(11) 570.937(13) 619.303(12)	0.0164(24) 0.037(3) 0.230(23) 0.0289(14) 0.110(6) 0.0267(13) 0.175(9) 0.0252(12) 0.0156(8) 0.0355(18)	JEF-2.2	Some beta emissions not included due to poor data quality

Nuclide	Half-life	Decay Modes	α Energy (keV)	α Emission Probability	β_max Energy (keV)	β_max Emission Probability	γ Energy (keV)	γ Emission Probability	Data Reference	Comments
F-18	1.828(2)h 0.076167(83)d	EC/β⁺					511[A]	1.936(4)	UKPADD;NPL	
Fe-55	2.735(22)y 999(8)d	EC					5.8877[X] 5.8988[X] 6.49[X]	0.082(8) 0.163(16) 0.033(3)	UKPADD	
Fe-59	44.502(5)d	β⁻			83(2) 131(2) 273(2) 466(2) 1565(2)	0.0009(1) 0.0143(7) 0.452(12) 0.531(14) 0.0018(4)	142.652(2) 190.0(2) 192.349(2) 335.0(1) 382.3(2) 1099.251(4) 1291.596(7) 1481.6(2)	0.0102(4) 0.00013(2) 0.0310(9) 0.00027(1) 0.00018(3) 0.567(13) 0.431(10) 0.00056(4)	UKPADD;NPL	
Fr-221	4.9(2)m (3.40(14))E-03d	α	5776(3) 5783(4) 5926(3) 5939(2) 5966(3) 5980(2) 6076(2) 6127(2) 6243(2) 6341.1(15)	0.0006(1) 0.00005(2) 0.0003(1) 0.0017(3) 0.0008(1) 0.0049(3) 0.0015(3) 0.151(2) 0.013(1) 0.834(8)			99.5(2) 118.2(2) 150.0(2) 171.3(5) 218.1(2) 283(1) 324(1) 359(2) 382(1) 409(1)	0.0012(4) 0.0004(2) 0.0008(3) 0.0008(3) 0.111(4) 0.0001(1) 0.0002(1) 0.0004(2) 0.0004(2) 0.0015(4)	UKHEDD	
Ga-67	3.261(1)d	EC					91.266(5) 93.311(5) 184.577(10) 208.951(10) 300.219(10) 393.529(10) 494.169(15) 703.110(15) 794.386(15) 887.693(15)	0.0296(6) 0.370(7) 0.204(4) 0.0233(6) 0.166(3) 0.0464(1) 0.00068(2) 0.000108(8) 0.000509(15) 0.00144(2)	JEF-2.2;NPL	

Nuclide	Half-life	Decay Modes	α Energy (keV)	α Emission Probability	β_{max} Energy (keV)	β_{max} Emission Probability	γ Energy (keV)	γ Emission Probability	Data Reference	Comments
Ga-68	1.1271(4)h 0.046963(17)d	EC/β+					511[A] 578.4(3) 805.9(1) 1077.4(1) 1261.3(1) 1883.2(1) 2338.0(4)	1.78(2) 0.00030(5) 0.00089(10) 0.030(3) 0.00090(10) 0.00130(14) 0.0000150(24)	JEF-2.2;NPL	
Ga-70	21.14(3)m 0.014681(21)d	β⁻ 0.9959(5) EC 0.0041(5)			441(3) 617(3) 1656(3)	0.0032(1) 0.0036(2) 0.9891(9)	176.17(2) 1039.20(8)	0.0029(1) 0.0065(5)	JEF-2.2	
Gd-148	75(3)y 2.74(11))E+04d	α	3182.79(2)	1.000					JEF-2.2	
Gd-152	(1.08(8))E+14y (3.9(3))E+16d	α	2140(30)	1.000					JEF-2.2	
Gd-153	240.5(7)d	EC					14.063(1) 54.193(1) 68.255(1) 69.673(4) 75.422(1) 83.367(1) 89.485(1) 97.431(6) 103.180(7) 172.852(1)	0.00024(6) 0.00026(4) 0.00015(3) 0.0246(7) 0.00080(4) 0.00198(6) 0.00074(7) 0.295(5) 0.211(6) 0.00036(3)	UKPADD	
H-3	12.33(2)y (4.5034(73))E+03d	β⁻			18.571(6)	1.000			UKPADD	
Hf-174	(2.0(4))E+15y (7(1))E+17d	α	2446(6)	1.000					UKPADD	
Hf-180m	5.5(1)h 0.2292(42)d	IT 0.997(1) β⁻ 0.003(1)					57.547(6) 93.325(12) 215.426(8) 332.275(11) 443.163(15) 500.697(13)	0.480(14) 0.171(4) 0.813(14) 0.941(17) 0.819(17) 0.143(4)	JEF-2.2;ENSDF	Emphasis placed on data from ENSDF

Nuclide	Half-life	Decay Modes	α Energy (keV)	α Emission Probability	β_max Energy (keV)	β_max Emission Probability	γ Energy (keV)	γ Emission Probability	Data Reference	Comments
Hf-181	42.38(6)d	β⁻			409.3(27)	0.07(3)	133.03(5)	0.42(3)	UKPADD	
					413.1(27)	0.93(3)	136.27(1)	0.058(2)		
							136.87(6)	0.0089(16)		
							345.91(3)	0.152(1)		
							475.94(3)	0.0071(1)		
							482.18(2)	0.806(2)		
							615.21(3)	0.0019(3)		
							619.05(4)	0.00026(2)		
Hg-197	2.692(25)d	EC					77.351(2)	0.179(5)	UKPADD;NPL	Uncertainties in gamma-ray data from NPL
							191.44(1)	0.0061(3)		
							268.79(1)	0.00038(2)		
Hg-203	46.595(13)d	β⁻			212.6(18)	1.000	279.1967(12)	0.8148(8)	UKPADD	
Ho-166	1.1167(8)d	β⁻			26.0(14)	0.00033(2)	80.57(1)	0.062(3)	JEF-2.2	Some beta emissions not included due to poor data quality
					194.1(14)	0.00297(12)	673.99(4)	0.00020(2)		
					396.6(14)	0.0095(5)	705.31(4)	0.00015(2)		
					1775.9(14)	0.477(24)	785.89(4)	0.00013(2)		
					1856.5(14)	0.51(2)	1379.40(6)	0.0093(5)		
							1581.90(8)	0.00181(9)		
							1662.40(8)	0.00116(8)		
							1749.9(1)	0.00025(2)		
							1830.60(15)	0.00008(1)		
I-121	2.12(1)h 0.08833(42)d	EC/β⁺					212.19(3)	0.84(9)	JEF-2.2	
							230.4(5)	0.0029(3)		
							319.7(5)	0.0104(11)		
							382.2(5)	0.0048(5)		
							471.5(5)	0.0086(9)		
							475.0(5)	0.0104(11)		
							531.9(3)	0.061(7)		
							594(1)	0.0037(4)		
							598.7(10)	0.0154(16)		
							1014.5(10)	0.0029(3)		

Nuclide	Half-life	Decay Modes	α Energy (keV)	α Emission Probability	β$_{max}$ Energy (keV)	β$_{max}$ Emission Probability	γ Energy (keV)	γ Emission Probability	Data Reference	Comments
I-123	13.2(1)h 0.5500(42)d	EC					158.97(5) 247.96(5) 281.03(5) 346.35(5) 440.02(5) 505.33(5) 528.96(5) 538.54(5) 624.57(5) 735.78(7)	0.833(4) 0.00071(3) 0.00079(3) 0.00126(5) 0.00428(15) 0.00316(11) 0.0139(5) 0.00382(13) 0.000833(3) 0.000616(22)	JEF-2.2;NPL	
I-124	4.18(2)d	EC/β+					511[A] 602.72(4) 645.82(4) 722.78(4) 1325.50(4) 1376.0(1) 1509.49(4) 1691.02(4) 2091.0(1) 2232.25(7) 2283.25(8)	0.46(16) 0.605(49) 0.0094(8) 0.100(8) 0.0143(13) 0.0166(2) 0.0299(2) 0.104(8) 0.0057(5) 0.0057(5) 0.0066(6)	JEF-2.2;NPL	Uncertainties in gamma-ray data from NPL
I-125	59.43(5)d	EC					35.50(1)	0.0666(10)	UKPADD	
I-128	24.99(2)m 0.017354(14)d	β⁻ 0.939(3) EC/β+ 0.061(3)			247(4) 542.3(41) 1255.4(39) 1682.0(39) 2124.9(39)	0.000005(1) 0.00012(1) 0.019(2) 0.15(1) 0.77(1)	442.91(7) 511[A] 526.62(10) 613.1(5) 743.5(2) 969.7(4) 1139.7(2)	0.16(2) 0.000040(4) 0.0154(14) 0.000024(6) 0.0014(2) 0.0038(5) 0.000096(13)	JEF-2.2;ENSDF	
I-129	(1.569(41))E+07y (5.73(15))E+09d	β⁻			150(5)	1.00	39.58(3)	0.075(2)	JEF-2.2;NPL	

Nuclide	Half-life	Decay Modes	α Energy (keV)	α Emission Probability	β_max Energy (keV)	β_max Emission Probability	γ Energy (keV)	γ Emission Probability	Data Reference	Comments
I-130m	9.0(1)m (6.25(7))E-03)d	IT 0.84(2) β⁻ 0.16(2)			379(10) 387(10) 480(10) 522(10) 530(10) 728(10) 874(10) 1392(10) 1902(10) 2488(10)	0.00022(3) 0.000099(14) 0.000051(8) 0.00102(14) 0.00019(3) 0.00035(6) 0.0051(7) 0.000065(10) 0.0115(15) 0.140(18)	536.09(2) 586.05(2) 1028.11(4) 1122.15(5) 1380.15(4) 1614.10(4) 1759.97(5) 1958.02(4) 1966.04(4) 2150.15(5)	0.157(20) 0.0107(17) 0.00039(7) 0.0017(3) 0.00036(6) 0.0045(7) 0.00030(7) 0.00019(3) 0.00052(9) 0.00021(2)	JEF-2.2;ENSDF	Uncertainties in data from ENSDF
I-131 (see also Xe-131m daughter)	8.04(1)d	β⁻			247.9(6) 303.9(6) 333.8(6) 606.3(6) 629.7(6) 806.9(6)	0.0213(3) 0.0062(2) 0.0736(10) 0.894(10) 0.0006(1) 0.0042(2)	80.183(10) 177.21(1) 284.30(1) 318.08(2) 325.78(1) 364.48(1) 502.99(1) 636.97(1) 642.70(1) 722.89(1)	0.02621(67) 0.002651(57) 0.0606(13) 0.000796(38) 0.002510(76) 0.812(17) 0.003609(86) 0.0727(16) 0.002197(52) 0.01804(39)	JEF-2.2;NPL	
I-132 (see also Te-132 parent)	2.283(8)h 0.09513(33)d	β⁻			738(2) 907(2) 964(2) 993(2) 1152(2) 1182(2) 1467(2) 1614(2) 2137(2)	0.135(9) 0.036(2) 0.079(6) 0.032(4) 0.025(3) 0.189(8) 0.085(8) 0.128(5) 0.186(8)	505.80(3) 522.7(1) 630.2(2) 667.718(7) 670(1) 671.6(2) 772.61(2) 812.4(2) 954.6(1) 1398.6(1)	0.049(1) 0.161(5) 0.135(4) 0.988(1) 0.044(3) 0.035(10) 0.754(15) 0.055(3) 0.176(6) 0.069(2)	UKPADD;NPL	Emphasis placed on data from UKPADD

Nuclide	Half-life	Decay Modes	α Energy (keV)	α Emission Probability	β$_{max}$ Energy (keV)	β$_{max}$ Emission Probability	γ Energy (keV)	γ Emission Probability	Data Reference	Comments
I-133	20.8(1)h 0.8667(42)d	β⁻			170(30) 374(30) 410(30) 462(30) 524(30) 708(30) 885(30) 1016(30) 1230(30) 1527(30)	0.00414(14) 0.0124(4) 0.00396(10) 0.0374(6) 0.0312(6) 0.0541(19) 0.0415(11) 0.0181(5) 0.835(18) 0.0107(5)	510.53(1) 529.87(1) 617.97(2) 680.25(2) 706.58(1) 856.28(1) 875.33(1) 1052.30(2) 1236.41(1) 1298.22(1)	0.0181(4) 0.863(17) 0.00539(12) 0.00645(17) 0.0149(3) 0.0123(3) 0.0447(9) 0.00552(17) 0.0149(3) 0.0233(5)	JEF-2.2	
I-134	52.6(4)m 0.03653(28)d	β⁻			1070(60) 1280(60) 1500(60) 1560(60) 1600(60) 1740(60) 1800(60) 1850(60) 2230(60) 2420(60)	0.019(2) 0.305(10) 0.065(4) 0.166(5) 0.037(2) 0.068(5) 0.11(1) 0.022(2) 0.032(9) 0.123(20)	405.451(20) 540.825(25) 595.362(20) 621.790(25) 677.340(30) 847.025(25) 857.290(30) 884.090(25) 1072.55(3) 1136.16(4)	0.073(4) 0.076(4) 0.112(6) 0.106(6) 0.078(5) 0.954(19) 0.070(2) 0.649(10) 0.150(8) 0.092(5)	JEF-2.2	
I-135	6.61(1)h 0.27542(42)d	β⁻			354(30) 456(30) 478(30) 618(30) 743(30) 920(30) 1033(30) 1146(30) 1253(30) 1451(30)	0.0141(5) 0.0479(15) 0.074(2) 0.0159(7) 0.080(3) 0.088(3) 0.218(5) 0.081(3) 0.077(4) 0.241(12)	546.56(2) 836.80(2) 1038.80(2) 1124.00(4) 1131.50(2) 1260.40(2) 1457.60(3) 1678.00(3) 1706.50(3) 1791.20(3)	0.072(3) 0.067(3) 0.080(3) 0.0365(15) 0.228(9) 0.289(12) 0.087(4) 0.096(14) 0.041(22) 0.078(3)	JEF-2.2	
In-111	2.8047(5)d	EC					171.28(2) 245.42(1)	0.9079(10) 0.9415(9)	UKPADD	
In-113m	1.658(1)h 0.069083(42)d	IT					391.69(1)	0.6489(15)	UKPADD;NPL	
In-115	(4.41(25)E+14y (1.61(9))E+17d	β⁻			497(4)	1.0000(1)			UKPADD	

273

Nuclide	Half-life	Decay Modes	α Energy (keV)	α Emission Probability	βmax Energy (keV)	βmax Emission Probability	γ Energy (keV)	γ Emission Probability	Data Reference	Comments
In-115m (see also Cd-115 parent)	4.486(3)h 0.18692(13)d	IT 0.9495(70) β⁻ 0.0505(70)			334.2(38) 831.5(37)	0.00048(2) 0.050(7)	336.24(3) 497.35(8)	0.458(1) 0.00047(1)	UKPADD	
Ir-191m	4.94(3)s (5.718(35))E-05d	IT					41.85(1) 47.05(3) 82.427(10) 129.431(5)	0.0000513(23) 0.000027(2) 0.00026(2) 0.29(2)	JEF-2.2	
Ir-192	73.831(8)d	β⁻ 0.9524(4) EC 0.0476(6)			51(4) 79(4) 256(4) 536(4) 672(4)	0.000032(5) 0.0108(6) 0.0555(4) 0.416(3) 0.481(3)	205.79549(6) 295.95827(12) 308.45692(13) 316.50791(13) 468.07152(24) 484.5780(4) 588.5845(7) 604.41464(21) 612.46564(20)	0.0318(12) 0.2873(20) 0.2975(21) 0.830(6) 0.477(3) 0.0314(1) 0.0448(3) 0.0809(5) 0.0526(4)	JEF-2.2;NPL; ENSDF	Gamma-ray energy standard (ENSDF)
K-40	(1.28(1))E+09y (4.675(37))E+11d	β⁻ 0.893(1) EC/β⁺ 0.107(1)			1311.6(5)	0.893(1)	1460.8(1)	0.107(1)	UKPADD	
K-42	12.37(2)h 0.51542(83)d	β⁻			75(3) 1097.5(18) 1684(2) 1996.5(17) 3521.1(16)	0.00067(9) 0.00055(12) 0.0035(4) 0.184(8) 0.811(8)	312.6(3) 694(1) 899(1) 1022(1) 1228(1) 1524.6(3) 1921(1) 2424(1)	0.00352(26) 0.000034(8) 0.000548(44) 0.000210(18) 0.000034(17) 0.189(8) 0.000431(45) 0.000208(31)	UKPADD;NPL	
K-43	22.2(2)h 0.9250(83)d	β⁻			422(10) 827(10) 1224(10) 1444(10) 1817(10)	0.022(1) 0.920(15) 0.036(5) 0.007(3) 0.015(3)	220.6(2) 372.8(1) 396.9(2) 404(1) 593.4(1) 617.5(2) 801(1) 990(1) 1022(1) 1394(1)	0.0409(20) 0.871(19) 0.1141(27) 0.001132(91) 0.1097(36) 0.804(22) 0.001481(93) 0.00331(62) 0.01873(81) 0.00105(18)	UKPADD;NPL	

Nuclide	Half-life	Decay Modes	α Energy (keV)	α Emission Probability	β$_{max}$ Energy (keV)	β$_{max}$ Emission Probability	γ Energy (keV)	γ Emission Probability	Data Reference	Comments
Kr-81	(2.1(1)E+05y (7.67(37))E+07d	EC					275.99(2)	0.0030(2)	UKPADD	
Kr-81m (see also Rb-81 parent)	13.2(1)s (1.528(12))E-04d	IT EC 0.000025(4)					190.53(4)	0.680(5)	UKPADD	
Kr-85	10.730(19)y (3.919(7))E+03d	β⁻			173.4(20) 687.4(20)	0.00437(10) 0.99563(10)	514.008(2)	0.00434(10)	UKPADD	
Kr-85m	4.480(8)h 0.18667(33)d	β⁻ 0.789(8) IT 0.211(8)			260.5(20) 711.3(20) 841.1(20)	0.00019(7) 0.0036(1) 0.785(8)	129.83(2) 151.16(1) 304.87(2) 450.83(2) 731.82(1)	0.0030(1) 0.752(7) 0.138(6) 0.00011(4) 0.000075(31)	UKPADD	
Kr-87	1.272(8)h 0.05300(33)d	β⁻			580.5(50) 928(70) 1077.7(50) 1334(100) 1474.6(50) 2148.4(50) 2310.9(50) 3044(70) 3486(50) 3889(50)	0.0049(4) 0.044(4) 0.0060(4) 0.094(7) 0.055(3) 0.0062(9) 0.0012(5) 0.073(4) 0.41(3) 0.305(22)	402.578(20) 673.83(8) 836.37(6) 845.44(4) 1175.40(8) 1338.007(7) 1740.52(8) 2011.88(10) 2554.8(2) 2558.1(2)	0.496(30) 0.0189(9) 0.0077(4) 0.073(4) 0.0111(6) 0.0063(5) 0.0204(9) 0.0288(19) 0.092(6) 0.039(3)	JEF-2.2	
Kr-88 (see also Rb-88 daughter)	2.84(2)h 0.11833(83)d	β⁻			142(17) 365(17) 521(17) 681(17) 1198(17) 1252(17) 1731(17) 2051(17) 2717(17) 2913(17)	0.0035(2) 0.0265(16) 0.67(3) 0.091(5) 0.0192(11) 0.0023(4) 0.0090(6) 0.0131(25) 0.0180(25) 0.14(4)	165.98(4) 196.320(15) 362.226(13) 834.830(3) 1529.77(3) 2029.84(40) 2035.410(18) 2195.840(7) 2231.77(2) 2392.11(4)	0.0310(2) 0.260(2) 0.0225(6) 0.130(2) 0.109(2) 0.0453(10) 0.0374(10) 0.1318(4) 0.0339(7) 0.346(2)	JEF-2.2	

Nuclide	Half-life	Decay Modes	α Energy (keV)	α Emission Probability	β_max Energy (keV)	β_max Emission Probability	γ Energy (keV)	γ Emission Probability	Data Reference	Comments
Kr-89	3.17(2)m (2.201(14))E-03d	β⁻			2064(60) 2332(60) 2529(60) 2770(60) 2932(60) 3236(60) 3400(60) 3606(60) 4353(60) 4930(60)	0.039(3) 0.143(9) 0.056(4) 0.031(3) 0.025(2) 0.100(9) 0.028(3) 0.036(4) 0.044(5) 0.22(4)	220.90(7) 497.51(30) 576.96(10) 585.80(7) 738.39(7) 867.08(7) 904.27(7) 1472.76(10) 1533.68(15) 1693.7(1)	0.199(11) 0.066(5) 0.056(3) 0.164(9) 0.042(2) 0.059(3) 0.071(4) 0.068(4) 0.051(3) 0.044(3)	JEF-2.2	
La-137	(6(2))E+04y (2.2(7))E+07d	EC					4.47[X] 31.817[X] 32.194[X] 36.4[X]	0.105(30) 0.214(10) 0.396(16) 0.144(9)	JEF-2.2	
La-138	(1.05(2))E+11y (3.84(7))E+13d	EC 0.664(5) β⁻ 0.336(5)			252(12)	0.336(5)	788.742(8) 1435.80(1)	0.336(5) 0.664(5)	JEF-2.2;ENSDF	Emphasis placed on ENSDF data
La-140 (see also Ba-140 parent)	1.6785(2)d	β⁻			1215(2) 1240.5(19) 1246.1(19) 1281.0(19) 1297.8(19) 1349.9(19) 1412.1(19) 1414.0(19) 1678.7(19) 2165.7(19)	0.0063(1) 0.110(2) 0.0567(4) 0.0109(8) 0.0553(5) 0.444(4) 0.0027(9) 0.0500(5) 0.204(5) 0.057(7)	328.76(6) 432.51(6) 487.02(6) 751.65(6) 815.78(6) 867.85(7) 919.53(6) 925.20(6) 1596.23(3) 2521.43(3)	0.206(1) 0.0291(2) 0.455(4) 0.0434(4) 0.234(2) 0.0552(5) 0.0268(2) 0.0695(4) 0.9542(5) 0.0344(3)	UKPADD	
Lu-176	(3.61(16))E+10y (1.32(6))E+13d	β⁻			187.9(21) 588.9(20)	0.009(2) 0.991(2)	88.35(5) 201.825(5) 306.88(5) 401.1(2)	0.13(4) 0.84(22) 0.93(19) 0.0084(36)	JEF-2.2	
Lu-177	6.70(2)d	β⁻			176.5(14) 248.2(14) 384.9(14) 497.8(14)	0.123(10) 0.0006(3) 0.11(2) 0.766(30)	71.642(3) 112.950(1) 136.725(2) 208.367(3) 249.674(1) 321.316(2)	0.00155(12) 0.0685(5) 0.00048(4) 0.111(4) 0.00213(15) 0.00253(12)	UKPADD	

Nuclide	Half-life	Decay Modes	α Energy (keV)	α Emission Probability	βmax Energy (keV)	βmax Emission Probability	γ Energy (keV)	γ Emission Probability	Data Reference	Comments
Mg-27	9.458(12)m (6.568(8))E-03d	β⁻			1594.9(13) 1765.5(12)	0.29(1) 0.71(1)	170.8(1) 843.7(1) 1014.4(1)	0.0084(10) 0.718(10) 0.282(10)	UKPADD	
Mn-53	(3.68(21))E+06y (1.344(77))E+09d	EC					5.4055[X] 5.4147[X] 5.95[X]	0.074(3) 0.147(5) 0.029(2)	JEF-2.2	
Mn-54	312.3(4)d	EC					834.827(21)	0.999758(24)	UKPADD	
Mn-56	2.579(3)h 0.10746(13)d	β⁻			250.4(9) 326.0(9) 572.8(9) 735.8(9) 1038.2(9) 1610.6(9) 2848.9(9)	0.00022(3) 0.0119(5) 0.00042(8) 0.146(3) 0.282(6) 0.00076(18) 0.559(10)	846.753(5) 1037.85(1) 1238.30(1) 1810.79(3) 2113.11(1) 2522.99(1) 2598.52(1) 2657.54(2) 2959.86(3) 3369.74(5)	0.9887(4) 0.00042(8) 0.0119(10) 0.275(6) 0.1434(30) 0.0103(4) 0.00022(3) 0.00672(20) 0.0297(10) 0.00158(10)	UKPADD;NPL	
Mo-99 (see also Tc-99m daughter)	2.748(1)d	β⁻			215(1) 227(1) 276(1) 285(1) 353(1) 436(1) 686(1) 823(1) 848(1) 1214(1)	0.0011(1) 0.00011(2) 0.000069(6) 0.000024(8) 0.0013(1) 0.161(5) 0.00042(7) 0.000025(20) 0.012(1) 0.824(10)	40.58(2) 140.511(1) 181.1(1) 366.4(1) 528.8(1) 621.2(1) 739.6(1) 778.0(1) 823.0(1) 961.0(1)	0.0104(4) 0.045(4) 0.0596(13) 0.0119(4) 0.00052(4) 0.00024(2) 0.119(2) 0.0420(12) 0.0129(4) 0.0096(4)	UKPADD;NPL	
N-13	9.965(4)m (6.9201(28))E-03d	EC/β⁺					511[A]	1.996(200)	UKPADD	
Na-22	2.603(3)y 950.7(11)d	EC/β⁺					511[A] 1274.54(4)	1.81(18) 0.9994(2)	UKPADD	

Nuclide	Half-life	Decay Modes	α Energy (keV)	α Emission Probability	β_{max} Energy (keV)	β_{max} Emission Probability	γ Energy (keV)	γ Emission Probability	Data Reference	Comments
Na-24	14.965(4)h 0.62354(17)d	β⁻			277.5(1) 1390.8(8) 4144.4(8)	0.00066(2) 0.99855(5) 0.00075(8)	998(1) 1368.630(6) 2754.030(14) 2870.3(10) 3867.37(50) 4238.9(10)	0.000014(3) 0.999936(15) 0.99855(5) 0.0000024(3) 0.000645(14) 0.000009(1)	UKPADD	
Nb-93m (see also Zr-93 parent)	16.13(14)y (5.89(5))E+03d	IT					30.82(17)	0.0000555(4)	UKPADD	
Nb-94	(2.00(25))E+04y (7.3(9))E+06d	β⁻			471.6(23)	1.000	702.622(19) 871.091(18)	0.9982(5) 0.9989(5)	UKPADD	
Nb-95	35.02(5)d	β⁻			159.8(5) 721.5(5) 925.6(5)	0.99951(13) 0.00017(8) 0.00030(5)	204.10(1) 561.72(2) 765.82(1)	0.00027(8) 0.00011(3) 0.9979(1)	UKPADD	
Nb-95m (see also Zr-95 parent)	3.61(3)d	IT 0.966(3) β⁻ 0.034(3)			340.7(5) 375.1(5) 957.2(5) 1161.3(5)	0.000038(20) 0.00072(9) 0.0242(8) 0.0091(9)	204.10(1) 235.68(2) 582.11(2)	0.0236(7) 0.251(5) 0.00056(7)	UKPADD	
Nb-96	23.35(5)h 0.9729(21)d	β⁻			212(4) 311.7(40) 432(4) 746.4(40) 748.6(40)	0.00030(15) 0.0060(3) 0.0070(4) 0.0280(14) 0.959(48)	241.4(2) 460.03(6) 480.68(8) 568.86(6) 719.54(15) 778.22(10) 810.25(7) 849.9(1) 1091.31(6) 1200.19(6)	0.038(3) 0.276(15) 0.062(5) 0.546(30) 0.071(5) 0.95(2) 0.097(8) 0.203(14) 0.48(3) 0.197(14)	JEF-2.2	
Nd-144	(2.1(4))E+15y (7.7(15))E+17d	α	1830(15)	1.000					JEF-2.2	

278

Nuclide	Half-life	Decay Modes	α Energy (keV)	α Emission Probability	β_max Energy (keV)	β_max Emission Probability	γ Energy (keV)	γ Emission Probability	Data Reference	Comments
Nd-147	11.02(2)d	β⁻			210.2(9)	0.022(2)	91.10(2)	0.277(17)	UKPADD	
					215.6(10)	0.00044(10)	120.50(7)	0.0038(5)		
					365.1(9)	0.149(1)	196.64(7)	0.0018(2)		
					406.9(9)	0.0080(6)	275.38(6)	0.0083(9)		
					485.6(9)	0.0062(4)	319.41(5)	0.0196(20)		
					805.0(9)	0.814(58)	398.15(6)	0.0083(9)		
							410.51(3)	0.0018(3)		
							439.91(6)	0.0118(11)		
							531.01(4)	0.127(8)		
							594.79(5)	0.0025(3)		
							685.89(3)	0.0085(9)		
Ni-59	(7.6(5))E+04y	EC/β⁺					6.915[X]	0.100(10)	UKPADD	
	(2.78(18))E+07d						6.930[X]	0.20(2)		
							7.65[X]	0.040(4)		
Ni-63	99(7)y	β⁻			65.87(15)	1.000			UKPADD	
	(3.62(26))E+04d									
Np-235	1.0845(33)y	EC 0.999986(2)					13.60[X]	0.373(40)	JEF-2.2	
	396.1(12)d	α 0.000014(2)					94.665[X]	0.00607(20)		
							98.439[X]	0.00984(28)		
							111.30[X]	0.00458(20)		
Np-237	(2.14(1))E+06y	α	4578(2)	0.0042(15)			29.37(2)	0.152(46)	UKHEDD-2.2:NPL	
	(7.816(37))E+08d		4640(2)	0.059(1)			57.115(50)	0.0038(5)		
			4659(2)	0.0058(2)			86.479(56)	0.123(15)		
			4665(2)	0.028(3)			88.04(16)	0.0014(2)		
			4766(2)	0.08(4)			94.66(5)	0.0064(11)		
			4771(2)	0.25(6)			117.68(3)	0.0017(2)		
			4788(2)	0.48(5)			143.21(3)	0.0043(5)		
			4804(2)	0.015(10)			151.37(4)	0.0023(3)		
			4817(2)	0.025(3)			195.09(2)	0.0019(2)		
			4874(2)	0.043(3)			212.415(25)	0.0015(2)		

Nuclide	Half-life	Decay Modes	α Energy (keV)	α Emission Probability	β_{max} Energy (keV)	β_{max} Emission Probability	γ Energy (keV)	γ Emission Probability	Data Reference	Comments
Np-238	2.117(2)d	β⁻			89.2(12)	0.0051(4)	101.93(4)	0.0027(2)	UKHEDD-2.2	
					221.9(11)	0.125(6)	882.63(6)	0.0087(6)		
					263.3(11)	0.495(16)	918.69(6)	0.0059(4)		
					306.4(12)	0.0059(3)	923.98(3)	0.028(2)		
					308.8(12)	0.0005(1)	936.61(11)	0.0040(2)		
					329.1(11)	0.0136(5)	941.38(8)	0.0054(3)		
					686.7(12)	0.0012(2)	962.77(3)	0.0070(4)		
					1247.8(11)	0.354(23)	984.45(5)	0.278(8)		
							1025.87(5)	0.096(8)		
							1028.54(2)	0.203(14)		
Np-239	2.355(4)d	β⁻			166(4)	0.000047(5)	57.27(2)	0.0015(2)	UKHEDD-2.2	
					210(2)	0.0148(9)	61.460(2)	0.0129(6)		
					216(2)	0.00007(1)	106.123(2)	0.272(8)		
					229(2)	0.00019(3)	209.753(2)	0.0343(15)		
					252(3)	0.000027(2)	226.41	0.0028(2)		
					330(2)	0.399(6)	228.184(2)	0.113(5)		
					392(2)	0.073(9)	277.599(2)	0.1438(14)		
					436(2)	0.514(20)	285.460(2)	0.0079(4)		
							315.880(3)	0.0157(7)		
							334.310(3)	0.0207(9)		
O-15	2.037(3)m (1.4146(21))E-03d	β⁺					511[A]	1.998(200)	JEF-2.2	Uncertainty in emission probability of annihilation radiation estimated to be 10%
Os-186	(1.9(13))E+15y (7(5))E+18d	α	2757.7(24)	1.000						
Os-191	15.4(1)d	β⁻			141.4(19)	1.000	41.85(1)	0.000051(2)	JEF-2.2	
							47.05(3)	0.000027(2)		
							82.43(1)	0.00026(2)		
							129.431(5)	0.29(2)		
P-32	14.27(4)d	β⁻			1710.4(6)	1.000			UKPADD;NPL	
P-33	25.4(1)d	β⁻			249(2)	1.000			UKPADD;NPL	

Nuclide	Half-life	Decay Modes	α Energy (keV)	α Emission Probability	β_{max} Energy (keV)	β_{max} Emission Probability	γ Energy (keV)	γ Emission Probability	Data Reference	Comments
Pa-231	(3.2760(110))E+04y (1.1965(40))E+07d	α SF (3.0(15))E-12	4678.6(9) 4734.7(8) 4851.8(9) 4934.4(9) 4951.0(9) 4986.2(8) 5013.5(8) 5029.6(8) 5032.2(8) 5059.1(8)	0.0161(7) 0.0847(40) 0.014(1) 0.030(4) 0.229(5) 0.014(2) 0.254(5) 0.20(2) 0.032(3) 0.110(5)			16.39(2) 18.95(2) 27.36(2) 46.37(2) 260.3(1) 283.690(13) 300.069(8) 302.669(6) 330.057(15) 340.77(7)	0.0022(1) 0.00354(7) 0.111(4) 0.00223(6) 0.00182(5) 0.0165(4) 0.0241(6) 0.0247(6) 0.0136(3) 0.00178(4)	UKHEDD-2.2;NPL	
Pa-233	27.0(1)d	β⁻			156.5(25) 173.7(25) 231.8(25) 273.5(25) 572.3(24)	0.251(11) 0.164(11) 0.485(87) 0.055(11) 0.045(26)	75.28(1) 86.59(1) 103.86(2) 271.48(8) 300.12(3) 311.98(3) 340.50(4) 375.45(4) 398.62(8) 415.76(4)	0.0132(4) 0.0197(12) 0.087(3) 0.0032(1) 0.0664(12) 0.3863(39) 0.0450(5) 0.0068(1) 0.0141(2) 0.0174(2)	UKHEDD-2.2;NPL	
Pa-234	6.78(3)h 0.2825(13)d	β⁻			387(8) 416(8) 437(8) 475.6(80) 476.1(80) 506(8) 647(8) 1072(8) 1130(8) 1175.2(80)	0.015(2) 0.089(20) 0.033(4) 0.27(5) 0.112(4) 0.066(7) 0.180(7) 0.021(10) 0.046(20) 0.022(10)[D]	131.3(2) 152.720(2) 227.2(2) 569.5(2) 733.4(1) 880.514(36) 883.237(33) 925.9(1) 926.72(5) 946.002(28)	0.163(20) 0.054(10) 0.052(10) 0.075(17) 0.064(9) 0.082(15) 0.086(15) 0.054(8) 0.067(13) 0.121(23)	UKHEDD-2.2	Beta energy of 1175.2 keV is an unresolved doublet

281

Nuclide	Half-life	Decay Modes	α Energy (keV)	α Emission Probability	β_{max} Energy (keV)	β_{max} Emission Probability	γ Energy (keV)	γ Emission Probability	Data Reference	Comments
Pa-234m	1.17(3)m (8.13(21))E-04d	β⁻ IT 0.0015(3)			367(12) 403(12) 469(12) 497(12) 685(12) 724(12) 1234(11) 1468(11) 1492(11) 2278(11)	0.00046(3) 0.000340(8) 0.00024(3) 0.00037(2) 0.00024(2) 0.00031(1) 0.0103(2) 0.0098(3) 0.0004(1) 0.975(1)	258.2(1) 742.814(22) 766.358(20) 786.272(22) 922.04(5) 1001.025(22) 1193.767(30) 1510.15(5) 1737.8(6) 1831.7(5)	0.073(3) 0.000935(37) 0.00319(8) 0.00048(4) 0.00012(2) 0.00835(11) 0.000131(6) 0.000130(4) 0.000212(4) 0.000173(4)	UKHEDD-2.2	
Pb-203	2.1621(8)d	EC					279.197(2) 401.325(10) 680.514(10)	0.810(7) 0.0356(19) 0.0072(4)	UKPADD;NPL	
Pb-204	(1.4(6))E+17y (5.11(22))E+19d	α	1933(2)	1.000					UKPADD	
Pb-209	3.253(14)h 0.13554(58)d	β⁻			644.6(12)	1.00(1)			UKHEDD 2.2	
Pb-210 (see also Bi-210 daughter)	22.3(2)y (8.145(73))E+03d	β⁻ α (1.9(3))E-08	3720(20)	0.0000000022(7)	16.5(5) 63.0(5)	0.82(8) 0.18(8)	46.50(2)	0.045(3)	UKHEDD-2.2	
Pb-211 (see also Bi-211 daughter)	36.1(2)m 0.02507(14)d	β⁻			102(6) 176(6) 264(6) 270(6) 293(6) 421(6) 541(6) 968(6) 1373(6)	0.00030(6) 0.00019(4) 0.00881(87) 0.00005(1) 0.00061(10) 0.00023(14) 0.0656(30) 0.0166(15) 0.908(4)	65.5(1) 313.8(2) 342.7(2) 404.85(4) 427.0(1) 481.1(4) 704.5(1) 766.35(20) 831.85(4) 1109.5(2)	0.00077(5) 0.00031(4) 0.00035(5) 0.0384(13) 0.0173(7) 0.00026(5) 0.0048(3) 0.0071(4) 0.0381(13) 0.00147(11)	UKHEDD-2.2	

Nuclide	Half-life	Decay Modes	α Energy (keV)	α Emission Probability	β_{max} Energy (keV)	β_{max} Emission Probability	γ Energy (keV)	γ Emission Probability	Data Reference	Comments
Pb-212 (see also Bi-212 daughter)	10.64(1)h 0.44333(42)d	β⁻			158(4) 334(4) 573(4)	0.051(2) 0.826(21) 0.123(23)	115.190(6) 123.435(12) 176.65(2) 238.625(6) 300.087(10) 415.28(2)	0.00596(8) 0.00011(6) 0.00050(5) 0.434(3) 0.0324(3) 0.0015(4)	UKHEDD-2.2	
Pb-214 (see also Bi-214 daughter)	26.8(9)m 0.01861(63)d	β⁻			191(12) 264(12) 496(12) 678(12) 735(12) 1030(12)	0.022(2) 0.0009(2) 0.0098(21) 0.482(7) 0.430(6) 0.056(6)	53.23(20) 241.91(3) 258.8(1) 295.2(1) 351.900(28) 480.5(2) 580.2(2) 785.95(20) 839.03(2)	0.0113(6) 0.075(3) 0.0046(11) 0.192(9) 0.369(17) 0.0033(4) 0.0035(5) 0.00842(12) 0.0057(6)	UKHEDD-2.2	
Pd-103 (see also Rh-103m daughter)	16.98(2)d	EC					62.43(4) 294.98(2) 357.41(2) 497.26(2)	0.0000106(7) 0.0000287(11) 0.000226(5) 0.000041(2)	UKPADD	
Pd-107	(6.5(3))E+06y (2.37(11))E+09d	β⁻			33.2(30)	1.000(1)			UKPADD	
Pd-109	13.430(14)h 0.55958(58)d	β⁻			204.9(20) 246.4(20) 253.2(20) 380.6(20) 391.5(20) 408.9(20) 414.0(20) 700.6(20) 804.5(20) 1028.0(20)	0.000017(5) 0.00018(1) 0.000016(3) 0.00032(1) 0.00021(2) 0.000018(2) 0.000042(4) 0.000057(19) 0.00020(4) 0.9990(1)	309.1(5) 311.4(1) 413(4) 415.2(3) 558.1(2) 602.5(1) 636.3(1) 647.3(1) 701.9(2) 781.4(2)	0.000049(15) 0.000319(9) 0.000066(10) 0.000107(10) 0.000024(3) 0.000080(5) 0.000100(5) 0.000244(7) 0.000031(3) 0.000112(12)	JEF-2.2	
Pd-112	20.3(2)h 0.846(8)d	β⁻			269.5(175)	1.000	18.5(5)	0.274(4)	UKPADD	

Nuclide	Half-life	Decay Modes	α Energy (keV)	α Emission Probability	β_{max} Energy (keV)	β_{max} Emission Probability	γ Energy (keV)	γ Emission Probability	Data Reference	Comments
Pm-144	363(14)d	EC					302.0(2)	0.0018(4)	UKPADD;NPL	
							477.0(1)	0.420(8)		
							583.0(2)	0.0019(2)		
							618.03(4)	0.986(10)		
							694.1(3)	0.0055(10)		
							696.51(1)	0.9949(2)		
							779.0(1)	0.0151(5)		
							814.0(1)	0.0055(3)		
							890.1(2)	0.0004(1)		
Pm-147	2.622(6)y	β^-			102.9(3)	0.000055(3)	121.22(2)	0.000276(8)	UKPADD	
	957.7(22)d				224.1(3)	0.999945(3)				
Pm-149	2.212(2)d	β^-			191(4)	0.0014(1)	22.51(1)	0.008(7)	UKPADD	
					240(4)	0.00035(2)	277.07(1)	0.00029(2)		
					243(4)	0.00050(4)	285.94(1)	0.031(2)		
					436(4)	0.00027(1)	558.37(1)	0.00015(2)		
					482(4)	0.00091(3)	568.38(2)	0.00019(2)		
					515(4)	0.00035(2)	590.89(1)	0.00069(7)		
					787(4)	0.034(1)	807.9(1)	0.00015(3)		
					796(4)	0.00027(2)	830.4(1)	0.00032(4)		
					1050(4)	0.25(20)	833.2(1)	0.00033(4)		
					1073(4)	0.71(20)	859.43(2)	0.00109(10)		
							881.94(5)	0.00024(2)		
Pm-151	1.17(1)d	β^-			309(5)	0.023(2)	100.01(1)	0.0253(23)	UKPADD	
					364(5)	0.060(3)	104.83(1)	0.0343(31)		
					446(5)	0.031(2)	167.75(1)	0.081(7)		
					741(5)	0.071(4)	177.16(2)	0.0356(32)		
					842(5)	0.404(8)	240.08(2)	0.0370(30)		
					863(5)	0.032(2)	275.21(2)	0.067(5)		
					1019.3(50)	0.081(10)	340.09(1)	0.22(1)		
					1082(5)	0.045(5)	344.91(1)	0.0209(16)		
					1182(5)	0.03(1)	445.68(1)	0.039(4)		
					1187(5)	0.08(1)	717.81(4)	0.039(4)		

Nuclide	Half-life	Decay Modes	α Energy (keV)	α Emission Probability	β_max Energy (keV)	β_max Emission Probability	γ Energy (keV)	γ Emission Probability	Data Reference	Comments
Po-208	2.93(4)y (1.070(15))E+03d	α 0.9999819(4) EC 0.0000181(4)	4233(2) 5115.0(16)	0.0000024(7) 0.9999819(4)			31.7(2) 63.3(1) 291.7(2) 538.5(2) 570.2(2) 601.8(1) 861.9(2) 899.2(1)	0.00000010(1) 0.0000014(2) 0.0000098(9) 0.0000025(2) 0.0000061(6) 0.0000053(5) 0.0000030(3) 0.0000024(7)	UKPADD	
Po-209	102(5)y (3.73(18))E+04d	α 0.9974(1) EC 0.0026(1)	4136(4) 4317(4) 4625(4) 4880(3) 4883(3)	0.0000056(4) 0.0000015(4) 0.0048(2) 0.794(10) 0.199(10)			185.2(4) 260.5(1) 262.8(1) 498.6(2) 576.2(1) 759.1(1) 761.4(1) 896.4(2)	0.0000003(1) 0.0022(1) 0.0007(1) 0.0000003(1) 0.0000005(1) 0.0000028(2) 0.0000018(1) 0.0025(1)	UKHEDD-2.2	
Po-210	138.376(2)d	α	4517(5) 5304.5(1)	0.000011(1) 1.00			803.1(1)	0.000011(1)	UKHEDD-2.2	
Po-211 (see also Bi-211 parent)	0.516(3)s (5.972(35))E-06d	α	6569(2) 6891(2) 7450(3)	0.00537(19) 0.00544(19) 0.98919(19)			328.2(2) 569.65(10) 897.8(1)	0.000032(11) 0.00536(2) 0.00520(29)	UKHEDD-2.2	
Po-212 (see also Bi-212 parent)	(3.00(2))E-07s (3.472(23))E-12d	α	8784.6(1)	1.000(1)					UKHEDD-2.2	
Po-213 (see also Bi-213 parent)	(4.2(8))E-06s (4.86(93))E-11d	α	7611(10) 8376(3)	0.00003(1) 0.99997(1)			779(1)	0.00003(1)	UKHEDD-2.2	
Po-214 (see also Bi-214 parent)	(1.65(3)E-04s (1.910(35))E-09d	α	6610(1) 6902.6(2) 7687.09(6)	0.0000006(2) 0.000104(6) 0.999895(6)			298(1) 799.7(1)	0.0000005(2) 0.000104(6)	UKHEDD-2.2	
Po-215	(1.78(1))E-03s (2.060(12))E-08d	α β⁻ 0.000004(2)	6950.1(20) 6956.7(20) 7386.4(8)	0.00022(4) 0.00034(7) 0.9994(2)	727(7)	0.000004(2)	438.7(3)	0.00048(9)	UKHEDD-2.2	

Nuclide	Half-life	Decay Modes	α Energy (keV)	α Emission Probability	β_max Energy (keV)	β_max Emission Probability	γ Energy (keV)	γ Emission Probability	Data Reference	Comments
Po-216	0.145(2)s (1.678(23))E-06d	α	5988.5(7) 6778.5(5)	0.000018(3) 0.999982(3)			804.9(2)	0.000018(3)	UKHEDD-2.2	
Po-218	3.05(9)m (2.118(63))E-03d	α β⁻ 0.0002(1)	6002.55(10)	0.999989(1)	256(13)	0.0002(1)	837(2)	0.000011(1)	UKHEDD-2.2	
Pr-142	19.13(4)h 0.7971(17)d	β⁻ 0.999836(8) EC 0.000164(8)			74.4(26) 583.2(26) 2158.8(26)	0.00023(5) 0.037(5) 0.963(5)	508.8(5) 642(1) 1575.6(5)	0.00023(5) 0.000021(8) 0.037(5)	JEF-2.2;ENSDF	Uncertainties from ENSDF
Pr-143	13.56(1)d	β⁻			191.9(14) 933.9(14)	0.000000012(4) 0.99999988(4)	741.98(4)	0.000000012(4)	UKPADD	
Pr-144 (see also Ce-144 parent)	17.28(2)m 0.01200(1)d	β⁻			254.6(26) 322.2(25) 342.7(26) 629.3(25) 811.8(24) 913.0(25) 924.8(25) 1436.6(25) 2301.0(24) 2997.5(24)	0.0000034(7) 0.0000091(7) 0.0000020(4) 0.0000025(8) 0.0100(2) 0.000083(7) 0.0000062(7) 0.000014(4) 0.0105(1) 0.979(7)	574.0(2) 624.8(1) 675.1(1) 696.5(1) 814.0(1) 864.4(1) 1388.0(1) 1489.2(1) 1978.8(1) 2185.7(1)	0.000016(4) 0.000011(1) 0.000026(2) 0.01342(13) 0.000032(2) 0.000023(2) 0.000066(3) 0.0028(1) 0.0000091(8) 0.0071(2)	UKPADD	
Pt-190	(6.6(3))E+11y (2.41(11))E+14d	α	3164(15)	1.000					JEF-2.2	
Pu-236	2.9(1)y (1.059(37))E+03d	α SF (8.5(18))E-10	5088.3(4) 5214.01(9) 5450.8(4) 5613.74(9) 5721.00(10) 5767.66(8)	0.0000027(6) 0.000006(2) 0.00002(1) 0.0018(2) 0.307(3) 0.691(3)			47.59(1) 108.98(2)	0.000668(13) 0.0018(2)	UKHEDD-2.2	

Nuclide	Half-life	Decay Modes	α Energy (keV)	α Emission Probability	β$_{max}$ Energy (keV)	β$_{max}$ Emission Probability	γ Energy (keV)	γ Emission Probability	Data Reference	Comments
Pu-237	45.3(2)d	EC 0.0000042(4) α	5098(7) 5155(7) 5259(7) 5302(6) 5335(6) 5356(6) 5610(6) 5650(6)	0.00000018(7) 0.0000027(8) 0.00000030(9) 0.00000524(4) 0.000019(1) 0.0000070(7) 0.00000042(4) 0.00000042(4)			26.34(2) 33.19(1) 43.43(3) 59.536(3)	0.0024(2) 0.00083(6) 0.000037(19) 0.0325(22)	UKHEDD-2.2	
Pu-238	87.7(2)y (3.2032(73))E+04d	α SF (1.86(6))E-09	4472.3(3) 4588.1(3) 4661.9(3) 4703.0(3) 4726.1(3) 5010.6(3) 5208.2(3) 5358.3(3) 5456.5(2) 5499.3(2)	0.000000012(1) 0.000000013(1) 0.000000056(5) 0.000000086(2) 0.000000085(1) 0.000000070(3) 0.000000030(1) 0.00102(2) 0.2884(6) 0.7104(6)			43.498(1) 99.853(3)	0.000395(8) 0.0000735(8)	UKHEDD-2.2	
Pu-239	(2.4113(30))E+04y (8.807(11))E+06d	α SF (4.4(4))E-12	5008(3) 5054(3) 5106.1(8) 5143.9(8) 5156.2(8)	0.00052(4) 0.00027(9) 0.1145(20) 0.1512(2) 0.7337(7)			38.660(2) 46.218(10) 51.624(1) 56.825(3) 98.78(6) 111.3(1) 129.296(1) 375.054(3) 413.713(5)	0.0001105(2) 0.00000737(75) 0.000271(5) 0.0001130(25) 0.0000122(4) 0.0000155(1) 0.0000631(6) 0.00001554(9) 0.0000147(1)	UKHEDD-2.2;NPL	
Pu-240	(6.563(7))E+03y (2.3971(26))E+06d	α SF (5.7(2))E-08	4863.6(5) 5021.5(5) 5123.62(25) 5168.30(15)	0.000113(3) 0.00089(2) 0.270(5) 0.729(5)			45.242(3) 104.234(6)	0.000447(7) 0.0000714(6)	UKHEDD-2.2	
Pu-241	14.4(1)y (5.259(37))E+03d	β⁻ α 0.0000245(8)	4896.5(12)	0.0000201(9)	20.81(20)	0.9999755(8)			UKHEDD-2.2	

Nuclide	Half-life	Decay Modes	α Energy (keV)	α Emission Probability	β$_{max}$ Energy (keV)	β$_{max}$ Emission Probability	γ Energy (keV)	γ Emission Probability	Data Reference	Comments
Pu-242	(3.735(11))E+05y (1.3642(40))E+08d	α SF 0.00000550(6)	4598.5(16) 4754.6(13) 4856.2(12) 4900.5(12)	0.0000086(7) 0.000307(14) 0.2348(17) 0.7649(17)			44.92(2)	0.000373(7)	UKHEDD-2.2	
Pu-244	(8.00(9))E+07y (2.922(33))E+10d	α SF 0.0012(1)	4545(2) 4589(1)	0.194(8) 0.805(8)			45(1)	0.00035(3)	UKHEDD-2.2	
Ra-223	11.43(2)d	α	5287.3(10) 5365.6(10) 5433.6(2) 5501.6(2) 5540.0(2) 5606.9(2) 5716.4(2) 5747.2(2) 5857.5(20) 5872(2)	0.0013(1) 0.0011(1) 0.023(1) 0.0080(2) 0.091(2) 0.242(4) 0.525(8) 0.095(2) 0.0032(6) 0.0087(17)			122.3(1) 144.2(1) 154.2(1) 158.6(1) 269.4(1) 323.9(1) 328.5(1) 338.3(1) 371.7(2) 444.9(1)	0.0119(5) 0.0372(25) 0.0604(35) 0.0072(5) 0.136(6) 0.0365(15) 0.00161(25) 0.0261(10) 0.0054(5) 0.0125(10)	UKHEDD-2.2	
Ra-224	3.62(1)d	α	5034.3(3) 5051.5(3) 5161.4(3) 5448.84(16) 5685.53(15)	0.000029(5) 0.000073(14) 0.000069(8) 0.0506(4) 0.9492(4)			240.987(5) 292.71(10) 404.2(2) 422.05(10) 645.52(10)	0.0397(5) 0.000060(7) 0.000021(5) 0.000029(5) 0.000052(9)	UKHEDD-2.2	
Ra-225	14.8(2)d	β⁻			322(13) 362(12)	0.69(6) 0.31(6)	40.0(10)	0.300(7)	UKHEDD-2.2	
Ra-226	(1.600(7))E+03y (5.844(26))E+05d	α	4160(2) 4191(2) 4340(1) 4601.9(5) 4784.50(25)	0.0000027(5) 0.000010(1) 0.000065(3) 0.0555(5) 0.9445(5)			185.99(4)	0.328(3)	UKHEDD-2.2	
Ra-228	5.75(3)y (2.100(11))E+03d	β⁻			15.5(40) 39(4)	0.35(1) 0.56(1)	30.5(2)	0.000135(32)	UKHEDD-2.2	Some beta and gamma energies not included due to poor data quality

Nuclide	Half-life	Decay Modes	α Energy (keV)	α Emission Probability	β_{max} Energy (keV)	β_{max} Emission Probability	γ Energy (keV)	γ Emission Probability	Data Reference	Comments
Rb-81 (see also Kr-81m daughter)	4.576(5)h 0.19067(21)d	EC/β⁺					190.32(3) 357.41(7) 446.15(2) 510.46(25) 511[A] 537.60(4) 568.90(4) 803.69(7) 834.73(5) 977.15(4) 1368.1(5)	0.640(14) 0.0076(2) 0.2327) 0.053(9) 0.573(6) 0.0223(16) 0.0058(2) 0.0083(2) 0.0081(2) 0.0056(2) 0.0095(9)	JEF-2.2	
Rb-86	18.63(3)d	β⁻ EC 0.000052(5)			697.6(19) 1774.3(19)	0.0883(6) 0.9116(6)	1076.68(4)	0.0883(6)	UKPADD;NPL	UKPADD data preferred
Rb-86m	1.017(3)m (7.06(2))E-04d	IT					556.0(2)	0.9818(5)	UKPADD	
Rb-87	(4.80(13))E+10y (1.753(47))E+13d	β⁻			273.3(19)	1.000			JEF-2.2	
Rb-88 (see also Kr-88 parent)	17.8(1)m 0.012361(69)d	β⁻			456(11) 464(11) 566(11) 795(11) 895(11) 1085(11) 2091(11) 2575(11) 3473(11) 5309(11)	0.0067(4) 0.0037(2) 0.00144(10) 0.0213(11) 0.00211(17) 0.00028(9) 0.0098(6) 0.133(7) 0.042(3) 0.780(14)	898.03(4) 1382.39(5) 1779.83(7) 1836.00(5) 2577.72(6) 2677.86(5) 3009.43(7) 3218.48(8) 3486.46(9) 4742.69(11)	0.1404(11) 0.0074(3) 0.00216(13) 0.214(3) 0.00180(9) 0.0196(3) 0.00244(9) 0.00214(6) 0.00131(4) 0.00143(6)	JEF-2.2	
Re-186	3.777(5)d	β⁻ 0.931(2) EC 0.069(2)			307.0(17) 937.3(17) 1074.5(17)	0.00049(4) 0.188(4) 0.743(4)	122.61(5) 137.157(8) 630.33(5)	0.00039(2) 0.082(3) 0.00023(3)	JEF-2.2;ENSDF	ENSDF data adopted for gamma-ray emission probabilities

Nuclide	Half-life	Decay Modes	α Energy (keV)	α Emission Probability	β_{max} Energy (keV)	β_{max} Emission Probability	γ Energy (keV)	γ Emission Probability	Data Reference	Comments
Re-188 (see also W-188 parent)	16.98(2)h 0.70750(83)d	β⁻			162.6(10) 178.6(9) 312.1(9) 354.3(9) 657.1(9) 662.0(9) 1033.3(9) 1486.7(9) 1964.6(9) 2119.7(9)	0.00053(5) 0.00108(7) 0.00040(3) 0.00186(10) 0.00521(24) 0.00078(7) 0.0064(3) 0.0160(14) 0.251(12) 0.716(13)	155.04(2) 477.96(3) 486.08(3) 633.00(5) 635.13(20) 672.51(3) 829.51(3) 931.32(3) 1132.35(4) 1610.43(5)	0.149(4) 0.0104(3) 0.00078(4) 0.0125(11) 0.0015(5) 0.00110(4) 0.00409(11) 0.00562(15) 0.00088(4) 0.00098(4)	JEF-2.2	
Rh-103m (see also Pd-103 parent)	56.115(12)m 0.038969(8)d	IT					39.756(6)	0.00069(2)	UKPADD	
Rh-105	1.474(2)d	β⁻			123.8(29) 247.0(29) 260.0(29) 566.2(29)	0.00042(5) 0.197(5) 0.053(2) 0.750(6)	38.7(2) 280.5(2) 306.25(3) 319.22(2) 442.38(4)	0.00027(5) 0.0019(2) 0.052(2) 0.192(5) 0.00042(5)	UKPADD	
Rh-106 (see also Ru-106 parent)	30.1(1)s (3.484(12))E-04d	β⁻			917(6) 1232(6) 1263(6) 1539(6) 1835(6) 1979(6) 2407(6) 2413(6) 3029(6) 3541(6)	0.00094(5) 0.00043(2) 0.00045(6) 0.0046(2) 0.00067(3) 0.0181(5) 0.101(4) 0.007(2) 0.084(6) 0.781(6)	428.5(1) 511.9(1) 616.1(3) 621.93(3) 873.5(2) 1050.4(2) 1128.0(1) 1194.5(3) 1562.3(1) 2112.5(3)	0.00074(9) 0.212(7) 0.0078(13) 0.1028(13) 0.0045(3) 0.0162(9) 0.00413(20) 0.00058(4) 0.00165(12) 0.00036(3)	JEF-2.2;NPL; ENSDF	ENSDF data adopted for beta-particle and gamma-ray emission probabilities

Nuclide	Half-life	Decay Modes	α Energy (keV)	α Emission Probability	β_{max} Energy (keV)	β_{max} Emission Probability	γ Energy (keV)	γ Emission Probability	Data Reference	Comments
Rn-219	3.96(5)s (4.583(58))E-05d	α	5783.7(20)	0.0001(1)			130.5(2)	0.0012(2)	UKHEDD-2.2	
			5948.1(20)	0.00006(6)			222(1)	0.00028(10)		
			6001.2(20)	0.000044(4)			271.3(1)	0.0993(99)		
			6154.8(20)	0.000006(4)			294.0(3)	0.00059(21)		
			6222.2(20)	0.00008(7)			401.8(3)	0.065(9)		
			6321.1(20)	0.0054(26)			516.8(8)	0.000227(7)		
			6425.0(10)	0.075(12)						
			6529.3(15)	0.0012(9)						
			6553.1(2)	0.115(15)						
			6819.4(3)	0.808(23)						
Rn-220	55.6(1)s (6.435(12))E-04d	α	5748.53(15)	0.00126(12)			549.74(5)	0.00126(12)	UKHEDD-2.2	
			6288.27(10)	0.99874(12)						
Rn-222	3.825(1)d	α	4988(2)	0.00072(21)			510(2)	0.0007(2)	UKHEDD-2.2	
			5489.66(30)	0.99928(21)						
Ru-103	39.26(2)d	β⁻			114(3)	0.00091(10)	53.29(2)	0.00374(21)	UKPADD;NPL	
					116(3)	0.067(1)	114.96(3)	0.000081(8)		
					229(3)	0.921(4)	241.85(3)	0.000151(16)		
					409(3)	0.00009(3)	294.98(2)	0.00265(20)		
					471(3)	0.0025(2)	357.41(2)	0.000091(28)		
					766(3)	0.0087(5)	443.80(2)	0.00374(28)		
							497.08(2)	0.913(39)		
							557.04(3)	0.0085(4)		
							610.33(2)	0.0584(20)		
							612.04(3)	0.000081(9)		
Ru-105	4.44(2)h 0.18500(83)d	β⁻			539(4)	0.0163(9)	262.83(10)	0.0657(14)	JEF-2.2;ENSDF	
					571(4)	0.0352(13)	316.44(15)	0.111(4)		
					595(4)	0.0061(6)	393.36(10)	0.0377(5)		
					947(4)	0.0398(15)	413.53(10)	0.023(2)		
					1110(4)	0.188(6)	469.37(10)	0.175(5)		
					1130(4)	0.169(6)	656.21(10)	0.021(3)		
					1192(4)	0.478(6)	676.36(8)	0.157(5)		
					1417(4)	0.005(3)	724.30(3)	0.473(5)		
					1447(4)	0.021(7)	875.85(15)	0.0250(9)		
					1523(4)	0.005(3)	969.44(10)	0.0210(7)		
					1786(4)	0.026(10)				

Nuclide	Half-life	Decay Modes	α Energy (keV)	α Emission Probability	β_max Energy (keV)	β_max Emission Probability	γ Energy (keV)	γ Emission Probability	Data Reference	Comments
Ru-106 (see also Rh-106 daughter)	1.008(3)y 368.2(11)d	β⁻			39.4(3)	1.000			UKPADD	
S-35	87.5(4)d	β⁻			167.50(2)	1.000			UKPADD;NPL	
Sb-124	60.24(9)d	β⁻			130(2) 203(2) 211(2) 611(2) 813(2) 866(2) 947(2) 1579(2) 1656(2) 2302(2)	0.0060(4) 0.0060(5) 0.088(2) 0.521(7) 0.0071(5) 0.041(1) 0.022(1) 0.050(4) 0.025(2) 0.223(12)	602.73(1) 645.86(1) 713.8(1) 722.78(1) 968.2(1) 1045.1(1) 1325.52(1) 1368.2(1) 1691.0(1) 2091.0(1)	0.978(1) 0.0740(7) 0.0234(3) 0.1097(12) 0.0192(4) 0.0186(2) 0.0155(5) 0.0260(8) 0.484(6) 0.0557(6)	UKPADD;NPL	
Sb-125 (see also Te-125m daughter)	2.7590(16)y (1.0077(6))E+03d	β⁻			95.4(20) 124.6(20) 130.8(20) 241.6(20) 303.4(20) 323.3(20) 445.7(20) 622.0(20)	0.134(1) 0.058(1) 0.180(2) 0.016(1) 0.398(3) 0.0008(2) 0.071(1) 0.142(2)	35.50(1) 176.33(3) 321.06(4) 380.44(3) 427.89(2) 463.39(1) 600.53(3) 606.66(3) 635.92(2) 671.42(1)	0.0424(3) 0.0676(6) 0.00409(4) 0.0150(1) 0.2927(15) 0.1037(7) 0.1765(12) 0.0496(4) 0.1116(1) 0.0178(2)	UKPADD	
Sb-126 (see also Sn-126 parent)	12.41(5)d	β⁻			222(33) 478(33) 501(33) 603(33) 684(33) 861(33) 906(32) 1175(32) 1454(32) 1896(32)	0.024(4) 0.309(20) 0.060(10) 0.0814(4) 0.045(6) 0.083(10) 0.042(7) 0.136(10) 0.023(4) 0.168(10)	297.3(1) 414.8(1) 572.5(6) 592.7(5) 666.34(1) 695.1(1) 697.1(6) 720.7(1) 856.8(3) 989.6(1)	0.050(3) 0.803(32) 0.064(3) 0.078(4) 0.997(2) 0.997(32) 0.309(21) 0.538(21) 0.172(6) 0.064(3)	UKPADD	

Nuclide	Half-life	Decay Modes	α Energy (keV)	α Emission Probability	β_{max} Energy (keV)	β_{max} Emission Probability	γ Energy (keV)	γ Emission Probability	Data Reference	Comments
Sb-127	3.84(3)d	β⁻			440(6)	0.014(4)	252.3(4)	0.082(6)	UKPADD	
					504(6)	0.052(2)	290.9(7)	0.019(2)		
					656(6)	0.013(6)	412.2(4)	0.035(5)		
					795(6)	0.077(4)	445.18	0.042(4)		
					798(6)	0.173(5)	473.3(3)	0.246(20)		
					895(6)	0.343(2)	543.2(5)	0.027(4)		
					949(5)	0.042(5)	603.7(8)	0.042(3)		
					1108(5)	0.225(20)	685.5(5)	0.352(18)		
					1240(5)	0.023(6)	697.4(5)	0.033(3)		
					1493(5)	0.020(5)	783.4(3)	0.147(10)		
Sc-46	83.79(4)d	β⁻			357.3(9)	0.999984(12)	889.277(3)	0.99844(16)	UKPADD	
					1477.8(8)	0.000016(12)	1120.545(4)	0.99874(11)		
Sc-47 (see also Ca-47 parent)	3.346(2)d	β⁻			441.2(19)	0.684(6)	159.37(2)	0.681(6)	UKPADD;NPL	
					600.6(19)	0.316(6)				
Se-75	119.64(24)d	EC					66.0523(9)	0.0110(2)	UKPADD	
							96.7344(10)	0.0341(4)		
							121.1171(14)	0.171(1)		
							136.0008(6)	0.588(3)		
							198.605(32)	0.0149(1)		
							264.6580(17)	0.590(2)		
							279.5431(22)	0.250(1)		
							303.925(15)	0.0131(1)		
							400.6593(13)	0.115(1)		
Se-79	(6.0(5)E+05y (2.19(18))E+08d	β⁻			150.7(18)	1.0000(1)			UKPADD	
Sm-145	340(3)d	EC					61.25(5)	0.1215(10)	UKPADD	
Sm-148	(7(3))E+15y (3(1))E+18d	α	1960(20)	1.000					JEF-2.2	
Sm-151	90(6)y (3.29(22))E+04d	β⁻			54.8(6)	0.0091(4)	21.532(8)	0.000314(14)	UKPADD	
					76.3(6)	0.9909(4)				

Nuclide	Half-life	Decay Modes	α Energy (keV)	α Emission Probability	β_{max} Energy (keV)	β_{max} Emission Probability	γ Energy (keV)	γ Emission Probability	Data Reference	Comments
Sm-153	1.929(2)d	β⁻			101.8(8)	0.00021(2)	54.193(1)	0.00049(7)	UKPADD	
					114.2(8)	0.00024(2)	69.673(4)	0.049(2)		
					126.6(9)	0.00010(1)	75.422(1)	0.0019(3)		
					171.9(8)	0.00069(4)	83.367(1)	0.0019(1)		
					173.8(9)	0.00063(4)	89.485(1)	0.00165(9)		
					635.5(8)	0.32(3)	97.431(6)	0.0076(4)		
					656.8(8)	0.0064(6)	103.180(7)	0.289(5)		
					705.2(8)	0.49(5)	172.852(1)	0.00075(4)		
					711.0(8)	0.0007(3)	531.40(6)	0.00061(4)		
					808.4(8)	0.18(2)	533.33(2)	0.00032(17)		
Sm-156	9.4(2)h 0.3917(83)d	β⁻			444(13)	0.55(5)	22.6(1)	0.08(6)	JEF-2.2	
					687(13)	0.034(23)	38.1(1)	0.032(5)		
					712(13)	0.45(5)	65.0(5)	0.015(4)		
							87.6(2)	0.24(7)		
							103(2)	0.014(5)		
							165.8(5)	0.147(23)		
							203.83(10)	0.23(4)		
							246.2(25)	0.013(3)		
							268.7(6)	0.025(5)		
							291.0(8)	0.030(6)		
Sn-113	115.09(4)d	EC					255.07(6)	0.0191(10)	UKPADD	
							638.0(1)	0.0000998(63)		
Sn-117m	13.60(4)d	IT					156.02(6)	0.0211(11)	UKPADD	
							158.56(2)	0.864(2)		
							314.58(4)	0.0000049(11)		
Sn-121	1.121(4)d	β⁻			388.9(24)	1.000			UKPADD	
Sn-121m	55(5)y (2.01(18))E+04d	IT 0.776(20) β⁻ 0.224(20)			358.1(25)	0.224(20)	37.13(1)	0.0185(17)	UKPADD	
Sn-123	129.2(4)d	β⁻			60(4)	0.0000098(23)	160.33(5)	0.000019(4)	UKPADD	
					136(4)	0.0000014(9)	1021.0(2)	0.0000194(4)		
					216(4)	0.000022(5)	1030.2(1)	0.00031(6)		
					308(4)	0.006(1)	1088.6(1)	0.006(1)		
					367(4)	0.00031(6)	1337.42(2)	0.0000076(17)		
					1397(4)	0.9937(11)				

Nuclide	Half-life	Decay Modes	α Energy (keV)	α Emission Probability	βmax Energy (keV)	βmax Emission Probability	γ Energy (keV)	γ Emission Probability	Data Reference	Comments
Sn-125	9.64(3)d	β⁻			62(6)	0.0025(1)	332.09(4)	0.0130(11)	UKPADD	
					75(6)	0.0020(1)	469.8(1)	0.0136(11)		
					110(6)	0.0058(5)	800.3(1)	0.0099(9)		
					348(6)	0.021(1)	822.4(1)	0.040(3)		
					367(6)	0.041(1)	915.5(1)	0.040(3)		
					460(6)	0.061(3)	1067.10(3)	0.0904(30)		
					1001(6)	0.0031(3)	1087.6(1)	0.0108(11)		
					1261(6)	0.028(3)	1089.25(4)	0.042(3)		
					1283(6)	0.0047(5)	1419.7(1)	0.00453(38)		
					2350(6)	0.825(40)	2001.8(1)	0.019(2)		
Sn-126 (see also Sb-126 daughter)	(1.0(2))E+05y (3.65(7))E+07d	β⁻			250(30)	1.0000(1)	21.6(6)	0.012(2)	UKPADD	
							23.3(6)	0.069(10)		
							42.6(6)	0.0043(7)		
							64.2(6)	0.090(14)		
							86.9(6)	0.083(13)		
							87.5(6)	0.397(20)		
Sr-85	64.849(4)d	EC					514.008(2)	0.9927(2)	UKPADD	
							868.98(5)	0.000124(5)		
Sr-87m	2.810(10)h 0.11708(42)d	IT 0.9970(8) EC 0.0030(8)					388.40(5)	0.8226(14)	JEF-2.2;NPL	
Sr-89	50.52(8)d	β⁻			583(3)	0.0000964(7)			UKPADD;NPL	
					1492(3)	0.9999036(7)				
Sr-90 (see also Y-90 daughter)	28.64(16)y (1.0461(58))E+04d	β⁻			546.2(20)	1.000			UKPADD;NPL	
Sr-91	9.52(6)h 0.3967(25)d	β⁻			404.6(40)	0.00237(18)	274.7(2)	0.0103(10)	JEF-2.2	
					477.3(40)	0.0148(11)	620.1(1)	0.018(2)		
					617.4(40)	0.0207(15)	652.3(1)	0.030(4)		
					703.6(40)	0.0037(3)	652.9(2)	0.080(9)		
					1104.1(40)	0.347(24)	749.8(1)	0.236(18)		
					1138.1(40)	0.0182(13)	761.4(1)	0.0057(5)		
					1378.6(40)	0.250(18)	925.8(2)	0.038(3)		
					1497.1(40)	0.0065(5)	1024.3(1)	0.334(23)		
					2031(4)	0.034(5)	1280.9(1)	0.0093(7)		
					2684(4)	0.29(5)	1413.4(1)	0.0098(8)		

Nuclide	Half-life	Decay Modes	α Energy (keV)	α Emission Probability	β_{max} Energy (keV)	β_{max} Emission Probability	γ Energy (keV)	γ Emission Probability	Data Reference	Comments
Ta-182	114.7(4)d	β^-			260.4(20)	0.293(6)	67.7500(2)	0.408(16)	UKPADD	
					303.4(20)	0.0013(3)	100.1065(3)	0.141(4)		
					326.1(20)	0.019(9)	152.4308(5)	0.074(4)		
					370.8(20)	0.0056(3)	222.1098(6)	0.074(2)		
					439.8(20)	0.201(14)	229.3220(9)	0.0367(15)		
					482.5(20)	0.021(2)	264.0755(8)	0.0351(11)		
					524.4(20)	0.394(18)	1121.301(5)	0.346(8)		
					556.2(20)	0.009(2)	1189.050(5)	0.161(4)		
					592.2(20)	0.038(14)	1221.408(5)	0.268(7)		
					1713.5(20)	0.018(9)	1231.016(5)	0.113(3)		
Tb-160	72.3(2)d	β^-			302(2)	0.00229(14)	86.79(1)	0.1316(62)	JEF-2.2;NPL	
					438(2)	0.0453(15)	197.03(1)	0.0515(19)		
					451(2)	0.0095(4)	215.65(1)	0.0395(15)		
					479(2)	0.100(4)	298.57(1)	0.269(11)		
					551(2)	0.0338(12)	879.36(1)	0.2946(84)		
					573(2)	0.470(16)	962.30(2)	0.0982(41)		
					681(2)	0.0020(4)	966.15(2)	0.2504(87)		
					788(2)	0.065(4)	1177.90(2)	0.1522(53)		
					871(2)	0.268(12)	1271.90(2)	0.0746(29)		
					1554(2)	0.0046(17)	1312.10(4)	0.02917(11)		
Tc-95m	61.0(21)d	EC/β^+ 0.96(1)					204.12(1)	0.662(12)	JEF-2.2	
		IT 0.04(1)					218.66(8)	0.000450(22)		
							252.95(1)	0.0640(13)		
							511[A]	0.0062(18)		
							582.07(1)	0.314(6)		
							616.49(2)	0.0134(3)		
							786.18(2)	0.0907(17)		
							820.61(1)	0.0493(9)		
							835.13(1)	0.279(6)		
							1039.25(2)	0.0291(6)		
							1620.20(4)	0.000391(21)		
Tc-97m	90.2(11)d	IT					96.6(1)	0.00316(5)	UKPADD	
Tc-99	(2.113(11))E+05y	β^-			203.9(14)	0.000016(4)	89.68(5)	0.0000065(15)	UKPADD;NPL	
	(7.718(40))E+07d				293.6(13)	0.999984(4)				

Nuclide	Half-life	Decay Modes	α Energy (keV)	α Emission Probability	β_{max} Energy (keV)	β_{max} Emission Probability	γ Energy (keV)	γ Emission Probability	Data Reference	Comments
Tc-99m (see also Mo-99 parent)	6.01(1)h 0.25042(42)d	IT β⁻ 0.000037(8)			113.9(14) 346.6(14) 436.3(13)	0.0000105(6) 0.000026(5) 0.000010(3)	89.68(5) 140.511(1) 142.68(1)	0.000010(2) 0.890(5) 0.00019(1)	UKPADD;NPL	
Te-123m	119.7(1)d	IT					88.46(3) 159.00(3)	0.00090(5) 0.8404(35)	JEF-2.2	
Te-125m (see also Sb-125 parent)	58(1)d	IT					35.50(1) 109.27(2)	0.0666(35) 0.00277(8)	UKPADD	
Te-129m	33.8(1)d	IT 0.69(4) β⁻ 0.31(4)			203(4) 322(5) 400(4) 554(4) 759(4) 835(4) 874(4) 908(4) 1604(4)	0.0015(1) 0.000022(4) 0.000006(3) 0.00038(3) 0.00010(8) 0.00029(2) 0.0073(2) 0.0307(5) 0.27(5)	27.79(3) 105.50(5) 556.6(1) 671.9(1) 695.89(5) 701.78(7) 729.57(4) 740.96(6) 817.03(6) 844.82(3)	0.00027(6) 0.0016(7) 0.00116(26) 0.00025(6) 0.0307(62) 0.00023(8) 0.00725(16) 0.00028(7) 0.00092(20) 0.00035(8)	UKPADD	
Te-131m	1.25(8)d	β⁻ 0.778(16) IT 0.222(16)			264(6) 318(6) 421(6) 431(6) 452(6) 508(6) 533(6) 545(6) 786(6) 2432(6)	0.011(2) 0.020(4) 0.026(3) 0.054(6) 0.371(19) 0.021(5) 0.161(12) 0.013(2) 0.026(9) 0.038(4)	102.06(1) 200.63(2) 240.93(1) 334.27(1) 773.67(3) 782.49(4) 793.75(3) 852.21(3) 1125.5(4) 1206.6(4)	0.0793(16) 0.0755(12) 0.0759(8) 0.0956(12) 0.382(4) 0.0778(12) 0.1385(20) 0.206(4) 0.1142(24) 0.0975(16)	JEF-2.2	
Te-132 (see also I-132 daughter)	3.23(3)d	β⁻			215(4)	1.000	49.72(1) 111.8(1) 116.3(1) 228.1(1)	0.147(9) 0.018(2) 0.0195(15) 0.88(1)	UKPADD	

Nuclide	Half-life	Decay Modes	α Energy (keV)	α Emission Probability	β_{max} Energy	β_{max} Emission Probability	γ Energy (keV)	γ Emission Probability	Data Reference	Comments
Th-227	18.718(10)d	α	5667.9(15) 5693(2) 5701.4(16) 5709(1) 5713(1) 5757.06(15) 5959.6(15) 5977.92(10) 6008.7(15) 6038.21(15)	0.0206(12) 0.0150(53) 0.0333(50) 0.0820(3) 0.0489(80) 0.203(20) 0.030(10) 0.234(20) 0.029(4) 0.245(30)			50.2(2) 79.8(1) 94.0(1) 210.6(2) 236.0(1) 254.7(2) 256.3(2) 286.2(1) 300.0(1) 329.9(2)	0.086(6) 0.020(2) 0.014(1) 0.009(2) 0.116(8) 0.0065(20) 0.074(5) 0.0155(8) 0.020(2) 0.028(2)	UKHEDD-2.2	
Th-228	1.913(2)y 698.71(73)d	α	5138.1(3) 5176.9(3) 5211.1(2) 5340.40(22) 5423.30(22)	0.00036(7) 0.0023(1) 0.0042(2) 0.276(9) 0.717(9)			84.373(3) 131.613(4) 166.411(4) 205.945(5) 215.984(5)	0.0124(3) 0.00125(6) 0.00105(4) 0.000184(9) 0.00260(5)	UKHEDD-2.2	
Th-229	(7.340(160))E+03y (2.681(58))E+06d	α	4763(2) 4797.8(12) 4814.6(12) 4837(2) 4845.3(12) 4901.0(12) 4967.5(12) 4978.5(12) 5050(2) 5052(2)	0.0063(6) 0.0127(10) 0.0930(8) 0.048(5) 0.562(2) 0.1020(8) 0.0597(6) 0.0317(4) 0.052(5) 0.016(2)			31.4(2) 43.99(1) 86.4(1) 107.11(1) 124.5(2) 136.990(4) 148.0(2) 156.41(1) 193.509(4) 210.8(1)	0.0245(6) 0.00762(17) 0.039(10)[D] 0.00809(12) 0.015(1)[D] 0.0118(2) 0.0109(2) 0.0124(2) 0.0441(6) 0.00318(4)	UKHEDD-2.2	Gamma-ray energies of 86.4 keV and 124.5 keV are unresolved doublets
Th-230	(7.54(3))E+04y (2.754(11))E+07d	α SF (2.5(25))E-13	4249(6) 4278(6) 4372(6) 4438.4(16) 4479.8(16) 4621.2(15) 4687.7(15)	0.0000005(2) 0.0000008(2) 0.00001(1) 0.00030(15) 0.0012(2) 0.234(1) 0.763(3)			67.672(2) 143.872(4) 186.053(4) 253.73(1)	0.0038(4) 0.00049(5) 0.000088(9) 0.00011(1)	UKHEDD-2.2	

Nuclide	Half-life	Decay Modes	α Energy (keV)	α Emission Probability	β_{max} Energy (keV)	β_{max} Emission Probability	γ Energy (keV)	γ Emission Probability	Data Reference	Comments
Th-231	1.0633(4)d	β⁻			142(2)	0.027(4)	25.64(2)	0.146(3)	UKHEDD-2.2	
					206(2)	0.124(13)	58.570(3)	0.0050(5)		
					215(2)	0.0125(21)	72.751(3)	0.0026(2)		
					287(2)	0.114(20)	81.228(3)	0.0085(3)		
					288(2)	0.365(45)	82.087(3)	0.0037(2)		
					305(2)	0.339(45)	84.214(3)	0.0671(10)		
							89.9(1)	0.0094(6)		
							99.278(3)	0.0012(1)		
							102.270(3)	0.0040(2)		
							163.101(5)	0.0155(10)		
Th-232	(1.405(6))E+10y	α	3830(10)	0.0020(8)			59(1)	0.0015(3)	UKHEDD-2.2	
	(5.132(22))E+12d	SF (1.4(5))E-11	3954(8)	0.23(3)			126(2)	0.00045(25)		
			4013(5)	0.77(3)						
Th-233	22.3(1)m	β⁻			433(3)	0.0056(6)	29.37(2)	0.025(3)	UKHEDD-2.2	
	0.01549(7)d				481(3)	0.015(2)	86.48(6)	0.027(4)		
					691(3)	0.017(4)	88.04(16)	0.030(10)		
					790(3)	0.003(1)	94.66(5)	0.0080(10)		
					797(3)	0.012(2)	162.504(12)	0.0032(4)		
					1076(3)	0.018(4)	169.162(10)	0.0034(3)		
					1150(3)	0.083(22)	440.94(4)	0.0023(4)		
					1158(3)	0.034(10)	459.222(7)	0.014(3)		
					1238(3)	0.50(5)	499.022(35)	0.0021(2)		
					1245(2)	0.30(5)	669.901(16)	0.0068(7)		
Th-234	24.10(3)d	β⁻			78(5)	0.028(5)	20.01(4)	0.000115(17)	UKHEDD-2.2	Emphasis placed on
					88(5)	0.0006(2)	62.88(4)	0.000048(6)	DOE/CPR2/41/1/21 9	DOE/CPR2/41/1/219
					98(5)	0.058(5)	63.30(4)	0.037(2)		
					99(5)	0.174(5)	83.31(4)	0.00071(7)		
					192(5)	0.739(5)	92.38(4)	0.026(2)		
							92.80(2)	0.026(2)		
							103.35(7)	0.000056(14)		
							108.00(5)	0.000078(27)		
							112.81(5)	0.0024(3)		
Ti-51	5.80(3)m	β⁻			1543.9(18)	0.070(11)	320.085(1)	0.942(9)	UKPADD	
	(4.03(2))E-03d				2152.5(17)	0.930(11)	608.57(7)	0.0132(20)		
							928.66(7)	0.057(10)		

Nuclide	Half-life	Decay Modes	α Energy (keV)	α Emission Probability	β_{max} Energy (keV)	β_{max} Emission Probability	γ Energy (keV)	γ Emission Probability	Data Reference	Comments
Tl-201	3.041(2)d	EC					30.59(4)	0.00258(10)	UKPADD;NPL	Emphasis placed on data from UKPADD
							32.15(2)	0.00260(13)		
							135.31(6)	0.0265(8)		
							141.18(7)	0.0007(1)		
							165.90(6)	0.00160(9)		
							167.46(4)	0.102(2)		
Tl-204	3.79(1)y (1.384(37))E+03d	β⁻ 0.978(2) EC 0.022(2)			763.4(2)	0.978(2)			UKPADD	
Tl-207 (see also Bi-211 parent)	4.77(3)m (3.313(21))E-03d	β⁻			524(6)	0.00246(40)	569.7(1)	0.00005(5)	UKHEDD-2.2	
					852(6)	0.00005(5)	897.7(1)	0.0024(4)		
					1422(6)	0.9975(5)				
Tl-208 (see also Bi-212 parent)	3.055(7)m (2.1215(49))E-03d	β⁻			514(4)	0.00050(6)	233.36(15)	0.0029(3)	UKHEDD-2.2	
					698(4)	0.00084(20)	252.61(10)	0.0078(3)		
					814(4)	0.00212(26)	277.358(12)	0.0637(12)		
					869(4)	0.00164(26)	510.77(10)	0.225(5)		
					1033(4)	0.0324(13)	583.191(2)	0.851(9)		
					1048(4)	0.00047(3)	722.04(12)	0.0024(2)		
					1074(4)	0.0029(2)	763.13(8)	0.0178(6)		
					1286(4)	0.244(8)	860.564(5)	0.126(2)		
					1519(4)	0.221(7)	1093.9(2)	0.0042(3)		
					1796(4)	0.494(21)	2614.533(13)	0.999(4)		
Tm-170	128.6(3)d	β⁻ 0.99854(2) EC 0.00146(2)			883.74(10)	0.240(10)	78.7(5)	0.000039(9)	JEF-2.2;NPL	
					968.00(10)	0.759(10)	84.257(2)	0.0326(16)		
Tm-171	1.92(1)y 701.3(37)d	β⁻			29.8(10)	0.02(1)	66.731(2)	0.0014(1)	JEF-2.2;ENSDF	Uncertainties in data from ENSDF
					96.5(10)	0.98(1)				
U-232	69.8(5)y (2.549(18))E+04d	α SF (8(3))E-13	4997.89(11)	0.000062(1)			57.78(5)	0.0199(2)	UKHEDD-2.2	
			5136.64(16)	0.00328(5)			129.082(13)	0.000682(4)		
			5263.50(15)	0.309(9)						
			5320.28(10)	0.688(9)						

Nuclide	Half-life	Decay Modes	α Energy (keV)	α Emission Probability	β$_{max}$ Energy (keV)	β$_{max}$ Emission Probability	γ Energy (keV)	γ Emission Probability	Data Reference	Comments
U-233	(1.59250(200))E+05y (5.8165(73))E+07d	α	4591(2) 4632(2) 4701(2) 4729(2) 4754(2) 4783.5(12) 4796(2) 4805(3) 4824.2(12)	0.0003(2) 0.0007(3) 0.00061(6) 0.0185(5) 0.0016(8) 0.149(2) 0.0011(2) 0.00051(5) 0.827(3)			29.192(1) 42.468(2) 53.59(5) 54.699(1) 97.14(5) 118.968(2) 146.35(2) 164.522(2) 291.354(4) 317.16(1)	0.00004(1) 0.0006(2) 0.00004(1) 0.00015(4) 0.00021(5) 0.000041(9) 0.000066(14) 0.000062(13) 0.000054(12) 0.000078(17)	UKHEDD-2.2	
U-234	(2.457(3))E+05y (8.974(11))E+07d	α SF (1.7(1))E-11	4603.8(9) 4722.6(9) 4774.9(8)	0.00199(2) 0.2842(2) 0.7137(2)			53.20(2) 120.90(2)	0.00123(2) 0.000342(5)	UKHEDD-2.2	
U-235	(7.038(5))E+08y (2.5706(18))E+11d	α SF (2(1))E-10	4217(3) 4325(3) 4368(10) 4396(3) 4415(3) 4440(5) 4506(5) 4556(3) 4598(3)	0.060(4) 0.048(6) 0.158(23) 0.58(6) 0.058(6) 0.006(2) 0.016(5) 0.024(3) 0.023(2)			109.16(10) 140.76(10) 143.76(10) 163.33(10) 182.61(20) 185.72(10) 194.94(10) 198.90(10) 202.11(20) 205.31(10)	0.0154(5) 0.0022(2) 0.1096(8) 0.0508(4) 0.0034(2) 0.572(2) 0.0063(1) 0.0042(6) 0.0108(2) 0.0501(5)	UKHEDD-2.2	
U-236	(2.3416(39))E+07y (8.553(14))E+09d	α SF (1.2(6))E-09	4335(5) 4445.3(10) 4495.5(10)	0.0015(1) 0.224(5) 0.775(9)			49.37(1) 112.75(2)	0.00067(5) 0.00020(2)	UKHEDD-2.2	
U-237	6.75(1)d	β−			148.5(12) 150.8(12) 187.0(12) 238(1) 252(1)	0.0060(3) 0.0022(1) 0.036(2) 0.522(20) 0.434(20)	26.34(2) 33.19(1) 51.005(40) 59.536(3) 64.832(40) 164.580(40) 208.000(10) 267.54(2) 332.354(20) 370.93(3)	0.0222(23) 0.0011(5) 0.00450(6) 0.345(8) 0.0131(3) 0.0187(5) 0.216(5) 0.0073(2) 0.0121(3) 0.00110(4)	UKHEDD-2.2:NPL	

Nuclide	Half-life	Decay Modes	α Energy (keV)	α Emission Probability	βmax Energy (keV)	βmax Emission Probability	γ Energy (keV)	γ Emission Probability	Data Reference	Comments
U-238	(4.468(5))E+09y (1.6319(18))E+12d	α SF (5.4(8))E-07	4041(7) 4150(5) 4198.5(50)	0.0023(7) 0.23(4) 0.768(40)			49.55(6) 110(5)	0.00064(8) 0.00029(10)	UKHEDD-2.2	
U-239	23.47(5)m 0.01630(4)d	β− SF (3.0(15))E-12			299(3) 419(3) 444(3) 601(3) 745(3) 815(3) 1145.2(25) 1188.2(25) 1231.8(25) 1262.9(25)	0.0022(1) 0.0025(1) 0.0026(2) 0.0022(1) 0.00058(6) 0.00072(6) 0.018(2) 0.688(14) 0.102(19) 0.178(29)	31.131(2) 43.533(1) 74.664(1) 117.772(7) 662.24(3) 748.08(4) 812.93(4) 819.22(4) 844.10(4) 964.30(4)	0.00075(17) 0.042(2) 0.481(10) 0.0013(4) 0.00178(4) 0.00101(2) 0.00077(2) 0.00144(3) 0.00159(3) 0.00087(2)	UKHEDD-2.2	
V-52	3.745(5)m (2.601(3))E-03d	β−			204(2) 503.5(20) 560.4(17) 814.0(18) 1010.9(17) 1207.9(17) 1606.1(17) 2541.6(17)	0.000025(14) 0.000018(9) 0.0004(1) 0.00008(1) 0.00116(2) 0.0057(1) 0.0004(1) 0.9922(2)	398.13(4) 647.55(5) 704.4(2) 935.54(3) 1333.67(3) 1434.09(1) 1530.69(3) 1727.65(7) 1981.22(4) 2337.6(2)	0.00008(1) 0.00024(2) 0.000018(9) 0.00061(3) 0.0059(1) 1.000(1) 0.00116(2) 0.00007(1) 0.00005(1) 0.000015(9)	UKPADD	
W-187	23.85(8)h 0.9938(33)d	β−			433(2) 448(2) 496(2) 540(2) 627(2) 687(2) 694(2) 801(2) 1178(2) 1312.5(18)	0.0053(3) 0.0047(1) 0.0013(2) 0.041(1) 0.543(5) 0.040(3) 0.041(3) 0.0010(6) 0.023(18) 0.30(2)	72.00(3) 134.25(1) 479.49(7) 511.65(5) 551.49(6) 618.28(6) 625.5(1) 685.74(5) 772.91(6) 864.6(1)	0.110(4) 0.087(4) 0.217(8) 0.0064(3) 0.050(2) 0.062(3) 0.0108(4) 0.27(1) 0.041(2) 0.0033(2)	UKPADD;NPL	Uncertainties in gamma-ray data from NPL

Nuclide	Half-life	Decay Modes	α Energy (keV)	α Emission Probability	β_max Energy (keV)	β_max Emission Probability	γ Energy (keV)	γ Emission Probability	Data Reference	Comments
W-188 (see also Re-188 daughter)	69.4(6)d	β⁻			58(3) 141(3) 180(3) 285(3) 349(3)	0.0083(5) 0.000087(18) 0.000067(4) 0.0015(8) 0.9900(9)	63.58(3) 85.31(6) 141.78(3) 207.86(4) 227.09(2) 290.669(13)	0.00109(16) 0.000024(8) 0.000064(8) 0.000080(16) 0.00221(8) 0.00402(12)	JEF-2.2	
Xe-127	36.44(7)d	EC					57.61(1) 145.25(2) 172.13(2) 202.86(1) 374.99(1) 618.4(3)	0.0131(8) 0.0429(16) 0.255(9) 0.683(5) 0.172(7) 0.000142(9)	UKPADD	
Xe-131m (see also I-131 parent)	11.87(5)d	IT					163.930(13)	0.0196(4)	UKPADD	
Xe-133	5.243(3)d	β⁻			43(3) 266(3) 346(3)	0.000113(5) 0.0087(9) 0.991(19)	79.617(5) 80.997(2) 160.614(3)	0.0027(3) 0.378(14) 0.00092(11)	UKPADD	
Xe-133m	2.19(2)d	IT					233.221(15)	0.100(2)	UKPADD	
Xe-135	9.09(1)h 0.3788(4)d	β⁻			96(9) 177(9) 550(9) 750(9) 908(9)	0.00123(4) 0.00075(4) 0.0312(10) 0.0068(3) 0.9598(3)	158.20(2) 200.19(10) 249.79(1) 358.39(4) 373.13(10) 407.99(2) 608.18(2) 654.43(2) 731.52(2) 812.63(3)	0.00289(10) 0.00012(5) 0.902(2) 0.00221(8) 0.00015(3) 0.00359(13) 0.0290(9) 0.00045(3) 0.00055(3) 0.00071(3)	JEF-2.2;ENSDF	
Xe-135m	15.29(5)m 0.01062(4)d	IT 0.997(3) β⁻ 0.003(3)					526.570(17)	0.812(5)	JEF-2.2;ENSDF	Uncertainties in data from ENSDF

303

Nuclide	Half-life	Decay Modes	α Energy (keV)	α Emission Probability	β_{max} Energy (keV)	β_{max} Emission Probability	γ Energy (keV)	γ Emission Probability	Data Reference	Comments
Xe-137	3.818(13)m (2.6514(90))E-03d	β⁻			1494(23)	0.0072(8)	298.00(7)	0.00119(9)	JEF-2.2;ENSDF	
					1495(23)	0.00100(15)	393.35(6)	0.00140(9)		
					2276(23)	0.0014(2)	455.490(3)	0.312(5)		
					2428(23)	0.00073(20)	848.95(6)	0.0062(3)		
					2560(23)	0.0038(5)	982.25(5)	0.00209(12)		
					2769(23)	0.0017(3)	1119.33(6)	0.00107(6)		
					2780(23)	0.00066(10)	1273.23(10)	0.0023(2)		
					3495(23)	0.0065(8)	1612.52(6)	0.00125(9)		
					3888(23)	0.304(30)	1783.43(6)	0.0041(2)		
					4344(23)	0.67(3)	2849.8(1)	0.00184(9)		
Xe-138	14.17(2)m (9.840(14))E-03d	β⁻			340(80)	0.0046(14)	153.75(3)	0.0595(13)	JEF-2.2	
					490(80)	0.0307(13)	242.56(5)	0.0350(7)		
					570(80)	0.095(4)	258.31(5)	0.315(7)		
					800(80)	0.327(13)	396.43(5)	0.0630(13)		
					810(80)	0.0028(3)	401.36(5)	0.0217(10)		
					2380(80)	0.201(7)	434.49(5)	0.203(4)		
					2420(80)	0.134(5)	1768.26(13)	0.167(4)		
					2570(80)	0.0560(21)	2004.75(14)	0.0536(13)		
					2810(80)	0.09(6)	2015.82(14)	0.123(3)		
					2820(80)	0.05(5)	2252.26(14)	0.0229(7)		
Y-88	106.630(25)d	EC/β⁺					511[A]	0.0040(4)	UKPADD	
							850.6(1)	0.00066(13)		
							898.042(4)	0.940(3)		
							1382.4(1)	0.00021(6)		
							1836.063(13)	0.9933(3)		
							2734.086(15)	0.0061(2)		
Y-90 (see also Sr-90 parent)	2.6713(25)d	β⁻			518.5(40)	0.000115(15)	1760.7(6)	0.000115(15)	UKPADD;NPL	
					2279.2(32)	0.999885(15)				
Y-91	58.7(1)d	β⁻			340.8(21)	0.0030(3)	1204.78(6)	0.0030(3)	UKPADD	
					1545.6(20)	0.9970(3)				

Nuclide	Half-life	Decay Modes	α Energy (keV)	α Emission Probability	βmax Energy (keV)	βmax Emission Probability	γ Energy (keV)	γ Emission Probability	Data Reference	Comments
Y-93	10.1(2)h 0.421(8)d	β⁻			430(20) 710(20) 970(20) 980(20) 1420(20) 1440(20) 1460(20) 1940(20) 2620(20) 2890(20)	0.00190(95) 0.0160(8) 0.000380(19) 0.000580(29) 0.00140(7) 0.00370(19) 0.00270(14) 0.0250(13) 0.0450(23) 0.903(45)	266.87(5) 680.3(1) 947.1(1) 1203.3(1) 1425.5(1) 1450.5(1) 1470.3(1) 1917.8(1) 2184.7(1) 2190.8(1)	0.068(4) 0.0061(3) 0.0194(10) 0.00103(6) 0.00238(14) 0.00333(20) 0.00067(4) 0.0140(7) 0.00155(9) 0.00171(10)	JEF-2.2	
Yb-169	32.01(2)d	EC					8.401(8) 63.119(7) 93.613(7) 109.78(7) 118.19(7) 130.52(7) 177.21(7) 197.95(7) 261.07(7) 307.73(7)	0.00352(30) 0.416(24) 0.0255(16) 0.1741(70) 0.01906(75) 0.1149(47) 0.2233(89) 0.359(14) 0.01684(66) 0.0987(38)	JEF-2.2;NPL	
Zn-65	244.26(26)d	EC/β⁺					511[A] 1115.546(4)	0.029(3) 0.5060(24)	UKPADD	
Zr-93 (see also Nb-93m daughter)	(1.53(10))E+06y (5.59(37))E+08d	β⁻			60.6(18) 91.4(16)	0.975(25) 0.025(25)			UKPADD	
Zr-95 (see also Nb-95m daughter)	64.03(3)d	β⁻			366(3) 399(3) 887(3) 1123(3)	0.545(5) 0.439(4) 0.011(1) 0.005(1)	724.199(5) 756.729(5)	0.439(8) 0.545(5)	UKPADD	

Nuclide	Half-life	Decay Modes	α Energy (keV)	α Emission Probability	β_max Energy (keV)	β_max Emission Probability	γ Energy (keV)	γ Emission Probability	Data Reference	Comments
Zr-97	16.90(5)h 0.704(2)d	β⁻			410.9(19)	0.0048(4)	254.17(15)	0.0129(14)	JEF-2.2	
					552.6(19)	0.056(4)	355.39(10)	0.0238(24)		
					602.7(22)	0.0066(10)	507.66(10)	0.053(5)		
					806.5(19)	0.0053(25)	602.42(5)	0.0137(14)		
					894.0(19)	0.0182(22)	703.70(5)	0.0104(19)		
					1110.0(19)	0.00717)	1021.2(2)	0.0104(19)		
					1407.5(19)	0.0415(5)	1147.99(10)	0.027(3)		
					1915.1(19)	0.881(7)	1275.88(10)	0.0095(9)		
							1362.47(10)	0.0133(19)		
							1750.46(10)	0.0118(14)		

APPENDIX

TABLE A1: SELECTED ISOTOPIC ABUNDANCES FOR ELEMENTS WITH RADIOACTIVE ISOTOPES, FROM [A1].

Radionuclide	Abundance (atom %)	Form of quoted uncertainty
^{40}K	0.011672 ± 0.000041	2s C
^{50}V	0.2497 ± 0.0006	se C
^{87}Rb	27.8346 ± 0.0132	2s C
^{87}Sr	7.0015 ± 0.0026	2s C
^{115}In	95.67 ± 0.04	?
^{123}Te	0.908 ± 0.001	2s
^{128}Te	31.687 ± 0.004	2s
^{130}Te	33.799 ± 0.003	2s
^{138}La	0.09016 ± 0.00005	2s
^{144}Nd	23.83 ± 0.04	2s
^{147}Sm	14.995 ± 0.001	2s
^{148}Sm	11.242 ± 0.001	2s
^{174}Hf	0.1621 ± 0.0009	2se
^{187}Re	62.602 ± 0.016	2s C
^{190}Pt	0.0127 ± 0.0005	?
^{234}U	0.00548 ± 0.00002	1s
^{235}U	0.7200 ± 0.0001	1s
^{238}U	99.2745 ± 0.0010	1s

Note: the data in [A1] are taken from a critical evaluation of available published data and represent best measurements from single natural sources. 1s, 2s – 1or 2 standard deviations, se- standard error, ? - error not defined and C - measurement has been calibrated and represents absolute value within the given uncertainty. For further details the reader is referred to [A1]

A1   P. De Bièvre and P.D.P. Taylor, *Table of the isotopic compositions of the elements*, Intl. J. of Mass Spectrometry and Ion Procs., 123, 149-166, 1993.

TABLE A2: THE PERIODIC TABLE

Reprinted with permission from the Handbook of Chemistry and Physics, 77th. Edition, Editor-in Chief, D.R. Lide, 1996, Copyright CRC Press, Boca Raton, Florida.

References
1. G.J. Leigh, Editor, Nomenclature of Inorganic Chemistry, Blackwells Scientific Publications, Oxfrod 1990.
2. Chemical and Engineering News, 63(5), 27, 1985.
3. Atomic Weights of the Elements, Pure & Appl. Chem., 66, 2423, 1994.

The elements 104-109 are now named as Rutherfordium (104), Dubnium (105), Seaborgium (106), Bohrium (107), Hassium (108) and Meitnerium (109).

Periodic Table of the Elements

New notation / Previous IUPAC form / CAS version

Key to Chart

Atomic number → **50** / Symbol → **Sn**	+2 +4 ← Oxidation States
1993 Atomic Weight → 118.710	-18-18-4 ← Electron Configuration

1 Group IA	2 IIA	3 IIIA IIIB	4 IVA IVB	5 VA VB	6 VIA VIB	7 VIIA VIIB	8	9 VIIIA VIII	10	11 IB	12 IIB	13 IIIB IIIA	14 IVB IVA	15 VB VA	16 VIB VIA	17 VIIB VIIA	18 VIIIA	Shell
1 **H** +1 -1 1.00794 1																	**2** **He** 0 4.0020602 2	K
3 **Li** +1 6.941 2-1	**4** **Be** +2 9.012182 2-2											**5** **B** +3 10.811 2-3	**6** **C** +2 +4 -4 12.011 2-4	**7** **N** +1 +2 +3 +4 +5 -1 -2 -3 14.00674 2-5	**8** **O** -2 15.9994 2-6	**9** **F** -1 18.9984032 2-7	**10** **Ne** 0 20.1797 2-8	K L
11 **Na** +1 22.989768 2-8-1	**12** **Mg** +2 24.3050 2-8-2											**13** **Al** +3 26.981539 2-8-3	**14** **Si** +2 +4 -4 28.0855 2-8-4	**15** **P** +3 +5 -3 30.97362 2-8-5	**16** **S** +4 +6 -2 32.066 2-8-6	**17** **Cl** +1 +5 +7 -1 35.4527 2-8-7	**18** **Ar** 0 39.948 2-8-8	K L M
19 **K** +1 39.0983 -8-8-1	**20** **Ca** +2 40.078 -8-8-2	**21** **Sc** +3 44.955910 -8-9-2	**22** **Ti** +2 +3 +4 47.867 -8-10-2	**23** **V** +2 +3 +4 +5 50.9415 -8-11-2	**24** **Cr** +2 +3 +6 51.9961 -8-13-1	**25** **Mn** +2 +3 +4 +7 54.93085 -8-13-2	**26** **Fe** +2 +3 55.845 -8-14-2	**27** **Co** +2 +3 58.93320 -8-15-2	**28** **Ni** +2 +3 58.6934 -8-16-2	**29** **Cu** +1 +2 63.546 -8-18-1	**30** **Zn** +2 65.39 -8-18-2	**31** **Ga** +3 69.723 -8-18-3	**32** **Ge** +2 +4 72.61 -8-18-4	**33** **As** +3 +5 -3 74.92159 -8-18-5	**34** **Se** +4 +6 -2 78.96 -8-18-6	**35** **Br** +1 +5 -1 79.904 -8-18-7	**36** **Kr** 0 83.80 -8-18-8	L M N
37 **Rb** +1 85.4678 -18-8-1	**38** **Sr** +2 87.62 -18-8-2	**39** **Y** +3 88.90585 -18-9-2	**40** **Zr** +4 91.224 -18-10-2	**41** **Nb** +3 +5 92.90638 -18-12-1	**42** **Mo** +6 95.94 -18-13-1	**43** **Tc** +4 +6 +7 (98) -18-13-2	**44** **Ru** +3 101.07 -18-15-1	**45** **Rh** +3 102.90550 -18-16-1	**46** **Pd** +2 +4 106.42 -18-18-0	**47** **Ag** +1 107.8682 -18-18-1	**48** **Cd** +2 112.411 -18-18-2	**49** **In** +3 114.818 -18-18-3	**50** **Sn** +2 +4 118.710 -18-18-4	**51** **Sb** +3 +5 -3 121.760 -18-18-5	**52** **Te** +4 +6 -2 127.60 -18-18-6	**53** **I** +1 +5 +7 -1 126.90447 -18-18-7	**54** **Xe** 0 131.29 -18-18-8	M N O
37 **Cs** +1 132.90543 -18-8-1	**56** **Ba** +2 137.327 -18-8-2	**57*** **La** +3 138.9055 -18-9-2	**72** **Hf** +4 178.49 -32-10-2	**73** **Ta** +5 180.9479 -32-11-2	**74** **W** +6 183.84 -32-12-2	**75** **Re** +4 +6 +7 186.207 -32-13-2	**76** **Os** +3 +4 190.23 -32-14-2	**77** **Ir** +3 +4 192.217 -32-15-2	**78** **Ir** +2 +4 195.08 -32-17-2	**79** **Au** +1 +3 196.96654 -32-18-1	**80** **Hg** +1 +2 200.59 -32-18-2	**81** **Tl** +1 +3 204.3833 -32-18-3	**82** **Pb** +2 +4 207.2 -32-18-4	**83** **Bi** +3 +5 208.98037 -32-18-5	**84** **Po** +2 +4 (209) -32-18-6	**85** **At** (210) -32-18-7	**86** **Rn** 0 (222) -32-18-8	N O P
87 **Fr** +1 (223) -18-8-1	**88** **Ra** +2 226.025 -18-8-2	**89**** **Ac** +3 227.028 -18-9-2	**104** **Unq** +4 (261) -32-10-2	**105** **Unp** (262) -32-11-2	**106** **Unh** (263) -32-12-2	**107** **Uns** (262) -32-13-2	**108** **Uno** (265) -32-14-2	**109** **Une** (266) -32-15-2	**110** **Uun** (269) -32-16-2									O P Q

*Lanthanides	**58** **Ce** +3 +4 140.115 -19-9-2	**59** **Pr** +3 140.90765 -21-8-2	**60** **Nd** +3 144.24 -22-8-2	**61** **Pm** +3 (145) -23-8-2	**62** **Sm** +2 +3 150.36 -24-8-2	**63** **Eu** +2 +3 151.965 -25-8-2	**64** **Gd** +3 157.25 -25-9-2	**65** **Tb** +3 158.92534 -27-8-2	**66** **Dy** +3 162.50 -28-8-2	**67** **Ho** +3 164.93032 -29-8-2	**68** **Er** +3 167.26 -30-8-2	**69** **Tm** +3 168.93421 -31-8-2	**70** **Yb** +2 +3 173.04 -32-8-2	**71** **Lu** +3 174.967 -32-9-2	N O P
**Actinides	**90** **Th** +4 232.0381 -18-10-2	**91** **Pa** +5 +4 231.03588 -20-9-2	**92** **U** +3 +4 +5 +6 238.0289 -21-9-2	**93** **Np** +3 +4 +5 +6 237.048 -22-9-2	**94** **Pu** +3 +4 +5 +6 (244) -24-8-2	**95** **Am** +3 +4 +5 +6 (243) -25-8-2	**96** **Cm** +3 (247) -25-9-2	**97** **Bk** +3 +4 (247) -27-8-2	**98** **Cf** +3 (251) -28-8-2	**99** **Es** +3 (252) -29-8-2	**100** **Fm** +3 (257) -30-8-2	**101** **Md** +2 +3 (258) -31-8-2	**102** **No** +2 +3 (259) -32-8-2	**103** **Lr** +3 (260) -32-9-2	O P Q

INDEX

311

—O—

—P—

Thorium, 1, 18, 21, 22, 68, 70, 71, 80, 83, 84, 149, 223, 229, 230, 237, 239
Thyroid, 161, 163, 164, 170, 211, 212
Ti-51, 299
TIMS, 80, 84
Tissue weighting factor, 157, 185, 218
Titanium, 50, 170, 230
Tl-201, 152, 300
Tl-204, 300
Tl-207, 300
Tl-208, 300
TLA, 145, 146, 147
Tm-170, 300
Tm-171, 251, 300
Tomographic studies, 168
Total dissolution, 67
Tracers, 61, 62, 66, 95, 142, 143, 144, 165
Transfrontier Shipment Regulations, 235
Transient equilibrium, 5
Transport of radioactive materials
    Type B package, 235
Transport of radioactive material, 234, 235
Transport of radioactive materials
    excepted package, 214, 235, 236
    Type A package, 214, 236
    Type B package, 214
Treaty on the Non-Proliferation of Nuclear Weapons, 236
Tritium, 2, 11, 22, 23, 24, 63, 69, 72, 94, 126, 127, 128, 140, 144, 149, 230, 233
Tropical year, 248
Type I error, 89, 90, 92
Type II error, 89, 90, 92

—U—

U-232, 82, 300
U-233, 82, 237, 301
U-234, 82, 204, 206, 208, 301
U-235, 82, 204, 206, 208, 237, 251, 301
U-236, 82, 301
U-237, 301
U-238, 82, 204, 206, 208, 237, 251, 302
U-239, 302
UK Activation-Product Decay Data Files, 247
UK Department of Environment Report, DOE/HMIP/CPR2/41/1/219, 247
UK Heavy Element and Actinide, 247
UKAEA, 239, 240
UKAS, 99, 100, 125
UKHEDD-2.2, 250, 253, 254, 255, 257, 258, 261, 262, 279, 280, 281, 282, 283, 285, 286, 287, 288, 291, 298, 299, 300, 301, 302
UKPADD, 247, 250, 251, 253, 254, 255, 256, 257, 259, 260, 261, 262, 263, 264, 265, 266, 267, 268, 269, 270, 271, 272, 273, 274, 275, 276, 277, 278, 279, 280, 282, 283, 284, 285, 286, 289, 290, 291, 292, 293, 294, 295, 296, 297, 299, 300, 302, 303, 304, 305
Uncertainties, 75, 86, 87, 98, 247, 248, 249, 250
United Kingdom Accreditation Service, 99, 125
UNSCEAR, 221
Unsealed source, 96, 133, 203, 210

Uranium, 1, 6, 18, 21, 22, 67, 68, 70, 71, 83, 84, 85, 124, 139, 148, 149, 196, 223, 229, 230, 237, 239
Uranium exploration, 139

—V—

V-52, 302
Valid Analytical Measurement, 62, 98
VAM, 62, 98

—W—

W-187, 251, 302
W-188, 155, 290, 303
Waste
    accumulation, 231
    disposal, 231
    storage, 231
Waste disposal, 148, 210, 213, 221, 223, 232
Whole-body monitor, 212
Wipe test, 210
Working standard, 94
World Health Organisation (International Reference Centre for Radioactivity), 94

—X—

Xe-127, 155, 303
Xe-133, 152, 155, 303
Xe-133m, 155, 303
Xe-135, 251, 303
Xe-135m, 251, 303
Xe-137, 304
Xe-138, 304
Xenon, 40
X-Ray Fluorescence, 141
XRF, 134, 141

—Y—

Y-88, 304
Y-90, 25, 155, 204, 206, 208, 295, 304
Y-91, 304
Y-93, 305
Yb-169, 305
Yield, 13, 15, 25
Yttrium, 71, 230

—Z—

Zinc, 159
Zirconium, 230
Zn-65, 25, 305
Zr-93, 278, 305
Zr-95, 25, 204, 206, 208, 278, 305
Zr-97, 306